Cost–Benefit Analysis and Project Appraisal in Developing Countries

Cost–Benefit Analysis and Project Appraisal in Developing Countries

edited by

Colin Kirkpatrick

Professor of Development Economics, Institute for Development Policy and Management, University of Manchester, UK

and

John Weiss

Professor of Development Economics, Development and Project Planning Centre, University of Bradford, UK

Edward Elgar

Cheltenham, UK • Brookfield, US

Published by
Edward Elgar Publishing Limited
8 Lansdown Place
Cheltenham
Glos GL50 2HU
UK

Edward Elgar Publishing Company
Old Post Road
Brookfield
Vermont 05036
US

British Library Cataloguing in Publication Data
Cost–benefit analysis and project appraisal in developing countries
1. Economic assistance – Cost effectiveness 2. Developing countries – Economic conditions
I. Kirkpatrick, C.H. (Colin H) II. Weiss, John
338.9'1

Library of Congress Cataloguing in Publication Data
Cost–benefit analysis and project appraisal in developing countries / edited by Colin Kirkpatrick and John Weiss.
Includes index.
1. Economic development projects—Developing countries—Cost effectiveness. 2. Economic development projects—Developing countries—Evaluation. 3. Economic assistance—Developing countries—Evaluation. I. Kirkpatrick, C.H. (Colin H.), 1944– .
HC59.72.E44C68 1996
338.9'009172'4—dc20 96–14169
CIP

ISBN 1 85898 346 0

Printed and bound in Great Britain by
Hartnolls Limited, Bodmin, Cornwall

Contents

Figures

Tables

Contributors

Ross Bull is Managing Director of Infrastructure Limited, London and resident adviser to the Project Management Unit, Ministry of Agriculture, Latvia.

S.I. Cohen is Professor of Economics at the Faculty of Economic Sciences, Erasmus University, Rotterdam, the Netherlands.

A.B. Czyzewski is Research Fellow at the Research Centre for Economic and Statistical Studies, and the Central Statistical Office, Warsaw, Poland.

Alfredo Lopes da Silva Neto is Lecturer at the University of Vicosa, Brazil.

Shanta Devarajan is Chief of the Public Economics Division of the Policy Research Department, The World Bank.

Jean-Pierre Foirry is Maitre de Conférence, Analyse de Projet, CERDI, University of Clemont-Ferrand.

Bernard Franck is Professor at the Faculté des Sciences Economiques, Université de Caen, France.

Mark Gray is Senior Lecturer in Economics at The Civil Service College, Ascot.

Erik Kijne is Consultant to the European Union, Directorate-General for Development.

Colin Kirkpatrick is Professor of Development Economics at the Institute for Development Policy and Management, University of Manchester.

Serge-Arno Klümper is Senior Economist, Directorate for Economic and Financial Studies, European Investment Bank, Luxembourg.

E. Kula is Senior Lecturer at the School of Public Policy, Law and Economics, University of Ulster.

Nicolas Lethbridge is Managing Director of Babcock and Brown, London.

Elio Londero is Economist at the Inter American Development Bank, Washington.

John D. MacArthur is Professor of Agricultural and Project Economics at the Development and Project Planning Centre, University of Bradford.

Oliver Morrissey is Senior Lecturer at CREDIT and Department of Economics, University of Nottingham.

David Potts is Lecturer at the Development and Project Planning Centre, University of Bradford.

Colin Price is Professor at the School of Agricultural and Forest Sciences, University College of North Wales, Bangor.

Lyn Squire is Director of the Policy Research Department, World Bank.

Sethaput Suthiwart-Narueput is Economist in the Public Economics Division of the Policy Research Department, The World Bank.

John Weiss is Professor of Development Economics at the Development and Project Planning Centre, University of Bradford.

Jon Wilmshurst is Chief Economist with the Overseas Development Administration.

Preface

The techniques and methodology of project appraisal in developing countries were introduced in the late 1960s since when both have been considerably expanded and refined. At the same time, much experience has been accumulated in the application of these procedures. The papers in this volume are evidence of the ways in which cost–benefit analysis (CBA) has developed in response to changes in economic circumstances and conditions over the past three decades.

The Development and Project Planning Centre at the University of Bradford was established in 1969, and has built up a worldwide reputation as one of the leading institutions involved with research and training relating to CBA and project appraisal in developing countries. The papers in this volume were originally presented at an international conference on Development Projects: Issues for the 1990s, held at the University of Bradford in April 1995 to mark the 25th Anniversary of the Development and Project Planning Centre.

The conference received financial support from the UK Overseas Development Administration. Thanks are also due to Pearl Golden and Mark Gargett for assistance in the organization of the conference, and in preparing the papers for publication.

CK
JW

PART ONE

Introduction

1. Cost–benefit analysis for developing countries

Colin Kirkpatrick and John Weiss

INTRODUCTION

One of the few issues on which economists are agreed is the key role of investment in the economic growth and development process. There is also general agreement on the need for the state to contribute to aggregate investment, even though views differ widely on the appropriate size of the public-sector contribution. Governments are charged with the responsibility of allocating capital to promoting development, and with selecting investments that will provide the maximum benefit to society. Public-sector investment decision making, however, is seldom easy. Setting aside the political pressures which can direct resources away from their economic-optimum pattern of allocation, there are many 'technical' economic issues to be resolved in deciding upon the best use of scarce investment resources. Public investment is often associated with significant externalities which are difficult to quantify. Uncertainty about the investment's future stream of benefits and costs adds to the planner's problems. Market values frequently diverge from the economic-efficiency values either because of market imperfections or government interventions and controls.

In an effort to deal with these problems, economists have elaborated a variety of techniques and approaches for the selection of public-sector investments in developing countries.[1] In the late 1960s and early 1970s, cost–benefit analysis (CBA) came to be regarded as the standard appraisal tool for public-sector investment choice. During the 1970s, serious attempts were made to implement some form of shadow pricing for project appraisal in the international development institutions and in national planning agencies. A sizeable proportion of development assistance was allocated to the training of analysts to conduct the appraisals, with the result that by the end of the decade most economists working on developing countries' problems were familiar with the shadow-pricing methodology and its use.

In the 1980s there was a marked decline in the theoretical development and practical use of shadow-pricing methods for appraising investment projects in developing countries. This decline can be traced to a number of factors: most significantly, the general shift in development policy toward market liberalization and 'getting the prices right' fostered the belief that the process of economic policy reform would allow market prices to reflect opportunity costs, thereby eliminating the need for shadow prices.[2] Consequently, a 'good policy environment' came to be regarded not just as a necessary, but also a sufficient, condition for satisfactory project selection.

By the end of the 1980s, there was a growing appreciation that the pendulum had swung too far, and a more balanced approach to project appraisal began to emerge.[3] It is now accepted that the cost–benefit appraisal of projects is complementary to market liberalization and policy reform. While it remains the case that one cannot have good projects in a bad policy environment, it is equally true that a good policy environment alone is seldom sufficient to ensure good project choice. The economic appraisal of projects using CBA continues, therefore, to have a central role in achieving economically efficient investment decisions, and hence more rapid economic growth in developing countries.

Since its establishment in the late 1960s, the Development and Project Planning Centre at the University of Bradford has built up a worldwide reputation as a leading institution involved with training and research associated with development projects. Project appraisal has been central to the Centre's activities, and staff have contributed significantly to developing both the methodology and pedagogy of CBA in the context of developing countries. At the same time, the work of the Centre has broadened to reflect the multidimensional nature of the 'development project'. Issues of project management, organizational and human resource development, participatory and process project analysis, and environmental impact assessment are now integrated into the Centre's activities, and are disseminated through the Centre's publications.[4]

The chapters in this volume were originally presented to the Centre's 25th Anniversary Conference, held in April 1995. The focus is on CBA and project appraisal in developing countries, and the papers cover both methodological issues and practical applications and case studies. The companion volume deals with environmental analysis, participatory and process appraisal, and the human resource and management aspects of development projects (Cusworth and Wilson 1996).

CBA FOR DEVELOPING COUNTRIES: AN OVERVIEW OF KEY ISSUES

CBA as developed in the context of developing countries (what we call here the development cost–benefit literature) was always influenced by two distinct traditions. On the one hand there was the legacy of welfare economics with its recognition of the intrinsic failure of markets, due for example to external effects, lack of information, public goods and indivisibilities. All of these are likely to be particularly important in the context of the sort of activities in which the public sector had traditionally invested in the developed-country context. Hence it was not surprising that from the 1950s onwards the need to appraise public-sector projects at prices that differed from those prevailing in markets and with a wider definition of benefits and costs than simply financial revenues and costs was recognized widely. Projects in the water sector in the US are usually identified as the early guinea pigs for simple economic or cost–benefit appraisals, but similar exercises followed for projects from other sectors, particularly transport, and for other countries.

On the other hand development economics had emerged as a distinct branch of economics by the early 1960s and development economists rightly felt that they had something distinctive to say about how conventional cost–benefit calculations should be applied in their territory. Their focus was on why market failure was considerably more pervasive and profound in the developing-country context; they singled out in particular the key markets for foreign exchange, domestic credit and unskilled labour and suggested that due to a combination of government controls and inherent structural rigidities these markets would fail to clear in a textbook fashion; the crucial consequence was that the key macro prices of the exchange rate, the interest rate and the unskilled wage would be a very poor reflection of the real worth of the resources concerned. Hence the conclusion from the developed-country context that financial appraisals at prevailing market prices would be inadequate as a guide to full costs and benefits to society was strongly reinforced by arguments about the prevalence of what came to be known at 'market distortions'.

During the late 1960s and early 1970s work on ways of adapting cost–benefit techniques to a development context was an area of rapid growth and relatively high prestige and some of the most eminent economists with an interest in development were involved: these included most notably A.K. Sen, Stephen Marglin, Partha Dasgupta, Arnold Harberger and Ian Little. The timing of this interest was not totally arbitrary; aid flows had begun to assume a quantitative significance at least for donors and there was a concern that projects should be selected and appraised appropriately. Further, at an intellectual level serious questions began to be raised about the rationality of economic policy in many developing countries, in particular the emphasis on what we can term a loose form of 'guided development' based around five-year plans, quantitative but normally unenforceable targets and various market controls. Naturally not all aid donor activities are either efficient or rational: aid tying, which has been a common pattern until relatively recently, was itself a form of distortion, whose implications are discussed in the chapter by Morrissey (Chapter 11).

Of the small group of cost–benefit theoreticians we have identified, Ian Little provided an eminent link between the two traditions, since his book on welfare economics (Little 1950) was a seminal work on the theoretical basis for market failures. Little went on to have a significant influence on thinking about economic policy in a development context, first through the publication of a major overview of industrial and trade policy, sponsored by the OECD (Little et al. 1970) and later through advisory work at the World Bank. The ideas in Little et al. (1970) on the need for policies based around comparative advantage and trade specialization were closely linked with the famous Little and Mirrlees (1968, 1974) approach to CBA and the clarity and almost missionary tone of Little et al. (1970) made it arguably one of the most influential academic publications on development policy.

This is not the place to provide a detailed survey of the development cost–benefit literature; one of the authors has already provided his own introduction (Curry and Weiss 1993) and several other introductory texts are available. Further, MacArthur in this volume (Chapter 8) summarizes much of the detail involved. However we do wish to stress a few points of theory, which will help us to place in context some of the later chapters in this volume. We take as a starting point something that can now be agreed fairly readily, but which initially exercised considerably those working in the area: that the alternative 'systems' of CBA, whether of UNIDO (1972), the better known Little–Mirrlees (1968, 1974) and its extension by Squire and van der Tak (1975), or the effects method (Chervel 1973) were saying essentially similar things and that the differences between them were far less significant than the similarities. The chapters by Franck and Foirry in this volume (Chapters 7 and 15), particularly the former, both compare the 'new' effects method with the more conventional approaches from the English literature and conclude that the differences are now relatively trivial. The image of distance remains the best explanation for the early debate. The journey from A to B can be measured in miles or kilometres; when the same distance is measured the result will look different depending on the unit chosen. Neither unit is right or wrong; what matters is that the link between them is understood and that there is consistency if the journey from A to B is to be compared with another journey from C to D.

The development cost–benefit literature accepted as obvious that the adjustments relating to externalities and other forms of market failure identified in the developed-country literature were necessary. It implied however that there were other quantitatively far more significant adjustments to be considered arising from the particular features of a typical developing country. We focus on three:

1. The need to use world prices as a measure of value for internationally traded goods.
2. The need to allow for a scarcity of domestic savings through a savings premium.
3. The need to identify and value the distributional effects of projects.

The first point arose from the fact that developing countries are typically small in relation to international trade and thus face a set of world prices that they themselves cannot influence (the 'small-country assumption'). Thus world prices represent the terms on which such countries can participate in trade; however circa 1970 domestic prices were typically widely divergent from world levels for similar commodities, primarily as a consequence of protectionist trade policies. The second adjustment was in response to the obvious point that savings levels in most developing countries were sub-optimal, in the sense that they were insufficient to finance the target investment levels deemed necessary to meet growth objectives; hence income that could be diverted into savings and by assumption used to fund productive investment was automatically assumed to be more valuable than income that was consumed immediately. Finally, the third point arose from the related observations of widespread poverty and highly unequal distribution of income in the typical developing country; the impact of a project on these parameters seemed of clear relevance in quantifying its net social value.

In varying ways these adjustments raised important questions of economic theory. We discuss these implications briefly in turn, before moving finally to questions of shadow-price estimation and alternatives to formal cost–benefit calculations.

USE OF WORLD PRICES

In one sense the greater use of world prices in appraisals, even for goods not actually imported or exported (provided of course they could be), was the single most significant contribution of the development cost–benefit literature. Squire et al. in this volume (Chapter 3) for example discuss the limited use of the Little and Mirrlees 'border-pricing methodology' at the World Bank and make it clear that whilst much of the sophisticated analyses that they and others were associated with were never operationalized, the world price rule for traded goods has been adhered to. However it is worth noting that this rule at first sight appears to violate one of the central canons of applied welfare economics that the value of a good is determined by its contribution to consumer welfare as measured by the compensating variation; that is the maximum the consumer would be willing to pay to receive a good (Mishan 1975; pp. 416–21). The full compensating variation is the amount paid plus any consumer surplus for non-marginal expenditures. As Londero in this volume (Chapter 4) reminds us, this precept remains valid even when it appears superficially to be violated by the world price rule. The reason is simply that if there are no changes in prices faced by consumers the compensating variation analysis ceases to hold, since consumers are neither better nor worse off as a result of project activity; with the small-country assumption the implication is that production or use of traded goods has no effect on domestic prices but simply affects foreign exchange reserves. Thus domestic production from an import substitute project replaces imports, whilst consumer prices, assumed to be the world price plus a given protective margin, remain unchanged; hence consumers are neither better nor worse off (assuming away any quality differences). Similarly, use of an exportable good by a project reduces export revenue, whilst consumer prices for the good, assumed to be determined by the world price plus the effect of any taxes or subsidies on trade, remain unchanged. Where consumer prices do change, for example, in the production or use of non-traded goods, the conventional willingness to pay approach still applies, although to express this in terms of world price units, as is required in the 'border-price methodology' of Little and Mirrlees, demands an extra and somewhat convoluted adjustment using a conversion factor for consumption.[5] The operational significance of this point is that changes in consumer welfare via changes in relative prices must be incorporated in cost–benefit calculations if all welfare changes are to be included, a point which has a particular significance for projects in non-traded sectors.

The difficulty of benefit valuation in non-traded activities where the simple world price rule will not apply directly has long been recognized. There are two conceptually distinct problems here: the first and empirically most significant is in deriving a meaningful estimate of benefit at domestic prices; the second involves the logically necessary step of converting this to a 'border-price equivalent' figure. In practice most of the effort of economists working on projects in such sectors has addressed the first of these questions and either ignored the latter or dealt with it only crudely. Quantitative benefit valuation for non-traded outputs normally involves either estimating cost savings on other forms of supply (where it is assumed that project output substitutes for higher-cost supply sources) or estimating consumer willingness to pay for additional output. The chapter by Klümper in this volume (Chapter 13) combines elements of both of these alternatives in a detailed case study illustration of benefit valuation for the water sector; here benefits are based on a combination of savings from high-cost private sources and new usage valued at expected tariffs plus estimated consumer surplus. Another example of an unorthodox project problem which is likely to become more significant in coming years is the appraisal of technical assistance projects, discussed by Gray in this volume (Chapter 16). Both chapters, whilst superficially quite different, are directly in the tradition of applied welfare economics taken over from a developed-country context and illustrate precisely the sort of exercise that project economists will be increasingly concerned with in the future.

SAVINGS PREMIUM

Use of a savings premium was a standard feature of both the so-called UNIDO and Little and Mirrlees approaches. Theoretically this adjustment emerged quite simply from the not unreasonable assumption of serious imperfections in capital markets in developing countries. Theoretically, ignoring the so-called 'isolation paradox', in a perfect capital market savers' time preference precisely matches the productivity of capital, so income used for consumption or savings purposes must be of equal value. Thus by definition a scarcity of savings relative to investment opportunities, as a result of the capital market failing to clear, implies that the productivity of capital at the margin exceeds the cost of forgoing consumption, that is savers' time-preference rate. Whenever this is the case there must be a positive savings premium; in the standard formulation this varies positively with the productivity of capital and the reinvestment rate from investment income and negatively with society's time-preference rate for consumption (the consumption rate of interest). Following the work of Marglin (1967) this approach led to the use of a social consumption rate of interest for discounting future benefits and costs combined with a positive savings premium applied to all savings used or created by a project (UNIDO 1972). It is now clearly understood that Little and Mirrlees did things back to front: by choosing to use savings rather than consumption as their unit they reduced the value of net consumption flows relative to savings and applied a discount rate that was based on opportunity costs, not social time preference. They later admitted that the whole series of adjustments, which followed logically from their choice of unit or numeraire, was made so that they could derive values for their discount rate that were in the range (typically 8 per cent to 12 per cent) that practical people (that is the World Bank) would find plausible.

There are two threads in this argument which we wish to pursue a little further. First, in much of the discussion the case for a positive savings premium was used interchangeably with that for a premium on government income. Much of the early methodology was written at a time when governments were still seen as engines of development, so that income in the hands of the government could be invested productively to bring in higher future consumption, or if it were not invested government income could be used for equally socially productive purposes. This assumption of a rational efficient government may be at odds with current orthodoxy, but it conveniently allowed Squire and van der Tak (1975, p. 106) to put forward the simplifying working assumption that all public income was equally valuable and that private savings and public income could be equated. Hence with these highly restrictive conditions a weight for public income could be derived following the Marglin formula for the savings premium. Things may look quite different from the perspectives of the 1990s where, for many, government activity is part of the problem, not the solution. However the case for a positive premium on government income continues to be argued by Squire et al. in this volume. Now there is significant difference in the basis for the premium. Instead of it being based on the returns generated on new public investment, which exceed the social time-preference discount rate, the case for the premium is now derived from the cost of raising income for the government from the private sector. The new rationale is bound up with the focus on the macro cost of a budget deficit in the open-economy macroeconomics literature that has dominated the structural adjustment debate (Weiss 1995); project income going to government means that distortionary alternative sources of income, whether higher taxes on the private sector or money creation, can be avoided. The avoided cost of these other sources of government income thus provides the measure of the premium on project income going to the government. For example, if it could be estimated that every dollar of tax revenue raised has a cost in terms of loss of allocative efficiency of 0.3 dollars this gives us a 30 per cent premium on additional government income.[6] Naturally, estimates for the efficiency losses due to taxation are subject to wide margins of error; in recognition of this Squire et al. suggest as a fall-back position that the net effect of a project on the government budget be estimated and different values for the premium experimented with. The concern is to avoid the overestimation of the benefits from projects that serve the private sector, but are financed significantly from the budget rather than by user charges; the argument is that only if the impact of such projects in terms of additional distortionary costs, either through taxation or deficit financing, is included will a full cost–benefit appraisal be undertaken.

The second point we wish to dwell on relates to the discount rate. Once a savings premium is used the appropriate discount rate will normally be the social time-preference rate for consumption. Indeed, as we have noted, such a discount rate must be known to establish the magnitude of the savings premium. Empirical attempts to estimate this elusive parameter are normally based on data on projected consumption per capita growth combined with an estimate of the rate of decline of the marginal utility of consumption plus another estimate of the pure impatience element in the discount rate. Even if this latter element is assumed away derivation of a rate still requires agreement on the subjective parameter relating to the marginal utility of consumption. Hence when the theoretical trappings are removed one is left with an essentially subjective value. This has not stopped some analysts from attempting empirical estimates. Such estimates are normally in the 1 per cent to 5 per cent range, since per capital consumption growth will rarely exceed 3 per cent annually and the conventional estimates of the elasticity of the marginal utility of consumption are typically between 1.0 and 1.5.[7]

However such discount rates are 'low' by conventional standards and thus this specification of the discount rate has received renewed attention as part of the revived debate on discounting stimulated in recent years by the issue of how to handle long-term environmental effects. It seems counter-intuitive if what everyone can agree are serious long-run environmental effects are discounted to insignificance by the application of conventional rates of 10 per cent or 12 per cent. Cline (1992) is an important recent example of this approach to environmental issues using a savings premium and a low consumption time-preference discount rate of 1.5 per cent.

Two proponents in this debate, Kula and Price, give their own individual views in this volume (Chapters 5 and 6); the former argues for his own 'modified discounting' approach, which does not assume that society can be treated as a single individual with an infinite life. The latter rejects conventional discounting based on 'a uniform negative exponential function', primarily in relation to (a) non-marginal values; and (b) resources that are not replaceable by products that are the fruits of economic growth.

The environment broadly defined appears to fall squarely under both headings (a) and (b). If environmental assets cannot be substituted by man-made capital the conventional argument that resources set aside today to cover environmental damage can grow over time at the discount rate to provide a fund to cover environmental loss in the future will cease to be valid. Further, in this case there would need to be some mechanism to ensure that potential compensation became actual so that those in the future affected by environmental damage really did benefit from the income generated by the fund. This would require a major form of earmarked taxation. Where conventional discounting procedures do not apply, alternatives include an environmental sustainability constraint (Markandya and Pearce 1994) and the use of a very low (although perhaps arbitrary) discount rate plus a savings or capital premium (Cline 1992).

INCOME DISTRIBUTION

For some, the most radical aspect of the development cost–benefit literature was its emphasis on the quantification and valuation of income flows to different groups to allow the calculation of a new measure of project worth that incorporated a project's distributional impact. The mechanics of how this might be done differed between the different systems. In many ways the approach in UNIDO (1972) of decomposing a project's net present value (NPV) into flows to different groups, some of which would gain while others lost, was both the clearest and easiest to operationalize. The alternative implied by Little and Mirrlees was to incorporate distributional effects in particular shadow prices, most notably the shadow wage. As Londero in this volume reminds us, such 'synthetic prices' give only a very partial insight into a project's distributional effects and in practice any systematic assessment of all distributional consequences requires an approach based on decomposing income flows.

There was also a subtle difference in the approach to income or more strictly consumption weights: following Little and Mirrlees (1974), Squire and van der Tak (1975) based their well-known approach on a simple, if somewhat mechanical, formula which derived the weight for a particular group from a comparison between a reference level of consumption, which in their formulation was the national average and the average for the group. The weight need not be simply the ratio of the two averages, since the ratio is raised by a power reflecting government preference for equality; however, as in the few operational applications of the approach this power is often set at unity, in effect the weight becomes a simple ratio.[8] The alternative to the use of a formula is to base weights on the revealed preference of decision takers for equality, as manifested in past project decisions where real income was traded off for redistribution; this was the recommendation in UNIDO (1972) and it is repeated in Brent (1990), although how this could actually be made workable is extremely unclear. The use of distributional weights was controversial on theoretical grounds with some eminent figures arguing that it violated the established principles of applied welfare economics, based on the potential compensation principle (Harberger 1978). By this logic a good project was simply one that generated sufficient income to be able in principle to compensate those whose incomes were adversely affected, without any guarantee that this redistribution actually took place. The response that not using income weights implied weighting all income flows by unity, which was as much a value judgement as any set of non-unitary weights, may well have been highly persuasive intellectually to those used to thinking about development issues, amongst which poverty alleviation has rightly had an important place. However practice on the ground never followed up this particular suggestion.

In this volume one of the key figures in the literature, Lyn Squire, with others, explains why the distribution weighting system he set out in Squire and van der Tak (1975) was never applied seriously at the World Bank. The difficulty in obtaining agreement on the weights to use and the technical problem of estimating the income flows for different groups are real practical obstacles. However he chooses here to stress another, intellectually more compelling, point: it was always recognized that using project selection as a means of redistributing income and reversing poverty was to rely on an indirect, possibly second-best policy instrument. Direct measures include special poverty-focused programmes and the use of the fiscal system to create redistribution. Squire et al. now suggest that distributional and poverty issues are best handled separately from decisions on individual projects. They argue that the composition of a government's public expenditure programme should be judged in the light of distributional targets; if the judgement is favourable the implication is that the World Bank and other donors can proceed with project appraisals that address primarily issues of economic efficiency without normally bringing in the distributional dimension, which is to be handled at a macro rather than project level. However, the authors argue that one aspect of the original weighting system should be retained. This exception refers to the assessment of how a project affects net government income; we have already noted their recommendation that a positive premium on government income should be experimented with.

Whilst for operational purposes it is fairly safe to dismiss the full system of income or consumption weights developed in the mid-1970s, this is not to say that distributional questions themselves should be forgotten.[9] There is now a well-developed methodology to trace through the distributional effect of a project, which can be applied even if the analyst chooses not to weight the different income flows with non-unitary weights but simply presents the results as part of the information derived from a project appraisal. Incidentally, as Franck in this volume reminds us, once an income distribution approach to CBA is adopted it is far easier to see the similarity between the conventional approach and the effects method. The chapters by Londero and da Silva Neto in this volume (Chapters 4 and 14) illustrate the approach; the former draws on material from a detailed book on distributional issues (Londero 1987), whilst the latter is a case study of a very large iron ore mine in Brazil.

We can identify several circumstances in which it might be highly appropriate to estimate unweighted the distributional effects of a project; one is the case Squire et al. have in mind where there is a tight government budgetary position and it is important to establish how government income is affected by a project. This is only a partial distributional analysis but the authors imply that this type of calculation should be carried out routinely. A second situation is where a project is targeted specifically at low-income groups, so that success will be judged in terms of how their income is affected. Here it will be necessary at the appraisal stage to estimate how the project will increase their incomes and to compare project costs with alternative means of achieving the same income change for the target group. A third possibility is where the project concerned has a major foreign investor presence; here it becomes essential to establish how much of the net benefits of a project remain within the national economy and what is the national return on national resources invested in a project. This perspective may have resonances of the 'bargaining model' approach to foreign investors, which has largely gone out of favour in the current climate; however in our view it retains relevance in the 1990s. An important example of this is the upsurge of privatizations, usually involving a combination of foreign and local capital, that has occurred in recent years in a wide range of developing countries. A cost–benefit approach to privatization was pioneered by Leroy Jones (Jones et al. 1990), and is illustrated for Poland, an economy in transition, in the chapter by Cohen and Czyzewski (Chapter 17).

SHADOW-PRICE ESTIMATION

As we have noted, a defining feature of the development cost–benefit literature was its initial focus on economy-wide distortions which meant that key macro prices such as the exchange rate or the interest rate for long-term funds failed to reflect underlying national opportunity costs. The policy framework implicit in this literature was that the factors that caused such distortions were not amenable to influence by the economic advisor and even less so by a modest project economist. Hence with direct policy reform off the agenda economic rationality would have to be introduced by the back door through the use of shadow prices in the process of project appraisal. It is worth recalling that the original idea was that for all developing countries using CBA, national shadow prices (or national economic parameters as they were often termed) would be estimated by a specialist local agency devoted solely to this task; these parameters would then be given to project analysts working for operational ministries or aid agencies for their use in appraisals. The specialist agency would then revise the national parameter estimates periodically.

Practice turned out to be quite different. A number of developing countries did have shadow-pricing studies carried out; for example, the Development and Project Planning Centre was involved in such exercises in Pakistan, Jamaica, Ethiopia, Nepal, China, Botswana, Sri Lanka and Malaysia in the period from the late 1970s to the early 1990s.[10] More recently there has been an interest in this exercise from Eastern Europe and a study has been done on Lithuania; the chapter by Potts in this volume (Chapter 19) summarizes the results of his work there. However, the exercise was typically carried out by external consultants (such as our Centre) rather than a specialist local agency and once estimated it was relatively rare for such parameters to be applied systematically by local ministries or enterprises; aid-financed projects from productive sectors generally had some form of economic appraisal, but as Squire et al. in this volume point out even for World Bank projects these were not always of a high standard and adjustments often tended to be *ad hoc* with shadow prices estimated for a particular project rather than being used consistently across an investment programme.

On the other hand, beginning in the 1980s there has been a major policy shift which, as Wilmshurst in this volume stresses (Chapter 2), has changed the conditions for the application of cost–benefit techniques in many countries. Economic reform, largely but not exclusively introduced in developing countries under the umbrella of structural adjustment financial packages, has introduced a far wider degree of market liberalization than the pioneers of the development cost–benefit literature ever anticipated. The preoccupations of the 1960s and 1970s with heavily overvalued exchange rates, subsidized credit and protected unskilled wages in many countries seem very far from relevant in the new climate of the 1990s. In effect in such countries the distortions that were amenable to policy control have been removed at source and the indirect route of circumventing them subtly through project-level decisions involving shadow prices no longer seems relevant. In other words the policy constraint assumed in the early literature proved to be far less binding than was originally thought.

Some words of caution are necessary to qualify this view. It should not be thought that economic reform of the type that has occurred in many countries over the last 15 years is sufficient to equate market and shadow prices and thus to largely remove the distinction between financial and economic project calculations. In the first instance the developed economy appraisal agenda that we noted at the outset, based on externalities and other forms of market failure, remains relevant; in addition it is misleading to assume that market-based reforms of the type we have seen remove totally the need for economic adjustments. Governments will rightly continue to impose taxes, grant subsidies and influence allocation decisions in various ways, all of which have implications for shadow prices, even if their influence is far less significant and less distorting than under earlier policy regimes.

We can give two simple illustrations of these points relating first to foreign exchange and second to labour. It is sometimes thought erroneously that reform in exchange rate policy, such as the introduction of a floating exchange rate, removes the need for shadow pricing foreign exchange or using a standard conversion factor in the border-price system; the argument is that if the exchange rate is market-determined why should any further adjustment be necessary? The answer is to allow for the effect of taxes and subsidies on the domestic prices of traded goods that can be purchased with foreign exchange. Since trade taxes are likely to remain an important source of revenue for most low-income economies well into the medium term, their influence on shadow pricing will remain relevant, even if they are imposed at a single uniform rate. Weiss (1994a) considers this point in more detail, arguing that a shadow exchange rate or standard conversion factor for use over the life of a project needs to be based on two adjustments: the level of the real exchange rate relative to its long-run sustainable value and the future average trade tax-subsidy rate. If no real exchange rate change is anticipated future tax policy towards foreign trade will determine the future value of the shadow exchange rate.

In relation to unskilled labour, market wages paid by new projects may move closer to national opportunity costs in a labour market in which minimum wage legislation is removed; however equality between the two seems unlikely for most developing countries until well into the medium term. To see this we can revert to the simple model of wage determination that lay behind the early thinking on shadow wages (Harris and Todaro 1970). This involved two sectors that can be termed rural and urban; the former supplies labour to the latter. If one assumes a protected urban wage (*Wu*) due for example to minimum wage legislation and an average income in the rural sector (*q*) then migration will continue until the expected urban wage (*p.Wu*, where *p* is the probability of a migrant worker obtaining employment) equals the rural workers income forgone, that is:

$$p.Wu = q$$

and

$$Wu = 1/p.q$$

In this model if *Wu* is fixed it is the change in unemployment, through its influence on *p*, that allows the equilibrium to be reached. Thinking such as this supported an argument for using market wage rates (*Wu* here) for shadow rates, since if we accept that the average rural income is a proxy for output forgone $1/p$ workers will leave the rural sector in response to a new job opportunity in the urban sector and $1/p.q$ gives total opportunity cost.

It should be noted that this argument can be used independently of labour-market reform removing minimum wages and other restrictions on wage flexibility. However removal of wage restrictions can be expected to bring down *Wu* and have some impact in raising *p*. Numerous complications can be introduced, but here we wish to stress only two points. First, it was always recognized that whilst average rural income may reflect a worker's own personal opportunity cost, it may be a poor proxy for marginal product which is the important concept for output forgone. Second, even if average and marginal products are close at market prices, distortions in product markets in the labour-supplying sector will mean that whilst *q* may be a proxy for labour's marginal product at market prices it will not be at shadow prices; for example if output forgone were an exportable subject to an export tax or a non-traded good produced under monopolistic conditions, market and shadow prices for the forgone output would differ and *q* would have to be replaced by *q.CF*, where *CF* is the conversion factor for the particular output forgone. Hence any residual product distortions in the labour-supplying sector should be reflected in the shadow wage, which will diverge from the market wage actually paid to labour. Use of a positive premium on government income as recommended by Squire further complicates the story (Squire 1989).

These qualifications relating to labour and foreign exchange are not meant to imply that economic reform will not reduce substantially the deviations between market and shadow wages or between official and shadow exchange rates. The conceptual point is that given the structure of actual economies it is expecting far too much of current reform programmes to remove the divergences between shadow and market prices completely.

If we are still going to need some shadow-price estimates, how feasible is it to derive estimates that are a better guide to resource allocation than the prices that are thrown up by newly liberalized markets? Shadow pricing at the project level for outputs and key inputs will certainly remain of significance. However we are now much less able to assert that our national shadow-price estimates relating to broad macro prices will be a superior guide to resource allocation, because the gap between market and shadow prices has been narrowed in many countries and because any operational set of national economic parameters will remain approximate and clearly subject to a significant margin of error. The case for putting a major effort into shadow-pricing studies is probably limited to economies in which the economic reform process has not yet been carried very far; some economies in transition, such as Lithuania discussed here in the chapter by Potts, may fall into this category.

Our techniques for estimating national shadow prices or economic parameters remain relatively unsophisticated, but they have improved in rigour over the years. After some initial partial estimates, when national parameters like those for unskilled labour and important non-traded sectors were estimated independently of each other, a more comprehensive and consistent methodology was developed. Following the pioneering work of Maurice Scott on Kenya (Scott et al. 1976), a clear statement of the semi-input–output approach with some very useful case studies was given by Powers (1981).[11] Since the mid-1980s all the shadow price studies conducted by the Development and Project Planning Centre have used semi-input–output analysis.

It is important to be clear on the strengths and weaknesses of this approach to national parameter estimation. On the positive side its main strength is that of consistency. Most sector and factor estimates are interdependent and thus require the solution of a set of simultaneous equations; to repeat the example noted above the value of unskilled labour will clearly influence the valuation of non-traded activities and, as part of national labour's forgone output, the value of non-traded sectors will in turn be one of the influences on the value of labour. On the negative side, however, even a quite large semi-input–output table requires an aggregation of fairly diverse activities and the sector values that emerge from this exercise are not always readily usable on individual projects because of the high level of aggregation; to give another simple example it may not be very useful to have a sector value for transport in general, when the project concerned moves all its output by rail. More fundamentally, however, through their use of fixed input coefficients such models can imply a very crude pattern of economic response to the demand changes created by new projects. Strictly, responses will depend on price changes and demand and supply elasticities; incorporating these requires a very much more sophisticated model of economic activity than that provided by semi-input–output analysis. An important illustration is the treatment of unskilled labour; where new labour is drawn from will have a major impact on the shadow wage and labour's conversion factor. Simply assuming, as is common, that it goes from agriculture to new projects, with existing employment in different agricultural activities providing the weights for labour-supplying sectors, could be quite misleading. These qualifications mean that despite the clear advantage in terms of consistency of treatment of different activities we still need to interpret shadow-price values from such studies with some care.

OTHER APPROACHES

Economists are now somewhat more humble in their approach to development projects. In part this is likely to be due to a clearer recognition than previously that certain types are not readily amenable to assessment by the economist's toolkit of techniques; Squire et al. in this volume draw attention to the significant number of World Bank projects not subject to an economic rate of return calculation. Similarly from an ODA perspective Wilmshurst in this volume points to areas in which a mixed team approach has replaced the narrower focus of the economist or financial analyst. In part also it is a recognition that development projects can be high-risk activities and that an embarrassingly high proportion of aid-financed (and by implication appraised) projects have gone badly wrong. The chapter by Weiss in this volume (Chapter 12) puts forward a simple stylized fact that 25 per cent of aid projects or thereabouts have 'failed' and discusses some of the implications of this relatively high project failure rate for *ex-ante* work.

Different conclusions can be drawn from this experience. On the one hand it can be argued that economic appraisals should be made more comprehensive and careful; on the other hand, however, others have concluded that an alternative approach is needed. Perhaps the most widely used alternative at present is some version of the logical framework; the chapters by MacArthur and Kijne (Chapters 9 and 10) consider various aspects of the framework. The latter focuses on a variant that is being applied by the European Commission, whilst the former discusses several variants and adaptations of the basic approach.

At one level the logical framework is no substitute for conventional quantitative appraisals; the framework can be seen as a statement of the 'story' of a project, either *ex-ante* or *ex-post*. Inputs, combined with various assumptions about how a project will operate, create outputs which in turn will lead to the achievement of various objectives. There is no reason why such a framework cannot be set out alongside conventional rate of return or quantitative calculations. At another level, however, it can be argued that there will be certain types of project which should be seen in terms of the achievement of a set of objectives, which cannot be converted readily into the monetary numeraire of conventional appraisals; examples of such projects can include those from social sectors, such as health and education, humanitarian aid, institution building and research-oriented projects. Cost-effectiveness analysis was seen as the conventional response to appraisal difficulties in such projects; however even this is not always straightforward where objectives cannot be specified narrowly at the outset. Setting out initial, perhaps sometimes loose, objectives in a project or logical framework may be the most effective way forward for the 'softer' type of project; the framework will probably be of less use in productive-sector projects, where objectives primarily, but not exclusively, relate to output expansion and income growth, which can be converted readily into a cost–benefit calculus. However at the *ex-post* stage, even for such productive activities, the framework approach may be of value in comparing initial objectives with achievements.

CONCLUSIONS

Our conclusion, and certainly that of the conference from which this volume comes, is that whilst the agenda has shifted significantly over the last 25 years there remains plenty for those working in the development cost–benefit field to consider and debate. The most profound trend has been the removal in many countries of what we can term 'first-order macro distortions'; this has meant, as we have argued, that whilst market and shadow prices will frequently continue to diverge, the extent of their divergence has been reduced substantially in many countries. The implications of this for the economist's role in economic appraisal are that time that might otherwise be spent worrying about national economic parameters can now be allocated to more project-specific issues, relating for example to markets, price trends for outputs and key inputs and externalities and, as we have suggested, distributional effects, including that on the government budget. The environmental front is where externality issues refuse to go away and it is a very safe prediction that environmental concerns will loom large in future debates on the application of cost–benefit techniques; as we have seen they are now influencing thinking on the discount rate.[12] In general, whilst cost–benefit work in the development context will continue to have its own distinctive perspective, these trends in a project-specific direction are likely to mean that the first of the two traditions we identified at the outset, that of applied welfare economics, is likely to become increasingly influential. Hence, whilst the toolkit of the development practitioner of cost–benefit will never be exactly similar to their equivalent working in a developed-country context, we speculate that there will be increasing overlap between the set of tools used regularly by both.

NOTES

1. For an introductory review of these various approaches, see Chowdhury and Kirkpatrick (1994). For a more detailed discussion see Curry and Weiss (1993).
2. The reasons for the decline in popularity of CBA in the 1980s are discussed in Kirkpatrick (1994).
3. The revival of interest in CBA and project appraisal is considered in Kirkpatrick (1994a).
4. The Development and Project Planning Centre contributions to the development project literature include Tribe and Yaffey (1992), Analoui (1994), Maddock and Wilson (1994), MacArthur and Weiss (1994), Kirkpatrick (1991), Curry and Weiss (1993), Weiss (1994c).
5. The treatment of willingness to pay in the Little and Mirrlees method is explained in detail in Ray (1984). Willingness to pay for foreign exchange was picked up in the UNIDO system through their specification of the shadow exchange rate, a point which some see as an advantage for their 'domestic price' approach (Londero (1987).
6. Squire in an earlier statement of the same point reports the results of a survey of studies from a range of countries. In recognition of the uncertainty there he recommends calculat-

ing a 'switching value' for the premium; that is the value it would have to take to make a project unacceptable by conventional criteria (Squire 1989, p. 1131).

7. The conventional formula is

$$i = gn + p$$

where i is the social rate of time preference for consumption, g is projected per capita consumption growth, n is the elasticity parameter of the government's marginal utility function with respect to additional consumption, and p is the pure rate of time preference. For estimates of i for Pakistan, see Weiss (1979) and UNIDO (1980).

8. The well-known formula for weight to group i (di) is

$$di = (ci/cr)^n$$

where ci is the average consumption of group i, cr is the reference consumption level (the national average or some other), and n is the elasticity parameter of the government marginal utility function with respect to additional consumption. Weiss's contribution to the literature on weighting involved the suggestion that cr could be set at the poverty line (Weiss in UNIDO 1980).

9. Not everyone has abandoned the case for distributional weights: Brent (1990) is an ardent advocate. Weiss (1994b) questions the feasibility of using consumption weights.
10. Weiss participated in all these studies, apart from the latter two in Sri Lanka and Malaysia. A summary of the results of these and studies by other researchers is in Curry and Weiss (1993, pp. 264–7) and MacArthur (1994).
11. The approach is surveyed in Weiss (1988).
12. Environmental papers delivered at the conference are published in the second volume, Cusworth and Wilson (1996). For a collection of papers on the environment and cost–benefit from a development perspective see Weiss (1994c).

REFERENCES

Analoui, F. (ed.) (1994), *The Realities of Managing Development Projects*, Aldershot, UK: Avebury.

Brent, R. (1990), *Project Appraisal for Developing Countries*, Hemel Hempstead, UK: Harvester-Wheatsheaf.

Chervel, M. (1973), 'Exercise in the Application of the Effects Method', *Industrialisation and Productivity*, no. 20, New York: UN.

Chowdhury, A. and C. Kirkpatrick (1994), *Development Policy and Planning: An Introduction to Models and Techniques*, London: Routledge.

Cline, W. (1992), *The Economics of Global Warming*, Washington, DC: Institute for International Economics.

Curry, S. and J. Weiss (1993), *Project Analysis in Developing Countries*, London: Macmillan.

Cusworth, J. and F. Wilson (eds) (1996), *Environment and Sustainable Project Development*, Cheltenham, UK: Edward Elgar.

Harberger, A. (1978), 'On the Use of Distributional Weights in Social Cost Benefit Analysis', *Journal of Political Economy*, **86** (2).

Harris, R. and M. Todaro (1970), 'Migration, Unemployment and Development: a two sector analysis' *American Economic Review*, **60**.

Jones, L., P. Tandon and I. Vogelsang (1990), *Selling Public Enterprises: A Cost-Benefit Methodology*, Cambridge, Mass.: MIT Press.

Kirkpatrick, C. (ed.) (1991), *Project Rehabilitation in Developing Countries*, London: Routledge.

Kirkpatrick, C. (1994), 'The rise and fall of cost benefit analysis: the role of project appraisal in managing development projects' in Analoui (1994).

Kirkpatrick, C. (1994a), 'New developments in project appraisal in developing countries: editor's introduction', Special Issue on Project Appraisal in Developing Countries, *Journal of International Development*, **6** (1).

Little, I.M.D. (1950), *Critique of Welfare Economics*, London: Oxford University Press.

Little, I. and J. Mirrlees (1968), *Manual of Industrial Project Analysis in Developing Countries, vol. 2*, Paris: OECD.

Little, I. and J. Mirrlees (1974), *Project Appraisal and Planning for Developing Countries*, London: Heinemann.

Little, I., T. Scitovsky and M. Scott (1970), *Industry and Trade in Some Developing Countries*, London: Oxford University Press.

Londero, E. (1987), *Benefits and Beneficiaries*, Washington, DC: Inter-American Development Bank.

MacArthur, J. (1994), 'Estimating Efficiency Prices through Semi-Input–Output Methods: a review of practice in available studies', *Journal of International Development*, **6** (1).

MacArthur, J. and J. Weiss (eds) (1994), *Agriculture, Projects and Development*, Aldershot, UK: Avebury.

Maddock, N. and F. Wilson (1994), *Project Design for Agricultural Development*, Aldershot, UK: Avebury.

Marglin, S. (1967), *Public Investment Criteria*, London: Allen and Unwin.

Markandya, A. and D. Pearce (1994), 'Natural Environments and the Social Rate of Discount' in Weiss (1994c).

Mishan, E. (1975), *Cost–Benefit Analysis*, London: Allen and Unwin.

Powers, T. (ed.) (1981), *Estimating Accounting Prices for Project Appraisal*, Washington, DC: Inter-American Development Bank.

Ray, A. (1984), *Cost Benefit Analysis*, Baltimore, Md: Johns Hopkins University Press.

Scott, M., J. MacArthur and D. Newbery (1976), *Project Appraisal in Practice*, London: Heinemann.

Squire, L. (1989), 'Project Evaluation in Theory and Practice' in H. Chenery and T. Srinivasan (eds), *Handbook of Development Economics, vol. 2*, Amsterdam: North Holland.

Squire, L. and H. van der Tak (1975), *Economic Analysis of Projects*, Baltimore, Md: Johns Hopkins University Press.

Tribe, M. and M. Yaffey (1992), *Project Rehabilitation in Adverse Environments*, Aldershot, UK: Avebury.

UNIDO (1972), *Guidelines for Project Evaluation*, New York: UN.

UNIDO (1980), *Practical Appraisal of Industrial Projects*, New York: UN.

Weiss, J. (1979), 'Project selection and the Equity Objective: the use of social cost-benefit analysis in Pakistan, *Pakistan Development Review*, **18** (2).

Weiss, J. (1988), 'An Introduction to Shadow Pricing in a Semi-Input–Output Approach', *Project Appraisal*, **3** (4).

Weiss, J. (1994a), 'Structural Adjustment, Real Exchange Rates and Project Appraisal', *Journal of International Development*, **6** (4).

Weiss, J. (1994b), 'Double Counting, Double Not Counting and Distribution Weights', *Project Appraisal*, **9** (4).
Weiss, J. (ed.) (1994c), *The Economics of Project Appraisal and the Environment*, Aldershot, UK: Edward Elgar.
Weiss, J. (1995), *Economic Policy in Developing Countries: the reform agenda*, Hemel Hempstead, UK: Prentice Hall–Harvester.

PART TWO

Perspectives on Cost–Benefit Analysis

2. An ODA perspective on the past and future of project appraisal*

Jon Wilmshurst

INTRODUCTION

This chapter reviews ODA experience from 25 years or more of project appraisal. The identification, appraisal and design of projects has been an important part of ODA work since the 1960s and the operational validity of this activity has been enhanced over this period.

The basic concept – the comparison between all costs and all benefits – should be a fundamental component of all public-expenditure decisions. We have always recognized that this cannot be undertaken in purely quantitative terms, that important considerations can be expressed only in qualitative assessments, and this qualitative aspect predominated in the early days. We did not have the tools to measure many of the costs and benefits foreseen beyond narrow financial analysis. But the systematic procedures introduced by economists in the 1970s for social cost–benefit analysis (CBA) completely altered this. Quantitative economic appraisal became the primary focus of project appraisal.

The first half of this chapter outlines the issues from the early days: the development paradigm and the controversies at the micro level. The second half traces the macroeconomic shifts of the 1980s, the consequent broadening of the scope of project appraisal and the key issues for the future. These developments have placed greater responsibilities on the practitioners of project preparation and appraisal.

THE DEVELOPMENT MODEL OF THE 1970s

It is almost impossible to avoid caricature in a short contribution which attempts to outline the development model of 25 years ago. Broadly, compre-

*The Overseas Development Administration (ODA) is the government department responsible for overseas aid in the UK.

hensive national planning was attempted in most developing countries with the public sector at the centre of resource allocation. The terms of trade were expected to decline for primary commodities and the manufacturing sector was seen as the engine for growth. But the private sector, domestic or foreign, was thought to be unwilling to provide investment funds in the necessary volume and unlikely to recognize the dynamic advantages of innovation.

The public sector needed, therefore, both to generate investment resources and to direct them to the best uses. The instruments for this were high taxes, import protection, foreign borrowing, administrative allocation of foreign exchange, price controls, subsidized interest rates and directed credits. The public sector was often the main innovator and investor.

The development of CBA in this environment had two pillars. One was recognition that the financial projections of investors – whether private or public – were too narrow because they took account of cash flows only as they related to the investor, not the wider effects for the country. The second contained an irony: CBA was needed because prices were considered to give incorrect signals, even though those prices were the result of the instruments used by government to direct resources.

ISSUES IN THE 1970s

The predominance of quantitative economic techniques meant that many of the issues raised in the early days were concerned with technical economic aspects. Considerable research was undertaken into shadow prices: for example, the accounting rate of interest, the shadow wage for unskilled (surplus) labour, foreign exchange and the premium to be accorded to uncommitted savings. The appropriate numeraire to use was a key issue and techniques for social (distribution) were prominent in the literature.

These particular problems have been largely solved, partly through innovation and partly by the changing environment. Issues which were important in the dirigiste era are less significant in the liberal 1990s. Social weighting is an exception, however. Underlying technical and philosophical problems have never been solved and the practical problem of obtaining the necessary data is probably insoluble for most projects. As a result, ODA has never used social weighting successfully in project decisions although full experiments were conducted in real project proposals.

The links between the results of project appraisals and the development plan were another technical concern. What should our response be if the plan gave one signal (e.g. build a machine tool factory) but appraisal gave the reverse (the net present value of the factory would be heavily negative)? The source of this dilemma originates in the irony mentioned above. The main

CBA techniques, i.e. OECD's Little and Mirrlees (1974) system, the UNIDO *Guide* (1978) and the World Bank's Squire and van der Tak (1975) methodology, were based, either directly or indirectly, on market-determined prices. The plan often assumed that current prices and market forecasts were a poor guide to the future and in any event the dynamic advantages to be captured from certain investments could not be measured in conventional CBA. Hence the plan was bound to conflict with individual project appraisals on occasion. In my view the fault was more likely to lie with the plan than the project appraisal. But this is subject to several caveats: CBA is an inexact science; it needs to take account of the policy context and infant industry and similar arguments are valid in some (carefully considered) circumstances.

Another group of issues related to the reliability of input data and forecasts. All CBA relies heavily on technical parameters: crop yields, design capacities, take-up rates, traffic flows, turn-around times, output per worker, class sizes, unit prices, and so on. Measurement errors are often high in the base year and the forecasting which is essential in appraisal introduces errors in both volume and price dimensions. The combined effect of these data problems can be enormous: as a simple illustration, forecasts made in the late 1970s for the oil price in the late 1990s were commonly around $50 per barrel. The current price is well under $20. In ODA experience, differences between project appraisals (*ex-ante*) and evaluations (*ex-post*) are more likely to be the result of such data problems than conceivable errors in shadow pricing. This data problem has not diminished with the passage of time. It is as important now as it was in the 1970s. But it is recognized more widely and techniques for sensitivity and risk analysis are now standard practice (without being a complete answer).

One other concern of a generation ago should be mentioned, because it still has considerable relevance. This is the broad issue of external effects. External *economic* effects have always been recognized as an important issue, relevant to the conflict between the plan and CBA which is discussed above. This aspect places a premium on the definition of the project for CBA purposes – the relevant boundary for project effects – an issue which is somewhat neglected in the literature but looms very large in practice. *Non-economic* external effects were not recognized so widely in the past but have become a major preoccupation in recent years. The problem is that most CBA adopts the conventions of national accounting. Items which are not captured in GDP measures – women's time, environmental effects, political freedoms, etc. – are not measured in CBA. This aspect is discussed further below.

THE CHALLENGES OF THE 1980s

The 1980s brought the debt crisis, structural adjustment and the collapse of central planning in Eastern Europe and the former Soviet Union. At the parochial level of project appraisal, the decade brought accumulating evidence that projects assessed as sound at the appraisal stage were underperforming badly at *ex-post* evaluation. What went wrong?

The macro and micro issues are linked, of course. The debt crisis resulted from failed economic policies, errors of national planning and lack of flexibility in an uncertain world. Economic reform (often termed structural adjustment) was a necessary response to this. But there were also non-economic causes at the macro level. A major factor was failure in the political field. Many governments were non-representative and self-serving. They did not submit themselves to normal democratic tests and often did not take account of the interests of the total population. We can assume that broad-based economic and social development was not always the central goal and that corruption influenced individual project decisions. At the extreme, projects could not succeed in the middle of civil wars.

Institutional and social aspects were other sources of failure. The direction of causality between these and wider policies is uncertain, but it is clear that projects were implemented in a setting of inappropriate prices and other incentives, weak financial capacity and management structures, low technical skills, poor accountability and inadequate consultation with project stakeholders.

The agenda for project appraisal therefore became more ambitious. Logically, the macro-policy, political, institutional and social setting had to be addressed first. At the project level, there were arguments for internalizing more of the externalities. Apart from casting the net wider in looking for project effects, this involved attempts to value activities previously assessed in qualitative terms only and also to incorporate in the overall project appraisal some kind of calculus for the total project effects.

Not all of this was new. For example, the Roskill Commission had undertaken far-ranging and imaginative valuations of almost everything relevant to the proposed Third London Airport in 1971. But such issues became more prominent in developing countries in the 1980s and the concern with the broader setting added an extra dimension. These concerns were reflected in two books from that period sponsored by ODA: its overall guide to economic appraisal, largely written by a member of Bradford University's Development and Project Planning Centre (ODA 1988), and a guide to the valuation of environmental effects (Winpenny 1991).

These developments also brought a more interdisciplinary approach to projects in the ODA. Previously a project team had usually comprised technical specialists and an economist, the latter responsible for both financial and economic aspects. From the mid-1980s onwards the requirements expanded. Social, institutional and environmental assessments were also needed. Existing professionals learned new skills and specialists in these new areas joined ODA's staff. Administrators had to manage more complex project cycle activities.

Economic reform also changed the roles of the public and private sectors, introduced privatization of parastatal enterprises and liberalized prices. One result of this was that nominal prices moved closer to opportunity costs as they became determined by market forces, reducing the importance of shadow pricing. It also meant that the private sector assumed the responsibility for financing a much higher proportion of total investment. One of the instruments which pushed developing countries towards private funding, particularly for infrastructure investments, was the OECD Helsinki Agreement on the use of officially supported export credits of 1992. This Agreement reduced the scope for public-sector funding by banning tied aid credits (defined as credits tied to donor procurement with a grant element in the range 35–80 per cent) for projects capable of being financially viable.

Nevertheless the public sector still has a major role in investment, particularly in the low-income countries because they are less attractive to foreign private finance, and CBA remains important. Even in economic infrastructure, for example, the public sector still finances 93 per cent of new investments although the private sector may be the direct provider (World Bank 1994). CBA is an essential tool for design and appraisal in this sector, in which developing countries invest $200 billion per year, and it is being applied increasingly in the education and health sectors. But the context and specific concerns have clearly changed dramatically since 1970 for both developing country governments and donors.

ISSUES FOR THE FUTURE

A striking feature of the past 25 years is the way in which project appraisal concerns have broadened and extended. Earlier concerns with how best to forecast the economic rate of return have given way to interest in a much wider range of factors thought likely to affect project impact. Focus on the design and appraisal at the project commitment stage has extended to monitoring and review throughout implementation, a more sustained concern with the project cycle. The next few paragraphs therefore outline the issues which are at the cutting edge of project appraisal today and probably deserve research interest. The broader setting is an important part of this. Key issues are outlined in the following paragraphs.

Given that stakeholder participation is now recognized as essential at the project level, how much account should be taken of the national or provincial political setting? At one extreme, governments may be so unpopular that a coup or civil war may stop normal activities. More conventional political changes can bring radical policy changes affecting exchange rates, prices, imports, etc. Sensible project appraisal takes into account such possibilities.

Institutional change in the sector may be more sensible than new investments. This issue has several aspects. The prior question is whether the sector should be in public or private hands. If the latter, the privatization project takes precedence and appraisal should look at the various options, with competitive supply arrangements as a primary goal. If this is impracticable, establishment of an appropriate regulatory regime for the private-sector monopolist requires careful assessment.

Linked to this, the new institutional economics introduces a further problem at the sector level. Benefits will result from, for example, financial restructuring without new investments (i.e. higher output from the same inputs or lower inputs for the same output). ODA has encountered several proposals of this kind and accepts their legitimacy, but there are virtually no case studies or other evidence to assist in determining the precise nature and scale of the benefits.

Sustainability of sponsor institutions is now recognized as an important determinant of project success. Financial analysis is part of this but broader structural and managerial assessments are also necessary. Such institutional awareness is now part of the toolkit for all professionals and many donors (including ODA) employ specialists in this field. But it is, perhaps, even further from an exact science than economics.

The more ambitious agenda of today has also taken appraisal into new areas at the project level. Investments in the social sectors – education, health and population, housing, domestic water and sewerage – are now subjected to much more careful analysis than 25 years ago. Quantification of benefits remains somewhat suspect, however, despite the research undertaken. Cost-effectiveness can be employed usefully but in practice outputs are seldom static or clear and this may not help much with overall resource allocation problems.

Humanitarian aid, which has taken an increasing share of donor resources in recent years, has not been appraised as rigorously as development projects in the past. In many cases the reasons are obvious – assistance has to be provided quickly in an emergency situation – but the build-up to humanitarian needs can be fairly slow, as in the case of drought. ODA has spent over £800 million on humanitarian needs of both the emergency and slow-onset varieties over the past three years and has commissioned several studies – for example, on the Bangladesh cyclone and the Southern African drought – in order to learn the lessons. It has also prepared guidelines for humanitarian aid projects (ODA 1994), but this branch of the appraiser's art is still in its infancy.

The process approach to project implementation has gained popularity in recent years without commensurate advances in appraisal techniques. This approach is typically used in the social sectors, research and institutional development projects and other projects with a strong 'people' dimension. The essential feature is that wider objectives are agreed at the outset but the exact modalities for achieving this are determined as the project proceeds in successive, flexible stages. Exact costs and benefits can seldom be determined at the outset, therefore, and appraisal and design need to be even more interactive than in 'blueprint' projects. Essential ingredients are limited commitments (e.g. pilot developments), milestone reviews and flexibility drawn wide enough to include termination of the project.

The trade-off between the results of different types of appraisal is hardly new, but deserves mention as the range of appraisal broadens. The technical, financial, economic, social, institutional and environmental appraisals should be complementary. For example, the economic returns are less likely if the social appraisal is negative. But there are obvious examples of conflict (e.g. sound economic forecast but weak cash flow, financially profitable but environmentally damaging), often as a result of externalities. How best to balance such conflicting signals is still a controversial area.

These potential conflicts in an interdisciplinary system also cast light on the definition of objectives. This obviously requires careful thought in the process approach – where both intermediate and final objectives are necessary – and it emerges from *ex-post* evaluations as an underlying problem for other kinds of project also. Was the water supply project intended to improve health or save women's time? Was humanitarian aid aimed at preventing starvation or helping agricultural production to resume? Is sustainability achieved if another donor supports the ensuing phase of a small enterprise development project? Precise definition of project objectives seems to be elusive yet it is a fundamental aspect of appraisal.

The appraisal of risk is also a familiar issue but again it takes on a new complexion as appraisal becomes more complex. Political, social, environmental and other risks were less familiar in the past. Better techniques are needed, particularly for the normal situation of inadequate data.

Most of these issues seem a far cry from the technical preoccupations of the late 1960s. One issue spans the years, however, overall resource allocation. The market is allocating more national resources now than in the days of central planning but the government budget is still an important instrument. Market failure is sufficiently pervasive to require government interventions of a non-financial kind also (e.g. competition policies and monopoly regulation, land use planning, environmental controls). The two-way link between micro analysis at the project level and macro policies affecting overall resource allocation remains fairly hit-and-miss. Research which established the link more transparently, particularly at the individual country level, would assist broader development.

OVERVIEW

Three main messages emerge from this review of the past 25 years: project appraisal has become more comprehensive, incorporating qualitative as well as quantitative aspects; it places correspondingly heavier demands on practitioners, and its relevance to individual investment and wider resource allocation decisions remains high. There is also a more mundane message for appraisers in the face of the wide technical agenda and the importance of the results. Perhaps the greatest appraisal skill of all is knowing when sufficient appraisal work has been undertaken to permit a soundly based decision.

REFERENCES

Little, I. and J. Mirrlees (1974), *Project Appraisal and Planning for Developing Countries*, London: Heinemann.

ODA (1988), *Appraisal of Projects in Developing Countries*, London: HMSO.

ODA (1994), *Humanitarian Assistance: guidelines on project proposals and project reports*.

Squire, L. and H. van der Tak (1975), *Economic Analysis of Projects*, Baltimore, Md: Johns Hopkins University Press.

UNIDO (1978), *Guide to Practical Project Appraisal*, New York: UN.

Winpenny, J. (1991), *Values for the Environment*, London: HMSO.

World Bank (1994), *World Development Report 1994*: *Infrastructure for Development*, London and New York: Oxford University Press.

3. Project appraisal at the World Bank

Shanta Devarajan, Lyn Squire and Sethaput Suthiwart-Narueput

> We have found that the extent to which [social cost–benefit analysis is] used and [has] real influence is not great, even in the World Bank
>
> Little and Mirrlees (1991)

Given this assessment of current practice by Little and Mirrlees, what steps, if any, should the World Bank take to put its appraisal of projects on a firmer analytical footing? In addressing this question we steer clear of the finer points of project appraisal – how to measure externalities, how to estimate shadow prices, etc. – and focus instead on two broad questions. The first is:

- What is the proper role for project evaluation in today's world where countries have reduced major economic distortions and are reconsidering the role of the state?

As we shall argue, this change in circumstances calls for a shift in the emphasis of project evaluation *away* from a concern with the precision of rate-of-return calculations to a broader examination of the rationale for and merit of public-sector provision.

The second question also moves away from a focus on rate-of-return calculations:

- Besides project evaluation, how else can economic analysis be used to ensure high-quality projects?

Here we suggest that pre-appraisal, sectoral analysis and especially reviews of sectoral public expenditure programmes can contribute substantially to the quality of projects approved by the World Bank. We address these two questions in later sections of the chapter. We begin with an assessment of the conclusion drawn by Little and Mirrlees regarding the current state of project evaluation in the World Bank. The final section offers some concluding thoughts.

THE CURRENT STATE OF PROJECT EVALUATION AT THE WORLD BANK

Before turning to a more qualitative assessment, we begin by examining the proportion of projects subject to evaluation and show how this has changed over time. For this we need to categorize projects according to their year of *approval*, that is, when the evaluation, if any, was done. Unfortunately, however, information on whether a project includes a rate-of-return calculation or not only becomes available on a systematic basis when the project is reviewed by the Operations Evaluation Department at the time of *completion* (that is, when the project loan is fully disbursed). As a result, the number of projects for which we have information falls off dramatically after 1985 – from 114 in 1985 to only 5 by 1989. Accordingly, we confine the analysis to the 15-year period from 1970–85. For obvious reasons, we also confine the analysis to *investment* projects – that is, we exclude all structural adjustment operations, all sectoral adjustment operations, and all technical assistance operations.

Figure 3.1 indicates a significant drop in the percentage of investment projects subject to the scrutiny of a rate-of-return calculation – from almost 70 per cent in 1970 to only slightly more than 40 per cent in 1985. Moreover, most of the decline has occurred in the 1980s. Taking 1980 as the swing year, the average share of projects subject to economic analysis fell from almost 70 per cent in the preceding five years to about 50 per cent in the subsequent five years.

At least three broad developments could explain this phenomenon:

1. *Sectoral shifts*. Traditionally, the World Bank has not calculated rates of return for projects in the social sectors or for financial-sector projects. An increase in the number of projects in these sectors could therefore explain the declining use of project analysis. The data do not support this view (see Figure 3.2). Sectors where rates of return are usually calculated such as agriculture, energy, industry, telecommunications and transport maintained their share in total approvals in that period. In fact, what has happened is a within-sector decline in the use of economic analysis especially in agriculture, energy, industry and transport. Post-1985 sectoral shifts may have become more important as more of our lending has been allocated to the social sectors and the environment – almost 20 per cent of lending in 1994 compared with less than 8 per cent in 1985.

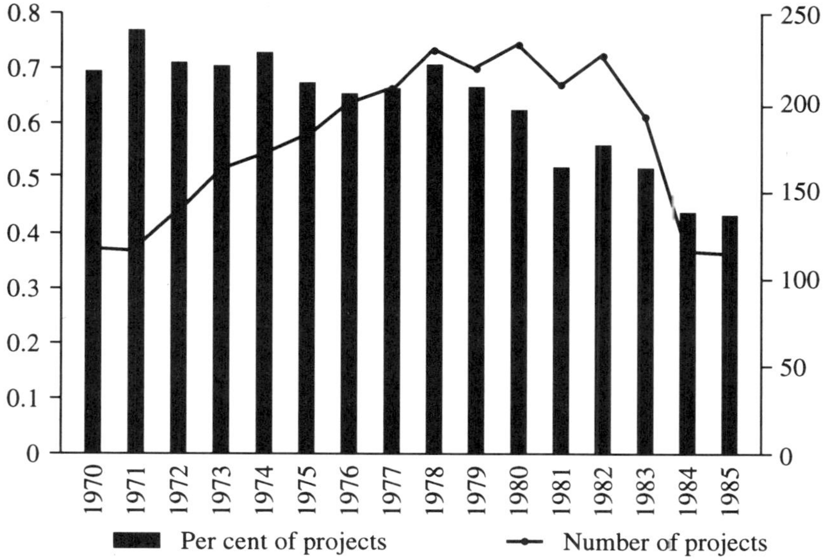

Figure 3.1 *Projects with IRR, 1970–85 (per cent of total number of investment projects)*

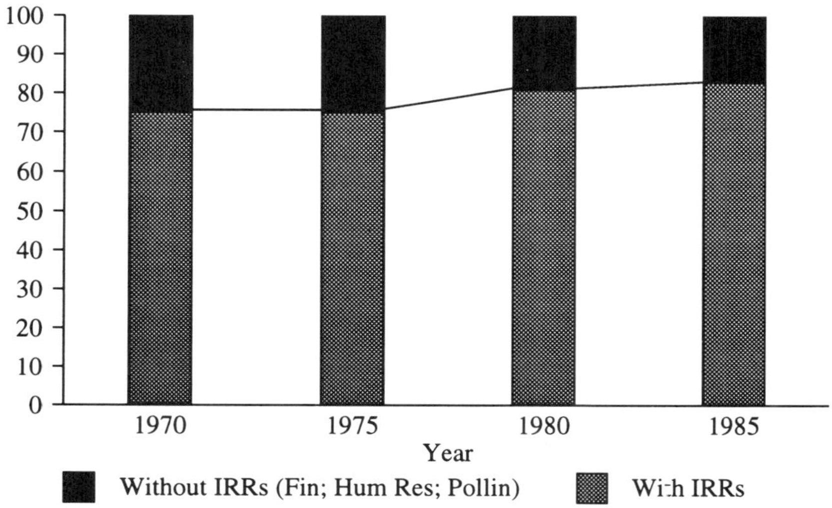

Figure 3.2 *Sectoral composition of projects (per cent of projects in sectors with v. without IRRS)*

2. *Quality control.* Before 1982 the World Bank had a fairly powerful central projects department that set standards for project appraisal and reviewed the quality of appraisal reports. The reorganization of the 1980s – especially that of 1987 – devolved much of the function of quality control to regional vice presidencies which were themselves the producers of the appraisal reports. Given pressures to lend, the incentives implicit in this organizational structure were unlikely to encourage the use of rigorous appraisal techniques.
3. *Other demands.* The decade of the 1980s saw the emergence of structural adjustment operations as an important and high-visibility activity for the World Bank. Between 1980–82 and 1986–88 the share of lending on these operations increased from 7 to 24 per cent. As a result, some of the Bank's best economists became absorbed in macroeconomic matters and attention to the details of investment projects declined. Over time, the number of recruits trained in project analysis also declined.

While obviously judgemental, it appears from the above that shifts in the sectoral composition of investment lending have contributed little to the declining use of project analysis and that the answer probably lies more in changes in the degree of central quality control and the emergence of other demands on the time of the economist. Interestingly, these new demands were focused on removing the very distortions that shadow prices were intended to correct for. Furthermore, as we show later, a less distortionary policy environment is associated with an increased probability of project success, perhaps reducing the need for careful CBA.

Little and Mirrlees appear to be correct therefore in their view that the extent to which project analysis is used at the World Bank 'is not great'. But what about the quality of the analysis when it is used? Judgements on this point are difficult to make precisely because there is no mechanism of central quality control that could be expected to monitor performance on a consistent basis. Nevertheless, two comments can be made, one of which is specific to the approach advocated by Little and Mirrlees while the other is more general.

The specific point concerns the use of distributional weights and the premium for public income. The evidence is clear: other than in a few experimental exercises distributional weights and public income premia have not been part of project analysis in the World Bank. Before asking why, it is important to clarify a key difference between distributional weights and the premium on public income. The need for distributional weights arises because of a concern with *distribution* whereas the need for a premium on public income arises because of a concern with the *efficiency* of resource allocation. To elaborate, imagine that in making its decisions about public investments the government decides to treat a marginal dollar accruing to each and every member of society as being equally valuable. This by itself is sufficient justification for the analyst to ignore *distribution weights*. Marginal benefits accruing to different members of society can be aggregated because they all have the same value. This notwithstanding, one might still want to use a *premium on public income*. Assume for example that at the margin public income is generated through an export tax. This will almost certainly impose a cost through its impact on the allocation of resources, which ought to be captured in appraising any project that makes a claim on public income and that therefore elicits a further increase in export taxation. This conceptual difference notwithstanding, the premium was widely seen as just another element of the system of distribution weights so that arguments for dropping distributional weights proper came to apply to the premium as well.

Why did the World Bank drop distributional weights (and by association the premium on public income)? At least three reasons can be advanced:

1. *Subjectivity*. The use of distributional weights requires a judgement about the value of marginal increases in income to different members of society which staff were extremely reluctant to make even though they recognized that the use of unitary weights for everybody was itself a value judgement.
2. *Practicality*. Many staff held the view that the actual task of identifying who benefited from World Bank projects with sufficient accuracy to make the application of distributional weights worthwhile was overwhelming.
3. *Efficiency*. A more compelling argument took the view that, while government should clearly be concerned about the distribution of income, project selection was not the most efficient instrument for pursuing this goal. This argument would claim that it is much more important for example to ensure that the broad allocation of public expenditure to different spending categories is more or less right than to worry about who benefits from every single project.

These arguments together with the disappearance of central quality control and the emergence of new demands on the time of economists were sufficient to ensure that distributional weights were never seriously used in the World Bank. And as noted above the premium on public income suffered a similar fate even though none of the arguments related directly to the premium and it has anyway a quite different conceptual rationale. We shall return to this point later.

With distributional weights and public income premia abandoned, we might characterize what remains of project evaluation at the World Bank, therefore, as the border price rule and sporadic use of a standard conversion factor, sectoral conversion factors being rarely if ever used. Given this more limited scope, how good is the Bank's project analysis? A general assessment of quality is possible thanks to a special review that was undertaken of the 92 investment operations for which rates of return were calculated and that were approved by the World Bank's board in 1991. The review tried to assess projects according to whether the underlying economic analysis was consistent with the calculations embodied in the rate of return. While obviously subjective, this approach rated the quality of project analysis as 'good or better' for 55 per cent of the projects, as 'marginal or acceptable' for a further 29 per cent, and as 'poor' for the remaining 15 per cent (Salop 1992).

That the ratings had some content is suggested by a follow-up study four years later that looked at the correlation between the rankings described above and the actual performance of the projects (Belli 1995). During implementation, supervision reports routinely provide a judgement on the likelihood that a project will be a failure. According to the study the probability that a project would be considered a failure dropped significantly as the quality of economic analysis at appraisal rose – if the project analysis was rated good or better the probability of failure was judged to be less than 5 per cent whereas it rose to more than 30 per cent if the analysis was rated poor. Although this exercise is subject to criticisms of simultaneity bias and omitted variables (i.e. the quality of analysis could indicate a competent project manager), it is the first attempt that we know of to provide some assessment of the value of good project appraisal.

The same study also updated the 1991 assessment of quality with the following results. Of the 112 projects approved in calendar year 1993 and subject to CBA, 20 per cent were rated good or better, 42 per cent were rated average or acceptable, 25 per cent were rated barely acceptable or marginal, and 13 per cent were rated as poor, an outcome not unlike that of the 1991 study. Given the previous finding about the percentage of projects subject to rate-of-return analysis, and the current finding that little more than half of the appraisals were considered good or better, we conclude that only around 25 per cent of projects are approved on the basis of good economic analysis.

PROJECT EVALUATION FOR THE 1990s

Given the disappointing assessment of current practice, what might one recommend to improve matters? Two steps seem worth pursuing: a more rigorous assessment of the underlying rationale for public sector intervention, and a reconsideration of the role of the premium on public income. Both arise from the changed circumstances in which project evaluation is to be practised. We first describe these changes and then move to the specifics of our two proposals.

Changed Circumstances

It is worth recalling that when Little and Mirrlees wrote their book governments were expanding public investment rapidly and much of that investment was in industry and related sectors. Indeed the first version of their book published in 1969 was titled *Manual of Industrial Project Analysis*. It is also worth recalling that at that time major distortions arising from trade policy and exchange rate policy were characteristic of many economies (see for example Little et al. 1970). It is not surprising therefore that an important focus for Little and Mirrlees was on techniques – especially the use of border prices and conversion factors – that addressed these concerns.

Moving into the second half of the 1990s, these concerns remain but in a much reduced form. Many countries are now grappling with the privatization of public enterprises rather than with new investment, and reforms of trade policy and exchange rate systems have reduced the distortions of most concern to Little and Mirrlees. In these circumstances, it may well be that the modest attention paid by the World Bank to sectoral conversion factors is a sensible allocation of the time of economists. On the other hand, more attention should be paid to the basic question of whether a project ought to be in the public sector or not. As we have noted, the composition of the World Bank's portfolio has shifted to more emphasis on basic infrastructure, social services, and environmental projects for which the rationale for public-sector provision is strong. But, there are still many projects entering the portfolio that could well be shifted to the private sector.

At the same time, the importance of macroeconomic stability is now widely accepted as a prerequisite for sustained development. And a prudent fiscal policy is central to macroeconomic stability. It follows that projects that place a burden on the budget have to be reviewed with care. Fiscal balance will require that the budgetary costs of these projects be recouped through some other tax instrument, which in turn will introduce *distortionary costs* somewhere in the economy. These costs ought to be included in the evaluation of the project which was of course precisely the original rationale for the premium on public income. Moreover, as the composition of projects shifts in favour of those with public costs and private benefits, the need for a careful assessment of budgetary impact and, in turn, of the distortionary cost of alternative sources of revenue will become greater.

Public–Private Choice

These changes – greater scrutiny of what types of activities ought to be undertaken by the public sector and the emergence of a more rational exchange rate and tariff structure – render the few aspects of the Little–Mirrlees approach to project evaluation that are practised at the World Bank less important. Indeed, instead of a concern with the calculation of the rate of return for a public-sector project, interest is now focused on whether a project ought to be in the public sector at all. However, the *principles* underlying Little–Mirrlees, not to mention other manuals on project evaluation (UNIDO 1972; Squire and van der Tak 1975), can be applied to the changed circumstances and new set of questions about the appropriate role of government. In particular, all the approaches to CBA require the project evaluator to specify the *counterfactual*: what would the world have looked like in the absence of the project? And this principle is relevant to the issue at hand whenever there is a private sector alternative to public provision.

To illustrate, assume that the government is contemplating an investment which produces private goods – a shoe factory, say. One possible judgement regarding the counterfactual is that in the absence of the public sector project nothing would have happened. In this case, the analyst should focus on a comparison of the costs incurred by the project and the benefits it is expected to yield. The use of border prices and conversion factors would obviously be relevant. Assuming that the evaluation points to a positive net present value (NPV), this project would be accepted. But the appropriate counterfactual might be that the private sector would have produced the shoes anyway (assuming the enterprise is profitable). In this case, the *net* contribution of the public shoe factory is zero, because the relevant comparison is between the private and the public sector project, and the NPV of the public-sector project (evaluated either at shadow prices or market prices) over and above that of the private-sector project is zero.[1]

While the shoe factory case may seem obvious, there are many World Bank projects where a private-sector alternative appears feasible and yet no private-sector counterfactual was specified. A quick survey of the titles of projects approved by the World Bank's board of directors indicates that only 13 per cent could be said to have an obvious public-sector rationale while many others seemed to have a strong private-sector characteristic (see Table 3.1 for examples). Of course, the title of projects is not an adequate basis for arriving at a definitive judgement, but it can reasonably be concluded that there is a need to consider the private-sector counterfactual more systematically. But on this, the 1995 report notes that 'In many cases, it was not possible to discern the *with* and *without* project situation on the basis of the

Table 3.1 Sample of IBRD and IDA projects with clear vs unclear public component: 1994

Org.	Country	Project title	Amount ($m)
		Projects with clear public component	
IBRD	Algeria	Emergency Desert Locust Control Project	30.0
	Brazil	AIDS and STD Control	160.0
	China	Shanghai Environment	160.0
	Indonesia	Dame Safety Project	55.0
	Jamaica	Tax Administration Reform	13.2
	Mexico	Second Primary Education	412.0
	Morocco	Environmental Management	6.0
	Peru	Basic Health and Nutrition	34.0
IDA	Chad	Health and Safe Motherhood	18.5
	Gambia	Capacity Building for Environmental Management	2.6
	India	Maharashtra Emergency Earthquake Rehab.	146.0
	Uganda	Sexually Transmitted Infections Project	50.0
		Projects with unclear public component	
IBRD	Bulgaria	Water Companies' Restructuring and Modernization	98.0
	China	Telecommunications Project	250.0
	India	Container Transport Logistics Project	94.0
	Korea	Financial Intermediation Project	100.0
	Malaysia	Second Rubber Industry Smallholders Dev. Auth.	70.0
	Papua New Guinea	Petroleum Exploration and Development Tech. Asst.	11.0
	Philippines	Leyte–Luzon Geothermal Project	113.0
	Romania	Industrial Development Project	175.0
	Tunisia	Private Investment Credit Project	50.0
IDA	Madagascar	Petroleum Sector Reform Project	51.9
	Mozambique	Gas Engineering Project	30.0
	Uganda	Cotton Subsector Development Project	14.0
Total 1994 IBRD and IDA loans and credits			20,836.0
IBRD and IDA projects with clear public component			2,747.3
Percentage of total loans and credits with clear public component			13.2%

information provided' in the appraisal report quite apart from whether a private-sector alternative was considered (Belli 1995, p. 15).

To be sure, specifying the private-sector counterfactual is not always straightforward. Yet, some principles can be invoked. First, if the project is producing a private good and is profitable at market prices so that there is good reason to believe the private sector will undertake it, then the difference between the factual and counterfactual should be zero. In this case there is no advantage to having the project in the public sector and the point can probably be established without a serious evaluation.[2] Second, at the other extreme we have the case of pure public goods. Here there is no prospect of private provision and hence no need to worry about a private-sector counterfactual. But pure public goods – defence for example – are relatively rare. And third, we have the case of market failure arising from externalities, indivisibilities, information failures and so forth. Here there may be a case for government intervention, but the private sector counterfactual will not necessarily be zero. Because this is the case which is likely to be most relevant to World Bank projects, we consider it in more detail.

When we have a market failure arising from, say, a positive externality, the private sector will provide some of the good, but not the socially optimal amount. In Figure 3.3, which is drawn for non-tradeables, the positive externality is captured by the marginal social benefit (MSB) curve lying above the marginal private benefit (MPB) curve. An example would be secondary education, which many would claim has significant positive externalities, although private secondary schools exist alongside public ones in many countries. In Figure 3.3 the private sector would provide up to q^* of the good on its own. The socially optimal amount, however, is q^{**}. (In the shoe factory example referred to earlier, the MSB and MPB curves coincide, so that $q^*=q^{**}$.)

In evaluating projects in sectors such as these, the analyst needs to establish two points. First, it is important to establish that public provision results in a greater supply of the good than would have occurred with just private-sector provision (that is, overall supply should exceed q^*). For if this were not the case, public provision would simply be crowding out private provid-

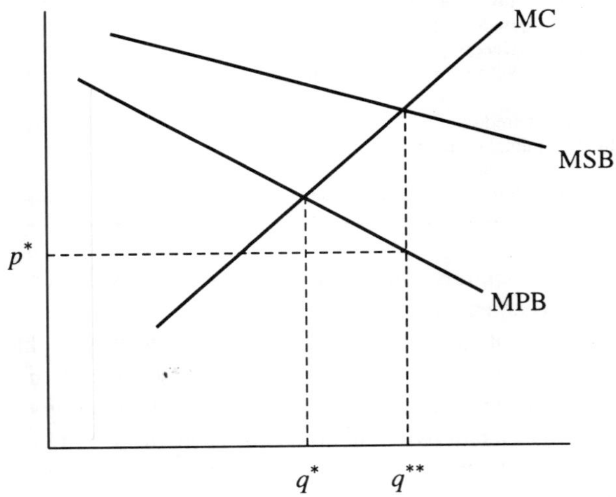

Figure 3.3 Public provision and the private-sector counterfactual

ers. The private-sector counterfactual would be equal to the project (assuming costs are the same) and the NPV of the public-sector project would be zero. And second, we should ensure that the project does not result in total supply of the good beyond q^{**} (that is, beyond the point where marginal costs exceed marginal social benefits). Thus, the relevant range for public provision in this sector is between q^* and q^{**}. We deal with the former (q^*) here because it bears on the issue of the private-sector counterfactual and confront the latter (q^{**}) in our discussion of the premium on public income.

Determining q^*, an unobserved counterfactual, is difficult but it may be feasible in many cases to arrive at an estimate using information on willingness to pay. Appraisal of the Leyte–Luzon Geothermal Project in the Philippines, a US$ 1.3 billion project, illustrates the idea. The economic analysis of this project includes an estimate of consumer willingness to pay based on current bulk energy tariffs in the Luzon system. In turn, this allows an assessment of what the private sector would have provided and determines the *minimum* level of public-sector supply. And as we shall see next it also has important implications for tariff policy.

Revisiting the Premium on Public Income

The premium on public income highlights the need to ensure that public-sector projects attempt to recover as much of their costs as possible from the private sector (that is, that an appropriate pricing strategy accompany the project's implementation). In Figure 3.4, we draw again on the Geothermal Project in the Philippines to show how a project's internal rate of return (IRR) changes with different pricing policies and different levels of the premium on public income. We calculate the IRR of the project for different values of the premium and differing pricing policies. If the electricity is sold at its market value and/or there is no premium on public income, the IRR for the project is 10.5 per cent. But any other combination of pricing policy and premium would result in a substantially lower IRR. In the extreme case, when the electricity is sold at 40 per cent of the market price, and the premium is 100 per cent, the IRR drops to 4.3 per cent, or by 60 per cent.

In the case of this power project it is reasonable to expect that full cost recovery is the appropriate goal, the rationale for public provision presumably being the size and indivisible nature of the project which make private provision difficult. Thus the premium may not be especially critical except as a reminder that less than full cost recovery imposes distortionary costs elsewhere in the economy. But, for many of those projects with a reasonable case for public intervention – basic infrastructure, primary education, rural health, and so on – full cost recovery is not likely to be a desirable goal. Thus, these projects will share a common characteristic: costs are borne by the public

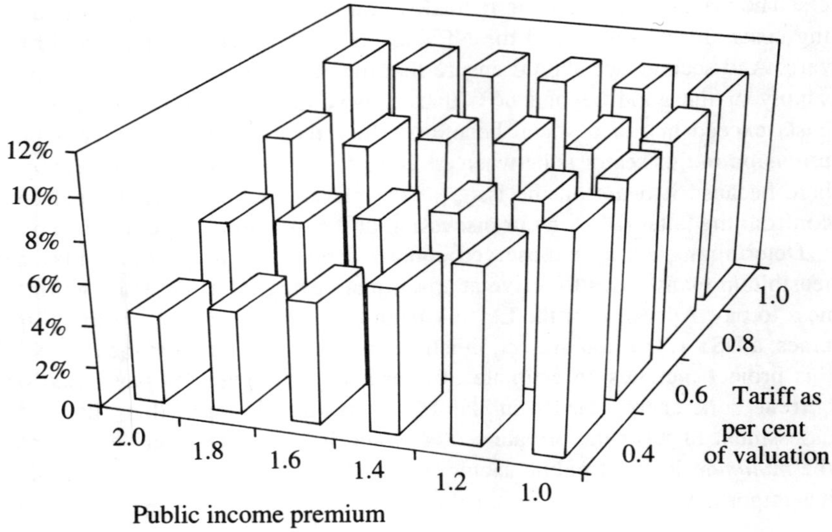

Figure 3.4 Leyte–Luzon Geothermal Project (IRR by premium on public income and tariff – base case IRR = 10.5%)

sector; benefits are enjoyed by the private sector. If there is a premium on public income (which is almost always the case, since governments resort to distortionary taxation for revenue), then the net present value of these projects will be lower than otherwise calculated. Put another way, since the World Bank has not used a premium (that is public costs and private benefits are treated equally), *it has systematically overestimated the NPV of these projects* (see Squire 1989).

Consider again Figure 3.3, which was drawn assuming no premium on public income. To the extent that there is a premium, the fact that the government suffers a fiscal cost (and hence a real cost implied by the need to generate revenue through some other means) causes the overall cost of the project to increase, shifting the MC curve upward and reducing the optimal supply to a level below q^{**}. Failure to consider the premium on public income results in a consistent oversupply of these goods to q^{**}. Note that once the premium on public income is taken into account, we may not want to accept a public project even though it produces between q^{*} and q^{**} where marginal social benefits exceed (private) marginal costs. Beneficiaries of the project could be the private sector while the costs could be borne by the public sector. These costs would need to be inflated by the premium, in which case they could exceed the benefits and lead to the project's rejection.

Of course, the analyst will never know the exact value of the externality. In principle, however, it is possible to estimate the cost associated with raising revenue from the least distortionary tax instrument. Estimates for developed countries range from 32 to 47 per cent in the US to 120 per cent in Sweden. Browning (1987) discusses four key factors that interact to determine marginal welfare cost and account for the wide variation in estimates. These include the elasticity of labour supply; the marginal tax rate; how (balanced budget) government spending affects actual labour earnings;[3] and the progressivity of the change in the tax structure that produces the incremental tax revenue.[4] In developing countries, the premium is likely to be even higher to the extent that these countries have access to a more limited set of tax instruments (e.g. trade taxes in low-income countries) which are highly distorting. On the other hand, if, as some believe, substitution elasticities are lower in developing countries, the deadweight loss from taxation will also be lower. Even in the absence of country-specific estimates, we suggest that it is still worth showing the net impact of the project on the government's budget and conducting sensitivity analysis for a plausible range of the premium.

IMPROVING PROJECT QUALITY INDIRECTLY

Focusing on rates of return or the immediate economic analysis of projects is one means, and presumably an important one, of improving the quality of projects. But other approaches may be as or more important. Here we examine two possibilities. The first is the positive counterpoint to the earlier observation that a concern with macroeconomic and structural reforms diluted the time and effort devoted to project evaluation. The consequent improvement in policy may have affected project performance positively. And the second emphasizes the importance of sector studies, the existence of which may improve the quality of future projects in that sector. In the following we explore both possibilities, offering some empirical evidence in each case.

The Policy Environment

To investigate the relationship between rates of return and the policy environment, Kaufmann (1991) looked at 1200 World Bank projects in 58 developing countries. He linked the re-estimated rate of return with various indices of policy-related distortions. The broad pattern is shown in Table 3.2: the lower the distortion, the higher the project's rate of return. This pattern is confirmed by his econometric estimation (which further controlled for country-specific factors, external shocks, etc.). For most of the policy distortions, a large

Table 3.2 Economic policies and the performance of projects

Policy distortion	Average ERR	Percent unsatisfactory (social-sector projects)
Trade restrictions		
Highly restrictive	13.20	28.10
Non-restrictive	19.00	0.00
Exchange rate		
Highly overvalued	8.20	37.00
Slightly overvalued	17.70	17.40
Real interest rate		
Negative	15.00	29.40
Positive	17.30	17.50
Fiscal deficit		
High	13.40	29.30
Low	17.80	11.30
Price distortions of tradeables		
High distortions	15.80	25.70
Low distortions	17.40	14.80

Source: Kaufmann (1991): Kaufmann and Wang (1995).

change in the index is associated with a three–seven percentage point difference in the rate of return. Furthermore, he showed that countries which moved from high to low distortions significantly improved the rate of return to their projects.

These results are both troubling and reassuring. They are troubling in so far as project evaluation techniques are in principle supposed to incorporate existing policy distortions. Thus, had the shadow prices for these projects been properly calculated, and appropriate project selection criteria followed, there should be no relationship between policies and rates of return. However, as we have seen, these techniques were used only on a limited basis. What these results indicate is that the 'costs' of not calculating the proper shadow prices are greater the more distorted is the economy. As such this confirms the appropriateness of the original Little and Mirrlees focus on key distortions and, by the same token, our suggestions to reconsider the emphasis in a changed world. At the same time, the Kaufmann results are reassuring in that the World Bank's increased emphasis on policy reform (possibly at the expense of better project analysis) may have yielded an unintended benefit: better returns on projects.

Kaufmann and Wang (1995) undertook a similar analysis for social-sector projects, where instead of rates of return (which are not usually calculated for projects in these sectors), they use an *ex-post* measure of the project's 'success'. Again, they find that the severity of the various distortions has a significant effect on project success with the percentage of unsatisfactory projects typically doubling as one moves from a low-distortion to a high-distortion environment (see Table 3.2).

Sectoral Analysis

The World Bank routinely carries out economic and sector work (ESW) on its client countries. Some recent econometric work (Schneider 1995) shows that the number of ESW reports on a country or sector contributes significantly to project success in that country/sector.[5] The percentage of successful projects (as determined by the Bank's Operations Evaluation Department at project completion) rises from 69 to 100 when the number of ESW reports increases from zero to four or more. Schneider's econometric results confirm that this relationship is statistically significant. Controlling for other factors, he concludes that one ESW report in a particular country and sector increases the probability of a project's success by nine percentage points, while two reports would increase it by 16 points.

Included in the Bank's ESW are reviews of public expenditures in particular sectors or the country as a whole. The reviews can be, and in some cases have been, used to inform project selection in the country or sector. These sectoral reviews are important because project-specific appraisal reports can (at best) only assess the rate of return or acceptability of the *project being appraised.* This is problematical for two reasons, both of which are especially important for multilateral lending agencies. First, the project being appraised may have been undertaken without external financing from a multilateral agency. In this case, the external funding is actually financing some other project which without the financing would not have been in the investment programme. This problem arises because financial resources are *fungible* at least to some extent. And second, even if the project would not have been in the investment programme without external funding, there is no guarantee that it is the *best* of all those projects not currently in the programme because of lack of financing. Yet the latter is the relevant question if the World Bank is to maximize the development impact of its lending.

The above argument calls for sector-wide reviews prior to project-specific appraisal and financing and perhaps explains an important part of the observed link between sectoral analysis and subsequent project success. To illustrate this point consider these two examples of sectoral public expenditure reviews (PERs). The Agricultural Expenditure Review of India (Pradhan and Perumalpillai-Essex 1993) examined several agricultural programmes as projects and calculated their economic rate of return. It concluded that two programmes – a fertilizer subsidy and a crop production scheme – had a zero rate of return because there was no justification for public provision of these goods (the benefits accrued directly to the individual farmers). Yet the bulk of central government expenditures were going to these two schemes. The study also pointed to the high rates of return in groundwater irrigation and extension services, recommending a reorientation of public expenditures in that direction. Similarly, an infrastructure public expenditure review of Peru calculated the economic rate of return of expanding each of the major road links in Peru. The results showed a large variation in the IRR. Using a cut-off rate of 12 per cent, the report was able to recommend dropping several road expansion projects, leading to a $275 million reduction in the government's road investment programme.

These reviews actually go beyond setting a good foundation for subsequent project appraisal – they also *improve the overall quality of the sectoral investment programme*. Moreover, if the result is a satisfactory programme, then the specific project financed and appraised in depth by the World Bank becomes less important. Rather, the World Bank could have the greatest development impact by associating itself with that project where World Bank knowledge and technical expertise is likely to be of most value. Alternatively, the World Bank could finance a time-slice of an agreed sectoral expenditure programme, an option that is receiving greater attention in the World Bank.

Furthermore, sectoral expenditure reviews can shed light on the two elements which we have identified as crucial for project evaluation in the 1990s, namely, the private-sector counterfactual and the premium on public income. In reviewing the government's expenditure programme within a sector, a sectoral expenditure review should identify areas where the private sector is providing, or can provide, the goods and services in question. For instance, a review of public expenditures in the health sector of Malaysia (World Bank 1992) noted that 62 per cent of spending by the Ministry of Health was on medical care (mostly private goods) and only 23 per cent was on public health, while the latter had a higher marginal impact on health status.[6] While sectoral expenditure reviews would not calculate the premium on public income, PERs that cover the entire government budget could in principle do so, in so far as they evaluate the government's budget constraint as part of the macroeconomic framework. At the very least, PERs should identify those countries where the gains from applying the premium on public income in project evaluation – or the losses from not doing so – are the greatest.

CONCLUSION

To some extent, the changed circumstances noted above vindicate the relatively limited attention the World Bank has paid to project appraisal. But at the same time those changed circumstances have also pointed to new priorities and raised old concerns that are not adequately addressed at present. In two areas we conclude that continuation of current practice, with in one case some tightening on quality, seems appropriate:

1. *Distributional weights*. The view that other instruments, especially the broad allocation of public expenditures and tax policy, are able to influence the distribution of income more efficiently than project selection, coupled with the practical difficulties of identifying income-specific project beneficiaries, leads to the conclusion that it is not worth revisiting the issue of distributional weights.
2. *Shadow prices*. The use of border prices and a standard conversion factor should be routine practice. Given the Kaufmann results, this point is especially important where economy-wide distortions remain significant. In addition, where the yes–no decision proves sensitive to the value of the standard conversion factor, further disaggregation – sectoral conversion factors – would be required.

More importantly, we suggest on the basis of this review that there are three areas where the World Bank should think seriously about improving its analysis in the interests of both its development impact and the quality of its portfolio:

1. *Public versus private*. Because the World Bank is still financing projects that appear to be producing private goods, a greater effort should be made to assess the feasibility of private-sector alternatives, including those that would prevail under regulatory or price (tax-cum-subsidy) policies. And even where there is a clear rationale for public provision, care should be taken to ensure that public provision results in a greater (that is, closer to optimal) supply than would be the case with private provision alone.
2. *Public income premium*. Because the World Bank is likely to be financing an increasing number of projects that are characterized by public costs and private benefits, the idea of incorporating a premium on public income in project appraisal should be reconsidered. Ideally, this should entail estimation of the premium at least in countries where the World Bank is investing in several projects or where the premium is likely to be especially large. This may be a task that could be most appropriately

undertaken by the Research Department. And finally, for all projects, whether it is possible to calculate a rate of return or not, and whether a country-specific estimate of the premium is available or not, the analyst should measure the impact of the project on the budget and explain what forms of cost recovery have been considered.

3. *Public expenditure reviews.* Wherever possible, the World Bank should allocate resources to reviews of sectoral expenditure programmes *before* embarking on the appraisal and financing of specific projects. Indeed, if a sectoral review has been undertaken, financing a time-slice of the programme may be the most effective use of World Bank funds.

Proposals such as these are unlikely to make much headway without a change in the structure of internal incentives. At a minimum, a reinstatement of a central projects unit both to provide assistance to project analysts and to exert a degree of quality control would seem to be required.

NOTES

1. Furthermore, if there is any added distortion from the public sector's need to raise funds, the return to the public investment is negative.
2. If the good is private but is not currently produced privately, then one would need to compare public provision with sale of project description (e.g. blueprints) to the private sector.
3. If the government provides a service that taxpayers would have otherwise purchased on their own, then the spending would be a perfect substitute for disposable income. By contrast, if marginal government spending provides no benefits to taxpayers, there is an income effect from the balanced budget spending operation that counters the substitution effect (Browning, 1987, p. 18).
4. The more progressive the tax change, the greater the marginal welfare cost. Raising additional revenue by increasing the rates of progressive taxes (e.g. federal income taxes) implies large increases in marginal tax rates (Browning, 1987, p. 19).
5. The study reviewed 431 projects for which project completion reports assigned ratings during the period July 1992–October 1994.
6. Regression analysis of infant mortality on various types of public medical expenditures showed that expenditures on safe water and immunization had a much higher impact than expenditures on public-provided doctors.

REFERENCES

Belli, Pedro (1995), 'Does Good Economic Analysis Lead to Better Projects?', mimeo, Washington, DC: World Bank.

Browning, Edgar K. (1987), 'On The Marginal Welfare Cost of Taxation', *American Economic Review*, **77** (1), 11–23.

Kaufmann, Daniel (1991), 'Determinants of the Productivity of Projects in Developing Countries: Evidence from 1,200 Projects', Background Paper for *World Development Report 1991*.

Kaufmann, Daniel and Yan Wang (1995), *Macroeconomic Policies and Project Performance in the Social Sectors: A Model of Human Capital Production and Evidence from LDCs*, Washington, DC: World Bank.
Little, I.M.D., T. Scitovsky and Maurice Scott (1970), *Industry and Trade in Some Developing Countries: A Comparative Study*, Development Centre of OECD, Oxford: Oxford University Press.
Little, I.M.D. and J.A. Mirrlees (1991), 'Project Appraisal and Planning Twenty Years On', *Proceedings of the World Bank Annual Conference on Development Economics 1990*, Washington, DC: World Bank.
Pradhan, Sanjay and Jeeva Perumalpillai-Essex (1993), *India: Public Expenditure Review Sector Report III: Agriculture*, Washington, DC: World Bank, South Asia Region.
Salop, Joanne (1992), *Economic Analysis of Projects: Towards a Results-Oriented Approach to Evaluation*, Washington, DC: World Bank.
Schneider, Robert (1995), *Economic Sector Work and Results on the Ground*, Washington, DC: World Bank.
Squire, Lyn and Herman G. van der Tak (1975), *Economic Analysis of Projects*, Baltimore, Md: Johns Hopkins University Press.
Squire, Lyn (1989), 'Project Evaluation in Theory and Practice', in H. Chenery and T.N. Srinivasan (eds), *Handbook of Development Economics, Vol. II*, New York: Elsevier Science Publishing.
UNIDO (1972), *Guidelines for Project Evaluation*, New York: UN.
World Bank (1992), *Malaysia: Fiscal Reform for Stable Growth*, Report no. 10120–MA, p. 40, Washington, DC: World Bank, Asia Region.

4. Reflections on estimating distributional effects

Elio Londero*

...Economics is not ethics, though it borders on ethics; the line between them is a place where it behoves us to walk very delicately. It is now quite clear that neither the First nor the Second Welfare Economics have been walking delicately enough.

J.R. Hicks, *The Scope and Status of Welfare Economics*

INTRODUCTION

This chapter is about lessons learned in developing and applying a methodology for estimating the distributional effects of investment projects in the framework of cost–benefit analysis (CBA). It starts with a brief account of the author's involvement with this subject, and the principles that guided subsequent work. An example illustrates an estimation of distributional effects and the information it provides. Then, main lessons learned from designing, applying and trying to disseminate the methodology are summarized, followed by the implications of estimating distributional effects for project preparation and design, for estimating accounting prices, and for data gathering and utilization. Finally, some lessons from implementation in an institutional setting are presented, as well as views on the implications for the teaching of applied welfare economics.

BACKGROUND

In 1980 the author became part of a group assigned the task of designing sector-specific guidelines for estimating the distributional effects of investment projects. A general methodology to that effect, based on the principles

*Opinions expressed in this chapter are those of the author and are not intended to represent the views of the Inter-American Development Bank. The author gratefully acknowledges comments by John MacArthur and Simón Teitel.

of CBA, was assumed to be in place (Powers and Howard 1979; Fontaine 1980). The role of the group was to adapt the methodology, essentially 'efficiency' analysis conducted in foreign exchange numeraire, to different types of projects (electricity generation and transmission, water supply, trunk and rural roads, irrigation, etc.).

Efficiency analysis is based on the so-called compensation principle, stating that if the winners can compensate the losers and still gain something we have an increase in 'economic efficiency'.[1] Note that if the poor lose 100 for the rich to gain 101, the compensation is *possible* and the project would pass the efficiency test even though the poor affected may be losing 50 per cent of their income for the rich beneficiaries to gain 1 per cent of theirs. Consequently, adding up the costs incurred and the benefits received by those affected is all that is required to know whether a project passes the 'compensation test'. In these circumstances, the distribution of costs and benefits among those affected becomes unnecessary. Alternatives to efficiency analysis require that the distribution of money measures of welfare changes brought about by the project be estimated (Londero 1987, chap. 1).

The group's objective was to provide the project analyst with the tools for showing the efficiency net present value of a project as the sum of the benefits received and costs incurred by those affected, classified between the public and private sectors, and then those belonging to the private sector classified in low income and other beneficiaries. A 'low income level' split persons in the two disjunct groups.

The process continued with reviewing the application of the methodology and guidelines, and advising practitioners on how to estimate distributional impacts in different projects and situations. This task led to a continuous learning on project-specific issues, as well as on the effects of a variety of practices, norms and regulations that contribute to shaping the distribution of costs and benefits.

At that time, the idea was conceived of communicating this experience to a wider audience. A book intended to provide the theoretical framework and to illustrate its application to a limited number of case studies was prepared, and published (Londero 1987).

A review of the literature undertaken in preparing the book revealed that, despite years of theoretical discussions on the use of distributional weights, there was very little information on deriving what at the time were called 'social prices' as a weighted sum of compensating variations.[2] Most of the discussions and applied research had been conducted around the estimation of 'synthetic prices',[3] which would comprise the net result of weighing and adding money measures of effects on different persons, as if distributional effects resulting from additional demands for, say, labour or foreign exchange were the most important ones in project analysis. Conversely, it seemed that other areas, such as the estimation of changes in consumers' surpluses, or the difficulties in estimating the distributional impact of changes in the prices of intermediate goods, had received considerably less attention.[4]

As regards applications, it seemed that only a few CBAs included estimations of distributional impacts,[5] and the main interest was in showing the difference in the final result of the authors' pricing proposals as compared with traditional efficiency analysis. Less attention had been paid to the discussion of the distributional effects of the project *per se*. In some instances, important distributional effects had been omitted.

There seemed to be more methodologically rich material in textbooks on public finance and among studies on tax and expenditure incidence,[6] despite the fact that CBA was frequently taught as part of public-finance courses. We shall see later on that this apparent incongruity may be explained by the prevalence of the efficiency paradigm.

The review of the literature revealed the importance of a methodological emphasis in the estimation of distributional effects *per se*. It also highlighted the usefulness of Hansen's (1974) approach of integrating financial and economic statements.[7] The method to be proposed would lead the analyst to start from a statement containing the present value of the financial flows of the project, and proceed to identify the persons who would be affected by it, and to quantify the amount by which they would be affected. Present values of project flows at efficiency prices would then be shown to be the sum of the compensating variations of those affected.

In pursuing these objectives, the author tried to follow four basic guiding principles:

1. Mishan's (1981a, 1981b) concern for keeping CBA firmly grounded in welfare economics.
2. Sen's (1972) approach to deriving accounting prices by identifying those affected.
3. Hansen's (1974) idea of an accounting consistency between economic and financial analysis.
4. The objective of presenting a method for estimating the distributional effects that would be general, serving more purposes than just distribution according to income brackets.[8]

Also, the basic method should be presented using the consumption numeraire, since it comes naturally from the definition of the compensating variation.[9]

AN EXAMPLE

An example of applying the method may serve to illustrate how distributional effects are estimated, and what a resulting estimation would look like.[10] The project consists of the introduction of gravity irrigation in an area where dry farming is practised. The government will be responsible for the construction, operation and maintenance of the system, as well as for providing the necessary agricultural extension services. Furthermore, it will be responsible for training and organizing producers in order to set up an agricultural cooperative that will provide three main services:

- leasing machinery and equipment to small farms;
- storing and marketing produce; and
- marketing seed, pesticides and fertilizers.

The government finances investment with budget funds and with a loan from a multilateral financing organization. However, since this loan would have been available and would have been used even in the absence of this specific project, the transfers between lender and borrower to which it gives rise are not *attributable* to the project, i.e. they would have existed without it. As for the cooperative, it will receive credits from the National Agricultural Bank (NAB) to finance its investment, including replacement. In addition, it will receive short-term finance, particularly during the first few years. Since these credits are granted at a real interest rate below the discount rate, the cooperative will receive a transfer equal to the difference between the present value of the credits received and the present value of the repayment flow.

Finally, the government will receive revenue for water charges and the cooperative income for the leasing of machinery and equipment, for storage and marketing services and for the trade margins on seed, fertilizer and pesticides. This revenue is the counterpart of the respective payments in the farmers' cost accounts which are shown in Table 4.1.

The first five columns of Table 4.1 correspond to the consolidation of the income changes attributable to the project, estimated under the assumption that the project affects only intramarginal producers without affecting prices (Londero 1987, section 7.3).[11] The first four columns are for the government, the cooperative and the two groups of farms. The fifth is for the National Agricultural Bank (NAB) and is included to complete the entries for the income flows between the cooperative, the farmers and the bank. The sixth column, 'Government (taxes)', is included to record the changes in government revenue from the taxes included in the prices of the goods purchased and sold, as well as those that account for the difference between the exchange rate and the accounting price ratio of foreign exchange. The government thus appears twice.

Table 4.1 Irrigation project

	Government	Cooperative	NAB	Small farms	Other farms	Gov. (taxes)	Workers	Total
GOVERNMENT & COOPERATIVE COSTS								
Cost of the irrigation system								
Foreign exchange	–849.8					–85.0		–934.8
Skilled labour	–198.0							–198.0
Unskilled labour	–119.2						35.8	–83.4
Taxes	–21.8					21.8		
Cost of support services								
Foreign exchange	–16.5	–108.8				–12.5		–137.8
Skilled labour	–45.3	–22.1						–67.4
Unskilled labour (FS)	–1.1	–8.3					2.8	–6.6
Unskilled labour (RS)		–3.4						–3.4
Taxes	–0.6	–10.9				11.5		
Purchases of seed, fertilizer & pesticides								
Foreign exchange		–603.6				–60.4		–664.0
Skilled labour		–106.9						–106.9
Unskilled labour (FS)		–92.0					27.6	–64.4
Taxes		–135.8				135.8		
Loan to the Cooperative		222.8	–222.8					
Repayments		–191.4	191.4					

FARMERS								
Sales								
Foreign exchange				134.4	622.5	75.7		832.6
Taxes				5.8	34.8	–40.6		
Non-traded vegetables				1,249.7	1,928.1			3,177.8
Production costs								
Foreign exchange				–28.8	–178.4	–20.7		–227.9
Skilled labour				–11.4	–14.0			–25.4
Unskilled labour (FS)				–12.0	–10.6		6.8	–15.8
Taxes				–7.8	–17.5	25.3		
Hired labour				–110.5	–452.9			–563.4
Purchased seed		166.7		–37.4	–129.3			
Machinery & equipment services		47.9		–47.9				
Fertilizers and pesticides		821.0		–354.0	–467.0			
Water costs	186.0			–68.3	–117.7			
Storage & marketing		126.6		–44.3	–82.3			
Loan received			–1,490.6	468.9	1,021.7			
Repayments			1,329.9	–430.4	–899.5			
Non-monetary income				–203.4	–37.4			–240.8
TOTAL ADDITIONAL INCOME	**–1,066.3**	**101.8**	**–192.1**	**502.6**	**1,200.5**	**50.9**	**73.0**	**670.4**

Source: Adapted from Londero (1987, table 12.14).

The first time, it appears as the source of expenditure on the irrigation system and support services, as well as the recipient of the water charges paid by farmers. In both cases, flows originating directly in the financial statements of the project are involved. The second appearance relates to the effects on tax revenue, and is included separately to facilitate interpretation of the vertical totals of the columns. Finally, the 'Workers' column is included to record the additional income which, as will be seen, explains the difference between the wages paid to unskilled workers in the formal sector of the economy and their income in the sector from which they come.

As regards the rows, the upper part of Table 4.1 contains irrigation and support services costs already broken down into their total requirements of non-produced inputs and transfers using a semi-input–output table. These costs are classified according to whether they are paid by the government or the cooperative. The costs for purchasing seed, fertilizers and pesticides by the cooperative are shown in the same way. Its income for machinery and equipment leasing, storage, marketing and sales of inputs to farmers is included in the lower part of the table as the counterpart of payments by farmers. The difference is that the sales of imported agricultural outputs and the purchases of the remaining inputs are shown broken down into their total requirements for non-produced inputs and transfers. The last row indicates the farmers' welfare loss due to additional work in their own farms, i.e. the project reduces underemployment.

To complete the income changes brought about by the project, only the effects of the net production of foreign exchange on the collection of taxes and the additional income of unskilled workers need to be included. It is estimated that for each $1.00 of additional foreign exchange, the government receives $0.10 in taxes as the net balance between greater receipts for imports and lower receipts for exports, i.e. the accounting price ratio of foreign exchange is 1:1. The change in tax receipts attributable to the use and production of foreign exchange is shown in the 'Government (taxes)' column. As for unskilled labour, a distinction has been made between wages paid in the formal urban sector (FS) of the economy (or equivalent) and in the rural sector (RS). This is because in the formal urban sector, wages are considerably higher than those in the informal sector due to high unemployment and widespread underemployment. Since, at the margin, unskilled labour comes from underemployment in the rural sector, the prevailing wages in this sector are taken as an approximation of the compensating variation of additional employment. Consequently, the difference between the two wages is shown as additional income for unskilled workers in the formal sector. In the rural sector, the wages paid are considered good approximations of the corresponding compensating variation, and thus no additional income is entered under this heading.

The sum of each column provides the real income change (sum of compensating variations) of the corresponding group. In order to obtain a measure of 'total' benefits attributable to the project, an aggregation criterion or interpersonal distributional value judgement is needed. If this value judgement corresponds to that of the operational version of efficiency analysis, an additional unit of income is equally valuable whatever the income level of the recipient, and the sum of the 'total' column will be the net benefits from the project at efficiency prices each time there is equality between the discount rate and the rate of return on marginal investment. The sum of this last column is all that is required by the operational version of efficiency analysis.

The estimation of distributional effects provides a wealth of additional information reflecting the combined effects of project-specific characteristics and more general economic policy measures. The project involves a sizeable transfer from the public to the private sector resulting mainly from water charges well below marginal costs, but also from real interest rates lower than the discount rate. As regards water charges, there seems to be a considerable margin for their increase without making farming unprofitable, although potential crop substitution effects of higher water charges prevent a strong inference from these results. Subject to the same caveat, farmers seem to be able to absorb an increase in real interest rates that would bring these rates closer to the discount rate. Within the private sector, benefits go primarily to owners of medium- and large-size farms as a result of land distribution in the area of influence. The cooperative is expected to be financially self-sufficient, and would continue to be so in the absence of the transfer through NAB financing. Since farming is not very labour-intensive and rural wages are estimated to be equal to alternative earnings, hired labour as a group is not an important beneficiary of the project. Finally, differences between market and efficiency prices are not an important part of distributional effects, but constitute a significant proportion of total efficiency benefits. Note that the closer water tariffs become to marginal costs and real interest rates to the discount rate, the greater the impact of differences between market and efficiency prices on the overall distributional effect.

If the interpersonal distributional value judgement were different from that of efficiency analysis, or the discount rate and the rate of return on marginal investment were not equal, this estimate of the distributional effects would be the departure point for calculating the 'total' net benefits. This calculation would require us to know the distribution of the *net* changes in income (Londero 1987, part III). This is the difference between the distribution of income changes generated by the project and by the alternative course of action. Since the decision to construct the irrigation system is the element that gives rise to all the other income flows, and since the funds financing its construction are those on which a decision is being taken, the alternative course of action is what corresponds to the *other* use that would be made of these funds if the project were not carried out. The income changes that this alternative use of funds would lead to, and their distribution, constitute the *without*-project situation.

MAIN LESSONS

Two important lessons may be drawn from designing, applying and trying to disseminate this method for estimating and presenting distributional effects. The first is that in most cases where benefits can be estimated, it is also possible to estimate distributional effects within reasonable margins of error.[12] Notable in this regard is that a reasonable estimate often provides a result that was not expected by less specialized economists and those not knowing the details of the project. That may be the case when beneficiaries are targeted, as in the introduction of services to specific communities, since the outsider expects to see the distributional impact of the average project in the sector, or when a project generates external effects reflected in the form of increased property values only partially captured through taxation. It may also occur when output does not affect the corresponding price, as in projects that mainly benefit intramarginal producers without affecting the margin, or those that affect marginal production costs without translating into price changes (Londero 1987, section 7.3).

The second lesson is that estimating distributional effects greatly improves the quality of economic analysis of investment and of policy advice in a variety of ways:

1. It forces a more thorough CBA. Since those affected are classified according to certain criteria, issues pertaining to differences in reactions among groups, such as different demand or supply price elasticities, are highlighted. For example, in the analysis of agricultural projects, focusing on distribution forces separate consideration to be given to different farm sizes when preparing farm-income statements, which in turn may lead to a more detailed analysis of the use, adoption, and rate of adoption of technology, contributing to a better accounting for differences in expected productivity increases among farms.
2. It helps in bringing up policy issues regarding transfers among agents, for example, the government's ability to capture additional rents through taxation, or transfers originating in promotional financing, differential taxation, or price discrimination.
3. It facilitates the discussion of alternative ways to address distributional concerns by forcing the analysis of incidence, and by enabling the sensi-

tivity analysis of alternative transfer instruments.

4. It contributes to improving the analysis of other allocative issues. For example, when rationing through prices is required to compensate for short-term shortages, it leads more naturally to accounting for the existence of different short-run elasticities for different groups.
5. It facilitates the review of CBAs, particularly when estimates are made in a framework in which the analyst moves from the financial to the economic statement of the project, presenting the latter as the result of sorting out transfers from real income changes. This way of presenting the results makes it considerably easier to spot the omission of costs or benefits, pricing mistakes, and double counting of costs or benefits.
6. It provides an appropriate framework for the appraisal of projects that affect residents of more than one country, such as foreign investments or integration projects.
7. Last, and certainly not least, it provides a less value-laden professional output, making it difficult for the analyst to hide behind efficiency considerations, and forcing the discussion of distributional consequences.

Estimating distributional effects is not an academic exercise. It is applied welfare economics in an environment where distributional considerations are very seldom taken into account as an integral part of the analysis, particularly in CBA. As a result, requirements for estimating these types of effect sometimes collide with long-standing practices in the collection and processing of data, and in the performance of economic analysis. Some of these implications are explored below.

IMPLICATIONS FOR PROJECT PREPARATION AND DESIGN

It is well known that project analysis begins during project preparation. Therefore, it is important to take into account distributional effects right from the start of project preparation, including the identification of alternatives and the gathering of specific data. Subsequently, distributional considerations should always be present while preparing financial flows, particularly in identifying the project's impact on those affected, classified according to the same criteria that will be used in the CBA. Only the allocation of transfers that explain the difference between market and efficiency prices should be left for the last step.

From a practical point of view it may be necessary during project preparation to obtain project-specific data that allow for the estimation of distributional effects. For example, farm budgets should be prepared by farm size, and traffic counts may need to be complemented with traffic surveys. In some cases it may be necessary to conduct project-specific surveys; in others, surveys that would be conducted anyway should be appropriately designed from the start to provide the necessary data.

Finally, estimating distributional effects would require that *estimates for different groups be kept separate*, and only aggregated in a final table showing the money measure of total welfare change.

IMPLICATIONS FOR THE ESTIMATION OF ACCOUNTING PRICES

Difficulties in estimating distributional effects may arise from the availability of accounting prices (or lack thereof), and from the way in which the results of existing studies have been communicated to the users. Just knowing the value of an accounting price is of little use for distributional purposes; it is also necessary to know the sources of the differences arising between accounting and market prices.

When pricing, it is difficult for the project analyst to identify and quantify transfers beyond those identified and quantified during the calculation of the accounting prices utilized. For this reason, when there is interest in distributional effects, it is necessary to take the appropriate measures *at the time accounting prices are estimated.*

When accounting prices are estimated using input–output techniques, particular attention has to be paid to the breakdown in the matrix for non-produced inputs and transfers (Londero 1987, part II). Treating primary inputs like labour or foreign exchange as partially produced inputs should be considered as a possibility (Londero 1987, chap. 13; 1994). Due to the greater disaggregation in the matrix of non-produced inputs and transfers imposed by these requirements, work beyond that needed to obtain accounting price ratios at efficiency prices will be required. In return, an early concern for the expected use of the resulting accounting prices would help to reduce mistakes from interpreting someone else's analysis, and may result in overall time savings.

When the valuation of inputs and outputs is direct, as could be the case for imported inputs or regional labour, the income changes recorded will be limited by the level of detail in the estimation of the accounting prices. For example, if in order to approximate the efficiency price of labour it is assumed that it is equal to wages in alternative employment, for distributional purposes no more income changes can be taken into account other than those resulting from the wage difference for the hired worker plus, if necessary, additional effects due to social security contributions. However, in many countries the estimation of accounting prices for labour may demand a more elaborate approach requiring detailed knowledge of the adjustment process that follows an additional demand for labour (Londero 1987, chap. 6).

IMPLICATIONS FOR DATA GATHERING AND UTILIZATION

Often, even though the analyst may try to consider the distributional aspects while preparing a project, he or she will find that the available data are insufficient. In that case, there are three alternatives: ignore the distributional effects; estimate them inadequately (with large margins of error); or delay the formulation of the project in order to obtain the relevant data. The last alternative is seldom chosen. Thus, concerns for distributional effects of economic policy measures (including investment decisions) should also be reflected in gathering basic data. Censuses and surveys should include questions on income levels; questions should be formulated in a way that is compatible with existing complementary data; and surveys should be designed so as to avoid problems of low statistical significance that arise when processing data classified according to, for example, income levels.

It may also be necessary to prepare analytical instruments considering the needs for estimating distributional effects. We shall briefly consider two examples.

The application of CBA to the field of selecting expansion plans for utilities (e.g. water or electricity) and, in particular, estimating the associated distributional effects, requires a considerable effort with regard to estimating demand functions.[13] In particular, the breakdown of residential demand by income groups and its separate projection is an important element in estimating the distributional effects. Each yearly figure in this projection can be conceptualized as the number of residential clients of a certain group times the average consumption per customer.[14]

In developing countries, customers who have no *access* to the good in question are mainly low-income people, and this access is determined principally by the utility's connection policy. Furthermore, elasticity of consumption per customer with respect to variables other than own price will in general be different for different income levels. Consequently, projections per group of customers should ideally take account of these effects. This requires an effort in estimating the number of customers for each group and year, and the corresponding functions for the consumption per customer.

As a result of the above, there will be different price elasticities of demand for each group. In particular, consumption per customer is expected to be less price-elastic as the customer's income level increases (Westley 1981, pp. 97–101).

Finally, there is the question of which part of the increase in the price for an intermediate good will be absorbed by consumers. It may be assumed that it is proportional to the expenditure on consumption of each group. However, the indirect content of the input in consumer baskets, that is, the direct and indirect requirements of the goods making up the basket, will not be identical for all groups. An approximation may be obtained by using the input–output model to estimate the indirect requirements for the input in question in the consumption basket. Then the share of the price increase that intermediate users are assumed to transfer to final consumers through prices can be distributed in proportion to the share of indirect consumption of each group of final consumers in total indirect consumption. That requires proper disaggregation in the transactions matrix, and household consumption classified by groups (Londero 1987, section 10.5).

In summary, concern for distributional effects should already be part of the data gathering process; if it is not, steps should be taken to remedy such omission. Also, when data including distributive information exist, they should be preserved throughout the different stages for preparing such data for publication, or when preparing analytical instruments, since it is normally cheaper to produce a subsequent version that aggregates across groups, than to return to the data in order to disaggregate by groups.

IMPLEMENTATION IN AN INSTITUTIONAL SETTING

Organizational problems are to be expected when introducing a requirement for estimating distributional effects. The first is the analyst's reaction to change, as they will be forced to modify their traditional approaches and work routines. This situation is made more serious by the fact that the traditional teaching of CBA is based on efficiency analysis, all of which leads to an almost certain need for retraining and closer supervision. At the same time, there is extra work to be accounted for when estimating the impact of a project on those affected. While most of this extra work should take place, as mentioned before, during project preparation, it is more likely to be pushed forward to the appraisal stage, when lack of adequate data becomes more difficult to compensate for, or proper manipulation of originally available data is no longer possible without incurring high costs.

A second important point is how the analyst perceives the relevance of estimating distributional effects to the project's future. In the cases the author is familiar with, estimates of distributional effects were not part of the decision criteria for accepting or rejecting specific projects. However, there was a cumulative goal for all projects analysed over a four-year period. Consequently, the relation between an individual project and an accumulated four-year result was distant. A situation such as this might be aggravated when analysts do not actively participate (or have responsibility) in selecting or preparing the projects to be analysed. Under such circumstances, good communication is essential between those with an overall view of goal achievement, and those in charge of selecting the projects.

A third and last group of considerations is the potential for inconsistent goals. For example, if investment goals for broad economic sectors coexist with distributional targets, conflicts may arise between sector investment goals and the objective of reaching a certain distributional effect. In a multilateral financial organization, this conflict could be intensified by the fact that the project universe is determined by the member country's investment policies. This situation becomes more difficult during periods dominated by fiscal considerations, when the investment budget becomes a very important adjustment variable. Obviously, when multiple goals are established, they must be consistent, and distributional goals are no exception to the rule.

IMPLICATIONS FOR THE TEACHING OF APPLIED WELFARE ECONOMICS

Many economists do not seem to be familiar with identifying, tracing and estimating distributional effects of price changes. There appear to be three main reasons for this state of affairs.

First, greater specialization in the study of economics and the greater monetary and academic recognition enjoyed by those devoted to short-term macroeconomic policy seem to have affected the interest in microeconomics in general,[15] and in applied microeconomic analysis in particular.[16]

Second, prevalence of the paradigm stating that efficiency results are what counts, and that distributional concerns should be addressed separately (perhaps through government tax and expenditure policies), has led to neglect of the fact that in order to deal with distributional effects they have to be known and estimated. Investment is a considerable part of government expenditure and has the additional important characteristic of shaping future current government expenditure.

Finally, the unavoidable discussion of ethical considerations in applied welfare economics gives the impression of a less *scientific*, more dilettantish approach.[17]

This state of affairs imposes additional responsibility on teachers of microeconomic analysis in general, and applied welfare economics in particular. Traditional teaching of efficiency analysis deprives welfare economics of its ethical content, and applied welfare economics of the instruments to raise those ethical concerns. A more distributionally-conscious approach would be more consistent with a tradition of controversy surrounding interpersonal welfare comparisons, and would also contribute to a better understanding of the ethical implications of intertemporal welfare comparisons.

From a more technical point of view, those with a background in estimating distributional effects would bring a perspective better aligned with the way policy measures are actually considered by policy makers; that is, who is affected, who wins, and who loses. Also, there are externalities to teaching the basic methods used for estimating distributional effects, since they apply to other fields of economics.

The above considerations speak in favour of a teaching method for applied welfare economics in which the so-called efficiency prescriptions are shown to be just a special case of a more general formulation of the problem. Such a method should address the behavioural assumptions and value judgements underlying the use of the compensating variation as the measure for the individual's welfare change. It should also address the technical and ethical difficulties involved in moving from measures of individuals' welfare changes to a measure of total or social welfare, as well as provide the foundations for estimating distributional effects.

CONCLUSIONS

Conclusions may be grouped in four main areas. First, by basing the analysis on the compensation principle, efficiency analysis makes it unnecesssary to estimate the distributional impact of projects. Alternatives to efficiency analysis require that the distribution of money measures of welfare changes brought about by the project be estimated. Those estimates are possible in most cases where benefits can be estimated. Obtaining those estimates tends to contribute to the quality of economic analysis and policy advice.

Second, the ability to better estimate distributional effects depends crucially on statistical offices taking those needs into account when gathering and processing data, project analysts appropriately handling data during the preparation of projects, and economists detailing transfers when estimating accounting prices.

Third, implementation would demand economists with a background in applied welfare economics broader than that provided by traditional efficiency analysis. Implementation in an institutional setting would require overcoming resistance to change, avoiding establishing inconsistent goals, and carefully monitoring project selection.

Finally, not enough attention seems to be directed towards the ethical considerations inherent in applied welfare economics, and there seems to be limited knowledge of how to estimate distributional effects. Devoting time to these subjects with students has external economies for other areas of applied economics.

NOTES

1. Useful presentations of the efficiency criteria are provided by Hicks (1939, 1975), Harberger (1971), and Mishan (1974, 1980, 1982). More critical approaches may be found in Dobb (1969), Meade (1972), Graaf (1975), and Sen (1979, 1987). Harberger (1984) proposes a 'basic needs' approach to supplement efficiency analysis.
2. A notable exception is that of Sen (1972).
3. Among others, UNIDO (1972), Little and Mirrlees (1974), Scott, MacArthur and Newbery (1979), and Hughes (1979a, 1979b, 1981).
4. For example, in explaining the concept of willingness to pay and its role in measuring benefits, the UNIDO *Guidelines* does not discuss willingness to pay as the result of adding compensating variations. In contrast, Wildasin (1988) discusses the distributional implications of seemingly insignificant price changes.
5. Among those were OECD (1969), Sen and Datta Chaudhuri (1970), UNIDO (1972, 1978, 1980), Hansen (1974), and Londero (1978, 1979).
6. For example, Hicks (1953), Musgrave (1959), Due (1968), or Musgrave and Musgrave (1976). Musgrave (1985) provides a historical account, and Kotlikoff and Summers (1987) a review of more recent developments.
7. In my own work (Londero 1987), I did not highlight Hansen's pioneering role in developing an integrated framework. I hope this note will be a first step in remedying that omission.
8. For example, distribution between residents and foreigners for the analysis of foreign investments, or distribution according to marginal propensities to save for the application of accounting prices of investment.
9. The use of the 'foreign exchange numeraire' has proven tricky even to the most knowledgeable; see Londero (1987, chap. 5).
10. The example is adapted from Londero (1987, chap. 12), which contains a more detailed analysis of this project, as well as others.
11. If prices were affected, changes in consumers' surpluses would have to be estimated, since minor price changes may carry significant distributional effects. See Londero (1987) and Wildasin (1988).
12. Londero (1987, chap. 16) provides a discussion of the reasons for this assertion, as well as a presentation of some of the difficulties involved. Powers (1989) reviewed the experience.
13. See Westley (1992).
14. Londero (1987, chap. 10) analyses this subject in more detail with reference to electricity generation.
15. The new industrial organization theory constitutes an exception.
16. In Sen's (1975) words, 'The system of recognition and acclaim that applies in the world of economics does not particularly encourage the preparation of works concerned with details, however important they may be for practical planning'.
17. Sen recalls Joan Robinson's thought that his '... interest for welfare economics and social choice theory reflected a clear failure to grasp what was really important ...' and hoped for him to '... get back to what she took to be serious economics. Capital theory, growth theory, distribution theory ...' (Klamer 1989, p. 139).

REFERENCES

Dobb, M. (1969), *Welfare Economics and the Economics of Socialism*, Cambridge: Cambridge University Press.

Due, J. (1968), *Government Finance: Economics of the Public Sector*, 4th edition, Homewood, Ill.: Irwin.

Fontaine, E. (1980), 'Los efectos indirectos de los proyectos, su evaluación y su impacto distributivo' (Indirect Effects of Projects: Their Evaluation and Distributional Impact), mimeo, Catholic University of Chile, Santiago de Chile.

Graaf, J. de V. (1975), 'Cost–Benefit Analysis: A Critical View', *South African Journal of Economics*, **43** (2), 233–44.

Hansen, John (1974), 'A Guide to the *Guidelines*: The UNIDO Method of Economic Project Evaluation', World Bank Staff Working Paper no. 166, Washington, DC: World Bank.

Harberger, A. (1971), 'Three Basic Postulates for Applied Welfare Economics', *Journal of Economic Literature*, **9** (3), 785–97.

Harberger, A. (1984), 'Basic Needs versus Distributional Weights in Social Cost–Benefit Analysis', *Economic Development and Cultural Change*, **32** (3), 455–74.

Hicks, J.R. (1939), 'The Foundations of Welfare Economics', *Economic Journal*, **49** (196), 696–712. Reprinted in Hicks (1981).

Hicks, J.R. (1975), 'The Scope and Status of Welfare Economics', *Oxford Economic Papers*, **27** (3), 307–26. Reprinted in Hicks (1981).

Hicks, J.R. (1981), *Wealth and Welfare*, Cambridge, Mass.: Harvard University Press.

Hicks, U. (1953), *Public Finance*, Cambridge: Cambridge University Press.

Hughes, G. (1979a), 'Shadow Prices for Project Appraisal in Morocco', mimeo, Washington, DC: World Bank.

Hughes, G. (1979b), 'Shadow Prices for Indonesia', mimeo, Washington, DC: World Bank.

Hughes, G. (1981), 'Conversion Factors and Shadow Exchange Rates', mimeo, Faculty of Economics and Politics, University of Cambridge.

Klamer, A. (1989), 'A Conversation with Amartya Sen', *Journal of Economic Perspectives*, **3** (1), 135–50.

Kotlikoff, L. and L. Summers (1987), 'Tax Incidence', in A.J. Auerbach and M. Feldstein (eds), *Handbook of Public Economics, Vol. II*, New York and Oxford: North Holland.

Little, I. and J. Mirrlees (1974), *Project Appraisal and Planning for Developing Countries*, New York: Basic Books.

Londero, E. (1978), 'Reestimación de los precios de cuenta de la inversión y de la mano de obra no calificada tomando en consideración ponderaciones de distribución interpersonal de ingresos. Su aplicación a un proyecto de carreteras' (Re-estimating Investment and Unskilled Labour Accounting Prices Taking Distributional Weights into Account: Application to a Roads Project), mimeo, Secretary of Planning, Guatemala.

Londero, E. (1979), 'Evaluación de la alternativa mano de obra intensiva para la construcción de caminos rurales de acceso versus la intensiva en maquinaria' (Evaluation of the Labour vs the Machinery Intensive Alternatives for the Construction of Rural Roads), in ILO-PREALC, *Construcción de caminos rurales con tecnologías de mano de obra intensiva en Guatemala* (Constructing Rural Roads with Labour Intensive Techniques in Guatemala), ILO–PREALC.

Londero, E. (1987), *Benefits and Beneficiaries. An Introduction to Estimating Distri-*

butional Effects in Cost–Benefit Analysis, Washington, DC: Inter-American Development Bank.
Londero, E. (1994), 'Estimating the Accounting Price of Foreign Exchange: An Input–Output Approach', *Economic Systems Research*, **6** (4), 415–34.
Londero, E. (1995), 'On Shadow Pricing Partially Traded Goods', presented to the conference *Development Projects: Issues for the 1990's*, Development Project and Planning Centre, University of Bradford, 6–8 April.
Meade, J. (1972), 'Review of *Cost–Benefit Analysis* by E.J. Mishan', *Economic Journal*, **82** (325), 244–6.
Mishan, E.J. (1974), 'Flexibility and Consistency in Project Evaluation', *Economica* (London), **41** (161), 81–96. Reprinted in Mishan (1981a).
Mishan, E.J. (1980), 'How Valid Are Economic Evaluations of Allocative Changes?', *Journal of Economic Issues*, **14** (1), 143–61.
Mishan, E.J. (1981a), *Economic Efficiency and Social Welfare*, London: Allen and Unwin.
Mishan, E.J. (1981b), *Introduction to Normative Economics*, Oxford: Oxford University Press.
Mishan, E.J. (1982), 'The New Controversy about the Rationale of Economic Evaluation', *Journal of Economic Issues*, **16** (1), 29–47.
Musgrave, R. (1959), *The Theory of Public Finance*, New York: McGraw-Hill.
Musgrave, R. (1985), 'A Brief History of Fiscal Doctrine', in A.J. Auerbach and M. Feldstein (eds), *Handbook of Public Economics, Vol. I*, New York and Oxford: North Holland.
Musgrave, R. and P. Musgrave (1976), *Public Finance in Theory and Practice*, 2nd edition, New York: McGraw-Hill.
OECD (1969), *Manual of Industrial Project Analysis. Volume II. Social Cost–Benefit Analysis*, Paris: OECD.
Powers, T. (1989), 'A Practical Application: The IDB Experience', in OECD–IADB, *The Impact of Development Projects on Poverty*, Paris: OECD.
Powers, T. and E. Howard (1979), 'A Methodology for Measuring and Recording the Distributional Effects of Projects in the Bank's Portfolio', *Papers on Project Analysis*, no. 10, Washington, DC: Inter-American Development Bank.
Scott, M., J.D. MacArthur, and D.M.G. Newbery (1979), *Project Appraisal in Practice*, London: Heinemann.
Sen, A.K. (1972), 'Control Areas and Accounting Prices: An Approach to Economic Evaluation', *Economic Journal*, **82** (325), 486–501.
Sen, A.K. (1975), 'Foreword' to A.S. Bhalla (ed.), *Technology and Employment in Industry. A Case Study Approach*, Geneva: International Labor Office.
Sen, A.K. (1979), 'Personal Utilities and Public Judgements: Or What's Wrong with Welfare Economics?', *Economic Journal*, **89** (355), 537–58.
Sen, A.K. (1987), *On Ethics and Economics*, New York: Basil Blackwell.
Sen, A.K. and M. Datta Chaudhuri (1970), 'Durgapur Fertilizer Project: An Exercise in Economic Evaluation', *Indian Economic Review* (new series), **5** (1), 43–70.
UNIDO (1972), *Guidelines for Project Evaluation*, New York: UN. Prepared by P. Dasgupta, S. Marglin and A.K. Sen.
UNIDO (1978), *Guidelines for Practical Project Appraisal. Social Cost–Benefit Analysis in Developing Countries*, New York: UN. Prepared by John Hansen.
UNIDO (1980), *Practical Appraisal of Industrial Projects. Application of Social Cost–Benefit Analysis in Pakistan*, New York: UN. Prepared by John Weiss.
Westley, G. (1981), 'The Residential and Commercial Demand for Electricity in

Paraguay', *Papers on Project Analysis*, no. 19, Washington, DC: Inter-American Development Bank.
Westley, G. (1992), *New Directions in Econometric Modelling of Energy Demand*, Washington, DC: Inter-American Development Bank.
Wildasin, D. (1988), 'Indirect Distributional Effects in Benefit–Cost Analysis of Small Projects', *Economic Journal*, **98** (392), 801–7.

PART THREE

Cost–Benefit Analysis: Methodological Issues

5. Social project appraisal and historical development of ideas on discounting – a legacy for the 1990s and beyond

E. Kula

The origins of project appraisal can be traced to *An Inquiry into the Nature and Causes of the Wealth of Nations* by Smith (1776) whose main message was that the pursuit of self-interest with the development of market opportunities is the key to economic growth which would lead to a great improvement in human well-being. Smith did not deny a role for the government provided that it does not become a burden on individuals when they work towards furthering their own interests. In the Smithian scheme of things there are only three legitimate roles for the government: judiciary, national defence and construction of public works which due to their nature could not be of much interest to the private sector. However, Smith did not admit too many projects into this category and suggested that once public works are completed the users should be charged an appropriate fee.

More than 60 years after the publication of the *Wealth of Nations* Dupuit (1844) began to puzzle about the real costs and benefits of public works with a view to ascertaining that such projects are truly beneficial to the community at large. He reasoned that all costs and benefits, including those which are not captured by operators, should be assessed before the construction of communal works – his particular example was a bridge. Economists now relate the concept of unpaid price to the consumer surplus and mark Dupuit as the first person to identify it. At a governmental level it was the US which first took an interest in the economic justification of public works, in particular land-based projects, since the advent of its reclamation programme in 1902.

There are at least four key aspects to communal project appraisal, all of which are controversial. These are: choice of a suitable appraisal method; pricing of inputs and outputs involved; discounting; and external effects, especially those which relate to the environment. This chapter looks at the historic development of ideas regarding the third item, discounting, and traces them to current problems which stem, almost exclusively, from neoclassical thinking.

MAJOR TIDES IN ECONOMIC THINKING

In the age of classical economics, dominated by Smith, Malthus, Ricardo and Mill, the fundamental relationships between population, capital accumulation, technological progress, and economic growth were analysed. The emphasis was on supply-side economics.

The Marxist school looked at the economic world from the viewpoint of class struggle. In *The Contribution of the Critique of Political Economy*, Marx (1859) argued that 'the history of all hitherto existing society is the history of class struggles. Freeman and slave, patrician and plebian, lord and serf, guildmaster and journeyman, in a word, oppressor and the oppressed, stood in constant opposition to one another'. In his lengthy analysis of the capitalist system Marx concluded that equality, genuine freedom and abundance were possible only in a classless society.

The third major wave of thought, led by Menger, Jevons and Walras, was the neoclassical school which put emphasis on *laissez-faire*, granting only a limited role to government in the management of the economy. Another aspect of the neoclassical tradition was that it replaced the supply-oriented theory of value with the demand-oriented concept of marginal utility.

The interventionist theories of Pigou (1920), Taylor (1928) and then Keynes (1936) changed the tide of economic thinking from neoclassical *laissez-faire* to intervention and allowed the state to regulate the economy by way of demand management. Keynes focused on the problems of unemployment at a time when the world was in the grip of the most damaging depression it had ever experienced. After the publication of the *General Theory* a good number of economists seized upon it avidly, seeking both to fathom its complexities and to spread its gospel. In the US the work of Keynes was used to justify the expansion of the nation's already existing portfolio of public works and deficit financing. The Keynesian macroeconomic policies were equally in fashion in the UK, especially after the Second World War, manifesting themselves in part in the growth of nationalized industries and a commitment to infrastructure projects. In some major public works such as the M1 motorway, the Tay and Severn Bridges, the Victoria Underground Line and the Cumbrian Coast Railway formal CBA was used for the first time in economic appraisal.

In the 1970s the power of Keynesian thought was losing strength largely because of the emerging problem of stagflation, when unemployment and inflation were growing at the same time, which made Keynesian demand management unconvincing. The monetarist school returned to the classical theory as the basis for their analysis of macroeconomic problems which contained, in the main, supply-side policies to encourage the development of free enterprise to boost output and employment. As monetarists began to lose ground in the 1980s post-Keynesians and neoclassical thinkers were trying to fill the vacuum. The former still see demand as playing the crucial role in determining the level of output, employment and inflation but pay attention to other factors such as cost, equilibrium unemployment and rational expectations. The latter maintain that demand management is totally ineffective given that in the short run aggregate supply and Phillips curves are vertical, prices and wages are, essentially, flexible and expectations are rational.

The theory of the interest rate which underpins discounting is an integral part of economic analysis in all major waves of thought. But from the viewpoint of project appraisal existing theories of discounting and problems associated with them are firmly rooted in the neoclassical tradition.

THE NEOCLASSICAL SCHOOL AND THE FOUNDATION OF CONTEMPORARY DISCOUNT RATE THEORY

There are two aspects of discounting: time productivity of surplus funds and psychological time preference of economic agents in their intertemporal decisions. Menger (1871) argues that a resource has a value because of individuals' expectation of its productive potential. Capital is valuable as it is a source of income; when invested it would enhance the owner's consumption capacity. That is, a given stock of capital, properly invested, physically grows over time, creating greater and greater consumption opportunities in future years.

The other aspect of discounting relates to individuals' psychology when they make intertemporal consumption decisions. It has been suggested that at any given point in time individuals have a tendency to undervalue, in a systematic way, their future satisfactions; the more distant the future gains the smaller value attached to expected utilities. More than 100 years ago Jevons (1871) argued that when it comes to the distribution of income over time individuals tend to undervalue their future needs. If that is so, what are the factors which make individuals behave in this fashion? The neoclassical tradition provides four answers; lack of imagination or myopia; primitive tendency or selfishness; risk; and diminishing marginal utility of increasing consumption.

Jevons (1871), with reference to the first item, suggests that to secure a maximum benefit in life all future incidents should have the same impact on us as present incidents regardless of their remoteness in time. But no human mind is constituted in this way and thus a future utility is always less compelling than a present one. Pigou (1929) is perhaps the best known economist in the time-discounting debate with his phrase of 'defective telescopic faculty'. When individuals have a choice between two satisfactions they will not necessarily choose the greater of the two, but will often devote themselves to acquiring a small benefit now in preference to a much larger one some years later. The main reason for this is that our telescopic faculty is defective and thus we see future pains as well as pleasures on a diminishing scale. As the years to which satisfactions are allocated become more remote, they will be represented by a continuously diminishing scale of magnitudes.

Böhm-Bawerk (1894) and Rae (1905) attribute part of the time discounting to primitive behaviour and selfishness. A tendency to prefer earlier consumption to a much larger one in the future is due to backwardness, which is most noticeable amongst primitive tribes and unruly groups in our society. The more primitive the tribe or the underclass the greater the preference for early consumption. According to some, this type of behaviour is, essentially, self-destructive. For example Rae (1905) argues that when I die, 'let the world burn', was an attitude of many wild and selfish communities in the past who quickly vanished from human history; see also Fisher (1930) and Strotz (1956).

The third reason which is given for time discounting is risk, which can be split into two parts: risk of not being alive in future when a consumption benefit is anticipated; and risk of saving/investment being lost due to various factors. Fisher (1930) is careful not to condemn all time discounting as irrational. Since all of us are mortal it is reasonable to exhibit a greater preference for a given consumption today than tomorrow, because we may not survive to enjoy it then. In effect, current survival is a precondition for acquiring future benefits, as termination of life now brings an end to the enjoyment of all deferred utilities.

Eckstein (1961) and Henderson (1965) see the possibility of calculating a pure time-discount rate based upon survival probabilities in which utility to be enjoyed at each future moment ought to be multiplied by the probability of being alive at that time. Since this probability falls with the remoteness of the period, a rational time-discount rate will emerge. At a societal level, a mortality-based time-discount rate for the community can be calculated by taking into account life tables, sex and age differentiated mortality rates and sex and age distributions of population. For actual derivation of this rate for various countries see Kula (1984a and 1994).

The second component parameter of risk is that although the individual who expects a consumption benefit at a future point in time may survive, his/her expectation may not materialize due to many factors. For example, savings deposited with a bank may be lost if the bank goes out of business (a recent example is BCCI); dividends expected from the purchase of a share certificate may not materialize if the firm runs into problems . Hicks (1946) argues that every investment is a gamble and thus the expected return must reflect compensation for risk taking which varies from person to person and from business to business.

The fourth reason given to justify a positive time-preference rate is the diminishing marginal utility of increasing consumption. If the income of a person increases steadily over time the satisfaction gained will also increase, but at a slower rate because each absolute addition to income yields a successively smaller increase in welfare. The diminishing marginal utility of increasing income is a much older concept than the pure time-discount rate; its source can be traced to the works of Dupuit (1844), Gossen (1854) and Jennings (1855). Despite its great potential in economic analysis this theory had gone unnoticed for a long period of time, which led Stigler (1972) to express concern that this was largely due to lack of professionalism in economics. More than 80 years after its first appearance in the literature Fisher (1927) used the diminishing marginal utility of increasing consumption to justify progressive income tax. Now this concept appears to be the backbone of models of the social discount rate.

The psychological time preference of individuals and the time productivity of capital were first brought into equilibrium via loanable funds by Fisher (1907 and 1930). Before him analyses of funds for consumption and production were conducted separately. In the revision of his book *The Rate of Interest*, which has a lucid subtitle, *As Determined by Impatience to Spend Income and Opportunity to Invest*, he emphasized that there are two distinct components of the discount rate. An extra unit of saving has two consequences; a reduction in present consumption by that amount and an increase in future production leading to a greater consumption opportunity.

In perfect competition market forces bring households' decisions to save into equilibrium with investors' plans to invest which, under certain conditions, results in a single rate of interest. By borrowing and lending at that rate market participants arrange their expenditure so that total satisfaction during the entire period for which their plans extend is at a maximum, as judged by their present preferences. Firms invest up to a point where the rate of return on capital projects, at the margin, is equal to the interest rate. Consumers' plans to save are brought into equilibrium with producers' plans to invest and the ruling interest rate reflects both the time preference of consumers and rate of return on capital projects.

BEYOND FISHERIAN SYNTHESIS

Fisher's interest rate theory, essentially static in its nature, was in later years elaborated by Feldstein (1964, 1972) who used a two-period analysis at a communal level containing a time-discount rate (the social time-preference rate) and a marginal productivity of capital (the social opportunity-cost rate). Fisher's model is a supply and demand determination of the interest rate; he emphasized on many occasions that it was not a superficial description of supply and demand but rather an analysis which traced the theory to its ultimate source in taste and technology; see also Samuelson (1967).

Fisher wanted to bring scientific rigour into economic analysis which, according to him, was essential to understand the great complexities of the subject. One way to achieve this was the use of mathematical models and he was one of the earliest economists to do so in his PhD thesis, *Mathematical Investigations in the Theory of Value and Prices*. Samuelson (1967) argues that this has been the greatest PhD dissertation ever written in economics. Around that time some philosophers such as Whitehead and Russell (1910) were arguing that any verbal statement could be put into mathematical notation and rigorously developed to its logical conclusion without confusion. Opponents of this idea quickly pointed out that in mathematical modelling of economic ideas there would be a substantial distortion of the truth by highly restrictive or even untrue assumptions (Fusfield 1976).

When Keynes became the editor of *The Economic Journal* in 1911, a position he retained for 33 years, he gave a great deal of encouragement to economists to write articles containing mathematical models. However, at that time not many economists had impressive mathematical skills, although this began to change gradually in later years. Harold Hotelling and Frank Ramsey were the earliest to demonstrate competent modelling skills in economics. The latter, with a great deal of encouragement from Keynes, published an article, a mathematical theory of saving, in *The Economic Journal* for the purpose of finding an answer to the question: how much of its income should a nation save? He concluded that the rate of saving multiplied by the marginal utility of money should always be equal to the amount by which the total net rate of enjoyment of utility falls short of the maximum possible rate of enjoyment (Ramsey 1928). In order to develop his model Ramsey made a surprising assumption that society is like a single individual who has an eternal life: 'In order to justify this rule it is, of course, necessary to make various simplifying assumptions: we have to suppose that our community goes on for ever without changing either in numbers or in its capacity for enjoyment or in its aversion to labour.' In his further elaboration of the model Ramsey even assumed that 'men, or rather, families, were to live forever', (Ramsey 1928, p. 558).

In later years, discussing Irving Fisher's capital theory at an individual level, Samuelson (1967) suddenly turns to a communal model by arguing that Fisher never faced up to an infinite period equilibrium model. 'Take the consumption-saving taster of the community: $U = \Sigma_0^\infty U(C_t)/(1+R)^t$ where U is communal utility, C_t is consumption at time t and R is the subjective communal discount rate', Samuelson (1967, p. 34). Obviously, just like Ramsey, Samuelson treats society as a single entity with an infinite life span.

Elsewhere, he develops a forestry model with an infinite chain of harvesting and replanting for both private and public sectors (Samuelson 1976). In addition, the forestry model is considered in a general equilibrium setting with reference to Frank Ramsey. 'And suppose a planner for this society acts to solve a Ramsey (1928) optimum-control problem, namely for t restricted to integral values, Max $\Sigma_{t=0}^{\infty} U[C(t), Q(t)]e^{-pt}$' where p is the communal discount rate. Marglin (1963) in his analysis of opportunity cost of public projects takes a similar view: 'We plan public projects to maximise their net present value at the marginal social rate of discount', then specifies a communal benefit function stretching from now to eternity (Marglin 1963, p. 278).

It is clear that Ramsey's paper on saving was a trend setter in the sense that it used an infinite-period communal utility function with a view that society is like a single individual who has eternal life. Since then Ramsey's mathematically convenient discounting, with its underlying assumption, has been widely used in many fields of economics from resource depletion (Hotelling 1931; Solow 1974) to economic growth theories (Mirrlees and Stern 1973). All the articles are too numerous to mention here. Perhaps the most infected area of economics is CBA, in theory and practice. In the next section practical problems created by the Ramsey–Samuelson type of discounting will be outlined with reference to communal project-appraisal practices in the UK.

DISCOUNTING IN PRACTICE – THE UK EXPERIENCE

Having realized the importance of discounting in economic policy making the UK government has been studying practical as well as theoretical developments in this field with a view to forming a national policy since the early 1960s.

In a 1967 White Paper (Cmnd 3437) it was recommended that publicly owned industries should use a *test rate of discount* of 8 per cent in their appraisal of all important projects. This White Paper also spelled out that this figure was broadly consistent with the average rate of return, in real terms, earned on a low-risk project in the private sector. In 1968 the rate was increased to 10 per cent; in 1972 it was reviewed but not changed.

The test rate of discount drew fire from a variety of sources on a number of issues. First, the rate was based entirely upon the concept of an opportunity-cost rate which is only one half of the theory; nowhere in the White Paper was there a mention of the other half, the social time-preference rate. As explained above, the neoclassical theory requires inclusion of both concepts in determining the communal rate and thus the test rate of discount was theoretically incomplete. Second, in estimating the social opportunity-cost rate the Treasury used an extremely crude measure by looking at the minimum return regarded as acceptable on a new investment by a large private firm. The communal rate of return on private capital was not adjusted either for market imperfections or for external effects. Third, a crude average rate of return, rather than the marginal one, was used in the choice of a figure for the UK. Finally, the money used for public projects was assumed to displace private investment rather than private consumption. If the government had borrowed the entire money from the capital market to finance its projects then the social opportunity-cost rate would have been relevant. However, in the UK the bulk of public projects have been financed by tax revenue, a large proportion of which comes from private consumption. The appropriate course of action in this case would be the use of the social time-preference rate.

The strongest objection to the test rate comes from the pro-forestry lobby who argued that the 10 per cent rate had ended all hopes of an economic rationale for forestry in the UK (Price 1973; Helliwell 1974). Indeed, some studies on forestry in the UK had revealed that only a low discount rate of the order of 2 per cent was required to justify afforestation (Land Use Study Group 1966; Hampson 1972).

All these criticisms of the test rate of discount turned out to be fruitful. The government conceded that in public-sector investment appraisal the chosen rate of discount should reflect ideas on the social time-preference rate as well as the social opportunity-cost rate. A justifiable figure for the former would almost certainly be below 10 per cent. Second, there was no point in imitating the private sector unless the rate of return there correctly reflected society's view of profitability. Third, it was hardly convincing to regard a public investment as diverting resources entirely from private investment rather than private consumption. In a 1978 White Paper (Cmnd 7131) the social rate of discount was reduced to 5 per cent, referred to as the required rate of return.

In the spring of 1988 the government revealed that since 1978 the rate of return in the private sector had risen to about 11 per cent. In the light of this, the government decided to raise the required rate of return for publicly-owned industries and public-sector trading bodies from 5 to 8 per cent in real terms before tax. The discount rate to be used in the non-trading part of the public sector should be based upon the cost of capital for low-risk projects in the private sector. In current conditions this indicates a rate not less than 6 per cent in real terms. In the government's view these proposals will ensure that the appraisal of public projects will be no less demanding in the non-trading sector than in the trading one (Hansard 1989).

THREE SPECIAL CASES

Forestry

The review process of the social discount rate was keenly watched by the forestry lobby in the UK. When the test rate of discount was replaced by the 5 per cent required rate of return in 1978 there was a sigh of relief. However, not everybody was happy as a substantial body maintained that even a 5 per cent discount rate was too high to justify the UK's forestry programme. In 1971 an interdepartmental government team was set up to carry out a CBA of UK forestry which revealed that even on the widest concept of profitability, including import saving, environmental, landscape and recreational benefits, a typical rate of return was no more than 4 per cent. After the 1971 cost–benefit study the government revealed its forestry policy that afforestation would continue as before (HMSO 1972). It was spelled out that this policy was guided by, but not based on, the conclusion of the cost–benefit study. With regard to the discount rate the Forestry Commission in the UK was given a target rate of return of 3 per cent; the Forest Service in Northern Ireland 5 per cent. These rates are still in operation.

Nuclear Power

The decades of expansion of nuclear power in the UK came to an abrupt end with the government statement of 3 November 1989 in which plans to build new pressurized water reactors were shelved mainly because of the diminished public support for the nuclear industry in general. The other reason for the policy reversal was the failure to sell the nuclear industry to the private sector. The privatization process of the electricity industry served the useful purpose of revealing not only how much nuclear electricity costs, but also its future liabilities. The private sector was quick to realize that the cost of generating power by way of nuclear reactors was much higher than fossil fuel plants and this cost has been going up over the years partly because of escalating costs of nuclear technology and partly due to the tightening of regulatory standards. The Energy Committee (1990) confirmed that on the basis of the evidence it received there had been a systematic bias in the Central Energy Generating Board's costings in favour of nuclear power by ignoring risks, failing to provide for contingencies, and putting forward best expectations rather than more cautious estimates. Furthermore, the private sector has seen the nuclear industry as an open-ended liability in view of reprocessing operations, decommissioning of nuclear plants and the disposal of nuclear wastes.

Apart from the 'front-end' stage which involves uranium extraction and delivery, a nuclear reactor's life goes through three phases: construction, operation and decommissioning. Furthermore there is the final stage of disposing of highly contaminated parts and wastes which is the most difficult and complicated part. The Energy Committee argues that in decommissioning the final return of reactor sites to green-field status will take place at least 100 years after the termination of power operations. In its economic calculations of decommissioning costs the Central Electricity Board has been using a 2 per cent discount rate which is well below the required rate of return.

The Railways

The UK government has a commitment to privatize British Rail's track and the rolling stock. The Treasury has calculated that on a replacement cost basis the track is worth about £7 billion. On the basis of an 8 per cent required rate of return for the tradeable £7 billion asset base Railtrack must earn £560 million per annum. In order to achieve this the operator must charge sufficiently high prices which are likely to make the rail service uncompetitive and reduce the interest amongst potential private buyers.

In order to make the privatization initiative attractive the Treasury has agreed to set Railtrack's initial rate of return at 5 per cent in 1994–95, rising by one percentage point a year until it reaches 8 per cent. This, the government believes, would encourage more private operators to bid for franchises under the government's privatization scheme.

Table 5.1 Identifying the social rate of discount

	%
Test rate, first proposal	8
Test rate, second proposal	10
Required rate of return	5
Current rate, tradeables	8
Current rate, non-tradeables	6
Forestry rate, UK	3
Forestry rate, Ulster	5
Decommissioning of nuclear industry	2
British Rail target rate 1994/95	5
British Rail target rate 1995/96	6
British Rail target rate 1996/97	7
British Rail target rate 1997/98	8

A summary of the UK's endeavours to identify the social rate of discount during the last three decades is shown in Table 5.1. Although the efforts of the UK government to identify an appropriate social rate of discount must be well appreciated, what has happened up to now is far from encouraging. The sharp fluctuations in the prescribed rate in a short space of time and the creation of many special cases must be highly damaging from the viewpoint of efficiency in resource allocation, a central problem in economics. No matter what is done, ordinary discounting which is based upon the Ramseian assumption does not fit. In the next section the Ramseian assumption that society is like a single individual will be changed, giving way to a new pattern of discounting.

MODIFIED DISCOUNTING

There are three main characteristics of the modified discounting method. First, society is not like a single individual who has an infinite life but comprises mortal individuals with overlapping life spans. Second, the nature of public-sector projects is that they provide a fixed and unalterable stream of net returns to society, the constituent members of which continually change by birth and death over time. Since there is no market for the beneficiaries to exchange their share of returns from a publicly-owned concern, they can only wait to acquire what is due to them (Broussalian 1971). Third, the public-sector policy maker acting on behalf of future as well as present generations treats all individuals, whether presently alive or yet to be born equally.

In order to derive discount factors based upon the modified method it is essential to make a set of assumptions, none too restrictive. First, the size of the community, life expectancies and age distribution are constant over time but individual members are mortal, replaced by birth and death. Second, imagine a public-sector project that throws off £1 net benefit over time. Third, £1 net benefit, as it becomes available, gets divided equally between the existing members of the community at the time. Then calculate a net present value for each single individual, whether alive now or yet to be born who will receive net benefits from this project. The summation of these individual net present values yields factors which are very different from the conventional method. Figure 5.1 shows the emerging pattern of discounting at a 10 per cent social interest rate over a 100-year period on the basis of a 73-year life expectancy. For a practical model to calculate these factors see Kula (1984b). There have been about two dozen articles debating modified discounting in the literature; for a summary see Kula (1994).

If the modified discounting method was used in economic analysis of *all* communal projects, long- as well as short-term, many theoretical as well as

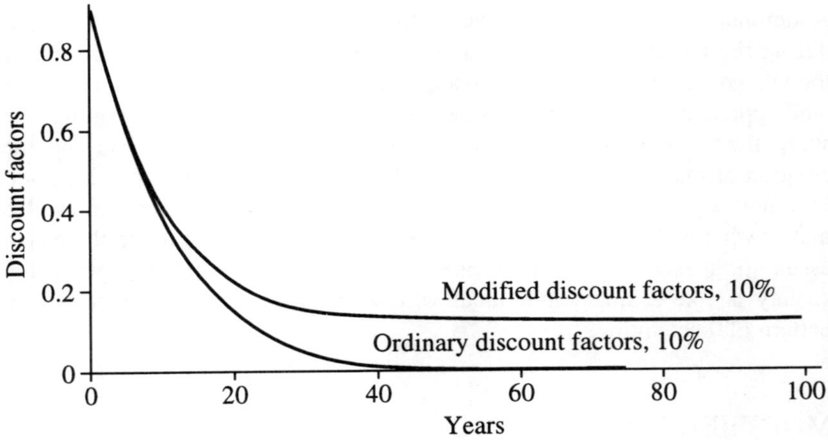

Figure 5.1 *Ordinary and modified discount factors at a 10% interest rate over 100 years*

practical problems mentioned above are likely to be eliminated. Furthermore, by doing so the communal decision maker would have the comforting thought that all generations, present as well as future, are treated equitably.

CONCLUSION

Although its principles have been established by economists, discounting is of interest to many subject areas such as psychology, philosophy, politics, development and environmental studies, as well as economics. There are two aspects to a discount rate; productivity of capital funds and subjective time preference of individuals in valuing a present consumption over a future one of the same magnitude. In the early part of the neoclassical age economists treated these concepts separately, but it was Irving Fisher who combined the two in a static analysis.

Frank Ramsey was the first economist to use the Fisherian discount rate in a dynamic communal model by assuming that society is like a single individual who has an eternal life. Since then this assumption has become the backbone of time-dependent economic analyses in many communal models in CBA, resource depletion, economic growth, determination of saving levels, etc.

When the UK government decided to establish a social discount rate for practical purposes in the 1960s many serious problems emerged. This chapter has tried to show that these problems are due to the Ramsey–Samuelson view of society: the community is like a single individual with an eternal life. Unlike Ramsey–Samuelson models modified discounting assumes a society with mortal individuals and overlapping lifespans. A comparison of ordinary and modified discount factors for 6 and 8 per cent social rates of discount is shown in Table 5.2.

Table 5.2 Ordinary and modified discount factors for 6% and 8% social rates of discount

	Ordinary discount factors		Modified discount factors	
Years	6%	8%	6%	8%
0	1.00	1.00	1.00	1.00
20	0.31	0.21	0.38	0.29
40	0.10	0.05	0.25	0.18
60	0.03	0.01	0.23	0.17
80	0.01	0.01	0.23	0.17
100	0.00	0.00	0.23	0.17

REFERENCES

Böhm–Bawerk, E.W. (1894), *The Positive Theory of Capital*, New York: Stedard.

Broussalian, V.L. (1971), 'Discounting and Evaluation of Public Investments', *Applied Economics*, **3**, 1–10.

Cmnd 3437 (1967), *Nationalised Industries: a review of economic and financial objectives*, London: HMSO.

Cmnd 7131 (1978), *Nationalised Industries*, London: HMSO.

Dupuit, J. (1844), 'On the Measurement of Utility of Public Works', translated from French in *International Economic Papers*, 1952, no. 2.

Eckstein, O. (1961), 'A Survey of Theory of Public Expenditure', in J. Buchanan (ed.), *Public Finances: Needs, Sources and Utilisation*, Princeton, NJ: Princeton University Press.

Energy Committee (1990), *The Cost of Nuclear Power*, London: HMSO, 7 June.

Feldstein, M.S. (1964), 'The Social Time Preference Rate in Cost-Benefit Analysis', *Economic Journal*, **74**, 360–79.

Feldstein, M.S. (1972), 'The Inadequacy of Weighted Discount Rates', in R. Layard (ed.), *Cost-Benefit Analysis*, London: Penguin Educational.

Fisher, I. (1907), *The Rate of Interest*, New York: Macmillan.

Fisher, I. (1927), 'A Statistical Method for Measuring Marginal Utility and Justice of Progressive Income Tax', in *Ten Economic Essays Contributed in Honour of J. Bates Clark*, New York: Macmillan.

Fisher, I. (1930), *The Theory of Interest as Determined by Impatience to Spend Income and Opportunity to Invest It*, New York: Macmillan.

Fusfield, D.R. (1976), *The Age of the Economist*, Foreman, Ill.: Scott.

Gossen, H.H. (1854), *Entwicklung der Gesetze des manschilchen Verkehrs*, 3rd edition, 1927, Berlin: Prayer.
Hampson, S.F. (1972), 'Highland Forestry: an evaluation', *Journal of Agricultural Economics*, **23**, 49–57.
Hansard (1989), *Investment*, **150**, no. (79), Col. 187, 5 April, London: HMSO.
Helliwell, D.R. (1974), 'Discount Rates in Land Use Planning', *Forestry*, **47**, 147–52.
Henderson, P.D. (1965), 'Notes on Public Investment Criteria in the United Kingdom', *Bulletin of the Oxford University Institute of Statistics*, February.
Hicks, J.R. (1946), *Value and Capital*, Oxford: Clarendon Press.
HMSO (1972), *Forestry Policy*, London: HMSO.
Hotelling, H. (1931), 'The Economics of Exhaustible Resources', *Journal of Political Economy*, **39**, 137–75.
Jennings, R. (1855), *Natural Elements of Political Economy*, London: Macmillan.
Jevons, W.S. (1871), *The Theory of Political Economy*, reprinted 1970, New York: Penguin.
Keynes, J.M. (1936), *The General Theory of Employment, Interest and Money*, New York: Harcourt.
Kula, E. (1984a), 'Derivation of Social Time Preference Rates for the United States and Canada', *Quarterly Journal of Economics*, **99**, 873–83.
Kula, E. (1984b), 'Discount Factors for Public Sector Investment Projects by Using the Sum of Discounted Consumption Flows Method', *Environment and Planning A*, **16**, 689–94.
Kula, E. (1994), *Economics of Natural Resources, the Environment and Policies*, 2nd edition, London: Chapman and Hall.
Land Use Study Group (1966), *Forestry, Agriculture and Multiple Use of Rural Land*, London: HMSO.
Marglin, S. (1963), 'The opportunity cost of public investment', *Quarterly Journal of Economics*, **77**, 274–89.
Marx, K. and F. Engels (1848), *Communist Manifesto*, London: Norton.
Menger, C. (1871), *Principles of Economics*, ed. J. Dingwall and trans. by Haselitz, New York: New York University Press.
Mirrlees, J.A. and N.H. Stern (1973), *Models of Economic Growth*, London: Macmillan.
Pigou, A. (1920), *Income*, New York: Macmillan.
Pigou, A. (1929), *The Economics of Welfare*, New York: Macmillan.
Price, C. (1973), 'To the Future – With Indifference or Concern?' *Journal of Agricultural Economics*, **24**, 383–94.
Rae, J. (1905), *The Sociological Theory of Capital*, London: Macmillan.
Ramsey, F. (1928), 'A Mathematical Theory of Saving', *Economic Journal*, **38**, 543–9.
Samuelson, P.A. (1967), Irving Fisher and the Theory of Capital, in W. Fellner (ed.), *Ten Economic Studies in the Tradition of Irving Fisher*, New York: Wiley.
Samuelson, P.A. (1976), 'Economic of Forestry in an Evolving Society', *Economic Inquiry*, **14**, 466–92.
Smith, A. (1776), *An Inquiry into the Nature and Causes of the Wealth of Nations*.
Solow, R.M. (1974), 'Intergenerational Equity and Exhaustible Resources', in Symposium on the Economics of Exhaustible Resources, *Review of Economic Studies*, Supplement, **41**, 29–46.
Stigler, G. (1972), 'The Adoption of the Marginal Utility Theory', *History of Political Economy*, **4**, 573–86.

Strotz, R.H. (1956), 'Myopia and Inconsistency in Dynamic Utility Maximisation', *Review of Economic Studies*, **23**, 165–80.

Taylor, F.M. (1928), Presidential Address to the American Economic Association, *American Economic Review*, **18**.

Whitehead, A.N. and B. Russell (1910), *Principia Mathematica*, Cambridge: Cambridge University Press.

6. Discounting and project appraisal: from the bizarre to the ridiculous

Colin Price*

INTRODUCTION

The broad basis and effects of discounting are well understood, and have been widely discussed: time preference; diminishing marginal utility of increasing consumption; the opportunity cost of investment funds. Other factors, such as long-term risk and uncertainty, while subject to some dispute, are regularly mentioned as a justification for discounting. Yet an increasing sense of disquiet can be felt among more thoughtful economists about the dramatic impact of discounting over long periods. In particular, the recent broadening of CBA to include environmental and cultural values, and even the value of life itself, has encouraged a closer look at the credentials of a technique which originated far away, in financial markets.

This chapter focuses, illustratively, on injury or damage to human interests caused or alleviated by projects or development strategies. Situations involving such factors – transport development, nuclear waste storage, loss of natural capital, global climate change – are central to the modern debate about economic evaluation. It analyses the features of such situations which make conventional discounting inappropriate, and broadens the discussion to other arenas where the justification of discounting, on closer examination, appears to fail.

Let us begin with another example of the bizarre effect of discounting. The risks associated with climate change are among the greatest faced by humanity. The spatial scale is global; the time scale is measured in centuries. The effect scale includes the loss of whole livelihoods, and indeed of lives. The discounting convention applied here is that adopted by the Department of Transport (1994) to value the possible loss of human life. The procedure is relatively sophisticated, in that the ruling 8 per cent discount rate is adjusted

*The author wishes to express his thanks to John Broome, Michael Jones-Lee, Erhun Kula and Ian Livingstone for supplying information for this chapter.

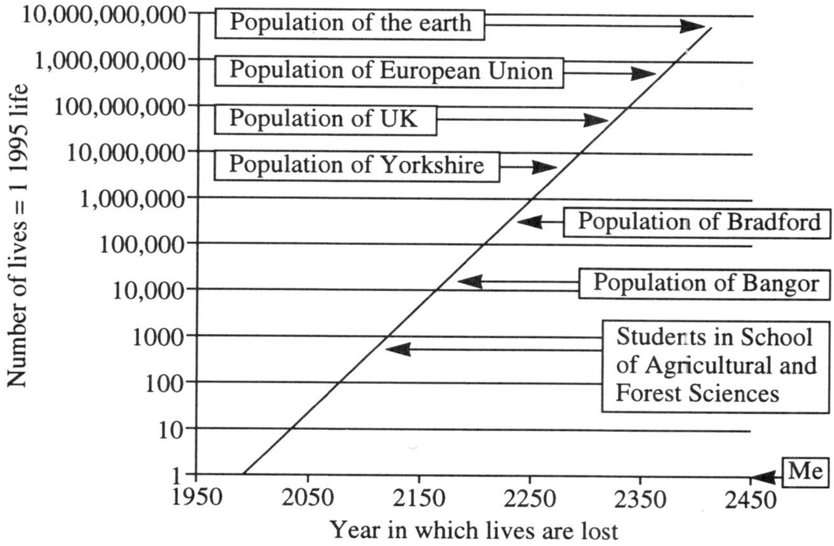

Figure 6.1 Discounting the value of human lives

downward by about $2^1/2$ per cent, to mirror expected growth in incomes. Nonetheless, the outcome is dramatic, as Figure 6.1 shows.

On the time scale relevant to the problem, the loss of livelihood or life of the entire population of the world has the same significance as the loss of a single livelihood or life in 1995. If it does nothing else, such a set of numbers must lead us to question the justifications given for undertaking the discounting operation.

Risk may be immediately dismissed as a basis for discounting in these circumstances. The convention of applying a premium to the discount rate for risky investments originates in capital markets, where the effect is to make such investments less likely to be adopted. In relation to climate change, the effect is perverse: a discount for risk, by devaluing the long-term costs of a business-as-usual scenario, makes this risky strategy *more likely* to be adopted. Justification, if it exists, must be sought elsewhere.

PREFERENCE FOR WHAT SORT OF TIME?

In a democratic society, a system of policy or project appraisal should respect the values held by individuals, including their apparent impatience for early consumption: this is the time-preference basis for discounting. Yet the meaning of time preference may not be as economists have interpreted it. The interpretations available depend on how choices are constructed, and in fact the data set habitually used by economists could hardly be more biased.

Historically, evidence about time preference has been derived from revealed choices in markets: in particular, evidence about risks to health and life has been drawn from studies of wages in risky occupations (Moore and Viscusi 1990). In recent years, however, such research has been supplemented by experiments using constructed choices, both real and hypothetical. Following is a series of such constructed choices, of the kind which purport to yield evidence for conventional time discounting, but which may have a very different interpretation.

Consider the choice between a permanent disability arriving at age 30 or at age 40 within an individual's life cycle. An expected preference for the second option might be presented as showing that people prefer to postpone disbenefits, as in conventional discounting. In fact, however, this preference shows no such thing. The only difference between the two situations is that the first involves an additional ten-year period of disability, without any compensating advantage. Preference for the second option indicates merely that disability is undesirable, and the less of it the better: it says nothing at all about the relative undesirability of disability early or late in time.

Next, consider a disability of given severity and duration, which may be experienced either between ages 15 and 20, or between ages 55 and 60. A preference for the second option might once again be taken as showing less weight given to later time periods. It might, however, as easily indicate that the particular disability would have more detrimental impact during the very active younger stages of the life cycle. It is, moreover, by no means certain that preference *would* be for the postponed disability: everyday observation indicates that many people prefer to get painful or distressing events 'over and done with' as soon as possible, thus reducing the period of apprehension felt about them.

But there is a further, and more persuasive piece of evidence to review. In retrospect many people express regret that good things have been brought forward in life and bad things reserved for later life. Contemplating a five-year disability in middle age, might one not wish that the disability was part of the past? Such a reversal of preference might indicate either superior information in later time, or a changed perspective. If the effect is one of information, then presumably the same reversed preference would have been expressed, had the information been available earlier: more informed decisions are (generally held to be) better decisions, in which case greater weight to *later* utilities and disutilities becomes the meaning of time preference. On the other hand, if changed perspective is the cause of reversal, we should acknowledge that preferences at a point in time are likely to be biased by their particular perspective, and provide a discounting relationship which is not representative of all relevant time perspectives. A much more consistent interpretation of time preference is that it represents a greater weight *to the present time* rather than *to early time*. Since all times become the present in due course, a balancing of perspective suggests that no particular weight should be given to early time, and the case for time-preference discounting vanishes.

Finally, consider a permanent disability to be experienced, not with reference to the individual life cycle, but rather early or late *in historical time*, without the person to suffer it being identified in the description of the choice. Here a new factor comes into play: less importance given to disability later in history reflects a lesser likelihood that any *presently living* individual would survive to join the set of people who might suffer the disability.

However, discounting does not represent even the selfish interests of presently living people accurately. Figure 6.2 shows the proportion of the present UK population expected to survive different periods into the future. Clearly the negative exponential of discounting fails to match the real survival prospects of such a population.

Some further weight to future generations might be given by the 'benevolent affections' (Rae 1834) which we feel for them. But, ethically considered, if future generations matter, they matter in their own right, and not according to the whim of present generations. As Sidgwich (1874) says: '... the time at which a man exists cannot affect the value of his happiness ... the interests of posterity must concern a utilitarian'.

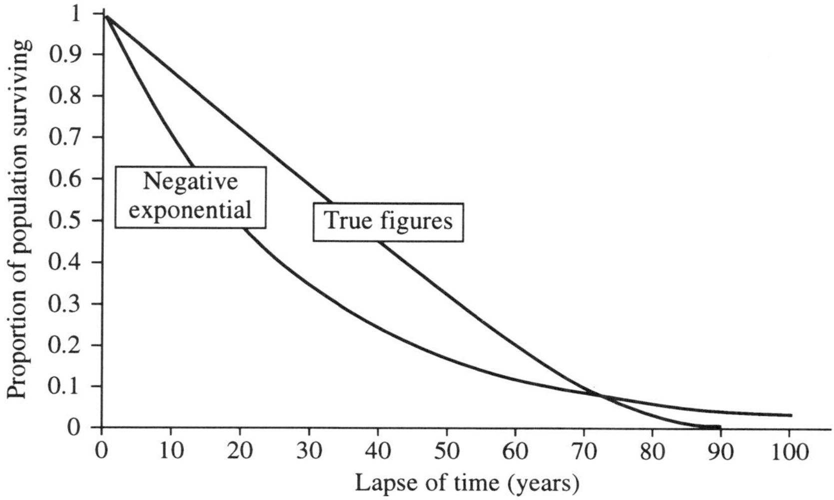

Figure 6.2 Survivorship of presently living people

The last-described choice situation is the one that most commonly confronts society; and it is impossible, from observing individual preferences, to distinguish in what mix the revealed time preference represents preference for short duration of disability, for disability late in the life cycle, for disability late in historical time, for disability to occur *other than now*, and for disability to occur *other than to oneself*. 'Late in historical time' is, from the viewpoint of society itself, the least reasonable of the interpretations; and yet it is the one embodied in time-preference discounting.

DISCOUNTING COMPENSATION FOR INJURIES

Notwithstanding the ambivalent indications of time preference, Parfit (1984) has argued that future injuries are less costly to provide compensation for, along the following lines:

- a given sum of money is acceptable as compensation for a certain injury;
- for future injuries, this sum may be provided by current investment of a smaller sum;
- the further into the future the injury occurs, the smaller the present investment needed to provide timely compensation;
- future injuries are hence of less significance.

Such an argument, however, ignores the effects of diminishing marginal utility. If consumption is greater in future, and if the marginal utility of consumption varies inversely with consumption (both being premises on which social discounting is widely justified), then the marginal utility of future consumption is less than that of present consumption, and a greater volume of consumption would be required to compensate for an injury of given severity. Broome (1994) asserts that the amount of investment required will be the same, irrespective of when the injury occurs.

This is not the case, however, with elastic marginal utility of consumption (marginal utility of consumption declines more rapidly than consumption rises). As future consumption rises, the required compensation rises more rapidly, and may become indefinitely large in the not-far-distant future (Price, unpubl.). The result is not unreasonable: once a certain level of affluence is achieved, no amount of additional consumption may be as valuable as the absence of an injury, as many people with relatively trivial injuries would testify.

In these circumstances the amount of money to be invested is *greater*, the further into the future the injury occurs, the implicit discount rate being

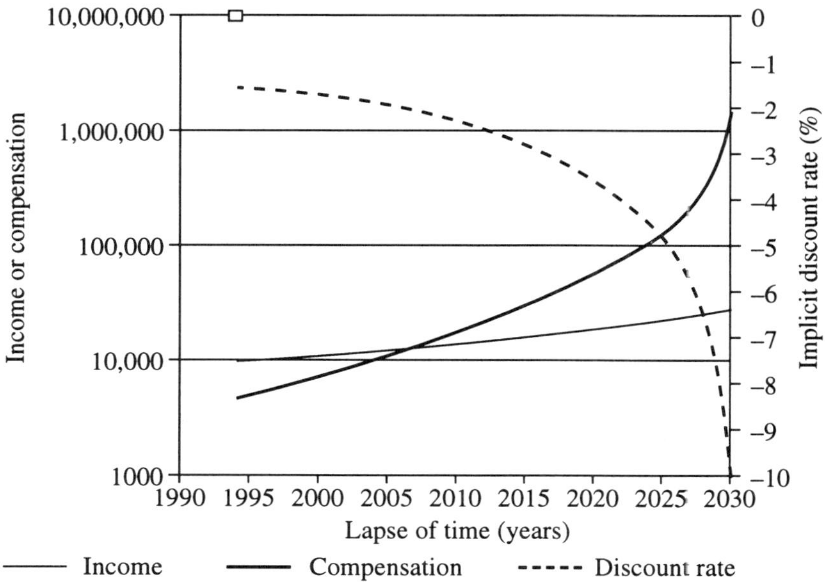

Figure 6.3 Compensation and implicit discount rate

negative, increasingly so, and eventually indefinitely so, as Figure 6.3 shows.

If adequate compensation cannot be paid (and clearly it cannot in this case), then the injury has to be evaluated on its own terms. A given injury may be of less consequence in future if remedial treatment improves through time, but no empirical or theoretical evidence suggests that such improvement would take place at the rate of return on investment, or at any other rate on which social discounting might be based.

It is not a little odd that diminishing marginal utility, the most intellectually respectable justification for social discounting, is in the case just described the reason why conventional social discounting cannot be applied.

ANALYSIS OF THE PROBLEM

The approach of conventional CBA to the problems above fails partly because the basis of discounting in time preference and risk are simply illegitimate. Partly, it fails because the legitimate consideration of diminishing marginal utility does not translate into conventional discounting when the relevant values have the following features:

1. They are non-marginal, in the sense that they entail not a small adjustment to the consumption of everyone, but a major change to the consumption (even loss of *all* consumption) of individuals.
2. They are not susceptible to transformation from or substitution by those increasingly abundant products which are themselves subject to diminishing marginal utility – and certainly not so susceptible at the present product–price ratio.

These features are quite characteristic of both the natural and the built environment, both of which are becoming common targets of project appraisal. From wildernesses to cathedrals, our aesthetic experience is of the following nature:

- Each individual site is a public good, whose destruction terminates non-marginal as well as marginal experiences.
- Each has its own character and human associations, so that one is not a substitute for another.
- To the extent that inter-site substitution is possible, it is limited by a carrying capacity, which, if exceeded, means that the site offers a poorer experience.
- It is in the nature of the experience that replacement by technological substitutes is not only inapposite, but even repellent.

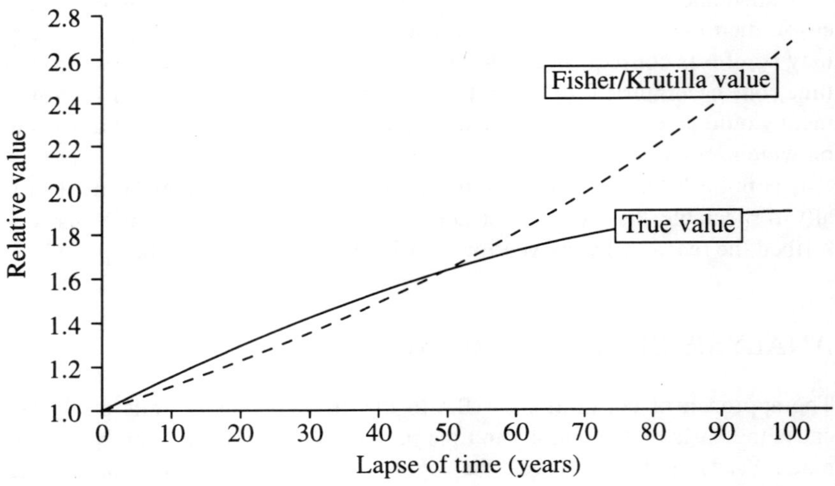

Figure 6.4 Future recreation values

Fisher et al. (1972), in a series of much-noted papers, have suggested that the problem of valuing public, non-substitutable resources can be addressed by increasing both the projected usage and the imputed price of natural environments, while continuing to discount normally. The effect, unfortunately, is to produce a profile of future values which under no combination of parameters will reflect the total utility of the resource (see Figure 6.4).

Once again, the only solution is to depart from conventional discounting and evaluate future costs and benefits on grounds of reasonable expectation of why and how they might change.

TROUBLE AT THE MARGIN

But it would be mistaken to think that the impropriety of discounting future consumption is confined to products where change is normally non-marginal. For some product/consumer combinations (electronic calculators for most purchasers; animal protein within the European Union; most material consumption for the top 50 per cent of income earners in the UK), technological change has greatly increased consumption per head, and diminished the marginal utility of producing one more unit.

Technology has not, however, been equally successful in promoting growth of consumption of all products, for all consumers. Environmental and cultural values are examples quoted above. The availability of basic material wants is also static or declining for many people. Figure 6.5 shows gross domestic product and protein consumption per head for a randomly selected developing country.

The discouraging GDP figures may actually present an overoptimistic picture, given that through time a greater proportion of formerly unrecorded subsistence production is included, and as a greater proportion of GDP may be required to service foreign debts. As for the remaining non-cash consumption, it is worth noting that shortage of fuelwood is widely perceived in Africa as 'the energy crisis that won't go away'.

Nor is this a problem confined to the developing world: the decline in nutritional standards and energy availability is shared by the poorest groups in the UK.

Nothing could be more ridiculous than discounting something that is becoming increasingly scarce on the grounds that it is becoming increasingly abundant. Yet project appraisal does not in general single out consumption by less favoured groups for different discounting treatment, despite the distortions introduced by use of a national mean discount rate (Price and Nair 1985), or a rate based on optimistic growth projections. Future impoverished generations do not have their poverty recognized on its own terms: on the

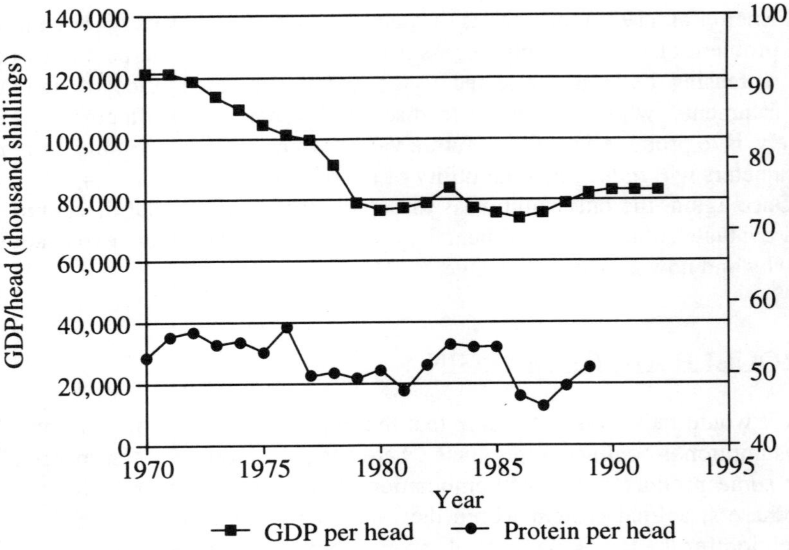

Figure 6.5 Consumption indicators in Uganda

contrary, their ability to meet their own needs is continually compromised as discounting progressively trivializes their resource base.

SUSTAINABILITY: OLD ILLUSION, NEW PACKAGE?

The modish justification for continuing to discount resource values, in the face of static or declining consumption per head, is this: exploiting a natural resource in the present provides revenue for investment in human-made capital (or environmentally compensating projects); the growth rate of consumption derived from such projects exceeds the growth rate of value of the natural resource; if future generations are to be provided with the greatest consumption, investment should be transferred to the highest-yielding forms; discounting at the rate of return on human-made capital ensures that retaining resources in low-productivity natural systems is seen as unprofitable; discounting is thus essential to protect the well-being of future generations.

The argument, a variant of the opportunity cost of capital basis for discounting, is superficially plausible. And yet for those old enough to recall the era of take-off into self-sustaining growth (Rostow 1956; Westoby 1962), the notion of pillaging natural capital to finance a compounding bonanza of investment and future consumption has a disconcertingly familiar ring. Many developing countries followed the prescription. Some fulfilled the prognosis, but many others did not, for reasons on which at least one of the practitioners later reflected ruefully (Westoby 1987).

What grounds have we to be optimistic that things will be different this time? Remarkably few. Characteristically, marginal propensities to save and reinvest out of revenues vary downwards from 25 per cent: using a World Bank protocol (Bruce 1976), a few years ago we even calculated a *negative* marginal propensity to save for Lesotho. And such neglect of investment and reinvestment appears to find official approval. In a World Bank publication on sustainability, El Serafy (1989) declares that 'the setting aside of part of the proceeds [of natural resource exploitation] in reinvestment is only a metaphor'. One is left wondering what kind of benefit future generations are expected to reap from this *metaphorical reinvestment*.

Nor can the developed nations be smug. Marginal propensity to save in the US has fallen from about 12 per cent to about 3 per cent over two or three decades. North Sea oil revenues do not appear to have financed the promised regeneration of (UK-funded) UK manufacturing industry. As for the future, does anyone seriously believe that collected carbon taxes will accumulate at compound interest over hundreds of years in an untouchable fund, to compensate the future sufferers from climate change? The excitement about the prospect of using carbon taxes to shift deadweight losses from conventional fiscal policy (Nordhaus 1994) hints at the readiness of governments to sell off the future's inheritance in lieu of current taxation, now that the historical family silver has mostly been pawned.

It is indeed a heavy irony that, because of high time preference – a preference, that is, for success *now* – governments have failed to turn natural resources into human-made capital, and thus have undermined the genuine justification for (limited) discounting offered by the transformation processes mobilized by invested and reinvested revenues.

DOES NOT-DISCOUNTING BRING ITS OWN BIZARRENESS?

Abandoning the familiar discounting protocol does have its problems. These do not, or should not, include the unleashing of a flood of environmentally destructive, but now-profitable investments. The environmental destruction will generally be of long duration, and as such it will weigh heavily against such investments under a no-discounting regime.

With some reinvestment and a rate of return on investment greater than whatever discount rate is held to be appropriate, the shadow price of investment funds threatens to become infinite (and, by comparison, the value of present consumption trivial). But this too is an empty threat, provided that marginal utility of consumption is elastic to consumption growth. If investment funds grow at a faster rate than consumption generally, they will ultimately come to dominate the growth rate of consumption, and as such will raise the consumption discount rate to a level that makes the value of all dependent future consumption finite. The argument is not dissimilar to the one under which even infinite future monetary compensation is insufficient to offset a disability giving finite present disutility.

Returning to the life-saving example, a further paradox impends if we discount the (investible) funds expended on life saving, but not the value of lives saved. Keeler and Cretin (1983) observe that, under such a dispensation, for every life-saving project there is another and superior one which involves delay of life saving, with intervening investment of funds, leading to greater life saving in a future period. Thus life-saving projects should be perpetually delayed. This might indeed be the implication. However, it is likely that the growth of life-saving funds would over time lead to diminishing returns from life-saving expenditure, as the most cost-effective options are successively taken up. An equilibrium would be reached, at which the growth of life-saving funds matched the growth in the marginal cost of saving a life, and in which present expenditure on life saving would continue to be made.

CONCLUSION

Livingstone and Tribe (1995) conclude that I conclude that no clear recommendation can be made with respect to selection of a discount rate. I do not believe that I conclude that at all. Instead, I conclude with great conviction and certainty that discounting by means of a uniform negative exponential function is contrary to reason and to judgement. The sooner we stop doing it in project appraisal, and seek a juster and more rational way to treat future values, the better.

This necessarily brief review has glossed over many arguments, counter-arguments and counter-counter-arguments, which are considered more comprehensively in Price (1993). These are details which I am happy to debate, at any length, at any time, in any forum. The issue is among the most significant of our age, and it is important that we devote whatever time is necessary to getting it right.

REFERENCES

Broome, J. (1994), 'Discounting the future', *Philosophy and Public Affairs*, **23**, 128–56.
Bruce, C. (1976), 'Social cost–benefit analysis', World Bank Staff Working Paper no. 239, Washington, DC: World Bank.
Department of Transport (1994), *Highway Economics Note 1: 1993 Valuation of Road Accidents*, London: Department of Transport.
El Serafy, S. (1989), 'The proper calculation of income from depletable natural resources', in Y.J. Ahmad, S. El Serafy and E. Lutz (eds) (1989), *Environmental Accounting for Sustainable Development*, Washington, DC: World Bank.
Fisher, A.C., J.V. Krutilla, and C.J. Cicchetti (1972), 'The economics of environmental preservation', *American Economic Review*, **62**, 605–19.
Keeler, E.B. and S. Cretin (1983), 'Discounting of life-saving and other non-monetary effects', *Management Science*, **29**, 300–306.
Livingstone, I. and M. Tribe (1995), 'The discount rate and the economic appraisal of projects with long time horizons', *Project Appraisal*, **10** (4).
Moore, M.J. and W.K. Viscusi (1990), 'Discounting environmental health risks: new evidence and policy implications', *Journal of Environmental Economics and Management*, **18**, S51–62.
Nordhaus, W.D. (1994), *Managing the Global Commons*, Cambridge, Mass.: MIT Press.
Parfit, D. (1984), *Reasons and Persons*, Oxford: Oxford University Press.
Price, C. (1993), *Time, Discounting and Value*, Oxford: Blackwell.
Price, C. (unpubl.), *Discounting Compensation for Injuries*, MS available from the author.
Price, C. and C.T.S. Nair (1985), 'Social discounting and the distribution of project benefits', *Journal of Development Studies*, **21**, 525–32.
Rae, J. (1834), *The Sociological Theory of Capital*, London: Macmillan, 1905.
Rostow, W.W. (1956), 'The take-off into self-sustained growth', *Economic Journal*, **66**, 26–48.
Sidgwick, H. (1874), *The Methods of Ethics*, London: Macmillan.
Westoby, J.C. (1962), 'The role of forest industries in the attack on economic under-development', *Unasylva*, **16**, 168–201.
Westoby, J.C. (1987), *The Purpose of Forests*, Oxford: Blackwell.

7. The effects method and economic cost–benefit analysis: substitutes or complements?

Bernard Franck

INTRODUCTION

The effects method of project appraisal (EM) was first developed during the 1960s as part of the work carried out by a French consultancy organization (SEDES) on behalf of various African countries. Its methodology was described in Prou and Chervel (1970) and later in a manual (Chervel and Le Gall 1976) which is now the official manual of project appraisal for the French authorities in charge of economic development overseas (Ministère de la Coopération, Caisse française de Développement). EM is therefore currently used in French-speaking African countries. Attempts have been made to apply it to France itself in the early 1980s (see Chervel 1992).

The method seems as first sight very different from traditional economic cost–benefit analysis (ECBA), the main point of difference being that it works with domestic market prices and not shadow prices. Unlike ECBA, its theoretical basis does not rely upon standard welfare analysis, but rather can be retraced to central planning models such as the Kantorovitch model of resource allocation. This is probably why EM has been largely ignored by the Anglo-Saxon world. There are very few writings in English about this method,[1] although the well-known paper by Balassa (1976) provides a critical evaluation of the so-called 'effects method'.

Nevertheless, EM has been taught in many seminars throughout the world, some of which were sponsored by prominent international organizations such as the World Bank (mainly EDI seminars for French-speaking participants) and UNIDO.[2] Some consultants' reports on projects financed by the European Development Fund use it and EM will be described in the next manual of project analysis written for the European Union.

We argue here that EM is not erroneous, as claimed by Little and Mirrlees (1990). Although it is still a minor competitor to ECBA, it is useful to restate the relative status of the two methods in project appraisal. This is not merely a theoretical matter: many country administrations and international institutions are involved in the training of people who will have to deal with economic appraisal of projects as administrators, civil servants or consultants. Which method(s) should they be taught?

Three different opinions can be identified on this subject among informed economists:

1. EM and ECBA are strictly interchangeable. If they start with the same set of assumptions and use the same data, they should lead to the same result. So either method can be used.
2. EM is more adapted than ECBA for some specific types of projects, or countries.
3. EM and ECBA do not have the same goals. They do not look at the same information and do not answer the same questions. So, ideally, both should be used when appraising a project.

After recalling the main specific features of EM, we shall discuss successively these three propositions.

MAIN CHARACTERISTICS OF THE EFFECTS METHOD

Let us recall first that EM chooses as its main criterion to appraise a project from the standpoint of society as a whole, the net or incremental value added generated by the project and distributed through the national economy.

The analysis of a project by EM involves a succession of steps leading to the computation of:

1. Direct value-added generated by the project for each year of its functioning.
2. Indirect value-added generated (mainly upstream).
3. Incremental value-added obtained by comparing the without- and with-project situations.

The discounted flow of incremental value-added is finally compared with the investment cost of the project to obtain a net present value (NPV) or an economic rate of return.

Step 1 is relatively straightforward, and can be calculated by looking at the income statement of the project and splitting the value of its production into three component parts:

- value of imported inputs (at cif prices, since duties are value-added accruing to the state);
- market value of locally produced inputs,
- value-added, which may be allocated according to the beneficiary: workers (wages), the state (taxes net of subventions), financial institutions (interest), project manager (profit).

The second step is harder and requires more information. It is argued that the increase in demand for local inputs used by the project will on most occasions be met by an increase in supply (whether these inputs are tradeable or not), thus generating further value-added, and additional imports. But this will also be true for the suppliers of the local inputs used by firms selling inputs to the project, and so on. If the process is (at least conceptually) carried on to its end, the value of the project output is finally broken down into only two elements: total value-added and total imports needed.

In practice, two methods can be used to estimate indirect value-added. The first is direct field enquiry, identifying sellers to the project, and estimating their value-added from their own accounts, and then trying to do the same backwards. Experience shows that very often, by concentrating on important items, a significant fraction of local inputs can be thus identified. The second method is to use an input–output table (in which imported inputs must be subtracted from total intermediate consumption). If such a table is available, we can obtain directly the total value-added included by unit of production for each activity by multiplying the vector of direct unitary value added, by the Leontief inverse of the input–output matrix. Applying these to the project's consumption of local inputs gives the amount of indirect value-added generated by the project. Indirect imports can be obtained by a similar operation, or by subtracting indirect value-added from the market value of these inputs.

There are several drawbacks, however, attached to the use of an input–output (I–O) table. When they exist, they are often old and inaccurate and therefore fail to describe the present and future structure of industries. Constructing a new I–O table is a time- and money-consuming task. Second, they give average technical coefficients which may be very different from those of firms actually involved in the project, especially if the aggregation level is high (this problem is similar to the choice between national versus project-specific parameters in ECBA). Third, by using them, it is implicitly assumed that at each round there will be an increase of production and no substitution effects. In other words, there is extra capacity available in each industry.

Taking these criticisms into account, the better method is probably to go as far as possible with the direct enquiry approach, using an I–O table only to estimate the residual elements of local consumption.

The third step is to estimate the incremental value-added. At the end of the second step, the total value-added created by the project has been evaluated. But there may also be value-added elements in the without-project situation which will disappear if the project is implemented. These must be subtracted to get the incremental value-added. This procedure is strictly equivalent to computing the opportunity value of outputs and the opportunity cost of inputs, as some examples will show:

1. If the project output is substituted for imports, the state will lose import taxes, and the corresponding amount must be deducted from the project value-added. Since we have already seen that imports generated by the projects are expressed at cif price, the method is equivalent to valuing traded goods at world price, and incremental value-added may be interpreted as a gain in foreign currency.
2. If the project hires workers who would have an alternative occupation in the without-project situation, the value-added suppressed by lost production must also be deducted. This is equivalent to computing a shadow wage rate.[3]
3. By the same line of reasoning, it can be seen that non-traded inputs are valued at their supply price if their production increases, and at market prices in cases of diverted demand.

Of course, the computation of incremental value-added is completely dependent on the description of the without-project situation. Traditionally, an assumption is made to simplify the analysis, according to which final demand of each good would be the same in the two situations. This is quite legitimate in a context of general planning, which is the optimal framework for the use of EM, but can sometimes be misleading, for instance, in the case of infrastructure projects. However, this assumption is not essential to the application of the method.

The comparison between discounted incremental value-added and the investment cost of the project is standard but raises one issue: since there are value-added elements in this cost, to be logically consistent these should be deducted to leave only the import content (direct and indirect) of investment as an actual cost to society. In practice this is seldom done, the explanation being that it is the total amount of capital needed which has to be mobilized, even if a part of the funds is recovered by national agents, and capital is fundamentally scarce.

Finally it must be pointed out that EM is not a single-criterion method. Other information is given, which may also be of interest to the political authorities: the number of jobs created by the project, and above all, the impact on income distribution. The redistributive effects of a project are particularly easy to identify when working with EM since, from the beginning, attention has been focused on new income flows. This is true of direct value-added, but also of indirect effects, since the total value-added included in local inputs may be split into its components, again using sectoral coefficients. For instance, at the end of the process, we can assess the effects of the project upon the government budget without extra computation. Direct effects may be disaggregated by distinguishing rural and urban households, modern and traditional firms, and so on. Regional effects may also be measured. But in EM these distributional effects are neither weighted, nor incorporated with efficiency effects in an overall criterion.

It should be clear by now that the economic analysis underlying EM is not heretical, and, by different ways, leads to reasonings which are very similar to those of ECBA. Can it then be said that they are equivalent?

EM AND ECBA AS PERFECT SUBSTITUTES

The formal equivalence of EM and ECBA can be demonstrated using a linear model of an economy with n goods and m production factors.

We use standard notations:

X, Y, M are the column vectors of production, internal final demand and net imports;
A is the matrix of technical coefficients;
F the matrix of factors utilization;
p and π the row vectors of domestic prices of goods and factors;
p^* and π^* the corresponding vectors of shadow prices;
v is the row vector of value-added at market prices by unit of production;
t is the row vector of taxes on traded goods.

The equilibrium condition between supply and demand is $X + M = AX + Y$. The definition of V gives $v = p\,(I - A)$, so that the total value-added in the economy is:

$$VA = vX + tM = p\,(I - A)\,X + tM = pY - (p - t)\,M.$$

Let us now consider a project as a marginal transformation, which does not affect prices or the final demand for traded goods. By differentiating the last equation, we get the incremental value-added generated by the project:

$$\mathrm{d}VA = p\mathrm{d}Y - p\mathrm{d}M \qquad (1)$$

Now the net social benefit at shadow prices, dB, is:

$$\mathrm{d}B = p^* \, (I - A) \, \mathrm{d}X - \mathrm{d}C^*$$

where dC^* is the marginal cost of production factors at shadow prices:

$$\mathrm{d}C^* = \pi^* \, F \, \mathrm{d}X$$

Let us look at factor k. Its marginal cost is $\pi_k^* \, (\Sigma_j f_{kj} \, \mathrm{d}X_j)$. But either factor k is scarce, and $\Sigma_j f_{kj} \, \mathrm{d}Xj = 0$, or its supply is not limited and $\pi k^* = 0$, so that dC^* = 0. Thus, finally

$$\mathrm{d}B = p^* \, (I - A) \, \mathrm{d}X - p^* \, \mathrm{d}Y - p^* \, \mathrm{d}M \qquad (2)$$

Is there a difference between (1) and (2)?

If we look first at a traded good, its market price is $p - t$, which is already its world price: for a non-tradeable good (for which no tradeable can be substituted), its shadow price is consumers' willingness to pay, and if there is no monopoly element on the market, it is equal to its market price. So, finally the expressions of dVA and dB are identical.

Of course, production factors and non-tradeable inputs will have shadow prices different from their market prices (they can be computed by semi-input–output analysis), but it does not matter, since these prices do not appear in the preceding formulae.

A good example of this equivalence is implicitly given in Chapter 9 of Curry and Weiss's (1993) manual. Here, the difference between the NPV at shadow prices of a project (a steel factory) and its NPV at market prices (going to equity holders) is broken down into income streams going to different groups affected by the project: government, labour, users of steel, suppliers of a non-traded input (iron ore), and lenders of capital. It is thus demonstrated that the net economic benefit of a project can be analysed as generation of income, that is value-added.

Nevertheless, there are two limits to the theoretical equivalence of the methods. First, we have not, until now, alluded to the shadow exchange rate (SER), since EM does not use the SER, or any other device accounting for the scarcity of foreign currency. This is deliberate, since the authors believe that the computation of an SER is completely arbitrary. Although, from a practical point of view, many project analysts share at least partially this view (see for instance Squire 1990) and also, under economic adjustment programmes, the range of countries which are opened to trade and for which the SER is now close to the official exchange rate has increased, this creates a gap between the two methods that cannot easily be bridged.[4]

Second, even a theoretical equivalence does not guarantee that in practice the results will be the same. All analysts have to make simplifying assumptions, and these will seldom be the same for the two methods. Let us for instance consider traded inputs used by a project. An ECBA analyst will assume that the new demand of such an input is entirely satisfied by imports, even if the good is locally produced.[5] An EM analyst on the contrary will assume that local production will increase as well, the proportion between imports and local inputs remaining constant (that is why EM works with an input–output matrix from which imported inputs are excluded, and why ECBA works with semi-input–output analysis). Both opinions can be upheld: the ECBA analyst will be right if local producers have no excess capacity and do not wish to invest; the EM analyst will be right if there is excess capacity (but in that case, why are there imports?), or if capacity is increasing. On the whole, EM may be considered as more optimistic, understating the occurrence of diverted demand, whereas ECBA is pessimistic, assuming, in the absence of other information, that the consumption of a local input is a real cost to society. It is likely that divergences will appear mostly concerning the choice or the use of national parameters such as the average shadow wage rate, or the input–output matrix, and not about project-specific parameters (but on this point, there could be as many arguments within methods as between).

Finally, it is not evident that everybody will be pleased with statements showing the similarity between methods. French economists (especially those working for governmental agencies) are rather prone to insist on the specificity of the 'French' method; Anglo-Saxon economists are inclined to look for good reasons to reject it. A compromise could be that EM and ECBA should not be applied to the same kinds of projects, or more globally, to the same kinds of countries.

IS EM EFFICIENCY DEPENDENT ON THE PROJECT OR COUNTRY TO WHICH IT IS APPLIED?

Project size is an important factor in assessing the relevance of EM. But it is the relative size of the project with regard to the national economy which is of interest, more than its absolute size. The larger it is, the more important and difficult it becomes to appraise linkage and other external effects by ECBA methods. These must somehow be internalized, which is a natural procedure in the context of EM.[6]

In contrast, it is not very interesting to apply EM to marginal projects: using EM to appraise the paving of a 50-mile gravel road is using a sledgehammer to crack a nut. For such projects, simple shadow pricing for unskilled labour and traded goods (as the World Bank usually did before 1975) will be easy and quite satisfactory.

As a second point, are there activities where EM would be particularly relevant? Perhaps EM is the right methodology for appraising large agricultural projects, because linkage effects may be important, and also because income redistribution effects may be complex, especially between governmental organisms which may be involved at different stages of the project operation (irrigation, input supply, credit, training, marketing). Thus it becomes necessary to estimate the budgetary incidence of the project on each of these organisms as well as the global effect on the national budget, but here also, it is the size of the project rather than its activity field that matters.

Third, a typology based on countries' characteristics could be considered. It has been suggested that EM could be relevant in small countries or islands,[7] arguing probably that in a small economy, any project will have a structural impact. This is not very plausible. The country size, as already noted, has no relevance by itself. What matters is the size of the project compared to country size and the scope of induced effects. Of course, a given project is liable to have a larger impact on the economy if the country is small, but in most cases, projects in small countries are also smaller than projects in large countries. Another point is that small countries are often more open in the sense that they utilize fewer natural resources: manufactured products have a higher import content so that linkages will be weaker and indirect effects negligible. Also, domestic transport and distribution costs are lower. The exactly opposite opinion, that EM is valuable for analysing projects in large countries or regional projects affecting several countries, could more easily be upheld.[8]

A more sensible distinction could be made not according to the size but to the institutional framework of the country. We have already said that the value-added concept fits easily into a planning procedure, where targets are expressed in terms of increments to the national income. EM ensures that decisions made at the macro and micro levels are consistent. So EM is at its best in countries where the planning process is extensive.

Finally, then, it seems impossible to rely on a typology of projects when assessing the relative efficiency of economic appraisal methods (at least when looking only at the productive sector), since the only feature of consequence is the extent of linkages, which is project-specific.

EM AND ECBA AS COMPLEMENTS

From this perspective, EM and ECBA do not ask the same questions. ECBA looks for a measure of the project's economic efficiency in a context of international trade. It gives the net economic benefit of the project if there is a systematic resort to the international market. EM shows the project's impact on growth, trade balance (since value-added is also an increase in foreign currency), the state budget, and income distribution. Though these objectives are always mentioned in traditional ECBA manuals, they attract considerably less attention than efficiency in resource allocation.

To deal with income distribution, the method suggested by UNIDO was to weight incomes accruing to different social groups, but it was hopeless to rely on political authorities to reveal their preferences about such weights. The Squire and Van der Tak (1975) method of integrating distributional effects into shadow prices ('social' shadow prices versus efficiency shadow prices) was so complicated and included so many arbitrary value judgements[9] that it was completely off-putting for field analysts. This method never gained more than experimental status within the World Bank, and interest for it slowly vanished (see Little and Mirrlees 1990; Ward and Deren 1991), although it was carried on more persistently by other institutions like the Inter-American Development Bank (see OECD 1989).

It cannot be denied, however, that income distribution considerations matter. The impact of a project on underprivileged groups is now looked at (as well as other considerations like gender and sustainability) by most institutions when appraising a project. EM is an efficient tool to approach such problems, since it does it at the same time as efficiency analysis.

In the other direction, some EM partisans suggest that analysis by this method could be followed by a further step where shadow pricing would be introduced. Practically, this would mean using world prices for all tradeables, even if non-traded, and valuing foreign exchange by means of a shadow exchange rate. The problem is that the assumptions are no longer identical, so we could have diverging appraisals of a project. For instance, several projects could eventually be ranked differently in the first and in the second step. This would be hard to explain to the political decision maker and make his or her final choice very difficult. So it seems a rather unhelpful way to proceed.

CONCLUSION

The fundamental equivalence of the EM and ECBA methods is intellectually reassuring: if both are conducted by qualified analysts, working with the same data, there should not be much difference between results. A discrepancy may occur when dealing with the foreign currency constraint, but even this could be for projects where most small cost and benefit items concern either traded goods (each of them being multiplied by the same factor) or non-traded goods (which should be much less frequent). It means also that the process of appraisal can be 'translated' from one method to the other, and this is sometimes the case in African countries where approaches are made to various institutions for funding. But this can be done only by analysts practising both methods.

From the training point of view, the answer to the question, 'Which methods should be taught', would then be:

- for the staff of international institutions, either is appropriate, but only one, since it would be awkward not to be able to compare projects appraised by different methods;
- for national administrators, both are necessary, the preferred method being liable to vary according to the weight of external and linkage effects.

But it is tempting to go further and to suggest that it would not be without value to put a touch of EM into ECBA, and vice versa. If income distribution matters, the computation of the amount and structure of at least direct value-added is useful information for the decision maker and is complementary to the computation of an economic rate of return (or NPV). Equally, when using EM, it is also possible, if foreign currency is scarce, to introduce a parameterized shadow exchange rate (or equivalently standard conversion factor). This would be easy, since the foreign trade elements appear clearly in the process. It could thus be seen if a project remains profitable for a reasonable range of values of this parameter.

In conclusion, the proposals in this chapter do not aim to bring about a revolution in project appraisal, but they could contribute to the search for a common language between analysts, and maybe add some power to their recommendations.

NOTES

1. The English translation of Chervel and Le Gall (1978) exists, but has been for a long time out of print. See also Chervel (1973).
2. It is worth mentioning that UNIDO published a manual in 1980 prepared in collaboration with the Industrial Development Center for Arab States (IDCAS), in which net value-added was considered as the operational criterion for measuring the contribution of a project to national income. In a further stage, however, the results were corrected by using an adjusted rate of exchange, accounting for the position of the balance of payments.
3. Initially, EM did not proceed this way, since the authors made an assumption of widespread underemployment of labour (or equivalently, zero shadow price of labour). This assumption was rightly criticized by Balassa (1976). But it can be dispensed with without any harm to the method.
4. It is possible to reconcile EM with ECBA on this point. To do so, an assumption must be made about who is the beneficiary of the foreign exchange premium. The most straightfor-

ward choice is to attribute it to the state, since it arises from the higher value put by the state than by private agents on foreign exchange. But certainly this correction does not fit in with the spirit of EM.

5. See for instance Curry and Weiss (1993, p. 175), 'by definition, where a project produces or uses traded goods, this will affect the foreign trade balance, not domestic production and income'.
6. An interesting case is that of rural roads projects, for which the traditional method of measuring economic benefits by road users' savings was recognized as unsatisfactory in the 1970s. The method now advised is to use a measure of producer's surplus or value-added (see for instance Carnemark, Biderman and Bovet 1976).
7. For instance in discussions around 1993 about a new manual of project appraisal for the European Union.
8. More generally, the view that small countries have peculiar problems has been much debated. See, for example, Srinivasan (1986) and *World Development* (1993).
9. A first question would be 'whose value judgements?', especially when the project is appraised by an international agency. It is clear for instance that when the World Bank takes a financing decision based on CBA, the value judgements used are those of the Bank (see Ray 1984).

REFERENCES

Balassa, B. (1976), *The Effects Method of Project Evaluation*, World Bank Staff Working Paper no. 231, Washington, DC: World Bank.

Carnemark, C., J. Biderman and D. Bovet (1976), *The Economic Analysis of Rural Roads Projects*, World Bank Staff Working Paper no. 241, Washington, DC: World Bank.

Chervel, M. (1973), 'Exercise in the Application of the Effects Method', *Industrialisation and Productivity*, no. 20.

Chervel, M. (1992), 'La méthode des Effects trente ans après', *Tiers-Monde*, **33** (132), 873–92.

Chervel, M. and C. Le Gall (1976), *Manuel d'évaluation économique des projets. La méthode des effets*, Paris: Ministère de la Coopération.

Chervel, M. and C. Le Gall (1978), *Manual of Economic Evaluation of Projects. The Effects Method*, Paris: Ministère de la Coopération.

Curry, S. and J. Weiss (1993), *Project Analysis in Developing Countries*, London: Macmillan.

Little, I.M.D. and J.A. Mirrlees (1990), 'Project Appraisal and Planning Twenty Years on', *Proceedings of the World Bank Annual Conference on Development Economics*, Washington, DC: World Bank, pp. 351–82.

OECD (1989), *The Impact of Development Projects on Poverty*, Paris: OECD Development Centre.

Prou, C. and M. Chervel (1970), *Etablissement des programmes en économie sous-développée: l'étude des grappes de projets*, Paris: Dunod.

Ray, A. (1984), *Cost–Benefit Analysis, Issues and Methodologies*, Baltimore, Md: Johns Hopkins University Press.

Squire, L. (1990), 'Comments on "Project Appraisal and Planning Twenty Years On" by Little and Mirrlees', *Proceedings of the World Bank Annual Conference on Development Economics*, Washington, DC: World Bank, pp. 383–5.

Squire, L. and H. van der Tak (1975), *Economic Analysis of Projects*, Baltimore, Md: Johns Hopkins University Press.

Srinivasan, T.N. (1986), 'The Costs and Benefits of being a Small, Remote Island, Landlocked or Ministate Economy', *The World Bank Research Observer*, **1** (2), 205–18.

UNIDO and IDCAS (1980), *Manual for Evaluation of Industrial Projects*, New York: UNIDO.

Ward, W.A. and B.J. Deren (1991), *The Economics of Project Analysis: A Practitioner's Guide*, Washington, DC: EDI Technical Materials, World Bank.

World Development (1993), Special Issue: 'Islands and Small States: Issues and Policies', **21** (2), February.

8. Shadow pricing without tears: how to estimate acceptable ERRs with minimal data

John D. MacArthur

DISTORTIONS AND EFFICIENCY SHADOW PRICES

The establishment of the Development and Project Planning Centre (DPPC) in 1969–70 was closely associated with the new interest at the time in economic appraisal. The seminal OECD work by Little and Mirrlees (1968) had recently been published, and considerable interest in it had been shown by the then Ministry of Overseas Development (ODM). ODM's interest was important, as their support was vital for the use of UK training fellowships to allow significant numbers of people in the target groups for in-service training courses – overseas officials – to come to Bradford to take part.

Reflecting the new interest in shadow pricing in the development economics community, much time was devoted to economic appraisal during the earlier courses that the Centre delivered. Perhaps as much as three of the twelve weeks of any course would be devoted to this topic. Training then partly centred around the current Overseas Development Administration (ODA) manual on the subject (ODA 1972; ODM 1978).

Since those early years, DPPC, like ODA, has appreciated that there is much more to project appraisal than economic analysis and shadow pricing. Project appraisal now has a wide agenda, and shadow pricing justifies less time in any course. Nevertheless, this remains a topic that is given significant space in courses for the productive sectors, industry and agriculture especially. Over the years, understanding of the topic has developed in DPPC and outside, with a steady flow of papers, textbooks, methodologies and manuals. Even in the 1990s, new books continue to be published.[1]

Since 1970, scores of officers and others have been introduced to the concepts and practice of shadow pricing. Significant in this group have been economists and desk officers in donor agencies, including ODA, the World Bank, and more recently the Commission of the European Union.

Despite all this attention and training, the principles of shadow pricing and economic analysis remain on the whole poorly understood. Perhaps even more serious is the fact that the methods are very little used, as Little and Mirrlees (1994) pointed out, with chagrin.

The fact that trainees still call for more simple procedures, which require less time and data, reflects the continuing failure of the technique to find a way into regular practice. This situation persists despite the significance of the topic that is acknowledged by everyone who understands the idea. Even where shadow pricing is used, it can be very cursory.[2]

Some of the blame for this failure may rest with the academic community, who have not found ways of reducing the many dimensions of economic revaluation into practical, meaningful steps whose requirements for time and data do not exclude them from all but the very largest and economically most significant projects.

This chapter, based on many years' personal experience of appraising projects, teaching the subject to economists and non-economists, and pondering how to make it simpler, attempts to outline a simple but possibly quite adequate approach to shadow pricing. For applications in the productive sectors, where revenue projects prevail and cost–income estimations are normal parts of project planning, a basic understanding of the principles and some thought about their implications can allow approximate shadow prices to be estimated which, in all but the most marginal cases, should allow an adequate estimate to be made of the economic rate of return. This does not call for too many data, or a great deal of time. The analyst who understands the basic ideas and these principles will be able to answer the economic appraisal question without too much difficulty and with sufficient accuracy.

SHADOW PRICES AND DISTORTIONS

Dreze and Stern (1994) define shadow prices for use to evaluate the net impact on welfare and public-sector projects as 'the social opportunity costs of the resources used (and correspondingly for outputs generated)' (p. 59). An economy is distorted if market prices and shadow prices do not coincide.

Considering distortion, they maintain first that it will exist if the distribution of income fails to be optimum. However, they further identify seven other 'sources of interference with the marginal equalities which are necessary for efficient allocation' (p. 61) – seven factors which we can say are also the source of distortions. These are:

1. Indirect or income taxes
2. Uncorrected externalities

3. Quantity controls
4. Controlled prices
5. Tariffs and trade control
6. Oligopoly
7. Imperfect information, transaction costs and missing markets.

Operational shadow pricing has been mainly restricted to making allowances for the last seven distortions. (Making allowance for distributional effects has never been effective.) The alternative and new values derived are 'efficiency shadow prices', which are our concern here.

Seven basic adjustment actions will always apply in efficiency shadow pricing for the valuation or revaluation of outputs and inputs identified in a project appraisal.[3] They stem from the main distortions listed, and the actions required to allow for them.

1. *Base the values of all traded goods (both directly traded and indirectly traded items) on their border prices.* For traded goods, the socially relevant opportunity is the possibility of gains from trade. Border prices represent the values at which the economy can buy from and sell to the international economy. Where this option exists, it should be used as the basis of valuation.[4]
2. *Remove the values of direct taxes and subsidies from the prices of all items.* Taxes – and subsidies, their converse – are treated as 'transfer payments'. Although they are financial payments they are not the cause of any associated resource use; they involve no social opportunity cost. Other transfer payments that share the same characteristic should also be excluded: interest payments, pure rents, and excess profits.
3. *Make an adjustment to allow for the discontinuity between international and domestic values caused by taxes on international trade.* Because trade taxes exist, the internal value of goods purchased (or forfeited) through a change in the availability of foreign exchange (FE) is more than the cost of the FE involved. The cost of the FE at market prices (the exchange rate) is expressed in terms equivalent to other domestic prices. To correct for the undervaluation of the effects of change in the stock of FE, either (i) FE must be valued upwards – through the use of a shadow exchange rate (SER) greater than unity – or (ii) domestic values must be reduced in relation to border prices, because the latter are more valuable. The standard conversion factor (SCF) that is used for the second adjustment will be less than unity. It is the reciprocal of the SER.[5]
4. *Value non-traded inputs at their long-term marginal cost of supply.* Generally the assumption is that the needs of the project for additional supplies of non-traded goods will be met from additional domestic sup-

ply.[6] The resource costs of this supply are the social costs attributable to the project. Because of economies of scale from existing plant, the resource costs for producing a small additional supply may be less than the market price. If, exceptionally, it is felt that the needs of the project will be met through diversion of inputs from another user, then the domestic market price of the items should be used, as a (minimal) reflection of the marginal value of lost output that the deprived user would have produced.

5. *Make allowance where necessary for the fact that the wages of some kinds of labour – especially formal sector unskilled labour – may be higher than their opportunity cost at market prices.* Some workers are able to secure wages that are fixed at rates higher than would be the free 'market-clearing' price for workers of the kind in view. Consequently, the market-price cost of these workers in the new activity can exaggerate the value of the loss in production arising from their shift from one sector to another. This only applies to unskilled workers in the 'formal' sector.[7]
6. *Taking account of these basic shadow-pricing requirements, calculate the border or market parity values of the goods and services used and produced by the project.* The market-price estimation of inputs and outputs will be in terms of the prices paid and received at the project. Shadow prices must be estimated at the same level. For all items, adjustments must be made for the various non-traded elements (transport, marketing and processing costs, including product losses) that will occur between the first point of availability (import or export point, production factory, etc.) and the project. Border parity prices are estimated for traded goods, and analogous factory or market parity prices are required for non-traded items.[8]
7. *Estimate the values of all consumer surpluses gained (and lost) in the with-project situation.* Many project outputs are provided free, and the same is true of many external effects. In other cases, products are sold at prices less than willingness to pay levels. These project consequences all have value that requires to be estimated and brought into the CBA, certainly where their value is significant in relation to other project values.

WHICH NUMERAIRE?

Shadow pricing involves estimating values other than those that exist in the market. The unit of measurement in which shadow-price values are expressed must be the value of a unit of currency used for some specific purpose in the domestic market. Since many market prices are distorted, one price must be specified as the reference unit – the numeraire.

For efficiency pricing, two numeraires have been proposed. Most popular and frequently used is the unit of domestic currency converted into foreign exchange through open channels, either in open markets or at the (controlled) official exchange rate. This is the 'world-prices' numeraire. All traded goods are immediately expressed at the cif/fob levels in terms of this unit.

The alternative numeraire is the value of the 'average' unit of currency spend on consumer goods in internal markets. This is the 'domestic-prices' numeraire. The base unit of value is the price of goods in an average consumer's shopping basket.

Which numeraire is best? Various arguments have been deployed. The world-prices numeraire has the advantage that most shadow pricing is applied to donor-funded projects, where the main source of external funding is for the supply of traded goods. These will be already expressed in border prices. Price adjustments will be required for only the minority of input items.

Another important operational advantage of the world-price unit has not been emphasized, but is relevant to the thrust of this chapter. This is that the world-prices numeraire uses as its base the most valuable of all resources, foreign exchange. Choosing the most valuable item as the basis of value means that, generally, all other values will be lower.

This fact allows a clear appreciation of what values shadow prices will or might take in relation to the market price for the same item: will they be the same, a little lower, or a lot lower? This substantial practical advantage is not obtained if the numeraire used is domestic prices.

CONVERSION FACTORS

Operationally, shadow pricing is most easily done by multiplying the market-price value of each item by a conversion factor (CF) to make the value transformation. The CF for each item will be estimated individually, and they are then brought into the calculation to transform the project statement of costs and benefits from market-price to efficiency-price terms.

The values that the CF takes is a reflection of the relationship of the shadow price to the market price. If the CF is greater than unity, the social cost of the item is taken to be higher than the market price: vice-versa if the CF is below one. This relationship is conceptually very important. Most of the following discussion will be based on the values of CFs for different items occurring in project analysis.

A classification of the types of element that occur on the output and input sides of most revenue projects is given in Table 8.1.[9] On both the output and

Table 8.1 Classification of market-project outputs and inputs by shadow-pricing class

Code	Item type	Basis of valuation
1	OUTPUTS	
1.1	*Traded*	
1.1.1	Direct exports	Border price, less project-to-port costs
1.1.2	Import substitutes	Border price, plus port-to-store costs, less project-to-store costs
1.2	*Non-traded*	
1.2.1	Capital goods	Market price
1.2.2	Intermediate products	Market price, plus consumer surplus if arising
1.2.3	Consumer goods	Market price, plus consumer surplus if arising
2	INPUTS	
2.1	*Traded*	
2.1.1	Direct imports	Border price plus port-to-project costs
2.1.2	Diverted exports	Border price less project-to-port costs
2.2	*Non-traded*	
2.2.1	Manufactured goods	
2.2.1.1	Incremental production	Incremental cost of supply
2.2.1.2	Diverted from other users	Market price
2.3	*Factors of production*	
2.3.1	Land	Market price if small Alternative net product if large
2.3.2	Labour – Skilled	Market price
2.3.3	– Unskilled formal	Opportunity cost plus necessary additional resource costs
2.3.4	– Unskilled informal	Market price
2.3.5	– Foreign	Market price

input sides, traded and non-traded items occur. On the input side factors of production also occur, all of which, except foreign labour, are normally non-traded.

The approach to valuation for each class of item is shown in the right-hand column, based on the seven basic adjustment actions described. The consequent levels of the CF (using a world-prices numeraire) for the different types of project item can be described, where no commodity-specific taxes or subsidies are assumed to occur.

Individual CFs for different items may be compared to two base measures: the numeraire – which is especially relevant to traded goods – and the SCF, whose value will be below the numeraire (i.e. less than unity) and which may be a more relevant benchmark for non-traded goods.

Traded Goods

By convention – through the choice of the numeraire – their border price equals their shadow price. The CF used to move from market price to shadow price therefore is 1.00 for the border price content.

This factor is applied only to the value of the good at the border. In project analysis, we value goods at the project site. By that stage, their prices will be a mixture of border price (CF = 1.00) and the cost of non-traded items (CF probably less than 1.00 – see below) involved in moving them between the port and the project, such as transport, market services and perhaps processing. If there are no commodity taxes or subsidies, or other significant transfer payments, the CF at the project level (what we call the border parity price) will generally be close to 1.00, probably a little higher for outputs and a little below for inputs.[10] Where the cost of transport is high in relation to the border price, the CF for traded outputs could be appreciably less than unity.

These general results will not apply with specific taxes or subsidies. Taxed exports will have CFs well above unity, while the CFs for subsidized exports will be well below 1.00, if the subsidy is substantial. For imports, the two factors work in opposite directions. Taxed imports will have a CF below the SCF, while imports that are subsidized will have CFs that are higher than the SCF, possibly higher than 1.00 if the subsidy is large.

Non-traded Goods

Because they contain elements of indirect taxes and other transfers (CF zero) and possibly some formal unskilled labour (CF less than unity), their CFs will almost always be less than 1.00. Commodities with a high specific tax (fuel is a common example) will have a relatively low CF. Subsidized commodities may have a CF higher than the SCF, and possibly higher than 1.00, indicating that the resource costs are more than the market price.

Labour

Wage labour will consist partly of formal-sector unskilled (FU) workers, so the CF may be less than unity. For most other kinds of domestic workers and foreign workers, the CF may be taken as close to the market price. Because non-foreign labour is a non-traded item, the SCF will generally also need to apply, leading to a labour CF a little less than the SCF.

The adjustments described above are the main elements for shadow-pricing items that have market prices. It follows from these points that, using a world-prices numeraire, the values of item CFs can be predicted in general though relatively narrow-range terms. As a consequence, first-attempt shadow pricing for revenue projects can be made simply from a qualitative idea of (1) the nature of the output or input item concerned, and (2) the structure of its pricing, especially whether taxes or subsidies are involved, and also whether prices are controlled. From this knowledge, and a basic understanding, acceptably accurate estimates of CFs could be made without the need for a great many new data and complex calculation.

Consider what values CFs for particular types of item can take. For project inputs, only a subsidy can give rise to a CF higher than 1.00. For traded goods without tax or subsidy, the CF may be close to unity, unless high transport costs are involved. For unsubsidized non-traded goods, the CF will be lower than 1.00. Application of the SCF itself will give a below-unity value. If there are specific taxes, economies of scale in supply, and a high content of FU labour in incremental production costs, the CF may be significantly below the SCF, with the lowest CFs of all for highly taxed input items – fuels are a common example already cited. If the non-traded item is subsidized, then the CF may be pushed above the value of the SCF, and possibly above 1.00 if the subsidy is very large.[11]

Where project benefits take the form of marketed outputs, similar principles apply if the items are traded goods. The project value will be the border price, adjusted for the cost of non-traded items incurred between the project and the border. In free-market situations, this will frequently give rise to CFs greater than 1.00. If the export is taxed, the CF may be well above unity, but if it is subsidized, the CF for the project-level price may be less than 1.00

For non-traded outputs, if there is a free market, the market value can be taken as a reflection of consumer willingness to pay. All that is required is application of the SCF.[12] The same is also true if the item is taxed or subsidized – whatever the origin of the price, if the market is just cleared at that price, the market price reflects marginal consumer valuation. However, if the price is fixed at levels below the market-clearing price, those obtaining the output will be in receipt of consumer surplus benefits.[13] In this case, the CF value will be higher than the SCF – possibly appreciably so, though this is uncommon.

Table 8.1 gave a basic account of the approach to valuation to be taken for the different main classes of project item that occur in revenue projects. A more detailed classification is given in Table 8.2, which allows for the three possible scenarios in each category: free-market price; a specific commodity

Table 8.2 The likely values of CFs for items of different types, using a world-prices numeraire

Code	Type of item	Relation to unity	Relation to SCF
1	OUTPUTS		
1.1	*Traded*		
1.1.1.N	Direct export, with no tax or subsidy	Slightly above	Well above
1.1.1.T	Direct export, with specific tax	Well above, possibly much above	Much above always
1.1.1.S	Direct export, with specific subsidy	Below, well below if subsidy large	Equal or close to, below if subsidy large
1.1.2.N	Import substitute, no tax or subsidy	Slightly above	Well above
1.1.2.T	Import substitute, specific tax	Below, well below if subsidy large	Equal or close to, below if subsidy large
1.1.2.S	Import substitute, specific subsidy	Well above, possibly much above	Much above always
1.2	*Non-traded, marketed*		
1.2.N	Free market	Below, at SCF	Equal to
1.2.C	Controlled market	Close to or above if much consumer surplus	Well above, much above if much consumer surplus
1.3	*No market*	No CF, shadow price has to be estimated indirectly and individually	
2	INPUTS		
2.1	*Traded*		
2.1.1.N	Directly imported, no tax or subsidy	Slightly below	Slightly above, equal or slightly below
2.1.1.T	Directly imported, import tax	Below, by slightly more than the tax level	Close to or below
2.1.1.S	Directly imported, import subsidy	Above, if subsidy is not very small	Well above
2.1.2.N	Diverted export, no tax or subsidy	Slightly above	Well above
2.1.2.T	Diverted export, export tax	Well above	Much above

Table 8.2 continued

Code	Type of item	Relation to unity	Relation to SCF
2.1.2.S	Diverted export, export subsidy	Close to, or below if subsidy large	Close to or equal
2.2	*Non-traded*		
2.2.1.N	Increased production, no tax or subsidy	Well below	Close to, below if imports content small
2.2.1.T	Increased production, item taxed	Much below	Below
2.2.1.S	Increased production, items subsidized	Close to or above, well above if subsidy is large	Above, perhaps much above
2.2.2	No new production or import, either with tax, subsidy or neither	Below, at SCF	Equal to
2.3	*Factors of production*		
2.3.1	Land	Below, at SCF unless land is a major cost	Equal to
2.3.2	Skilled labour	Below, at SCF	Equal to
2.3.3	Unskilled formal labour	Well below	Below, unless high indirect costs
2.3.4	Unskilled informal labour	Below, at SCF	Equal to
2.3.5	Foreign labour	A little below	Close to or a little above
2.4	*No market*	No CF, shadow price has to be estimated indirectly and individually	

tax; and a commodity subsidy. The third and fourth columns of the table indicate what value the CF for an item of that kind can be expected to take, in relation to the numeraire and the SCF.

In Table 8.2, the relations of the item CF to the numeraire and the SCF are expressed qualitatively. The progressive measures of departure from these values, and possible ranges of difference implied by the terms, are: slightly above or below – say up to 0.10 different; well above or below – say 0.10 to 0.20 different; and much above or below – a difference of more than 0.20.

The likely values indicated for each item in the table are based on the comments made above. Two new categories have been introduced in the transfer from Table 8.1 to Table 8.2, namely output and input items where there is no market. In these cases, there is no market price, so there is nothing in a financial statement of costs and benefits to which a CF can be applied. Indirect methods for valuing these items have to be used. These methods are likely to involve estimating a demand curve or a cost level, both based on domestic market prices for the economy concerned. To represent these values in world-prices numeraire terms, the SCF (or CCF) will need to be applied to the estimated non-market values.

It is suggested that reference to Table 8.2 will be of great value to project analysts who wish to estimate the economic internal rate of return (ERR) of a project for which a comprehensive statement of costs and benefits at constant market prices has been used to estimate an IRR. The procedure would be first, to identify the main cost and benefit items (often there will be only three of four important inputs, and one or two main outputs), and second, to decide in which of these categories each item occurs. The effect of revaluation on total costs and total benefits can then be estimated, and a firm position taken on whether, after shadow pricing, the IRR will be higher or lower than before. The variables that have the largest single effect on any rate of return are those related to output. Estimating the CF for the output will be a very important step in estimating the effect of shadow pricing on the returns from the project.

IS THIS APPROACH REALLY MAKING ECONOMIC ANALYSIS SIMPLER?

The procedure suggested here as being simple but correct may not appear to everyone to be so easy. Eight different categories of output were listed, and 15 different types of input. Any combination of items from these categories is in principle possible in a project. In fact some of these categories are very uncommon, especially in donor-assisted investment projects. There, the outputs will commonly be traded, using a mixture of traded and non-traded inputs. Unless the item is protected by an import tax, the CFs for the output are likely to be higher than the CFs for inputs, so shadow pricing is sure to make the result better. Remember only a subsidy can make the CF of a non-traded input higher than 1.00. Most CFs for these items will be well below the numeraire, often also below the value of the SCF.[14]

In summary, the levels of the CF for any market item can be predicted from consideration of the elements that make up its market price. Knowledge of the underlying features of shadow pricing and of the characteristics of each item allow the effects of shadow pricing to be predicted with considerable confidence, without in fact any shadow prices or CFs being calculated. Even when these numbers have been estimated, there should be no surprise about the results. The effects of shadow pricing are entirely predictable. This is true of both the direction of change from the IRR calculated at market prices, and possibly also in the extent of the change that shadow pricing could bring.

The methods suggested here will very often be quite sufficient for economic appraisal at early stages in the project sequence (MacArthur 1994b) – that is, at the stage of project identification, and also when pre-feasibility studies are undertaken. More comprehensive shadow pricing, with numerical estimates, may be more suitable in a full feasibility study, but there are instances where even at that stage informed knowledge of what the CFs of the main items will be can be quite sufficient to show whether a project is socially valuable, without the need to resort to numbers.

Despite continuing interest in the subject, it remains the case that little shadow pricing is done. This chapter suggests that much more could be done towards meaningful economic analysis in an approximate but acceptable way, especially in connection with revenue projects.

The use of simplified methods could release much of economists' time for other pressing questions. Of much greater relevance to donor staff are the questions of how to undertake satisfactory forms of economic analysis for non-revenue projects. Trainees in most of the commissioned training courses that DPPC has been conducting say that knowing how to handle revenue projects is not their problem. They deal with very few such projects in current portfolios. They need advice on the appraisal of initiatives in all those sectors where the product is not a market good; that is where the main benefits (and some of the costs) are external. This is where the attention should increasingly be focused. This is where the new manuals are required.

NOTES

1. Ward and Deren (1991), Curry and Weiss (1993), Perkins (1994) and Dinwiddy and Teal (forthcoming 1995) are some of the latest texts.
2. Little and Mirrlees (1994) describe the apparently widespread situation in the World Bank where all traded goods are valued at international prices, and all other values are adjusted with an SCF of 0.8, a general value possibly usable irrespective of country. Short of doing no analysis at all, things can't get much more basic than this!
3. The 'basic principles' outlined in this section are the operational implications of the nature of the distortions and the theories underlying how they arise and how they might be allowed for. This account does not attempt to explain the underlying theory. Curry and Weiss (1993) and Perkins (1994) give comprehensive basic accounts of the issues. ODA (1988) gives an operational view, with a background of the ideas behind the methods. More fundamental theoretical discussion is to be found in the papers in Part 1 of Layard and Glaister (1994). The place of CBA theory in the wider context of development economics is explained in Dinwiddy and Teal (forthcoming).
4. A discussion once took place on the difference between traded and tradeable goods. Papers in the OUIES Symposium (1972) are early examples. This paper takes the position

that border prices are relevant only if, during the lifetime of the project, trade will be a relevant option. If, through edict, trade will not be permitted, the item affected should be treated as non-tradeable. With structural adjustment and the liberalization of trade, the number of situations where a good is tradeable but not traded should diminish steadily. The issue is much less important in the 1990s than it was in the 1970s.

5. Here we use the SER to refer to the ratio of the shadow to the official exchange rate, or the conversion factor for foreign exchange. The SCF reflects the general relation for goods that are actually traded between their prices inside the country and their prices in international markets. Two alternative formulae are suggested for its estimation (see for example ODA 1988, pp. 31 and 32). One is based only on imported goods; the other takes exports as well as imports into account. The view is taken here that the first of these methods will frequently be the most relevant for poor countries, especially those with a weak export base. Changes in foreign exchange availability in such economies will mainly or entirely affect the level of imports, and will have little direct effect on the levels of exports. For this reason, the SCF that reflects the general relation between international and domestic prices for imports only is the most relevant general CF to use.
6. ODA (1988) contains a list (p. 24) of the most common non-traded goods and services that enter into productive projects.
7. The extent of this distortion is diminishing with the liberalization of labour markets, in parallel with many other 'structural adjustment' changes.
8. Border parity prices are calculated from the border price, with the costs of the non-traded components added or subtracted as relevant. This gives the price at the project level that is 'in parity' with a given border price. The procedure for this estimation is illustrated, for example, in ODA (1988) and in Gittinger (1982).
9. A classification of project inputs and outputs that is in some respects similar to the one developed in this chapter is given in Gittinger (1982; pp. 282 and 283).
10. The producer prices of some traded commodities can be subject to transfer costs of various kinds to which the title 'tax' is not applied, but which nevertheless have the same effect on social efficiency as taxes. Formal measures of this kind include reserve fund levies, surpluses to public-sector marketing agencies and other devices of the kind. Informal mark-ups/deductions also exist in those rents obtained by import licensees who are able to take advantage of artificial scarcities that arise when effective import-restriction systems apply – a scarcity premium that they can collect.
11. Some of the highest CFs ever calculated have been for subsidized non-traded items, especially power. MacArthur (1994a) gives a summary of the values of CFs estimated in comprehensive studies to measure sets of CFs, using sophisticated methods. For example, a CF of over 3 was estimated for power in Egypt, where electricity sales were very heavily subsidized.
12. In principle, the CF to be used here would be the consumption conversion factor (CCF), which reflects the general relation between the typical basket of consumer goods and the numeraire. CCFs have been estimated in a few cases where sets of CFs were derived simultaneously (see MacArthur 1994a), but they are seldom available, and are very difficult to estimate. Use of the SCF instead is normal practice.
13. The evidence for a price below market-clearing levels will be queues, black markets and other non-market means for allocation of the available quantity amongst interested consumers.
14. This point is illustrated in MacArthur (1994a), where the results of the calculation of sets of CFs for 13 economies are summarized.

REFERENCES

Curry, S. and J. Weiss (1993), *Project Analysis in Developing Countries*, London: Macmillan.

Dinwiddy, C.L. and F.J. Teal (forthcoming), *Principles of Cost–Benefit Analysis for Developing Countries*, Cambridge: Cambridge University Press.
Dreze, J. and N. Stern (1994), 'Shadow prices and markets: policy reform, shadow prices and market prices', in Layard and Glaister (1994).
Gittinger, J.P. (1982), *Economic Analysis of Agricultural Projects*, 2nd edition, Baltimore, Md: Johns Hopkins University Press.
Layard, R. and S. Glaister (1994), *Cost–Benefit Analysis*, 2nd edition, Cambridge: Cambridge University Press.
Little, I.M.D. and J. Mirrlees (1968), *Manual of Industrial Project Analysis in Developing Countries*, vol. 2, Paris: OECD.
Little, I.M.D. and J. Mirrlees (1994), 'The costs and benefits of analysis: project appraisal and planning twenty years on', in Layard and Glaister (1994).
MacArthur, J.D. (1994a), 'Estimating efficiency prices through semi-input–output methods – A review of practice in available studies', *Journal of International Development*, **6** (1).
MacArthur, J.D. (1994b), 'The project sequence: A composite view of the project cycle', in MacArthur and Weiss (1994).
MacArthur, J.D. and J. Weiss (eds) (1994), *Agriculture, Projects and Development*, Aldershot, UK: Avebury.
ODA (1972), *A Guide to Project Appraisal in Developing Countries*, London: HMSO.
ODA (1988), *Appraisal of Projects in Developing Countries: A Guide for Economists*, London: HMSO.
ODM (Ministry of Overseas Development) (1978), *A Guide to the Economic Appraisal of Projects in Developing Countries*, London: HMSO.
OECD (1972), *Manual of Industrial Project Analysis in Developing Countries: Volume II – Social Cost Benefit Analysis*, Paris: OECD Development Centre.
OUIES (Oxford University Institute of Economics and Statistics) (1972), 'Symposium on the Little–Mirrlees Manual of Industrial Project Appraisal in Developing Countries', *OUIES Bulletin*, **34** (1).
Perkins, F. (1994), *Practical Cost Benefit Analysis*, London: Macmillan.
Ward, W.A. and B.J. Deren (1991), *The Economics of Project Analysis: A Practitioner's Guide*, Washington, DC: EDI of the World Bank.

9. Logical frameworks today – increased diversification of the planning format

John D. MacArthur

INTRODUCTION

The logical framework (LogFrame), and various derivatives, have become established instruments in project and programme planning since they were first taken up by USAID in the early 1970s. Many development assistance agencies have since adopted some form of the LogFrame matrix, while almost all of the remainder have adopted the basic ideas and language of this approach.

During the 1970s, and the early 1980s, LogFrames followed a fixed, widely common pattern. However, by the mid-1990s the situation has become diversified, with many forms of LogFrame in use. Whereas in the 1980s the planning consultant could ask of a client agency 'Do you use a LogFrame?', the question now has to be 'Which form of LogFrame do you use?' Both for learners and for non-dedicated users, the LogFrame business has become very diverse and perhaps confusing. This chapter looks at some of the different forms that are currently in use, with comment on the diversifications adopted.

ORIGINS AND EARLY FORMS[1]

LogFrames began when, under commission from USAID, Practical Concepts Inc. (PCI) devised the simple 4 × 4 matrix that everyone is familiar with. Figure 9.1 presents this basic form. The vertical logic describes the four-level structure of objectives: inputs – outputs – purposes – goals. The logic of separately identifying these different levels of objective was quickly appreciated, and the approach was taken up in the Department of State, with the Canadian International Development Agency (CIDA) following after only a few years. The importance of the corresponding features of the horizontal dimension – assumptions about non-project factors, indicators of attainment, and means of verification – were also widely appreciated and adopted by

PROJECT DESIGN SUMMARY
LOGICAL FRAMEWORK

PROJECT TITLE:____________________

NARRATIVE SUMMARY	OBJECTIVELY VERIFIABLE INDICATORS	MEANS OF VERIFICATION	IMPORTANT ASSUMPTIONS
Programme or sector goal: The broader objective to which this project contributes:	Measures of goal achievement:		Assumptions for achieving goal targets:
Project purpose:	Conditions that will indicate purpose has been achieved: end of project:		Assumptions for achieving purpose:
Outputs:	Magnitude of outputs:		Assumptions for achieving outputs:
Inputs:	Implementation target (type and quality):		Assumptions for providing inputs:

Source: CIDA (1980)

Figure 9.1 The basic logical framework matrix

development assistance agencies.[2] Furthermore, even though there was no summary matrix table in the project documentation of the World Bank and some of the regional development banks, LogFrame terminology was taken up by them, and adopted. More recently, several non-governmental organizations have adopted the format. LogFrame is an essential feature of development planning in 1995.

INNOVATIONS DURING WIDESPREAD ADOPTION

Some of the LogFrame ideas crossed the Atlantic in relatively intact form, and by the mid-1980s many European bilateral donors had taken up the idea. However, innovations were being introduced affecting both the use and the shape of the matrix.

The ZOPP Innovations[3]

These began with the introduction in 1983 of the ZOPP procedures, a new departure that brought in two major changes from the established 'North American' LogFrame model.

Team activity in problem analysis and project design

Following ideas developed with Team Technologies Inc., GTZ took up the integrated planning approach of objectives-oriented project planning. The starting point for project definition and planning was team operations. Discussions in groups helped to identify and clarify development problems in a chosen subsector or problem area from the viewpoints of all of those parties who were invited to take part in the democratic brainstorming sessions on which ZOPP was based. Problems were identified which were seen as inhibitors to the attainment of agreed objectives. These problems or constraints were then converted into opportunities for action. A logical hierarchy of actions and effects was defined from them to fill what PCI had called the 'narrative summary' column of the LogFrame, what ZOPP calls the project planning matrix.[4]

The recognition of activities as LogFrame elements

The brainstorming approach to LogFrame definition and preparation as the starting point of planning was the first of the ZOPP innovations. Also significant to the practicalities of project planning and matrix construction was the addition to the ZOPP project matrix of the hierarchy level 'activities'.[5] Following a well-established procedural step of project management planning – called work breakdown structure – the ZOPP architects made the valuable insertion of activities as a hierarchy stage between the output and input levels. This follows the logic of project planning and costing. Outputs that will meet agreed objectives are defined. Operational activities are then specified that will allow the outputs to be produced. Activities are in all sound cases the base units for budgeting, so it made sense to incorporate this level of actions into the narrative summary. Inputs were not displaced – in the ZOPP project matrix they became the verifiable indicators for the activities. The specification of inputs was merely moved sideways, taking up position at the foot of the second column of the matrix, not the first. The basic form of the ZOPP matrix is illustrated in Figure 9.2.

Recent Changes in the ODA LogFrame

By the mid-1990s, the preference for activities over inputs as the base level has gained widespread acceptance, certainly on the east side of the Atlantic. ODA was a relatively late adopter of the LogFrame idea (1986), and the format taken up was virtually the same as the USAID form, with anglicized column headings and horizontal titles. However, in 1993 (under the influence of Team Technologies) ODA adopted a revised LogFrame format, which incorporates activities as the floor level of the narrative summary column (Team Technologies 1994).

The new generalized LogFrame is now in use by ODA, and many training courses for ODA and clients' agency staff have been held. The current matrix is illustrated in Figure 9.3.[6] In the vertical hierarchy, it identifies activities that lead to outputs, which allow the attainment of purposes which will contribute to the achievement of singular, pre-defined project goals. The headings of the four columns remain as in North American format – Narrative summary; Objectively verifiable indicators; Means of verification; and Important assumptions.[7]

NORAD's Version of the EU Format

Important differences persist, however, between the different LogFrame matrices that are currently in use. In the late 1980s, the Norwegian Agency for International Development (NORAD) introduced a further simplification, by combining the two indicator columns, to create a 4 × 3 matrix (Figure 9.4). It is likely that this pattern will be adopted by NORAD's recent client on LogFrame matters, Japan International Cooperation Agency.

A new LogFrame was introduced for use in the European Union[8] in 1993 (CEC 1993). In this presentation, the assumptions column has been pushed down one step, departing from the basic simplicity of the 4 × 4 square that earlier prevailed (Figure 9.5). This modification helps to clarify the often unclear relation of the cells in the assumptions column to levels in the

Deutsche Gesellschaft Technische Zusammenarbeit (GTZ) GmbH	PROJECT PLANNING MATRIX (PPM)
SUMMARY OF OBJECTIVES/ACTIVITIES	OBJECTIVELY VERIFIABLE INDICATORS
OVERALL GOAL to which the project contributes: The wheat production in the Sudo Province doubled.	INDICATORS that OG is reached: Wheat production in Sudo (quality Reference '81') is (in kt): '82 '83 '84 '85 '86 '87 220 260 300 340 380 400
PROJECT PURPOSE: Draught animals in the Sudo Province effectively used in agriculture.	INDICATORS which show the achievement of a successful PP: The selected draught animals are used in the following numbers: '82 '83 '84 '85 '86 '87 1000 3000 5000 7000 9000 10000
RESULTS/OUTPUTS: 1. Effective combination of animal breeds, cultivation methods and local conditions determined. 2. Farmers cooperatives in operation. 3. Farmers trained. 4. Animals distributed and trained. 5. Agric. implements provided to the farmers (demand satisfied).	INDICATORS, describing the Results: 1. Before 12/'82, one or more combinations determined, which suit the Sudo Province's conditions, so that a 100 % (increase of yields or of farmer's incomes is reached by using animal traction. 2. A set number of farmer cooperatives (with specified levels of organization, functioning and membership) operational at point T1 in time. 3. Y number of farmers with positive results successfully completed their training (in relation to the skills and level of knowledge of the curriculum) at point T2 in time. 4. Z number of selected animals broken-in and trained for field work at point T3 in time and, with the help of credits (with repayments from revolving funds + surplus income in yr 1), provided to the cooperative during the first year. 5. Q tons of selected wheat seeds, R tons of specified fertilizers and Z tons of particular pesticides (plus sprayers) provided to the cooperatives at point T4 in time.
ACTIVITIES 1.1 Build and staff experimental stations. 1.2 Conduct studies, obtain necessary end results. 2.1 Design cooperatives (organization + function). 2.2 Implement recruiting campaign for farmers. 2.3 Start cooperatives and solve starting difficulties. 3.1 Work out curriculum and provide good trainers. 3.2 Conduct training course. 4.1 Select necessary number and breeds of animals. 4.2 Develop credit system and implement it. 4.3 Buy animals, train and deliver them. 5.1 Estimate necessary agric. implements. 5.2 Coordinate availability of implements with the Ministry. 5.3 Depending on their progress, provide farmers with implements.	SPECIFICATION of Quantities and Unit/Costs for each Individual Activity: Total Budget: (in 1000 %) 1982 '83 '84 '85 '86 '87 Running costs 5 5 5 5 5 – Purch. Animals 25 25 25 25 25 – Total 30 30 30 30 30 – (See attached budget for Personnel and Cost details).

MANAGEABLE FACTORS
If these activities are carried out,
then these results/outputs are obtained

DEVELOPMENT HYPOTHESIS
If these results are obtained,
then the project purpose is achieved
If the project purpose is achieved,
then a contribution is made towards the goal

Figure 9.2 The GTZ project matrix

Project Title: Agricultural Production in Sudo Province Project No: 4712 Est. Project Duration: 5 years Country: Kwaziland	PPM prepared on (date): 1985
MEANS/SOURCES OF VERIFICATION	IMPORTANT ASSUMPTIONS
– Quarterly bulletin of the Statistics Dept. of the Min. of Ag. – Ad random tests by project staff.	For sustainability of Overall Goal 1. World Bank Project fulfills its objectives (develop new land and increase the average farm size). 2. The aimed increase of agricultural production is not essentially influenced by changed sectoral and intersectoral priority setting of the Min. of Ag. and the Government. 3. The Min. of Agric. successfully extends the use of draught animals or of suitable machines to other areas of Kwaziland. 4. See point 1 and 3 below (Results).
– Yearly counts by project staff. – Ad random tests by Animal Husbandry Expert.	For achievement of the OG: 1. See point 1 below (Results) 2. See point 3 below (Results) 3. See point 5 below (Activities)
1. Test date. 2. Regular reports by project staff. 3. Records from trainer teams. 4. Records from Animal Training Sections. Records from Credit Sections. 5. Records from the Extension Service of the Ministry. Reports from the Section for Production Inputs.	For the achievement of the PP: 1. Weather conditions (e.g. rainfall, temperature) remain on normal levels in the whole Province. 2. Farmers accept using the animals and implements in the recommended way. 3. Major economic factors (prices of means of production, price of wheat) do not change considerably (or at least remain within x % range from this year's prices). 4. See point 5 below (Activity level).
Information from the accounts.	For obtaining the Results: 1. At least one practical (workable) combination (of animal breed, cultivation method and local conditions) can be found. 2. The farmers have no insurmountable objections (e.g. cultural, economic) to joining a cooperative. 3. Sufficient good trainers are available. 4. No essential rise in the price of the animals. 5. Min. of Ag. provides the appropriate production implements in sufficient quantities at the right time.

Source: GTZ (1987)

Narrative summary (NS)	Verifiable indicators (OVI)	Means of verification (MOV)	Important Assumptions
Goal:			(Goal to supergoal):
1 Small farmer income increased.	1.1 Economic value of increased agricultural production @ 11,156kMK per annum by end 1998. 1.2 Economic value of increased animal production @ 140kMK per annum by end 1998.	1.1 M&E Unit household surveys. 1.2 M&E Unit household surveys.	1
2 Improved social well-being of rural farm families.	2.1	2.1	
Purpose:			(Purpose of Goal):
1 Small farmer agricultural and livestock productivity and production increased.	1.1 Total farmer productivity increased by: Maize 200 Kg/ha Sorgum 400/Kg/ha 1.2 Total farmer production increased by: Maize 39,000 m/tons Sorgum 4,300 m/tons Cattle 300 p/a	1.1 M&E Unit annual surveys. 1.2 M&E Unit annual surveys.	1 Export/import parity for crop prices remains constant.
Outputs:			(Output to Purpose):
1 Extension services centers and administrative improvement program operational.	1.1 5 centers and 3 sub-centers staffed and equipped and providing medium and short term training to farmers. 1.2 Research trials conducted and information dessiminated.	1.1 Site inspections Training records 1.2 Research results	1 Farmers will adopt new seed packages and methods at a rate of 33%. 2 Research results work under normal on-farm conditions. 3 Increased soil fertility can be sustained.

2 Small farmer credit program operational.	2.1 Ag. credit fund lending 5.3 million in medium term loans from 91–98.	2.1 Bank documents	
3 Infrastructure development program completed.	3.1 62Km rural farm to market roads reconstructed to DRIMP standards. 3.2 88 shallow wells built. 3.3 1000 water taps installed. 3.4 16 bore holes reconstructed. 3.5 3 health facilities operational.	3.1 Transportation records Site survey 3.2 Construction reports Site surveys 3.3 M&E Unit household surveys 3.4 Construction reports Site surveys 3.5 Health center records	
4 Monitoring & evaluation program established.	4.1 M&E Unit established and staffed and collecting performance data.	4.1 Quarterly project reports	
Activities: 1.1 Hire 4 SDOs and 53 field staff 1.2 Conduct in-service training 1.3 Procure equipment 1.4 Identify, hire contractor. 1.5 Construct service center. 1.6 Rehabilitate RTZ hdqtrs. 2.1 3.1 4.1	Commodities 300000.00 Technical Assis. 200000.00 Training 500000.00 Personnel 125000.00 1125000.00	1.1 Extension center records 1.2 1.3 1.4 1.5 1.6 2.1 3.1 4,1	(Activity to Output) 1 Implementation follows project construction schedule. 2 Inflation rate is 5% p/a. 3 Value of MK against int'l currencies constant.

Source: Team Technologies Inc. (1994). Model project supplied (incomplete) with the software.

Figure 9.3 Project logical framework AGMALAWI

1. DEVELOPMENT OBJECTIVE The higher-level objective towards which the project is expected to contribute (Mention target groups)	1. INDICATORS Measures (direct or indirect) to verify to what extent the development objective is fulfilled. (Means of verification should be specified)	1. EXTERNAL FACTORS Important events, conditions or decisions necessary for sustaining objectives in the long run
2. IMMEDIATE OBJECTIVE The effect which is expected to be achieved as the result of the project (Mention target groups)	2. INDICATORS Measures (direct or indirect) to verify to what extent the immediate objective is fulfilled (Means of verification should be specified)	2. EXTERNAL FACTORS Important events, conditions or decisions outside the control of the project which must prevail for the development objective to be attained
3. OUTPUTS The results that the project management should be able to guarantee (Mention target groups)	3. INDICATORS Measures (direct or indirect) which verify to what extent the outputs are produced (Means of verification should be specified)	3. EXTERNAL FACTORS Important events conditions or decisions outside the control of the project management, necessary for the achievement of the immediate objective
4. ACTIVITIES The activities that have to be undertaken by the project in order to produce the outputs	5. INPUTS Goods and services necessary to undertake the activities	4. EXTERNAL FACTORS Important events, conditions or decisions outside the control of the project management necessary for the production of the outputs

Source: NORAD (n.d.)

Figure 9.4 The NORAD project matrix

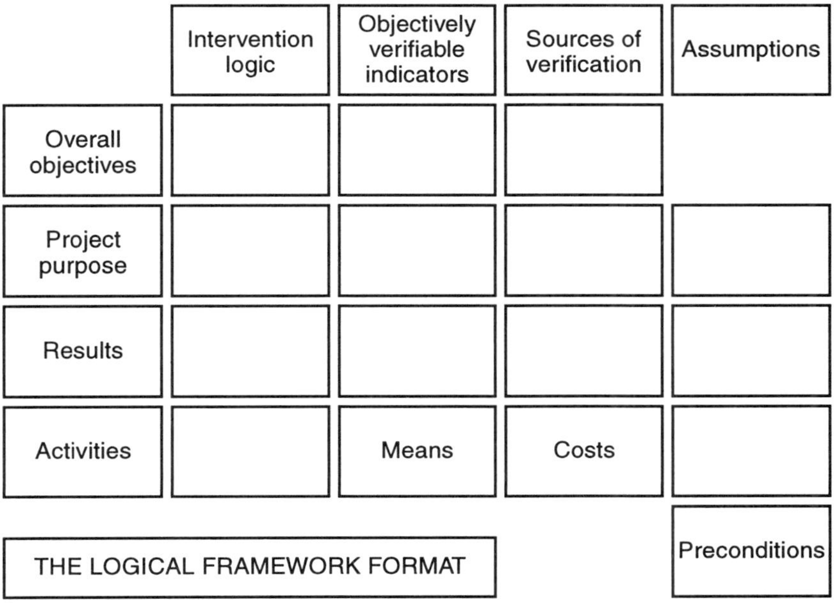

Source: CEC (1993)

Figure 9.5 The logical framework format of the CEC

narrative summary, one of the limitations in existing formats to which Wiggins and Shields (1995) draw attention.

The Broader Approach for UNDP/GEF Projects

Perhaps the most significant change from the 'classic' summary matrix format has been that adopted by the United Nations Development Programme (UNDP) for its projects under GEF – the Global Environmental Facility.[9] In this case, the LogFrame is restricted only to the narrative summary sections of other forms. Within these projects, one overriding objective is defined, though if required with many purposes.[10] For the attainment of each purpose there may be a number of outputs, and for each output there will be one or more contributing activities.

The major innovation of this form is in the presentation. The hierarchy of the vertical relationships – activities contributing to outputs that contribute to purposes – is reflected in a hierarchical arrangement with outputs and activities listed in sub-sections at two levels under the relevant purposes. A specimen representation of the presentation structure is in Figure 9.6.

Header information			**1**
Brief Description			**1**
A. CONTEXT			**2**
B. PROJECT JUSTIFICATION			**6**
C. DEVELOPMENT OBJECTIVE			**12**
D. IMMEDIATE OBJECTIVES, OUTPUTS AND ACTIVITIES			**12**
IMMEDIATE OBJECTIVE 1			
Output 1.1			
Activities for Output 1.1	1.1.1		
		1.1.2	
Output 1.2			
Activities for Output 1.2	1.2.1		
		1.2.2	
Output 1.3			
Activities for Output 1.3	1.3.1		
		1.3.2	
		1.3.3	
IMMEDIATE OBJECTIVE 2			
Output 2.1			
Activities for Output 2.1		2.1.1	
		2.1.2	
		2.1.3	
Output 2.2			
Activities for Output 2.2		2.2.1	
		2.2.2	
Output 2.3			
Activities for Output 2.3		2.3.1	
		2.3.2	
		2.3.3	
		2.3.4	
		2.3.5	
		2.3.6	

Figure 9.6 Structure of a UNDP/GEF project document to illustrate the dominance of LogFrame sections

Source: UNDP/GEF Project Document. 'VietNam: Conservation Training and Biodiversity Action Plan' (n.d. – probably 1992).

A further difference in this format is the release from the summary matrix presentation. Thus, entries at all four levels can be as long and discursive as is necessary to describe the objective in view. As a consequence, the project description in this LogFrame format can extend over many pages.[11]

This pattern allows a very systematic description of the project. It achieves this by allowing an understanding of the logic of the hierarchy of objectives and activities that is very much easier seen than in conventional forms, where the eye has to move from one box (and page[12]) to another to see what are the related items at lower/higher levels, and how they relate.

Another major difference between this presentation and the more 'classical' forms used elsewhere is the separation of the narrative summary section from indicators and assumptions. These are of course mentioned in the UNDP/GEF project documents, but not in direct relation to the project description.

Perhaps this format is seen as the most appropriate for UNDP/GEF types of development activity. However, this is obviously an agency-influenced preference. As with other types of project from the same stable, IBRD/GEF projects still contain no matrix at all, neither in summary form nor extended.

While reservations may be expressed about the separation of description from indicators and assumptions, there is no doubt that the close association in a hierachical account of the purposes, outputs and activities is of great potential value in designing the project. This author has already found it of great value in teamwork for the design of a complex participatory, poverty-focused agricultural project. The client agency (which used the basic 4 × 4 model) had some difficulty adjusting to the unaccustomed form of an early design presentation in the format illustrated in Figure 9.6. However, the design team found the arrangement of ideas in this way was a most valuable structure for developing the project logic in a comprehensive manner. Preliminary experience suggests that the UNDP/GEF format is most valuable for use in preliminary stages of project design, both as a planning tool and as a means of explaining the hierarchy to other parties. As the final or only LogFrame type of presentation, it suffers from the separation of narrative structure from indicators and assumptions, two of the main virtues of the matrix method that other users have seen. However, those requiring the 'classical' format for final project proposals might see virtue in proposing this mode of structured design and presentation as a valuable tool for early stages of project preparation. As both Wiggins and Shields (1995) and Ackroyd (1995) emphasize, the preparation of a succession of LogFrame drafts is an established feature of project planning in agencies that use the technique fully. This applies both to pre-investment planning and to replanning during implementation, especially in 'process' projects.

LINKING THE LOGFRAME TO SOFTWARE FOR PROJECT PLANNING

A recent development from the base of LogFrame methods has been the preparation of integrated PC software that covers a wide range of elements in project planning. This has now been developed to the stage where existing software can be used for the preparation of an entire project proposal document.

A main manifestation of this situation is the TeamUp software developed by Team Technologies (1994), and introduced by ODA in late 1993 for widespread use in projects that they finance. Now in its second version,[13] the basis of the software is the definition (in the first step) of a hierarchy of goals, purposes and outputs. These would be derived, as the software name suggests, from ZOPP-like team-based explorations of problem tree analysis and their conversion into action proposals.[14]

The hierarchy of elements at these three levels that stem from the separate team sessions are drawn, in the first of eight steps of the integrated software, into a linked diagram, using Windows methods. The defined elements provide the basis for Step 2, the preparation of a 4 × 4 square LogFrame matrix, the core of the software. Figure 9.3 illustrates this format. The hierarchy components defined in Step 1 become the top three boxes of the NS column of the matrix. The remaining 13 LogFrame boxes have to be filled in as part of Step 2. A complete LogFrame is thus prepared – over a long period of time!

A further six steps go on to elaborate detailed features of a TeamUp project plan. They are as follows:

3. Performance plans
4. Stakeholder analysis
5. Work breakdown structures
6. Organizational responsibility chart
7. Gantt chart
8. Project budget.

Experience of this relatively new software package has yet to be evaluated. However, there can be little doubt that the development of integrated PC software for project planning, based on LogFrames, is likely to continue. The introduction of the subsequent six steps as complementary components is an innovation that will cause discussion and clarification. Nevertheless, the software now taken up by ODA points in a direction in which further development can be expected to be seen.

CONCLUSION

When systematic training courses in project planning and appraisal were first held in the late 1960s/early 1970s, the LogFrame idea had not been developed. The emergence and importance of the approach and technique were recognized by its inclusion in courses in the mid-1970s.[15] During the intervening years, LogFrame ideas have gradually been widely adopted. In the mid-1990s, they are an established feature of the project planning scene, and of training in project planning courses.[16]

However, during the last ten years, there has been growing diversification and development from the core idea. This has taken three main forms:

- diversification of the structure and appearance of the basic four-row, four-column matrix;
- the association of LogFrame development with participatory team methods;
- the beginnings of steps to integrate LogFrame drawing with other project planning forms on specialized PC software packages.

Based on the almost 'inspired' innovative planning tool that PCI proposed in 1971, a diverse and deepening project planning style has developed around the LogFrame core. Change and elaboration of the method continue.

In view of the diversity and wide reaches of these developments, there is perhaps now a need for an international review of formats, practice and experience with LogFrames, both as tools for project planning and management and for the purpose for which they were originally proposed, as an aid to *ex-post* evaluation.

NOTES

1. A fuller account of the development of LogFrame ideas is in MacArthur (1994).
2. Ackroyd (1995) provides a recent report on adoption of the technique in 1993 by yet another agency, the African Development Bank.
3. ZOPP is an acronym based on the initials of the German-language form of the term 'objectives-oriented project planning'.
4. A full introduction to ZOPP methods is in GTZ (1988).
5. Wiggins and Shields (1995) provide a recent comment on the logical value of this development.
6. This illustration is taken from the Team Technologies (1994) software. It is based on a printout of the incomplete LogFrame that is provided for illustration with the ODA customized version of the basic software.
7. When ODA adopted the Logframe in 1986, some different terms were used. The matrix as a whole was referred to as the 'project framework'; the two higher levels in the 'project structure' (left-side) column were 'wider objectives' and 'immediate objectives'; and the

two indicator columns had different descriptions. Wiggins and Shields (1995) contains an illustration of this original ODA format.

8. This was the European Community at the pre-Maastricht ratification time of publication.
9. It is not known whether this format is more widely adopted in UNDP. Use of this format has so far been seen by us only in GEF project documents.
10. Limitations on the number of goals and purposes allowed in LogFrames is a point of difference between different adopting agencies. A single goal is a quite common constraint, but restriction to only one or two purposes is also a feature in some cases. This point is discussed in MacArthur (1994).
11. In a draft UNDP/GEF project discussed in an early 1995 workshop in Amman, 18 of the 45 pages of the most recent draft project document were devoted to this extended LogFrame-type material.
12. Although the original concept was for a single page summary, and this was often relaxed formally to allow a second page, many LogFrames used in practice now extend to multiple pages.
13. PC/TeamUP 2.0. See Team Technologies (1994).
14. Basic elements of the procedure are described in the associated manual.
15. LogFrames became a feature of training courses in the Development and Project Planning Centre from 1975, following the Centre's first contacts with the Evaluation Division of USAID in February 1974.
16. They have even become the subject of doctoral theses. An example is Famiyeh (1991).

REFERENCES

Ackroyd, D. (1995), 'Steps towards the adoption of the Logical Framework Approach in the African Development Bank: some illustrations for agricultural sector projects', *Project Appraisal*, **10** (1).

Analoui, F. (ed.) (1994), *The Realities of Managing Development Projects*, Aldershot, UK: Avebury.

CEC (1993), *Manual on Project Cycle Management*, Brussels: CEC.

CIDA (1980), 'Guide for the use of the Logical Framework Approach in the Management and Evaluation of CIDA's International Development Projects', Hull, Canada: Canadian International Development Agency.

Famiyeh, J. (1991), 'The Logical Framework Concept in Agricultural Policy Planning', unpublished PhD thesis, University of Bradford.

GTZ (1987), 'ZOPP in brief', mimeo, Eschborn: Deutsche Gesellschaft für Technische Zusammenarbeit.

GTZ (1988), 'ZOPP – an introduction to the Method', Eschborn: Deutsche Gesellschaft für Technische Zusammenarbeit.

MacArthur, J.D. (1994), 'The logical framework: a tool for the management of project planning and evaluation', DPPC New Series Discussion Paper no. 42, University of Bradford, also published under same title in Analoui (1994).

NORAD (n.d.), 'The Logical Framework Approach (LFA): Handbook for Objectives-oriented Project Planning', Norwegian Agency for International Development, Oslo.

Team Technologies Inc. (1994), 'PC/TeamUP 2.0 Software Manual', Chantilly VA: Team Technologies.

Wiggins, S. and D. Shields (1995), 'Clarifying the "logical framework" as a tool for planning and managing development projects', *Project Appraisal*, **10** (1).

10. Project-cycle management (PCM): a tool for aid effectiveness

Erik Kijne

INTRODUCTION

The European Commission manages development assistance of about ECU 5 billion per year.[1] This is about one quarter of the annual portfolio of the World Bank, or a little over twice the size of the UK bilateral aid programme. In voting an aid programme of this size, the member states of the European Union endeavour to reinforce relations with more than 100 countries worldwide as part of an emerging common foreign and security policy. Poverty alleviation is generally the central objective of this aid, while the primary focus of aid to the more developed or emerging economies tends to be on integration into the world economy. Aid managed by the European Commission is probably the most scrutinized aid anywhere in the world with controls exercised by the European Parliament, national parliaments, the European Council of Ministers, the European Court of Auditors, and also checks by teams of internal auditors and evaluators.

In the 1970s and 1980s discussion on aid often turned to the question of volume and how this might be increased. In the 1990s, however, the focus of the aid debate falls squarely on the issue of quality in times of demanding budgetary convergence criteria within the European Union, high unemployment levels and social exclusion on our doorsteps, combined with new foreign policy demands. Words such as *effectiveness* and *sustainability* have entered everyday vocabulary.

Only recently, the European Commission reacted to evaluation findings of aid projects which highlighted confused and unrealistic objectives, inadequate attention to risk, poor monitoring, weak sustainability prospects and insufficient participation by beneficiaries in the aid process. Contacts with members of the Wappenhans Task Force reviewing World Bank experiences and contacts with several bilateral and multilateral agencies revealed that the Commission was not alone in these difficulties.

A drive to improve the quality of development aid was launched. Again, in common with the rest of the donor community, we soon learned that this is not a 100-day or even 1000-day miracle. Improving aid quality is about changing mind sets, and takes time. Overcoming vested interests, prejudices and cultural barriers, both in our institutions and in the developing world, is the order of the day.

The starting point for this drive was the development of new tools – guidelines, handbooks and training programmes – with the project-cycle management (PCM) methodology at the centre of this process. As evaluations revealed inadequacies in project design mainly due to poor project identification and preparation, the primary goal of introducing the PCM method in the European Commission was to improve the quality of financing proposals. This is achieved through improved consultation and analysis of the beneficiary situation, the preparation of feasible and sustainable plans using the logical framework and incorporating lessons from project evaluations, and the transparent presentation of the proposal in a standardized format. Ultimately the goal is to improve the effectiveness of aid through better-quality management and decision making.

This chapter presents the mechanics of PCM and then reviews present and potential applications of the method in the various phases of the project cycle.

THE MECHANICS OF PCM

Project-cycle management (PCM) is based on six principles:

1. *Project cycle.* The PCM method distinguishes clear phases in the project cycle. In these phases the roles of stakeholders are clearly defined and the decisions to be made are laid down.
2. *Beneficiary focus and ownership (client orientation).* PCM raises beneficiary orientation of projects by focusing on the problems of the beneficiaries and implementing agencies. A detailed problem analysis is made during the identification of a project, and the type of intervention is selected on the basis of the needs of beneficiaries and the parties involved.
3. *Logical framework planning.*[2] The PCM method produces a transparent project design derived from the logical framework approach. Such a logical framework matrix focuses explicitly on the project purpose and incorporates the services to be provided by the project (results). An important aspect of the logical framework is the notification of assumptions and preconditions required to initiate activities and achieve the various objectives (results, project purpose and overall objectives).
4. *Sustainability.* Right from the planning phase, the results and activities derived from the logical framework plan are tested for sustainability. If

necessary for the assurance of the sustainability of the project, additional results, activities, assumptions and preconditions are incorporated into the plan.
5. *Transparent, standardized documentation.* PCM introduces a standardized format for all project documents, providing a clear set of quality criteria for financing proposals.
6. *Framework for learning and decision taking.* PCM provides the European Commission and partner organizations with a systematic framework for learning from experience on the basis of improved monitoring and evaluation practices. The lessons learnt are to be incorporated in sectoral policies, and also in national and regional indicative programmes which serve as guidelines for the identification of new projects.

The underlying mechanics of these six principles are explained in more detail below.

The first principle, the six phases of the project cycle, is presented in Figure 10.1. This section of the chapter will first elaborate on the mechanics of the second, third and fourth principles of PCM which offer a potential to improve the quality of the information presented in the standardized documents (fifth principle).

In the third section the applications of PCM through the introduction of possible instruments in the various phases of the project cycle are explained (sixth principle). Figure 10.1 also presents the various documents prepared in each of these phases and the instruments available to produce these documents. These are shown in Figure 10.1 by circles. The diamonds visualize assessment exercises to judge the quality of the respective documents that form the basis of adequate decision making.

The introduction of the PCM has mainly focused on the identification and formulation phases dealing ultimately with the preparation of financing proposals. In these phases the following three steps apply in an iterative way:

- Analysis
- Project design
- Documentation

On the basis of the information presented at each phase of the project cycle, a decision has to be made on whether or not to proceed. In addition to the quality criteria derived from the PCM application instruments and means are being developed to facilitate improved decision making in each project phase. The proposed adjustments to the decision making procedures are presented in a later section.

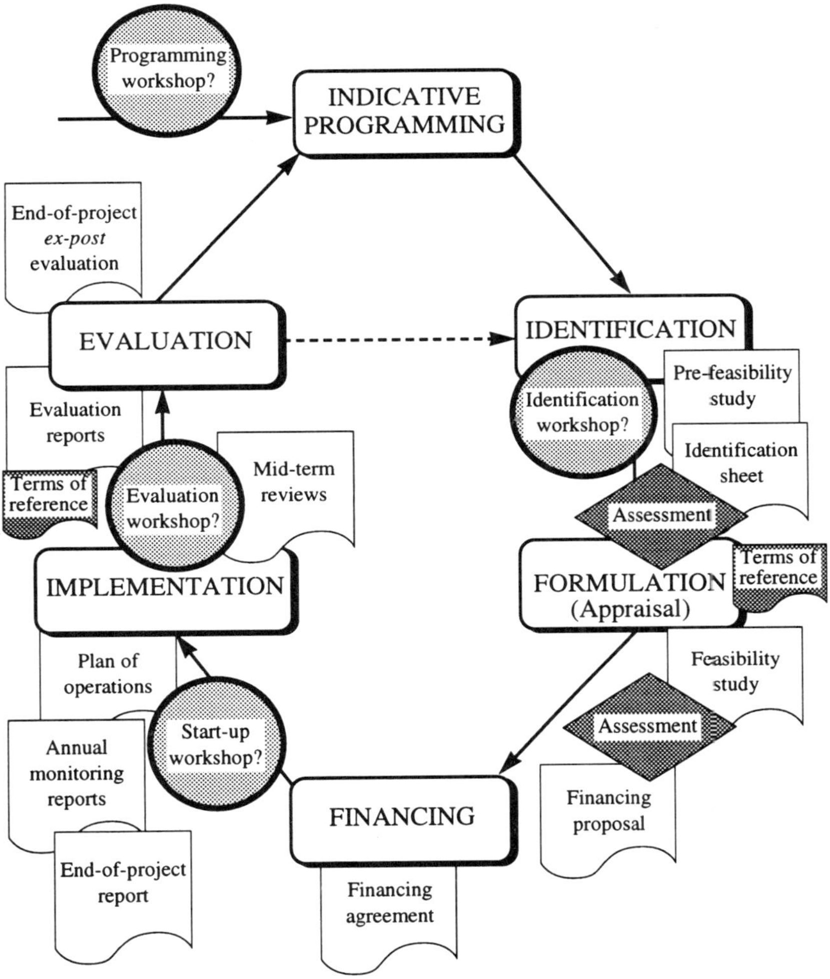

Figure 10.1 Applications of the PCM method in the project cycle

Analysis

In the first phase of the project cycle, which is known as project identification, it is crucial to analyse the situation of the beneficiaries. In the subsequent project phases the situation of the beneficiaries must be checked and any changes identified. The analysis is comprised of three steps.

1. *Identification of parties involved (stakeholders*). On the basis of the entity, the area or sector identified for a possible intervention, an inventory and analysis is made of the beneficiaries, sub-groups (gender) and implementing agencies.
2. *Problem identification and analysis.* The problems as perceived by the various stakeholders must be identified and analysed. The problems are then linked together in a *cause–effect relationship* to produce a *problem tree*. This problem analysis must be done in the identification phase, and the evolution of these problems with time should be constantly monitored during project implementation.
3. *Objective analysis*. Based on the problem analysis, the project objective can be analysed by reformulating the problems into objectives and placing them in a hierarchy of *means–ends* relationships to produce an *objective tree* of all objectives to be achieved through the project and by

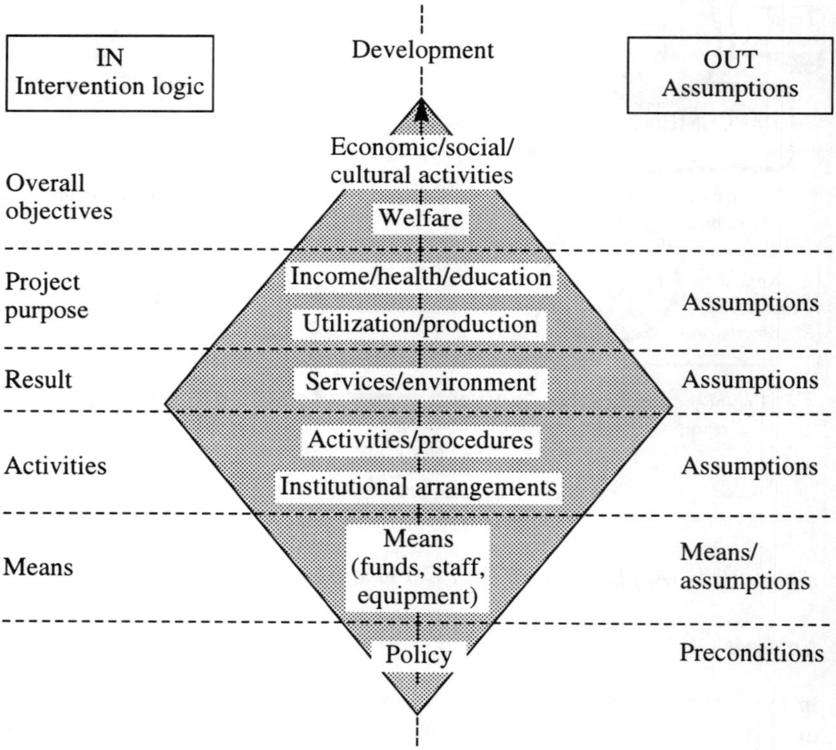

Figure 10.2 Model of the hierarchy of project objectives and the link to the logical framework

others. The objective tree displays the objectives at various levels related to the stakeholders in the project: government, implementing agencies and beneficiaries. A model of such an objective tree can be presented in a diamond shaped form as shown in Figure 10.2. At the bottom of the diamond, objectives related to government policy and implementing agencies are presented. Achievement of these objectives enables these organizations to carry out activities that deliver services to the beneficiaries. Only when the beneficiaries are satisfied with these services and are able to use them do they benefit from the project (the services here are income, health, education). When these objectives are fulfilled welfare is achieved, which in turn creates the conditions for new economic, social and cultural activities and ultimately development is achieved.

Project design

The logical framework is one of the tools incorporated in the PCM method, and is thus a major link in the introduction of quality management. The logical framework has been criticized as being too much of a blueprint approach and like many such tools it has certain limitations. In its simplest form logical framework is a throw-back to 'planning by objectives' in the early days of management science. But it should not be forgotten that the progress enjoyed by industrialized countries today is the result of advances in management and technology, to name but two fields. Management by objectives, which are time-bound and measurable, is as valid a concept now as it was for the early management scientists. So too, logical framework is a tool to aid dialogue. It cannot replace dialogue; nor can it usurp classical economic and/or other appraisal or evaluation methods.

There are six steps in preparing a project design following the logical framework approach:

1. Make clusters of objectives on the objective tree and identify alternatives.
2. Establish the focus of the project in terms of the project purpose.
3. Identify the project results and assumptions (design a comprehensive package).
4. Identify activities, assumptions and preconditions.
5. Adjust and update the plan on the basis of the sustainability factors.
6. Prepare an activity schedule and responsibility matrix.

We discuss these in turn.

Make clusters of objectives on the objective tree and identify alternatives

The objective tree represents a hierarchy of objectives which are the basis for planning. The branches of the objective tree represent clusters of related objectives and a selection has to be made of which clusters the project will address and which are outside the control of the project. The selection of objectives to include (IN) and those to exclude (OUT) is referred to as the scoping of the objective tree. Figure 10.2 shows the link between the objective tree and the logical framework matrix. This helpful tool demonstrates the separation of objectives from the tree on the basis of the decision to be either IN the project design or to be OUT as an assumption or precondition. The respective objectives are placed at various levels in the matrix. These levels are determined by whether the objective is offering a direct benefit to the beneficiaries (project purpose), the economy and government (overall objectives) and by the services offered by the project to the beneficiaries (results). Objectives in the objective tree positioned below these results are reformulated as activities.

Establish the focus of the project in terms of the project purpose

The first issue addressed by PCM is the project purpose, that is the objective directly related to the needs of the beneficiaries. The project purpose must be stated in terms of benefits to the beneficiaries – *why they need the project.* The project purpose must not be expressed in terms of services provided but must be determined in terms of the *utilization of these services* by the beneficiaries.

Identify the project results and assumptions (design a comprehensive package)

In order to achieve the project purpose, a number of services may need to be made available. Some of these services may be supplied by the projects, and are referred to as the project results. Other services which cannot be made available by the project but which are nevertheless essential to achieving the project purpose should be assumed to be supplied by external agencies. These are referred to as assumptions which are outside the control of the project. With a clear focus on the needs of the beneficiaries as specified in the project purpose, the required results and assumptions (supporting external objectives) can be identified. For example:

- A hospital designed and built to solve health problems is unlikely to achieve its goal if the people it serves continue to depend on contaminated water supplies.
- A credit fund set up to boost productivity of small industrial enter-

prises may not be effective if production factors and markets are not accessible (assumptions).

Planning from the project purpose down will generate additional objectives required to achieve the higher-level objective. This system of *planning by objectives* offers a tool for identifying a number of assumptions, which after assessment, may have to be incorporated into the project design. This system differs from *planning by activities*, which is based on the preconceived 'logical' effect of services the project has to offer. This reasoning is often derived from vested interests. The difference between objective- and activity-oriented planning is illustrated in Figure 10.3. The thick arrows visualize the thinking process. As such 'bottom–up' or activity-oriented planning may leave out important factors that are discovered though 'top-down' objective-oriented planning.

When making the shift from the objective tree to the logical framework matrix as presented in Figure 10.4, planning starts with the identification of the project purpose. Following the objective-oriented planning downwards all objectives required to achieve the project purpose are identified. Those selected for achievement by the project (IN) are placed at the corresponding level in the left column of the matrix, while the objectives to be achieved by others are placed in the right column as assumptions (OUT). Assumptions are external factors not under the control of the project but which must be met in order to achieve the project objectives. Preconditions are external factors that

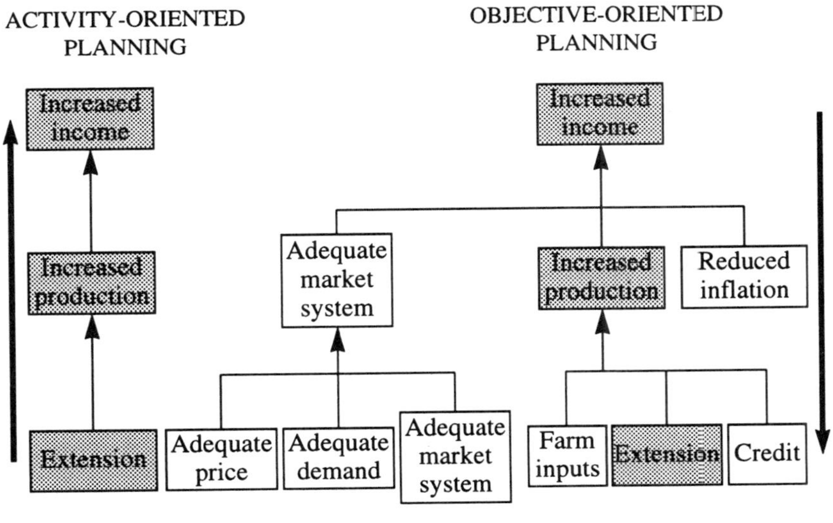

Figure 10.3 Activity- versus objective-oriented planning

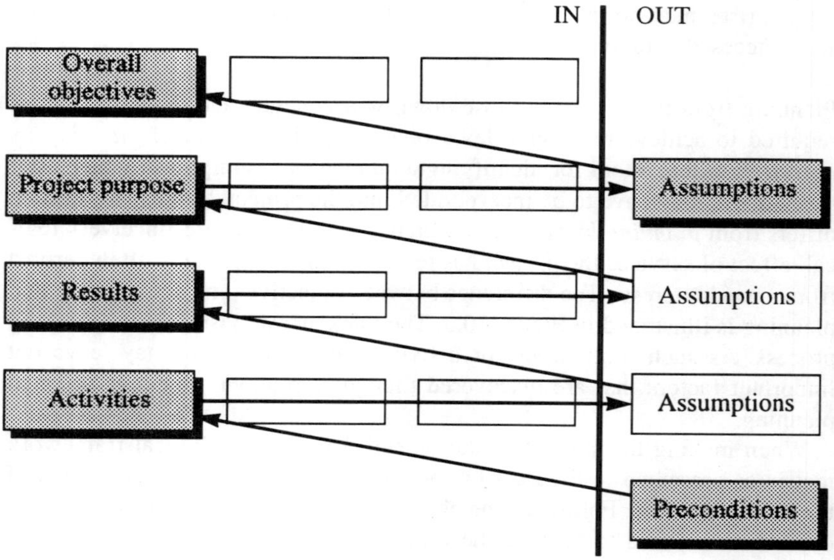

Figure 10.4 Matrix of project objectives (IN), assumptions and preconditions (OUT)

must be complied with before the project activities can start. Policy requirements are often identified as preconditions and form a critical element in the initial negotiations on the project agreement.

Identify project activities, assumptions and preconditions

The decision on whether to include a condition in the left or right column of Figure 10.4 is determined by running the conditions through the questions posed in the algorithm presented in Figure 10.5. Following this procedure, the first question assesses the importance of the condition in achieving a higher-level objective. It may either be excluded or further tested on whether the condition is achieved without further project involvement. When this is certain to happen the condition can be excluded from the matrix. When it is likely the condition should appear as an assumption and when it is unlikely it should be checked whether the project can affect this condition. If this is the case the condition should be part of the project design and as such be shifted into the first column of the matrix. If the project will have no authority or means to affect this critical condition then the condition is called a *killer assumption*. From the technical point of view the project is likely to fail. So if a killer assumption is identified, then the project design has to be changed or the project should be rejected.

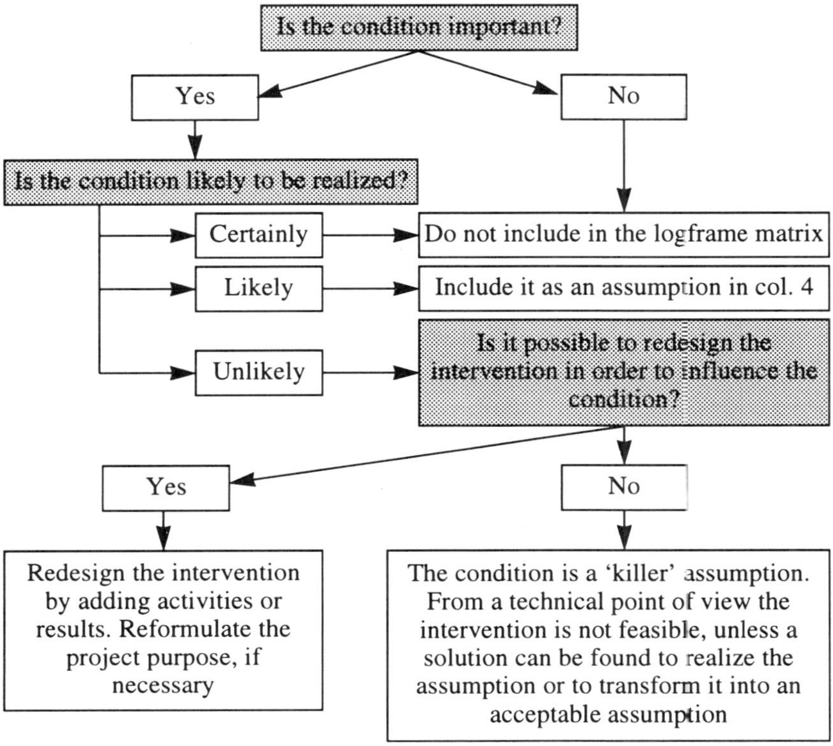

Figure 10.5 Algorithm to assess conditions

Once all the project results have been identified, the activities required to achieve each result can be defined. Again, external conditions required to carry out the activities are identified. After testing each of these on the algorithm above, some assumptions may have to be fulfilled before the activities can commence. These crucial assumptions are referred to as *preconditions*.

Adjust and update the project plan on the basis of sustainability factors
In this step of the designing of the project, the factors which determine its sustainability are incorporated in the logical framework matrix. Once it has been clarified that the project addresses the real problems of the beneficiaries by offering the required services, due attention should be given to ensuring that these services will be sustainable after the development assistance ceases. All too frequently, there is inadequate commitment by the implementing agencies, insufficient management capacity, or the means are not made avail-

able by implementing agencies or governments to continue operation after a project is completed.

The principle of phasing a project with different results achieved consecutively during implementation is shown in Figure 10.6 The incorporation of additional results required to achieve the project purpose may lead to extension of the implementation phase of the project.

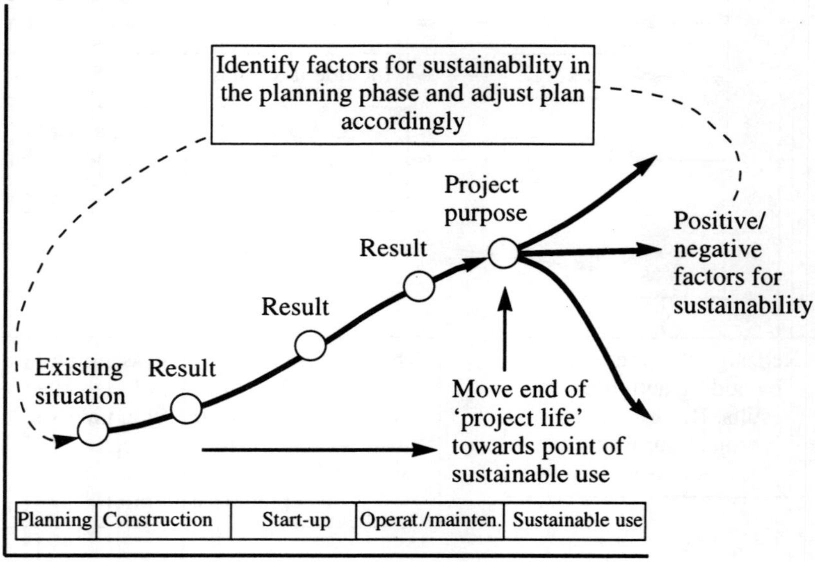

Figure 10.6 Visualization of achievement of objectives during project implementation

Factors relevant to the sustainability of development projects are:

- Policy support
- Appropriate technology
- Environmental protection
- Sociocultural aspects/gender issues
- Institutional and management capacity in the public and private sectors
- Economic and financial rationale.

The project results and corresponding activities are assessed on the basis of the sustainability risk factors listed above. This may lead to the inclusion of the additional preconditions, activities, assumptions or even results in the plan or LogFrame matrix (see Figure 10.7).

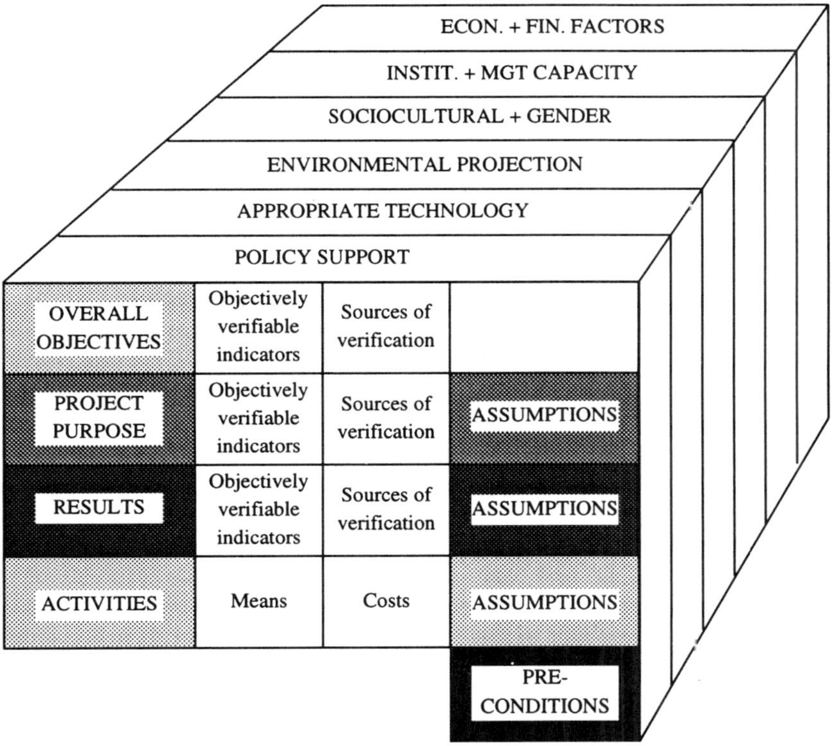

Figure 10.7 Factors for sustainability incorporated into the logical framework matrix

The inclusion of the sustainability check on the LogFrame planning is a significant conceptual addition introduced by the PCM method. Corrective measures to ensure the sustainability of a development project may be included in its design. If these factors are beyond the control of the project, they are included as *assumptions*, which have to be fulfilled by external agents. Close scrutiny of such factors often leads to modification of the project design. For instance, the approach or technology proposed may have to be modified, cost recovery systems may have to be included, or institutional development activities incorporated. Furthermore, an analysis of the assumptions may well indicate that the implementation of policy measures by the recipient government is a *precondition* for the ultimate success of the project.

Prepare activity schedule and responsibility matrix

A rough indication of the phasing of a project should be attached to the financing proposal. At the start of the implementation phase, a detailed activity schedule setting out responsibilities distributed among the involved parties on an annual basis must be prepared by the implementing agency as part of the plan of operations to cover the total project period.

Documentation

One of the strengths of PCM is that project documents prepared in the phases of the project cycle are presented in a standardized format covering all issues including the assumptions on which the project is based. The standarized format, as presented below, offers transparency and facilitates an improved institutional memory in the donor agencies. In organizations with constant staff transfers, short, concise and transparent project documents enable rapid understanding of the dossiers, which provide clear insight into the evolution of projects.

At each stage in the project cycle, the information in the respective documents is examined, revised where necessary and carried forward to the next stage. This system makes the project concept and context in which it operates clear and visible, and thus enables improved project monitoring and evaluation.

The basic format for project documents is as follows:

1. **Summary**
2. **Background**
   - 2.1 Government/sectoral policy
   - 2.2 Features of the sector
   - 2.3 Beneficiaries and parties involved
   - 2.4 Problems to be addressed
   - 2.5 Other interventions
   - 2.6 Documentation available
3. **Intervention**
   - 3.1 Overall objectives
   - 3.2 Project purpose
   - 3.3 Results
   - 3.4 Activities
4. **Assumptions**
   - 4.1 Assumptions at different levels
   - 4.2 Risks and flexibility
5. **Implementation**
   - 5.1 Physical and non-physical means

- 5.2 Organization and implementation procedures
- 5.3 Timetable
- 5.4 Cost estimate and financing plan
- 5.5 Special conditions; accompanying measures taken by the government

6. Factors ensuring sustainability

- 6.1 Policy support
- 6.2 Appropriate technology
- 6.3 Environmental protection
- 6.4 Sociocultural aspects/gender issues
- 6.5 Institutional and management capacity, public and private
- 6.6 Economic and financial rationale

7. Monitoring and evaluation

- 7.1 Monitoring indicators
- 7.2 Reviews/evaluations

8. Conclusions and proposals

This format should be seen as a checklist of relevant issues rather than as an administrative harness. Some units in the European Commission have adjusted and detailed the format to meet specific information needs (Food Security Unit; NGO Unit, Human Rights and Democracy).

QUALITY MANAGEMENT IN THE PROJECT CYCLE

The procedures as described illustrate practical applications of PCM; the examples given refer in particular to the procedures as applied in aid to the African, Caribbean and Pacific states managed by the European Commission.

Although as yet not formally adopted by the European Commission in Brussels, some delegations in ACP states are proposing to use PCM in the formulation of national and regional indicative programmes which set out the European Union intentions for development assistance in a specific country or region. As a result of applying the PCM method, indicative programmes will focus more on the achievement of overall objectives in macroeconomic and social terms in specified sectors. A major component of the indicative programmes will be matching these wider sectoral approaches and geographical focus with the policy frameworks of the recipient government. These policy considerations will appear as preconditions in the various related projects and programmes.

Identification Phase

Project proposals are assessed in the identification phase by field staff of the delegations in conjunction with staff from the National Authorising Office and preferably also by staff from the line ministry involved in the case of a public sector project. Depending on the complexity of the projects and the interests involved, the delegations may be assisted in the assessment by an independent moderator. On the basis of the quality of the proposal and its match with the indicative programme, a project proposal may be turned down, returned for improvements, or processed for the formulation phase.

Assistance may also be provided in improving a project identification document through the organization of a participatory planning workshop with stakeholders, and conducted by an independent moderator. Participatory planning workshops are encouraged in identifying the formulating projects, especially complex projects. This is a very useful means of identifying and verifying the problems and issues to be addressed and to suggest possible solutions. Such workshops have the additional benefit of stimulating the commitment of implementing agencies and the beneficiaries through their involvement in planning. In additions, they may generate the basic information needed for feasibility studies and ultimately the drafting of a financing proposal.

Early in the identification phase an identification sheet is prepared by the delegation. It is proposed that the identification sheet and the proposal are screened by a multidisciplinary panel at policy level to be established in the Commission in Brussels. Following the go-ahead by this panel, the formulation phase can be initiated with the preparation of terms of reference for a feasibility study by the delegation or the desk officer.

During this phase, the PCM focal points will become involved. The focal points will comprise persons selected from geographic, technical and other units in the European Commission, and will be trained in the PCM method. Their task is to assist colleagues in the application of the PCM method in assessing project proposals and preparing terms of reference.

Formulation Phase

In the formulation phase of a project, a feasibility study may have to be carried which will include a draft financing proposal prepared in the standardized format for project documents. The intervention proposed will be based on an assessment of alternative and detailed design studies. The project purpose and the results will be specified in terms of objectively verifiable indicators and assumptions identified and quantified. The draft financing proposal is drawn up by the delegation in the field and sent to Brussels for approval.

The standardized format for project documents as part of the PCM method ensures that the essential information justifying the proposed project is presented. It is also becoming common practice to include a logical framework matrix, which facilitates rapid assessment of the project design.

The guide for assessing financing proposals offers elements for critical assessment of the quality of the document. Inconsistencies in the logic and unrealistic perceptions of the assumptions and preconditions often justify further information gathering or study. A proposal should give sufficient information, and justification on the following points:

- *Relevance* Is the project sufficiently justified within the context of its environment (problems identified versus objectives proposed)?
- *Focus* Has the project selected the right offer compared to alternatives?
- *Design* Are the services offered by the project (results and corresponding assumptions sufficient to achieve the project purpose (comprehensiveness)? Are the proposed activities sufficient and appropriate to achieve the results?
- *Ownership* Are the implementing agencies and beneficiaries sufficiently committed to the project?
- *Sustainability* Has the project a reasonable chance of being sustainable?

It is suggested that the draft proposal will be screened by the future operation and policy panels and only after their approval will the final version of the financing proposal be written, either by the delegation or the desk office.

Financing Phase

All financing proposals will be presented in a concise document of a maximum eight pages following the standardized format. These documents will emphasize the functional specification (objectives to be achieved) rather than the technical specifications (activities to be carried out). More transparent financing proposals adhering to the standarized format will facilitate judgement and decision making in the financing committees. These improved documents offer an adequate opportunity for the member states to understand more clearly the development initiatives of the European Commission and to become more committed to their success.

Implementation Phase

The preparation of a plan of operations at the start of the project implementation will need to be institutionalized. A participatory start-up workshop may assist in determining the detailed activities and responsibilities of the implementing agencies. Such a workshop will generate an ownership feeling and thus a stronger commitment of the parties involved to successful implementation of the project.

A project monitoring sheet to be completed annually by the delegation has recently been introduced, and a more comprehensive system will be developed. Because the PCM method describes projects in terms of objectives which are quantified by indicators, the method also facilitates project monitoring and evaluation. In principle, monitoring and evaluation become a matter of assessing the achievements according to the objectively verifiable indicators defined on the basis of the project purpose and results. In addition, this approach makes it easier to monitor key activities during project implementation. Monitoring reports are prepared periodically by project staff or consultants and reviewed by delegation staff. These reports will, in due course, follow the standardized format of the PCM method. The information provided will give a periodic overview of project performance and indicate where adjustment is required.

Evaluation Phase

A model terms of reference for evaluations is available which matches the PCM criteria with evaluation themes, such as relevance, efficiency, effectiveness, impact, sustainability and lessons learnt. Consultants contracted by the European Commission for evaluation missions are offered training in the PCM method to enable them to respond adequately to the requirements of terms of reference based on this method.

Problems are sometimes encountered in evaluating projects which have not been formulated according to the PCM method. Very often, these projects do not have clearly formulated objectives with objectively verifiable indicators against which to evaluate the project. In such cases, consultants together with the project implementors are required to work out the project objectives and their indicators.

The results from evaluations are transposed into feedback mechanisms to improve programming and preparation of projects and programmes.

THE RESULTS SO FAR

A little over two years into the process, the Commission is about to start an evaluation of experience to date with the PCM method. The introduction of PCM has been supported by the dissemination of 20,000 introductory manuals to professionals involved in development aid. An extensive training programme has also been conducted for about 2000 national planning officers from developing countries and professional staff in delegations and in the European Commission in Brussels. In addition, bilateral development organizations and consultancy associations in various European countries have received training in the PCM method.

Enormous progress has been made in informing, sensitizing and training. Virtually all professional staff throughout Directorate General Eight now apply the main principles of PCM in their daily work. The effectiveness of this effort to date is reflected in the greatly improved quality of financing proposals and evaluation studies. Pre-feasibility study work (problem analysis) is increasingly using participatory workshops and the quality of the resulting studies is improving.

Application of the PCM method in work plans and related monitoring has received little attention as yet. Future emphasis will certainly focus on the application of the method in the implementation phase.

The PCM approach sits comfortably in the aid environment of the 1990s where donors have reached a general consensus on setting poverty alleviation and sustainable development as overall objectives, with human rights and democracy as essential preconditions to achieving these objectives. It is also encouraging that planning by objectives using time-bound indicators is gaining currency particularly with donors, as is realism about the objectives of development aid and the time required for change.

It is widely recognized that the logical framework principles at the heart of the PCM method are well adapted to project situations. This is less obvious in the case of programme aid and other forms of non-project aid. The applicability of PCM is currently being tested in a country-level evaluation, in relation to structural adjustment support and in STABEX operations. It is too early to report on the outcome but we are convinced that the method has an important role.

THE FUTURE

The PCM work programme for 1995–96 foresees an intensification of training and applied workshop activity in beneficiary countries. It also includes the establishment of focal points within the European Commission. These persons will be instrumental in the application and institutionalization of the PCM method. Thought is being given to the installation of formal mechanisms for quality screening of financing proposals at policy and operational levels. Furthermore, plans are being developed to produce more detailed methodological guidance particularly for those involved in the monitoring of projects and programmes.

PCM might be a universal tool but to be effective it must be used in conjunction with other tools, such as economic and financial analysis methods, institutional appraisal techniques, gender, environmental criteria and participatory planning techniques not involving the logical framework. The Commission is developing updated guidelines and accompanying training packages in virtually all these fields. DPPC, Bradford, is one of the partners in developing new materials in economic and financial analysis. Furthermore, to ensure that the various techniques are not divorced from practice, guides for a number of key sectors will be developed around the PCM integrated approach which will guarantee improved linkages between formulation and evaluation. In this way, stakeholders' concerns, the establishment of verifiable indicators and mechanisms for feedback of lessons from experience when properly integrated throughout the project cycle should improve the quality of monitoring and evaluation. This in turn will assist decision makers and increase the sustainability prospects of our aid.

NOTES

1. Latin America and Asia 10 per cent; Mediterranean 7 per cent; Eastern and Central Europe 24 per cent; Africa, Caribbean and Pacific 33 per cent; food aid/humanitarian/NGOs 26 per cent.
2. Logical framework is a planning tool presenting the objectives, related activities and corresponding assumptions and preconditions of the project or programme design at different hierarchical levels in a matrix format, see also Chapter 9 of this volume.

11. Evaluating concessionality in tied aid projects

Oliver Morrissey

INTRODUCTION

The considerable literature on the procurement tying of aid largely focuses on the place of tying within donor aid policy (e.g. Jepma 1991; Morrissey et al., 1992). Less attention has been paid to analysis of the costs to the recipient countries. There are two distinct ways in which tied aid can undermine the value of aid to the recipient: overpricing and distorting the nature of aid. There are *a priori* reasons to believe that procurement prices under tied aid will be somewhat higher than prices under fully untied aid. Competition for tied aid contracts is limited, usually to a few donor firms, whereas untied aid can in principle be sourced on the world market where competition is more intense. Empirical evidence suggests that tied aid prices are some 10–15 per cent higher than competitive world prices (Jepma 1991, 1992). Tying also limits the choice open to recipients. In particular, it restricts recipients to using the products and technology supplied by the donor, which are not always the technologies most appropriate to the needs of the recipient.

This chapter applies the general argument of Morrissey and White (1993), regarding the concessionality of tied aid, to the specific issue of projects financed by tied aid, especially those financed from the UK's Aid and Trade Provision (ATP). To what extent does the fact that the aid is tied reduce the economic benefit of the project to the recipient? First, we present a simple theoretical framework for analysing the overpricing disadvantage associated with tied aid, evaluated against both the advantage of access to concessional finance and to foreign exchange. Then we consider the implications of this analysis for the evaluation of a tied aid project, arguing simply that any overpricing due to tying directly reduces the measured net benefit of a project. Finally, we draw some conclusions.

TYING: AN ANALYTICAL FRAMEWORK

We are concerned with the general case where aid is both procurement-tied – the receipt of aid is conditional upon the purchase of goods and services from the donor – and project-tied – the aid must be used to finance specific expenditures. Morrissey and White (1993) begin their analysis with a simple question: 'What is the value of an amount of aid granted to a country?' To answer this, we need to know the discounted present cash value of the aid, which must be compared to some reference value. Two choices of reference value are common. First, one can compare it to an alternative source of project funding, namely commercial borrowing. Financial flows are officially defined, by the Development Assistance Committee (DAC) of the OECD, as aid if the grant element is at least 25 per cent (the grant element for commercial borrowing being zero). Second, one can compare aid with alternative sources of foreign exchange, in particular: is foreign exchange in the form of a given amount of aid worth more or less than the same amount of foreign exchange in the form of export revenue? We address both types of comparison.

Aid versus Commercial Borrowing

The grant equivalent of an aid flow is its face value less the present value of total repayments (interest and amortization). For a pure grant, the grant equivalent is equal to the face value of the flow. The grant element (G) is:

$$G = (F_A - R_A)/F_A \qquad (1)$$

where F_A = face value of the aid loan or grant, and R_A = present value of repayments. When aid is a pure grant, then $R_A = 0$ and $G = 1$; therefore the grant element is 100 per cent. At the other extreme, a loan with an interest rate equal to the discount rate implies $F_A = R_A$ and $G = 0$. The DAC norm is that the grant element for aid to least developed countries (LLDCs) should be at least 86 per cent over three years; only France failed to achieve this target in 1990 while ten donors reached the 100 per cent level (DAC 1991). The grant element is only the first stage in determining the value of aid. Donors tend to tie or partially tie a significant portion of their aid: only Switzerland, Japan and Sweden can declare half or more of their aid to be formally untied, whereas for five countries less than 15 per cent is untied (DAC 1991). Had the recipient gained additional funds through a commercial loan they would have been able to procure at world prices, which are expected to be lower than tied aid prices. The grant equivalent of the aid should be adjusted accordingly to 'deflate' the face value of the loan by the extent of overpricing. The formula for G thus becomes:

$$G_T = [(P_W/P_D)F_A - R_A]/F_A \quad (2)$$

where G_T is the value of the grant element when aid is tied; P_W the world price for goods procured for the project; and P_D the donor price for goods procured under an aid-financed project. Clearly, $G_T < G$ if $P_W/P_D < 1$; that is, the grant element adjusted for tying will be lower than the unadjusted grant element provided that, as we would expect, the prices paid for aid-financed goods exceed those of the same goods purchased through world markets. For overpricing to be such that the recipient would be better off borrowing on commercial terms and procuring the goods on the world market we require $G_T < 0$ or, from (1) and (2):

$$1 - (P_W/P_D) > G \Rightarrow G_T < 0 \quad (3)$$

Now, define $P = (P_D - P_W)/P_W$, a measure of percentage overpricing, then manipulation with (3) yields $G_T = G - [P/(1 + P)]$ and:

$$[P/(1 + P)] > G \Rightarrow G_T < 0 \quad (4)$$

Considering the DAC norm for G as 0.86 (and noting that this is generally exceeded, at least for LLDCs), then tying would have to increase prices by over 600 per cent if the excess prices were to offset the grant element. This is far in excess of even the upper-bound estimates of the impact of tying on prices. Even the minimum grant element in aid of 25 per cent (and it is rarely this low in practice) implies that tying would have to increase prices by more than 33 per cent to offset the concessionality of aid. This too is greater than empirical estimates of the degree of overpricing due to tying. Tying does reduce the concessional value of aid, but aid remains preferable to commercial loans.

The algebra for the grant element in mixed credits such as ATP differs from that for normal aid. This arises because the aid (F_A) is in the form of a pure grant ($R_A = 0$) and the associated credit (F_C) is at a subsidized rate (R_C). Incorporating tying:

$$G_C = [(P_W/P_D)F - R_C]/F \quad (5)$$

where G_C = grant element in ATP (where $F = F_A + F_C$), and R_C = subsidized repayment stream in ATP, when $R = R_A + R_C$; $R_A = 0$.

Following (4), only if $[P/(1 + P)] > G_C$ will the excess prices due to tying offset the concessionality of mixed credits. From Equation (5) it follows that R_C and F_A/F_C (the terms of the associated non-concessional finance and the aid share of the total flow) are the two factors to quantify in evaluating the 'value for money' of mixed credits.

Aid versus Exports as a Source of Foreign Exchange

Thus far we have considered whether or not the recipient would be better off to borrow the funds commercially rather than accept aid. An alternative source of foreign exchange is of course to export. Aid and exports are not direct substitutes, but they are alternative sources of foreign exchange. Views regarding which alternative is of most benefit can influence policy choices (as indeed can policies pursued influence the benefit of each alternative). In the aid versus trade literature developed by Johnson (1967) and Thirlwall (1976), one dollar of aid is deemed to command resources in excess of the one dollar. The rationale for this view is that in the absence of the foreign exchange (provided through aid) domestic resources would have to be devoted to the (relatively inefficient) production of goods that can now be imported. The aid inflow, F, permits a more efficient reallocation of resources. It is assumed that unit domestic production costs more than the unit price of the goods in the world market, implying an excess cost of import substitution (c, which is positively related to, although not identical to, domestic resource cost). Thus the 'worth' of an aid inflow, allowing for tying and the grant element, is $(1 + c)G_TF$.

The net worth of foreign exchange earned from exports (X) is cX: resources used in the production of export goods must be reallocated from other domestic production but, because of the excess cost of import substitution, these exports command more goods at world prices that if the resources were devoted to producing goods for domestic consumption. The measure cX is the excess of foreign exchange earned from export production over the foreign exchange value of resources used in export production.

For a given amount of foreign exchange ($F = X$), aid will be more valuable than trade if $(1 + c)G_T > c$. Combining with Equation (4), Morrissey and White (1993) present two conditions under which aid is preferred:

1. Aid is preferred to non-concessional borrowing and untied procurement if:

$$G > [P/(1 + P)] \Rightarrow G_T > 0 \tag{6a}$$

2. Aid is preferred to exports as a source of foreign exchange if:

$$G - [P/(1 + P)] > c/(1 + c) => G_T > c/(1 + c) \quad (6b)$$

As $c > 0$, the latter is the stronger condition: a given aid bundle is more likely to be superior to commercial borrowing that it is to exports.

Figure 11.1 illustrates the 1992 position for ATP, where $G = 0.4$ and all ATP is project and procurement tied. The right side of Figure 11.1 shows the value of G_T for $G = 0.4$, given percentage overpricing (P): the curve $G_{0.4}$ is a plot of $G_T = 0.4 - [P/(1 + P)]$, as embodied in equation (6a). Hence, if the grant element ignoring overpricing is 0.4 then, overpricing of 67 per cent (where the $G = 0.4$ curve cuts the horizontal axis, at point M) fully offsets the benefits of tied aid compared to untied non-concessional finance. If overpricing exceeds 67 per cent then $G_T < 0$ and the country should not accept aid. It is easy to show that the higher G then the higher the extent of overpricing must be before aid should be rejected.

In the left-hand segment of Figure 11.1, the curve I illustrates the mapping of c on the horizontal to $c/(1 + c)$ on the vertical (which is also G_T). Aid is preferred to trade if $G_T > c/(1 + c)$, which is the case for points above and to the right of I; trade is preferred to aid for points below and to the left of I (in both cases assuming $P = 0$). Restating the basic condition following equation (6b) as trade is preferred to aid if $G - (P/(1 + P)] < c/(1 + c)$, then even if overpricing were only 10 per cent ($P = 0.1$ in Figure 11.1), a lower-bound

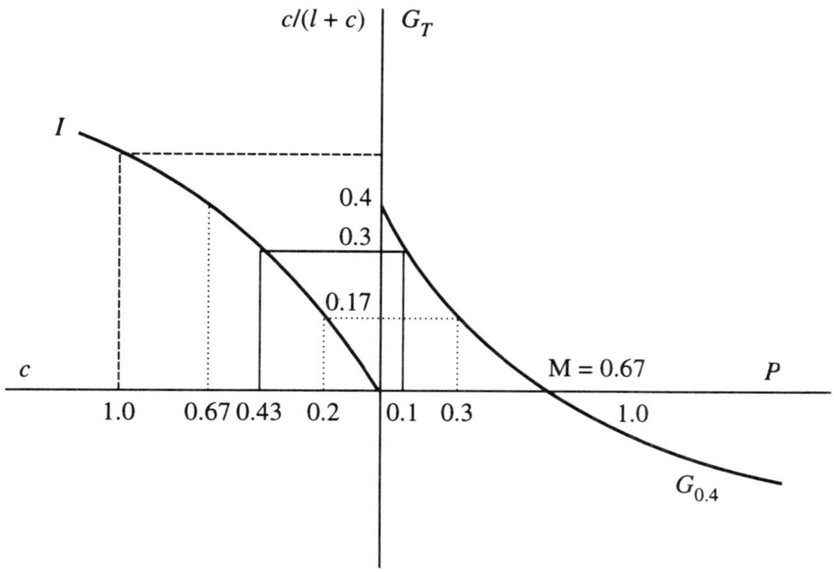

Figure 11.1 Concessionality trade-offs for mixed credits

estimate, c in excess of 0.43, implies trade is to be preferred. Figure 11.1 also illustrates that for overpricing as high as 30 per cent, inefficiency in excess of 0.2 implies trade is preferable to tied aid. Given the empirical estimates of overpricing due to tied aid, which could certainly be in the range 10–20 per cent in the 1980s, we can easily envisage situations where mixed credits would be of less benefit, evaluated as concessionality, than foreign exchange earned through exports.

Our results demonstrate that for mixed credits, overpricing of more than 67 per cent would be required to offset concessionality, which we would not consider typical. Assuming no overpricing, recipient inefficiency in excess of 67 per cent ($c > 0.67$ in Figure 11.1), which is not implausible if protection is high,[1] implies that recipients would benefit more from exports (because resources used in inefficient import-substituting industries are diverted to competitive export industries) than from mixed credits. Assuming overpricing of 10 per cent, recipient inefficiency exceeding 43 per cent would indicate that exports are preferable to aid.[2] It is clear from Figure 11.1 that as overpricing increases, lower values of c will trigger trade being preferred to aid: in general, trade is quite likely to be preferable to mixed credits under plausible assumptions.

EVALUATION OF TIED ATP PROJECTS

When introduced in 1978, the UK's Aid and Trade Provision (ATP) was available principally in the form of mixed credits whereby, according to DAC rules, a given minimum percentage of the offshore value of a project was covered by a cash grant (aid out of the ATP budget) and the remainder was financed by commercial loans (for a review see Morrissey 1991). The DAC guidelines specify the minimum G but not the maximum. Assuming the interest on the commercial loan to be equal to the discount rate, then (ignoring overpricing) the share of grants in the credit is equal to the grant element of the credit in its entirety. This can be demonstrated easily. The overall grant element, G, is a weighted average of the grant element of the loans, G_L, and of grants, G_G:

$$G = wG_L + (1 - w)\, G_G \tag{7}$$

where w is the share of loans in the credit. But $G_G = 1$ by definition and $G_L = 0$, by our assumption that the interest rate equals the discount rate. Hence $G = 1 - w$. There is also a further subsidy to the recipient country because the interest rate charged on G_L is less than the market rate, and therefore less than the discount rate (but data are not available to incorporate this empirically).

The overall grant element in mixed credits has risen steadily from 0.32 in 1988, to 0.35 in 1989 (following the DAC agreement for a higher minimum) and 0.40 in 1992, reflecting the likelihood of the minimum being exceeded for LLDCs (Morrissey and White 1993). In the context of the excess pricing discussed earlier, the increasing value of *G* suggests that ATP mixed credits are of increasingly concessional benefit to recipients. This is a positive trend. However, the analysis of the previous section also shows that tying may reduce the benefit of ATP projects. In principle, aid in an ATP project provides a good, or the inputs which can be used to produce an output, which may be an importable, exportable or non-tradeable. In practice, some 80 per cent of ATP finances capital inputs, mostly plant and engineering machinery, more than half of which are used to produce non-tradeables (such as physical transport and communications infrastructure or power generation and transmission); less than 10 per cent of ATP provides final goods, usually vehicles (Morrissey 1991).

While aid may be granted for an investment project because the recipient faces a savings gap, we shall assume that the binding constraint is a foreign exchange gap. This implies that the benefit of the aid is as a cheaper form of paying for imports than debt; (6a) applies and ATP is preferable to a commercial loan. Were the project output to be an exportable (which is not common), there would be a future benefit in relaxing the foreign exchange gap. In situations where the foreign exchange gap is not binding, domestic welfare requires evaluating aid according to (6b) and the net benefit of aid is less obvious. On the assumption that the foreign exchange gap declines with economic growth, it follows that tied aid is less beneficial to more developed LDCs, although ATP has tended to go to the relatively richer LDCs (Morrissey 1991). Let us now consider a more specific case where tied aid provides the inputs for a project to produce non-tradeable outputs.

The previous section presents only a partial-equilibrium analysis. In a general-equilibrium setting one could envisage other (indirect) effects which alleviate or exacerbate the implied trade-off between aid and trade. For example, assume that the goods procured under tied aid are inputs to the production process. Tying then impacts like an import restriction: the effect is similar to a tariff on inputs, in that it increases prices, but is like a quota as the rents accrue to foreign firms rather than the recipient government. In the absence of a (compensating) output tariff, this would be equivalent to imposing a negative effective tariff on value added in the using sector, which would therefore be less competitive. As much tied aid, especially ATP, goes to infrastructure projects, this would have the effect of increasing the price of non-tradeables (hence a Dutch disease effect). The point is that tying can introduce or increase price and resource allocation distortions in developing countries.

The standard economic justification for aid is to relax a saving and/or foreign exchange gap. In a dynamic setting, aid projects relax the former by funding necessary investment, in which case evaluation is against (6a), and relax the latter by facilitating the production of exportables, in which case (6b) applies. Few aid projects, and very few ATP projects, invest directly in export industries (with the exception of primary commodities) but can relax the foreign exchange gap in two ways. First, by funding infrastructure, they can reduce the necessity for future capital good imports, but tying can increase the price of non-tradeables in the process. Second, the project may produce importables; here the net impact on welfare depends on the relative efficiency of domestic production; the implication of (6b) is that the LDC would be better to reallocate its resources to produce those exportables at which it is relatively efficient. If aid does not support this, and especially if aid reinforces a tendency for relatively inefficient production of importables, its net benefit (concessionality) is reduced and may be eliminated. The simple point is that in evaluating aid projects the potential reduction of concessionality associated with tying should be taken into account.

CONCLUSIONS

We have presented a simple framework to show that while excess tied prices reduce the concessionality of tied aid and mixed credits, the overpricing is unlikely to be so much as to offset the benefits of concessionality. From the recipients' viewpoint, mixed credits are preferable to loans at a market rate but generally less preferable than bilateral aid, even if tied, which has a higher grant element and, other things equal, has greater concessionality. But in addition to aid and commercial borrowing, developing countries have a third possible source of foreign exchange, namely exports. The advantage of exports is assumed to be the diversion of domestic resources away from inefficient import production. We demonstrate that the condition for preferring trade over aid implies that, at quite feasible values for excess pricing, exports may be preferable to associated finance or possibly low-concessional aid. It follows that policies directed towards export orientation are preferable to dependence on associated finance; where tied aid acts against export orientation (in supporting importables rather than exportables) it may act against the long-term interests of LDCs.

In considering ATP projects specifically, which have a lower grant element than other forms of tied aid, another potential problem was introduced regarding non-tradeables. Developing countries need to invest in physical (and human) infrastructure and, when they face a savings gap, aid is justified (and preferable to commercial loans even if tied). However, if prices are higher under tied aid (than under either untied aid or commercial loans, both allowing procurement at world prices) the effect is to increase the (net resource) cost of non-tradeables. This introduces a relative price distortion in the LDC, which may exacerbate existing anti-export bias (due to protection and/or overvaluation). In the context where programme aid, from the World Bank and bilateral donors, is increasingly associated with policy conditions to reverse anti-export bias, it is at least undesirable that project aid may act in the opposite direction. The untying of project aid, which will tend to increase concessionality, would have the general benefit of rendering programme and project aid more consistent in terms of achieving the development aims of aid.

NOTES

1. Recent evidence suggests that in the early 1990s, even after trade policy reforms, average nominal tariffs were about 15 per cent for Latin America: 25 per cent for East Asia; 38 per cent for sub-Saharan Africa; and in excess of 40 per cent for five out of 25 countries listed, three in South Asia (Dean et al. 1994).
2. Given $G = 0.40$, then $P = 0.1$ implies $G_T = 0.30$. It follows that any $c > 0.43$ will lie to the left of I.

REFERENCES

DAC (1991), *Development Co-operation 1991 Report*, Paris: OECD.

Dean, J., S. Desai and J. Riedel (1994), 'Trade Policy Reform in Developing Countries Since 1985: A Review of the Evidence', Washington, DC: Word Bank (mimeo: forthcoming as a Working Paper).

Jepma, C. (1991), *The Tying of Aid*, Paris: OECD.

Jepma, C. (1992), 'EC-Wide Untying', University of Groningen: IDE Paper.

Johnson, H.G. (1967), *Economic Policies Towards Less Developed Countries*, London: Allen and Unwin.

Morrissey, O. (1991), 'An Evaluation of the Economic Effects of the Aid and Trade Provision', *Journal of Development Studies*, **28** (1), 104–29.

Morrissey, O., B. Smith and E. Horesh (1992), *British Aid and International Trade*, Buckingham: Open University Press.

Morrissey, O. and H. White (1993), 'How Concessional is Tied Aid?', University of Nottingham: CREDIT Research Paper 93/13.

Thirlwall, A. (1976), 'When is Trade More Valuable Than Aid?', *Journal of Development Studies*, **13** (1), 35–41.

12. Project failure: the implications of a '25 per cent rule'

John Weiss

INTRODUCTION

For a considerable time international agencies and those professionals working in the projects field have been aware of the simple fact that many projects fail to meet initial expectations and that at present a significant proportion can be said to 'fail' in some sense. This is evidenced by various forms of project completion reports and *ex-post* studies and is reflected at a macroeconomic level in low rates of economic growth despite relatively high investment ratios. In thinking about issues it can be useful to set out arguments by reference to 'stylized facts' that, whilst simplifications of reality, reflect the essential elements of a case. For this chapter we choose to put forward a simple stylized fact that from the portfolio of projects of an international development agency 25 per cent have failed; this is our '25 per cent rule'. We base our case for the existence of such a rule on our personal experience, that of other professionals working in the field and from a reading of project completion reports. To give one example, if we take the *ex-post* studies carried out by the Operations Evaluation Department of the World Bank over the period 1980–90 the proportion of projects classed as 'unsatisfactory' is approximately 25 per cent (World Bank 1991).[1] However the important point is not the precise percentage, which will clearly vary over time and between agencies, but the fact that failures relate to a significant proportion of projects. This stylized fact may help to explain the so called 'micro–macro paradox', referred to frequently in the literature on aid, whereby apparent success at the project or micro level appears to have a very weak impact on macroeconomic performance. Our suggestion is that micro success is perhaps less widespread than is often thought and that weak macro effects may be wholly compatible with project level performance.

In this chapter we try to explore some of the implications of this relatively high 'failure rate'. We begin by considering how, conceptually, failure can be identified; we then consider evidence on sectoral variations in failure rates. Third, we consider different causes for project failure, both internal and external to projects themselves. The new policy environment introduced widely in developing countries through various stabilization and adjustment programmes is meant to address at least some of these issues and we discuss how it may affect project performance.

The final section considers the implications of the earlier discussion for *ex-ante* appraisal techniques, particularly in relation to risk analysis.

MEANING OF PROJECT FAILURE

In theoretical terms the meaning of success and failure at a project level is clear. The conventional *ex-ante* criteria of net present value (NPV) and internal rate of return (IRR) indicators can be applied to actual project data to determine if on the basis of outcomes a project has generated a return that exceeds the opportunity cost of the resources it uses; in other words whether at an appropriate discount rate its *ex-post* NPV is positive or its *ex-post* IRR is above the discount rate. In principle there is an issue as to how the discount rate should be specified, since it can be either an opportunity cost or a social time-preference rate, where the opportunity cost of investment funds is covered by a savings premium. Nonetheless the key point is that a single discount rate should be used for projects from all sectors. This requires that all types of project benefit must be directly comparable; hence there must be a means of converting heterogeneous benefits into a common unit for comparison across sectors.

For traded activities, in principle, there is little difficulty since output values are given by world prices although there may be additional effects relating to externalities or distributional changes that have to be expressed in world price equivalents; well-known problems arise for projects in non-traded sectors, however. In principle, willingness to pay, converted to its equivalent value in units of foreign exchange, provides the measure of output value, so that, for example, willingness to pay by users of a new road can be compared directly with export revenue from a rubber plantation. In practice, there is a widely held view that it is more difficult to capture benefits in some sectors than in others; if, for example, the generated traffic from a new road or the health benefit of a water-supply project are real but largely 'unquantifiable', benefits from projects operating in particular sectors may be systematically underestimated relative to benefits from projects producing largely tangible traded output. This has led to the practice of applying lower discount rates to certain non-traded activities whether in infrastructure or social sectors. If this approach is adopted *ex-ante*, then it is also likely to be applied *ex-post* to judge project success, so that the test applied to a project varies between sectors.

However, it is clear that this operational expedient of using different discount rates for projects from different sectors has no basis in theory, unless one assumes a rigid budget constraint for each sector, so that marginal projects in each sector have different opportunity costs. Under-recording of benefits, which lower discount rates attempt to allow for, need not be related systematically to time, which is what is implied by the use of a lower discount rate, and the problem is best treated directly on the benefit side by attempting to capture the real effects involved. Nonetheless while the theoretical position is clear, because of genuine difficulties on the benefit side caution needs to be exercised in interpreting the results of estimates of 'failure', where *ex-post* NPV or IRR results are compared with a single test rate of discount.

Whilst the standard economist's analysis of project failure assumes that all project effects can be expressed in quantifiable terms and incorporated in *ex-post* calculations of project worth, there is an alternative way into the problem that stems from the increasingly common logical framework approach.[2] Here the initial objectives a project was designed to serve are identified and at the *ex-post* stage the achievement of these objectives can be assessed. Naturally it may be possible to quantify trade-offs implicit in the different objectives and convert a project's contributions to these objectives to a common monetary unit, so that conventional cost–benefit calculations can be applied. However for some, the advantage of the logical framework approach is precisely that it does not attempt to convert potentially complex and diverse effects into a single unit; hence from this perspective failure must be identified on explicitly judgemental grounds, as the non-achievement of specific objectives set out at the *ex-ante* stage of the project.

Finally it is also necessary to comment on a third approach to the problem of 'failure'. This identifies failure, somewhat narrowly, with financial insolvency. It is clear that a project in financial difficulties, that for example cannot repay creditors or meet the wage bill of its workers, will often have failed to contribute adequately to its wider objectives. Nonetheless it is necessary to caution against an automatic equation of financial and wider economic failure. Projects with a poor financial performance can still be economically viable where:

- full economic benefits are not captured by the project itself (for example due to taxes, external effects or forms of control);
- the project is a least -cost means of meeting a specific social objective, such as subsidizing a particular target group;
- the project's costs have a significant tax component.

What is obviously the case is that a project in financial difficulties will require these to be overcome, if it is to continue in operation. The normal recommendation would be that those in the economy who benefit most from a project should contribute most to its financing (unless there are explicit distributional reasons why this is not appropriate) and project financial reform should bear this principle in mind. However, the important general point is that we cannot assume that all projects that have been closed or which have needed major financial restructuring have been 'failures' in the sense of failing to meet economic objectives; many may well have been, but the point is that the link is not automatic.

However, whichever definition of failure is applied, failing projects should be a serious cause for concern; where projects fail in the economist's sense (under our first definition) they result in a misallocation of resources and a lower real income level in the economy as a whole than would otherwise be the case. Even where overall real income is not reduced, which may be the case with projects under our second and third definitions of failure, there will still be problems in terms of target groups not served or distributional and possibly macroeconomic effects, where financial losses have to be covered by higher taxes, government borrowing or some form of private saving. Hence a high failure amongst development projects must be a cause for concern.

EVIDENCE ON PROJECT FAILURE

Our initial assertion is that roughly 25 per cent of projects in the portfolio of international agencies can be said to be failures. Precise checks of the reasonableness of this stylized fact require a detailed examination of project files and an agreed definition of failure. World Bank evidence cited above follows the first of the three approaches we have noted, since *ex-post* IRRs are compared with a single cut-off discount rate of 10 per cent.

Support for our generalization comes from other sources as well. For example Cassen (1986, p. 109) surveys evaluation studies from a number of aid agencies and comes to a broadly similar conclusion that some 65–75 per cent of projects are 'satisfactory', whilst the remainder are 'problematic'. The Food and Agriculture Organization (FAO) experience is surveyed in Edwards (1991) and that of the International Finance Corporation (IFC) in IFC (1989); IFC data suggest an even higher failure rate since, from a sample of 110 projects covered by either completion reports or *ex-post* studies more than 26 per cent had economic returns of zero or less and about 50 per cent had returns below 10 per cent. However this picture is likely to be distorted since the sample seems biased towards problematic projects

However, of almost equal interest is the sectoral distribution of failures; a second stylized fact for which we think there is evidence is that projects in

Table 12.1 Sectoral distribution of unsatisfactory projects 1987–90

Sector	Number of projects	% unsatisfactory
Agriculture	324	44
Transport	105	17
Industry	41	56
Telecommunications	22	9
Power	64	16
Water	55	29
Total	611	35

Source: World Bank (1991, table 2.13).

the infrastructure field in general (including here power, water, telecommunications, roads and ports) have had lower failure rates than projects in the directly productive sectors of industry, mining, agriculture and tourism. In support of this we cite the same World Bank study; Table 12.1 summarizes the distribution of 'unsatisfactory projects' (those with IRRs below 10 per cent) between sectors.

The overall failure rate is rather higher than our 25 per cent because it appears that returns worsened for projects assessed in the second half of the 1980s and the figure we cited earlier is the average for the decade. The sectoral distribution shows a clear tendency for a higher rate of unsatisfactory projects to be found in industry and agriculture; industrial projects in particular appear to have been subject to critical difficulties. Taken at face value these results provide support for what became the conventional emphasis of aid programmes in the 1980s with much new project lending directed towards infrastructure schemes, rather than new productive-sector projects

In part some of this superior performance within infrastructure may be due to a less critical form of *ex-post* assessment being applied to such projects. It may be obvious if productive-sector projects are in difficulties with low capacity working, unsold stocks and mounting debts, for example; it may be less clear, however, that traffic is not using a road or that water-supply capacity is under utilized. Nonetheless it seems unlikely that all the divergence in sector outcomes could be explained as a form of evaluation bias, particularly since the point about under-recording of benefits, noted above, argues for a bias against rather than a bias in favour of infrastructure. Explanations must be speculative; one possibility is that in many countries there had been a long-term decline in the stock of capital assets in the infrastructure sector (roads that needed repair, power plants that needed rehabilitation and so forth) so that there was a strong suppressed demand for these activities; another is that infrastructure activities are less sensitive to their external operating environment than are productive projects and that in general in the 1980s the external environment created serious difficulties for projects in many countries. We elaborate further on this point below as part of a wider discussion on causes of project failure.

CLASSIFICATION OF CAUSES OF PROJECT FAILURE

In simple terms we can think of project failures as arising either from internal (project-specific) causes or from external factors related to the environment in which a project operates; additionally within this latter category we can distinguish between factors relating to the national and international environments faced by a project. Put simply the distinction would be that internal factors are within a project's own control, whilst external factors are not; further national external factors can be influenced by the domestic policies of non-project agents, whilst international external factors are outside the control of national agents and are determined by international forces.

Considering internal factors first, there will be a range of influences on a project's performance stemming from the way it is organized, owned and managed. Generalizing across sectors is difficult because of the different problems that can arise, but we can identify as important influences the incentive structure of a project, the technology used and the project's institutional or organizational structure. Thus projects can fail if they give inadequate incentives to the workers, managers, suppliers or other project participants; alternatively they may fail if workers, managers or other participants cannot master the technology involved; finally failure can arise where the organizational structure is inadequate and appropriate managerial control cannot be exercised. There is a whole set of issues lying behind these points and these factors may well be interrelated, so that their presence becomes a characteristic of, as much as an explanation for, a poorly run failing project.

The external project environment can be of major significance; however it needs to be viewed at different levels. What we term the national level relates to conditions within both the sector in which a project is located and the national economy. The national environment relates to issues like pricing policy, the control exercised by sponsoring ministries over parastatal projects, the internal market, the availability of inputs, whether local or imported, the exchange rate and the cost of domestic finance; the external environment relates to factors like external demand for project outputs, the price and availability of imports and international interest rates. Hence projects may fail where national policies are inappropriate, for example with tight bureaucratic controls that stifle managerial initiative, or with an overvalued exchange rate

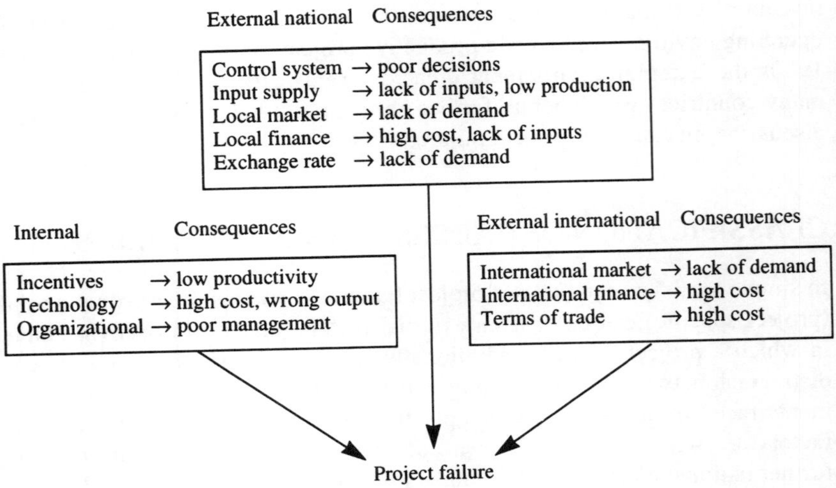

Figure 12.1 Cause of project failure

that prevents the growth of new exports; alternatively international factors over which the economy has little or no control, such as declining export prices or rising interest rates on foreign loans can cause serious difficulties. Figure 12.1 gives a schematic representation of the different factors.

In terms of the distinction raised earlier regarding infrastructure and productive sector projects, generalization across such a wide range of activities is potentially misleading; however there may be some validity in the argument that in the 1980s infrastructure projects were less prone to the negative influence of factors arising from a hostile external environment, particularly at the international level. As predominantly non-traded activities, their demand will be affected only indirectly by exchange rates or by international income changes and they are clearly not subject to international price fluctuations on the output side, although movements in input prices, particularly for energy products, can be important.

POLICY CHANGE TO ADDRESS PROJECT FAILURE

Policy within the majority of developing countries underwent a major shift during the 1980s. In part this reflected a need to remove serious macroeconomic imbalances – the so-called stabilization side of reform; in part also various supply-side measures, now conventionally labelled adjustment policies, attempted to alter the behaviour of domestic agents in a way that creates a more efficient use of resources and an acceptable long-run rate of growth. Taking these dimensions in turn, in principle, both should help to address problems of project failure. First, stabilization is meant to stabilize the macro-economic environment, which is part of the national external environment we have identified. The goal is stable and realistic real exchange rates and interest rates that allow an efficient allocation of foreign exchange and domestic credit; hence demand-side problems for projects created by overvalued local currencies, and supply-side problems arising from shortages of foreign exchange for productive inputs and financial difficulties created by fluctuating and nominally high interest rates are to be addressed by improved economic management; further, to the extent that stabilization is accompanied by a revival of economic growth, projects serving the domestic market will see a more favourable demand situation. In reforming the price system stabilization and adjustment programmes have also attempted to address the problem of economic distortions that so concerned those working on project appraisal in the 1970s and early 1980s. Overvalued exchange rates, high and varied trade taxes and controls on wage and interest rates were held to give profoundly incorrect price signals to enterprises; this meant that what might make sense for the enterprise in profit terms need not be economically desirable. Hence the possibility of economic failure in apparently profitable enterprises and the reverse situation noted above of financially unprofitable but economically viable projects.

Perhaps even more fundamental are the attempts to change the way in which enterprises operate with a view to addressing some of the internal problems of project management. Crucial here are attempts to decentralize decision taking for parastatals, so that government ministries no longer attempt to direct and control parastatals as offshoots of civil service departments. In an environment in which parastatals are granted greater freedom to set prices and decide production it is expected that some of the problems of project institutional structure will be overcome; further, where projects are no longer bound by civil service pay scales or by government controls on the prices they can offer customers, the expectation is that the problem of lack of adequate incentives will be addressed. Privatization has also emerged as a strategy to overcome managerial failings within the public sector, although it is misleadingly simplistic to assume that internal problems are related only to public-sector projects.

For private-sector projects the main mechanism for overcoming internal failings is the so-called 'enabling environment'; this requires the removal of the most intrusive of the controls on private sector activity (for example price ceilings for sales or import licences to access foreign goods) combined with the general programmes of market liberalization relating to interest and exchange rates and trade policy, in particular. Where private firms face a more competitive market environment due, for example, to the removal of barriers to foreign trade or the ending of directed credit programmes for the domestic banking sector, the expectation is that internal managerial shortcomings will have to be reduced if firms are to survive.

Project appraisal techniques, rather than go out of favour, have seen something of resurgence; for example a number of adjustment programmes have had training components aimed specifically at strengthening the capacity of the banking sector to appraise loan requests. The procedural change from previous emphases is that now it is the banking sector, whether the central bank, development banks or commercial banks, that is to scrutinize loans; this is in contrast with the earlier focus on government ministries whose planning staff would examine the validity of investment proposals from enterprises. However in the new environment the expectation is that the 'first-order distortions' relating to exchange rates, interest and wage rates will be largely removed, so that the shadow-pricing adjustments that dominated discussions of economic analysis for projects in developing countries in the 1970s and early 1980s will become less significant.

However, whilst there is a direct link between the new thrust of policy in many developing countries and measures to reduce project failure, there are several reasons why, in the short term at least, it may be difficult to reduce the failure rate on aid-financed projects much below the 25 per cent norm we have identified from past experience. First, the ultimate success of the conventional stabilization and adjustment package in raising long-run growth remains controversial. Considerable ingenuity has gone into means of demonstrating that economies introducing such measures have done better than countries in similar initial difficulties that did not go down this path; the result has been largely inconclusive with at best the identification of a few successes and rather more ambiguous cases. A very detailed example of this type of exercise is the World Bank study on Sub-Saharan Africa (World Bank 1994). Hence if the policy path on which many countries have embarked fails to deliver a more stable domestic macroeconomic environment the problems that we identify under the external–national heading may not diminish substantially.

Second, relatively high failure rates are in one sense expected from market-oriented production systems; if competition is to be a driving force for economic change in a process of 'creative destruction', some producers will fail as a natural concomitant of the success of others. The relatively high 'death rates' amongst small and medium enterprises in developed economies are evidence of this.

Third, an important set of causes of project failure remains outside the reform agenda; these are the external international factors we have identified. Many of the low-income developing countries suffered seriously from terms of trade movements in the 1980s, as world prices of several primary commodities in either processed or unprocessed form declined substantially. Projects exporting rubber, cocoa and sugar, for example, all saw major declines in export revenues that no doubt contributed to the failure of many projects of this type. The shift to a greater export orientation has been very widespread amongst developing countries and there are well-known reasons to justify this, relating to foreign exchange constraints on growth and the negative incentive effects created by a trade system based on tight import controls. However, it is important to stress that at the project level an export orientation is in no sense a guarantee of success. Successful export growth for manufactures and other non-traditional products requires a focus on product quality and the establishment of adequate marketing links; for primary exports it requires a specialization in products whose price trend is in a favourable direction. A shift in the investment portfolio towards a greater export orientation magnifies the risk of failure due to unfavourable external international factors; however, equally it may serve to reduce internal inefficiency within firms and thus reduce some of the causes of internal failure. Hence the net effect will be ambiguous and will vary between cases.

Finally, there is a class of project for which many of our earlier comments may be inappropriate. These are social-sector projects, for example in health or education sectors; critics of conventional adjustment assert that this type of project is particularly vulnerable under adjustment programmes, because the financial restrictions imposed on government activity, on the grounds of macroeconomic balance, starve this type of non-revenue-generating project of funds, regardless of whether the rhetoric of reform acknowledges the importance of social priorities. In a number of countries there has been considerable discussion of introducing charges for use of schools and hospitals to allow a higher proportion of revenue to be raised from users rather than from general taxation. It remains an open question how far such charges are in fact compatible with the long-run success of such projects, where here we define success in the logical framework sense of providing services to a particular target group, since the charges may simply ration many of the target users out of the market. Hence arguably it is by no means obvious that conventional adjustment programmes, as currently implemented, are compatible with the long-run success of certain types of non-revenue-generating project.

EX-ANTE APPRAISALS: WHERE THE 25 PER CENT RULE CONTINUES TO APPLY

Our argument is that it is unrealistic to expect the new reform programmes, even if they work effectively in their own terms, to remove the general validity of our stylized fact that a significant proportion of new projects, even those subject to the relatively close scrutiny of aid donors, will fail in at least one of the senses in which we define failure above. Naturally there is nothing inevitable here, in that 25 per cent can become 20 per cent or 15 per cent over time. However reality suggests that *ex-ante* appraisals must address the point that things can go seriously wrong for a significant proportion of projects. What does this imply for *ex-ante* project work? The issue relates primarily to what can be done to address 'appraisal optimism' – the phenomenon which appears to dictate that for a high proportion of projects assumptions made at appraisal are more optimistic than actual outcomes. For international agencies the reasons are familiar, with pressure to disburse loans sometimes overriding critical judgements. Apart from a stress on realism in assumptions adopted, can anything else be done? The standard technique of sensitivity analysis is only a partial solution if its application simply becomes routine, so that the effect of changes in a few key parameters (typically 10 per cent either way) on project viability is assessed. This type of application is only helpful if the implications of the results of sensitivity calculations are addressed to ensure that problematic changes do not in fact occur.

One way around the problem, which has been discussed extensively in the literature over the years, is to adjust the discount rate applied to projects to allow for risk of failure; in others words to place a risk premium on the discount rate that becomes higher than would otherwise be the case. The theoretical flaws with this procedure are well known; essentially the case against it is that there is no reason to believe that risk of failure rises exponentially over time, which is what is implied by a higher discount rate; so that by raising the discount rate to adjust for risk the choice between projects with different time profiles of net benefits is distorted.

Potentially more fruitful is the application of risk analysis techniques, which allow a focus on individual project parameters that may be subject to risk. Such techniques have become considerably more accessible in recent years due to the development of microcomputers.[3] They have the well-known advantages of allowing changes in many or all project variables at the same time and of presenting results in terms of a probability distribution of measures of project worth; so that we will know that there is an x per cent probability of a project IRR being below 10 per cent, for example. Alternatively project results can be presented on the basis of confidence intervals, so that for example there may be a 90 per cent probability that the IRR lies within a certain range of the initial 'best-estimate' figure. There are undoubted difficulties of application relating to the specification of probability distributions of values for key variables and for possible correlation between changes in key variables; however, in situations in which a significant proportion of projects will fail, for one reason or another, it may be of interest to have project results summarized in terms of an estimated probability of failure.

The key issue is whether the inherent riskiness of a project should influence decision taking. If uncertainty and the risk of failure are ignored the conventional criteria of acceptance are based on a comparison of single values for a project's NPV and IRR with the test discount rate. With uncertainty, in principle, a similar procedure can be applied by reducing uncertain benefits and costs to 'certainty equivalents' and comparing the NPV and IRR measures derived from these with a single discount rate. In this adjustment the risk of project failure can be allowed for by applying a risk-aversion parameter which places different weights on income, not on the basis of time (as in the discount factor), but in relation to the condition or state in which income is received; in other words income received at a time of economic depression will have a higher value than income received at a time of prosperity. This weight is totally independent of distributional considerations and reflects attitude to risk. In principle such weights can differ between decision takers.[4]

A convenient assumption is that for public-sector projects risk-aversion parameters are not relevant, since risks will be pooled over large numbers of individuals and projects.[5] It is well known that this is not inevitably a valid procedure, however, where projects are large relative to total economic activity and where returns are procyclical, so that a project would be in difficulties at the same time as other projects. There is a strong case for not accepting such non-marginal projects, if their probability of failure is above the average probability for other projects in the portfolio. In such a situation a risk calculation will be useful to establish whether such large projects add to the risks inherent in normal project activity. In addition the risk-pooling argument assumes that particular groups are not affected disproportionately by any projects. Thus losses on one project will be offset by gains on another for all relevant categories of project beneficiary. This is clearly a simplification, particularly in relation to the project's external effects. Thus conceptually it is by no means clear that the risk-pooling argument removes the need to consider the variability of project returns on government-related projects.

In practice calculation of certainty equivalent benefits and costs using a numerical weight to capture risk aversion is rarely, if ever, attempted. However in some instances use is made of risk-analysis calculations, which present results in terms of a probability distribution of IRR or NPV outcomes, and this approach should be considered for wider use.

Risk calculations can be conducted at different levels of detail. In the simplest form the analysis uses no more data than those required for a sensitivity analysis, except that all key variables are allowed to vary simultaneously within a specified range with equal probability of occurrence within that range.[6] A fuller analysis allows for different probability distributions for variables and for the possibility of correlation between them. The key difficulty is in identifying appropriate probabilities for key project variables; the two basic alternatives are to rely on 'expert opinion' or past data where reasonably long time series of observations are available. The latter approach has a particular relevance for primary commodity producing projects, which have been rendered high-risk by international commodity price fluctuations.

The comparison between a decision informed by a risk analysis and the conventional treatment is illustrated in Figure 12.2. OQ shows the combinations of expected IRRs and risk, defined as the probability of a return below a risk free test rate of 10 per cent, for a set of projects. It is drawn rising so that higher expected returns are associated with greater probability of failure. If risk is not considered only projects that achieve a 10 per cent return or more are acceptable. However, if risk is incorporated in the assessment the information on the horizontal axis must be used; hence as shown, a project with an expected return of 12 per cent might not be acceptable if its probability of failure, at 25 per cent, is judged by the appropriate decision taker to be too high.

Operationalizing this approach requires someone to determine an acceptable risk level. If aid funds are involved with private projects there will be a tendency to allow private investors to make their own judgements, which occurs anyway regardless of whether a formal risk calculation is carried out. In principle, if an acceptable risk level is to be identified, like the opportunity cost of capital, it should be a country-specific parameter. However as rules of thumb rather than precise calculations tend to predominate in operational

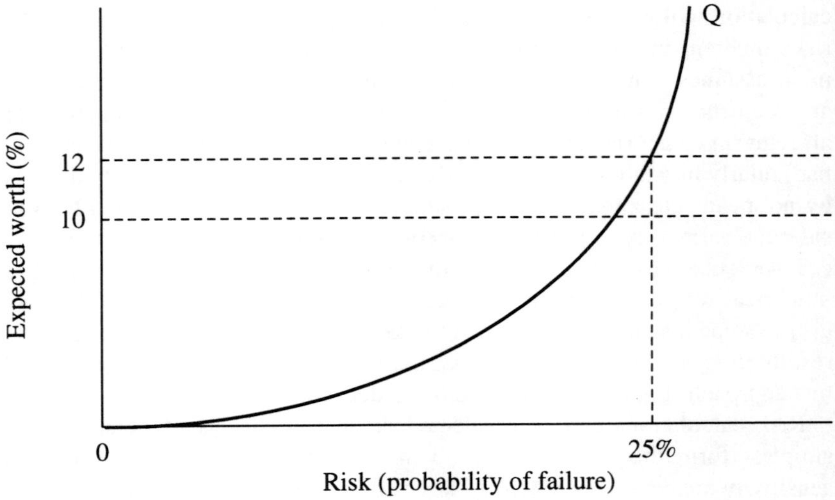

Figure 12.2 Decision criteria with risk

work, there is a case for using the average failure rate on an agency's existing programme, whether 25 per cent or another figure, as the minimum acceptable risk level for large non-marginal projects.[7]

Our conclusion is not that a full risk analysis should be carried out as a normal procedure for all projects; this would certainly be 'overkill'. We argue that it has a role as a means of coping with the problem of project failure, in certain well-defined non-marginal situations, where projects are large, prone to risk and there is adequate information on which to base judgements relating to probabilities for different parameters. In addition simpler risk calculations can provide additional information to that derived from sensitivity analysis at little or no extra effort and cost.

Aside from this modest addition to their toolkit, what other ways have project analysts for coping with what we know are high failure rates? Realism in assumptions about technical, managerial and external factors is obviously important, as is appropriate use of sensitivity analysis to inform on what needs to be strengthened if unfavourable outcomes are to be avoided. Apart from this, the removal of major macroeconomic distortions in many countries has meant that economists can shift their attention away from shadow-pricing adjustments to issues relating to markets, benefit valuation for non-traded sectors (like health, housing, water, transport and power) and externalities. All of these pose complex and serious issues for *ex-ante* work and there is a significant agenda here for research that will, we hope, lead to further operational refinements and lower failure rates.

NOTES

1. An overview of World Bank experience is the well-known Wapenhans report (World Bank 1992).
2. On the logical framework, see Wiggins and Shields (1995) and MacArthur (Chapter 9, this volume).
3. Savvides (1994) introduces risk analysis and discusses a computer programme that attempts to overcome the problem of correlation between variables.
4. Following Bierman and Smidt (1988; pp. 403–4), formally the certainty equivalent return is

$$CEr = r(s).p(s).a(s)$$

where CEr is the certainty equivalent return, $r(s)$ is the return in state s, $p(s)$ is the probability of s occurring, $a(s)$ is the risk adjustment factor for state s. However, different projects will have different distributions of possible returns and their variance gives a measure of project-specific risk. Hence formally project risk can be measured by $\text{VAR}r = (r - \hat{r})^2$ where $\text{VAR}r$ is the variance of project returns and $\hat{r}$ is the expected value of returns; thus for all s:

$$\text{VAR}_r = (r(s) - \hat{r})^2\, ps.$$

5. This is often described technically as the Arrow–Lind theorem. For projects involving governments, where risk adjustments are ignored on the grounds that risks can be pooled across society, a = 1.0 for all possible states or conditions: this simplifies *CEr* to the conventional expected value calculation. For a textbook discussion of the theorem and its limitations see Pearce and Nash (1981, pp. 74–7).
6. In a very useful paper Clarke and Low (1993) show how this simple form of risk analysis can be applied in a LOTUS spreadsheet. Its main limitations are that it assumes a rectangular probability distribution and zero correlation for all variables .
7. The ODA have been thinking along similar lines and have issued a guidance note which suggests that a simple form of risk analysis be carried out and that a 30 per cent probability of failure should be a cut-off point; with risk at this level project design should be reconsidered as a means of increasing the chance of success. In effect this is a '30 per cent rule'. I am grateful to John Roberts of ODA for drawing this point to my attention.

REFERENCES

Bierman, H. and S. Smidt (1988), *The Capital Budgeting Decision*, New York: Macmillan.

Cassen, R. and Associates (1986), *Does Aid Work*? Oxford: Clarendon Press.

Clarke, R. and A. Low (1993), 'Risk Analysis in Project Planning: a simple spreadsheet application using Monte-Carlo techniques', *Project Appraisal*, **8** (3).

Edwards, D. (1991), 'Improving Agricultural Project Design' in C. Kirkpatrick (ed.), *Project Rehabilitation in Developing Countries*, London: Routledge.

IFC (1989), 'The Development Contribution to IFC Operations', Discussion Paper no. 5, Economics Department, International Finance Corporation, Washington DC.

Pearce, D. and C. Nash (1981), *The Social Appraisal of Projects: a text in cost–benefit analysis*, London: Macmillan.

Savvides, S. (1994), 'Risk analysis in investment appraisal', *Project Appraisal*, **9** (1).

Wiggins, S. and D. Shields (1995), 'Innovation in the practice of planning agricultural and rural projects clarifying the logical framework', *Project Appraisal*, **10** (1).

World Bank (1991), *Annual Review of Evaluation Results*, Washington, DC: World Bank Operations Evaluation Department.

World Bank (1992), *Effective Implementation: Key to Development Impact*, Washington, DC: Portfolio Management Task Force.

World Bank (1994), *Adjustment in Africa: Reforms, Results and the Road Ahead*, New York: Oxford University Press for the World Bank.

PART FOUR

Practical Applications

13. Analysis of water-supply projects in practice*

Serge-Arno Klümper

AMBITIOUS GOALS – UNSATISFACTORY RESULTS

Access to clean water for all has been an outstanding goal since the 'water-supply and sanitation decade' of the 1980s. Significant investments have gone into the sector to reach that goal. In the Mediterranean, for example, a region known for its low renewable water resources, water investments have typically accounted for 10–20 per cent of public sector investment, equivalent to perhaps 2–4 per cent of GNP.

Yet, despite the considerable investments allocated to water supply, not only have we so far failed to reach the goals set, but rising demand for fresh water has generated new problems:

- Millions of people in developing countries still face daily problems in obtaining water for domestic use.
- The cost of new water supplies is continuously rising, a cubic metre of water provided by 'the next project' being in some cases two to three times more expensive than that of current supplies.
- Many public water utilities are unable to guarantee a reliable service delivery, because of a lack of revenue.
- Deteriorating water quality is becoming an increasingly serious issue in many places.
- Last but not least, competition over water for alternative uses is getting more severe and often leads to conflicts.

Why is this?

Apparently the disappointing results do not stem from an insufficient level of investment in the water sector. Rather it is the quality, the efficiency of these

*The opinions and conclusions expressed in this chapter are those of the author and do not necessarily reflect the position of the European Investment Bank.

investments which has to be blamed. Given that the decision to invest in a particular water project is based somehow on a more or less thorough assessment of the project, something must be wrong with the way most investments in water-supply expansion tend to be appraised. In order to identify those weaknesses, I shall briefly review the main characteristics of the traditional approach to water-project analysis.

TRADITIONAL APPROACH TO WATER-PROJECT ANALYSIS

In most cases the analysis only tries to demonstrate that the project under review is the least-cost solution to meet assumed 'requirements', taken as given, without going any further. The question of whether the project is worth financing as a whole, i.e. whether the additional supply is really needed or not, is not addressed.

Sometimes a financial internal rate of return (FIRR) is calculated and compared to the opportunity cost of capital. Alternatively, the average incremental cost (AIC) is computed and set against the prevailing or the projected tariff. Where the FIRR is higher than the opportunity cost of capital or the AIC lower than the tariff, it can be said without further analysis that the water investment is not only financially viable but economically justified, based on the assumption that the economic benefits of the project are at least as high as the financial ones.

Unfortunately, in practice this happens to be the case only for a small percentage of water projects; most are not financially viable. Whenever the condition is not met, the analyses tend to refer to non-quantified benefits for additional justification. But it cannot be assessed whether, if quantified, those benefits would have made the projects economically viable. It only indicates how high the non-quantified benefits ought to be. Another approach uses the AIC to value the additional supply. However, without properly taking the matching tariff increase into account in the analysis of demand, one ends up justifying any supply expansion.

In the rare cases where a full economic analysis is attempted the value of the consumer surplus is often estimated in an inconsistent way. Generally this is due to insufficient knowledge of the 'without-project' situation, where unconnected households' water consumption tends to be met from a variety of sources (Lovei 1992).

In all cases, water demand, determined by requirements, is almost invariably taken as given. Demand is either extrapolated from past trends or projected based on a normative per capita requirement and population growth. No account is taken of the factors that drive water demand, e.g. the price of water. Accordingly, project revenues are obtained by estimating water sales independently and multiplying that by the projected tariff.

Further average incremental cost estimates are not systematically used to assess current tariffs and propose necessary adjustments.

If we look for the rationale underlying this approach we find a set of assumptions which are increasingly questioned on the grounds of empirical evidence.

REVISING SOME ASSUMPTIONS

Demand vs Requirements

One of the most misleading concepts is that of water requirements or needs. It is still widely referred to when designing water-distribution systems. Statements like 'the per capita consumption of x litres per day is too low' are commonly used to justify water-supply expansion. In some cases, current consumption levels are not even known precisely and additional investments are simply based on assumed consumption 'standards' of an increasing population.

The problem with these standards deriving from the well-known 'basic needs' approach is that they can only concern, if at all, a minor fraction of total water consumption. Basic requirements for human survival, i.e. for drinking, are very low. They are generally admitted to lie in the range between 3 and 6 litres per capita and per day. Consumption which goes beyond that amount varies enormously from one setting to another. In fact, beyond requirements for drinking, the level of water consumption is determined, as for any other commodity, by a great number of factors, of which the most important are:

- *The socioeconomic and demographic characteristics of the household*, including level of income and assets, education of family members, occupation, size and composition of family, etc.
- *The service level and quality* (individual connections, standpipes, continuous or intermittent supplies, metered or unmetered connections).
- *The price of water*, both financial and in terms of time required to collect it.

Given that water demand is not fixed, but endogenously determined by a number of factors, and given also that there can be more or fewer losses of water on its way from the source to the final consumer, gross figures of *per capita availability* of water for regions or countries do not make much sense, either. Fixing a minimum needed amount of water, like the 500 cubic metres per capita per year claimed by some authors, overlooks the many possible adjustment mechanisms, which include reduction of losses, recycling, reduction in agricultural use, changes in consumer behaviour, investments in new water-saving technology and the like. Neither does it take into account other non-conventional sources of supply (e.g. desalination of sea water, water imports).

Response to Price

Among the various factors that determine water demand, price stands out as a particular important one, due to its potential contribution to a more efficient allocation of water. Basic consumer-demand theory (and common sense) suggests that the quantity of water consumed varies inversely with the price of water, following a downward-sloping demand curve. So increasing the price would, all other factors aside, reduce water consumption, thus improving water conservation. However, whether this potential can be effectively tapped or not crucially depends on the degree of responsiveness of changes in quantity demanded to changes in price. A convenient measure of this response is the price elasticity of demand.[1]

The traditional view is that water, being an absolute necessity in domestic use, has a fixed unit consumption and does not react to price changes. Price elasticity of water demand is assumed to be almost zero. The historical legacy of very low charges in many countries, which leads consumers to disregard water as a noticeable cost, lent support to this assumption (Winpenny 1994). On these premises, tariffs cannot be used as a mean of rationing demand.

However, this view is increasingly challenged by substantial empirical evidence that price elasticity of demand for water is significantly greater than

Table 13.1 Estimation of price elasticities

Price elasticity of demand	Region	Study
–0.5	Selected countries	Martin and Thomas (1986)
–0.3 to –0.7	Developed countries	Bhatia et al (1993)
–0.2 to –0.8	Developing countries	Al Quanaibet and Johnston (1985)
–0.7	Zimbabwe	World Bank (1993)
–0.4	Kenya	World Bank (1993)
–1.5	India	World Bank (1993)
–0.7	Brazil	World Bank (1993)
–0.7	Pakistan	World Bank (1993)

zero. Table 13.1 gives some recent estimates of this relationship. Based on these results and others it seems wise to adopt an educated guess for the price elasticity of demand for water in the range of –0.2 to –0.8. Failure to do so would lead to highly questionable results, particularly if, for instance, a real tariff increase is expected.

The Value of Water

In an attempt to justify water projects which are not financially viable, reference is often made to the alleged existence of substantial, health-related positive externalities, not captured by the willingness to pay (WTP) of the user. Because they are declared difficult or impossible to assess, no attempt is made to quantify them.

The argument goes as follows: observed WTP would understate the real value to society of additional water supply, because only health benefits known to users would be reflected in their WTP. This would leave two kinds of 'external' benefits unaccounted for: those unknown to users; and benefits to others through reduced disease transmission. Given that these are difficult to quantify, they would simply be assumed to be big enough to justify the investment.

However, regarding the first, experience suggests that health benefits will not materialize, and thus not be relevant, unless consumers understand the relationship between water and health and use water properly. As to the second point, people most affected by disease transmission are those living in the same household and probably their benefits are reflected in consumers' WTP (Lovei 1992).

Other 'additional' benefits often put forward in favour of a water project include: time savings because water would be carried over shorter distances, and fuel cost savings because less boiling would be required. Since these benefits are usually the reason why consumers might be willing to pay for piped water in the first place, adding them to the WTP would lead to double counting (Lovei 1992).

This leaves us with consumers' WTP for water as the main benefit of a water supply project. It comprises most of the expected benefits. It is easy to quantify, provided some research is done on the without-project situation. And it is usually quite high. Whenever the WTP was observed or inferred from surveys, it was found to be considerably higher than the prevailing tariff and the full economic cost of supply.

Revising these assumptions has led to a new approach in the analysis of water-supply projects which is much wider in scope and puts more weight on the efficient allocation of water.

NEW APPROACH TO WATER-PROJECT ANALYSIS

Instead of looking for the most cost-effective way of satisfying assumed needs, the needs themselves are now questioned and analysed. Is the size and the timing of the investment right or is it oversized or premature? Would it be possible to postpone the investment by taking appropriate measures to better manage demand? Is the project viable, i.e. will sales eventually cover capital and current costs of the investment? Given shortage of funds, is the ranking of projects the right one?

In order to answer these questions the new approach to the economic analysis of water-supply projects goes well beyond a simple least-cost analysis. It comprises a demand forecast, an assessment of the relevant water balances, a full CBA and a comparison of water tariffs with marginal cost of supply.

To illustrate these different steps, reference is made to a potable and industrial water-supply project recently financed by the European Investment Bank (EIB). It concerns the extension of the water-supply network in six locations affecting about 3 .7 million inhabitants in a Mediterranean country. Capacity increases by 36 per cent. The goal of the extension is more to connect a larger number of people to the network than to lead to an increase in consumption per capita.

Demand Analysis

Demand analysis is the first step, whose obvious objective is to assess future demand. Simple extrapolation of past trends is inappropriate because it fails to take into account the impact of the various factors affecting demand. Wherever enough statistical data are available, forecasts are therefore based on explanatory methods linking per capita water demand to these factors, the most important of which are: real per capita income, real tariff, and composition of customers. Standard simple or multiple regression analysis can generally provide good estimates of the relevant parameters.

The case study is a good example of how responsive water demand is to price. Since 1981 tariffs have been steadily increased, now being about 2.5 times higher in real terms than in 1980. At the same time per capita consumption has decreased markedly, despite a rise in per capita income. On the basis of historical time-series data a number of regressions were run and finally the following elasticity coefficients were retained:

- income elasticity: 0.5
- price elasticity: –0.5
- elasticity of per capita demand with respect to network expansion: –0.01

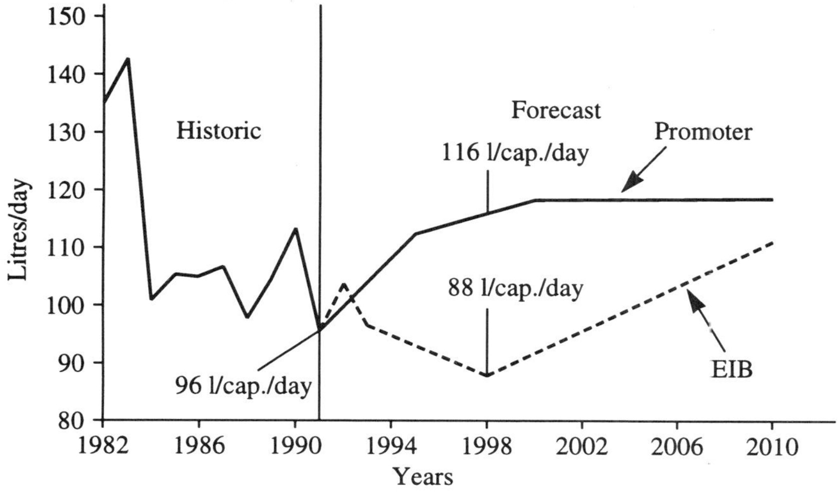

Figure 13.1 Forecast of per capita demand

For the project in question we found that the water demand projections of the promoter were too optimistic as they were based on the extrapolation of the long-term past trend (see Figure 13.1) and did not take into account recent and projected increases in tariff. Our analysis shows a much slower growth and in fact a fall in consumption per head for the first years of the forecast period, corresponding to the impact of recent and projected tariff increases.

Assessment of Water Balances

Once per capita demand has been estimated, required production, the relevant variable for the next step, is easily obtained by aggregating over served/connected population, though due attention must be given to the impact of any expected reduction in physical losses.[2] Comparing demand (required production) to present (without-project) and future (with-project) capacity allows us to assess how water balances, i.e. the difference between demand and supply, evolve over time in both cases.

Figure 13.2 gives a schematic view of the most important concepts. In the without-project situation a deficit to be covered appears from 'first year of deficit'. The project leads to a step increase in capacity which allows the deficit to be satisfied up to a point ('first year of deficit with project') after which demand would have to be rationed until new capacity was provided. Two points are worth emphasizing here. First, additional capacity should

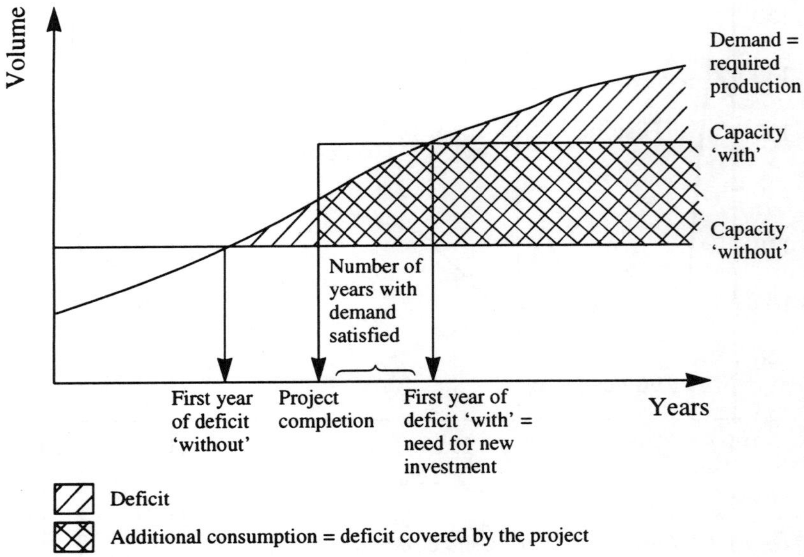

Figure 13.2 Water balance – additional consumption

not be confused with additional consumption. Whereas the former is given by the technical characteristics of the investment, the latter is variable depending on water demand, and can be much lower in case demand has been overestimated. In the figure the dark shaded area represents the additional consumption made possible by the project. Another point highlighted by the diagram is the period during which demand is satisfied by the project (number of years with demand satisfied). This will depend on the trend of demand relative to the capacity of the project. The faster the growth of demand the earlier the date at which a new deficit will arise in the with-project situation and new investments would be necessary. Hence, this stage of the analysis is important for two reasons: it allows us, first, to assess whether the proposed *timing* of an investment is realistic and, second, to determine whether the *sizing* of a project is well adapted to the expected development of demand. Less costly alternative solutions can thus be identified.

For the project in hand Table 13.2 summarizes the results of this stage of the analysis. For each scheme we have the increase in capacity as a result of the project, the rate of increase in water production required to satisfy demand, the first year of deficit without the project and the year until which the project will be able to satisfy additional demand. Notice that in one case – scheme 6 – the first year of deficit without the project is 1999. That means

Table 13.2 Water balance result

	Scheme 1	Scheme 2	Scheme 3	Scheme 4	Scheme 5	Scheme 6
Additional capacity (in %)	25	35	1000	60	50	76
Required production growth rate (in %)	4.5	3.4	5.0	3.8	3.4	3.9
First year of deficit without project	1992	1994	1992	1992	1993	1999
First year of deficit with project	2000	2003	2013	1999	2009	2012
Number of years with demand satisfied	8	9	21	7	16	13

that this component of the project is premature and could be delayed for a few years without giving rise to unsatisfied demand.

Cost–Benefit Analysis

However, to be in a position to accept or reject a project, the additional consumption has to be valued and compared to the cost. This is done by means of CBA.

In a first approximation the additional volume of water consumed yearly over the lifetime of the project can be valued with the water tariff. Subtracting the cost stream yields the net financial cash flow of the project Since the economic rate of return (ERR) is generally at least as high as the financial internal rate of return (FIRR), the project is justified if the FIRR is not less than the opportunity cost of capital or if the net present value of the cash flow is positive.

If we apply this approach to the project at hand, only the schemes 2, 4 and 6 appear to be economically justified. For the others ERRs are extremely low and in two cases are negative.

Does this mean that the other schemes are not justified? Certainly not. While this simplified approach provides a cost-effective way of quickly identifying viable projects, it cannot be used to reject a project, given that the financial revenue stream only provides a lower bound for the expected economic benefits. Nor is it appropriate if an order of priority has to be assigned to a set of possible projects. In these cases it is necessary to complement the simplified approach by taking into account the true WTP of the households that will benefit from the project.

Where incremental supply aims merely at satisfying increased demand of already connected households this does not make much difference. The WTP of those consumers for the additional water supply will be close to the additional water bill.[3] But wherever previously unconnected customers are to be served with piped water (probably the rule in most developing countries) economic benefits might be much higher than additional financial revenues.

This is mainly due to the high WTP of unconnected households. When piped water is not available, people usually rely on a variety of water sources like vendors, wells, rivers, ponds, springs and rainwater. Both the quality and the price of water from these sources are different, and each source serves different needs. The failure to take these sources into account amounts to assuming that the without-project consumption of these customers is zero, which is clearly unrealistic.

To illustrate this point, consider scheme 3 (see Table 13.3). Only 37 per cent of households are connected to the potable water network. The remainder get their water from vendors and wells and their consumption per head is

Table 13.3 The willingness to pay of unconnected households (connection rate 37%)

	Connected household	Unconnected household
Specific consumption	66 l/cap/day	40 l/cap/day
Source of supply	Piped water	Well, spring or oued 60% → 1.39 ECU/m^3 Water vendors 40% → 4.63 ECU/m^3
Price/cost	0.37 ECU/m^3	2.68 ECU/m^3

much lower. The water tariff paid by connected households is 0.37 ECU/m^3, while the price paid by non-connected households is much higher – about 2.68 ECU/m^3. This is the average willingness to pay of non-connected households for one m^3 of water and is calculated as a weighted average of the costs from wells or springs and water vendors (see Table 13.3).

Once piped water becomes available, it is a potential substitute for water from all other sources. Hence, the quantity of water supplied by the project can be divided into two parts: one replaces the previous sources and the quantity of water they provide; the other part is a net increase in water consumption. Figure 13.3 gives a comparative-static view in any given year of the project's life, between the with- and without-project situation. In this figure, which shows the demand curve of a representative consumer,[4] the first part is *Qv*, whereas the second part is (*Q*2 – *Q*1).[5] How can these benefits be quantified?

1. Benefit of the first part is equal to the savings of economic resources[6] by consumers who do not need to use the former water sources any more. After the amount and cost of replaced water are estimated, the calculation of the resulting savings is relatively straightforward: it is the product of the quantity replaced and its weighted average unit cost (the area represented by *OQvD*1*pv* in the figure). Notice that the price *pv* does not necessarily represent a market price, but could well be the average opportunity cost of resources spent on supplying water by traditional means (that is a shadow price).
2. Benefit of the second part is the WTP for the net increase in water consumption (area *Q*1*Q*2*D*3*D*2). Estimating those benefits is more comp-

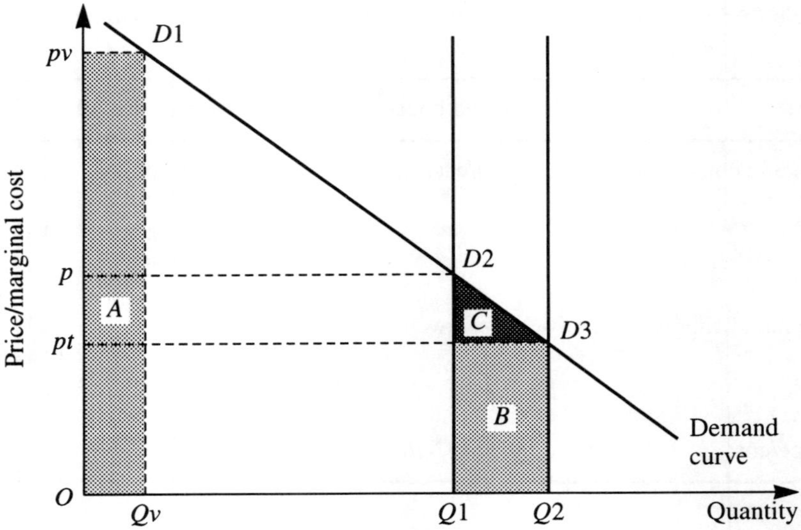

pv = price/cost of traditional water sources (well, oued, water vendors)
p = price of water without project (weighted average of all sources)
pt = piped water tariff
Qv = water consumption from traditional sources
*Q*1 = total water consumption without project (all sources)
*Q*2 = total water consumption with project

Savings of economic resources (*A*) — *A* = *Qv pv*

Economic value of net increase in water consumption (*B* + *C*)
of which water bill: — *B* = (*Q*2 – *Q*1) *pt*
and consumer surplus: — *C* = ½(*p* – *pt*) (*Q*2 – *Q*1)

Figure 13.3 Economic benefits of piped water supply

licated as it requires knowledge of the shape of the demand curve for piped water. In principle this is clearly defined: since piped water can serve all water needs, its demand curve is the aggregate of the water demand curves for each need. In practice, though, this aggregation is usually difficult because available information of prices and quantities does not allow us to know more than a single point on each demand curve. Being thus unable to properly aggregate over the underlying demand curves, we do not know exactly what price (*p* in the figure) belongs to the total consumed quantity of water in the without-project situation (*Q*1 in the figure). As a practical approximation it can be assumed that this price (*p*) is equal to the weighted average[7] of the prices/costs of water from the various sources, including the prevailing water tariff for piped water already consumed by a fraction of the population affected by the project.[8] In the case of scheme 3, for example, it is the weighted average of 0.37 and 2.68 ECU/m^3. The high-quantity–low-price point (*D*3) can be determined by the tariff projection (*pt*) and the corresponding water sales (*Q*2) estimated in the analysis of demand. Since the demand curve is assumed to be linear between the quantities *Q*1 and *Q*2, the average economic value of one unit of incremental water is equal to the average of the two prices *p* and *pt*. The benefit due to the net increase in water consumption is then equal to the average economic value calculated accordingly, multiplied by the total net increase in water use.

Performing this exercise for each year of the project's life yields the benefit stream, which in turn leads to the net economic cash flow, after subtraction of the cost stream. The NPV or the ERR can then be used as usual to decide whether or not to make a particular investment or to rank several competing projects.

Table 13.4 compares the results of the simplified approach, using tariffs as a measure of benefits, with those from the detailed method based on WTP. As can easily be seen, when ERRs are calculated by the second and more rigorous method, all components of the project appear to be economically justified (the lowest ERR is 10 per cent). Notice also that the difference between the results of the two methods tends to be larger the lower the initial connection rate is. This is quite plausible: the lower the connection rate, the more consumers there will be with a high willingness to pay, thus increasing the projects' benefits.

Table 13.4 Economic rate of return

	Scheme 1	Scheme 2	Scheme 3	Scheme 4	Scheme 5	Scheme 6
Short-cut method	**3.3%**	30.6%	**–1.4%**	8.1%	**–1.1%**	8.0%
Detailed method	11.5%	34.0%	15.8%	17.7%	10.1%	13.0%
Connection rate	84%	84%	37%	84%	65%	82%

Another interesting point about this approach is that it changes the priorities in water development. Traditionally, what is done is to rank possible investments in water supply according to their unit cost of provision (cost per m^3 or per inhabitant); taking those with the lowest unit costs first. With the second approach what matters is the net benefit per additional m^3 or per inhabitant. A project which would be postponed because of its high unit cost might well get priority because of the high WTP of households presently relying on very expensive sources of water. Whether such an economically justified investment will eventually also become financially viable crucially depends on the way this high WTP is tapped by adjusting the water tariff accordingly. This brings us to the last step.

Analysis of Water Tariffs

The appraisal of an investment in water-supply expansion is a good opportunity to analyse the level of tariffs. It allows us to compare the cost of provision with the price of water and to identify whether tariff adjustments are necessary and, if so, to make suggestions to this effect. There are two broad categories of issues that have to be considered. The first is the financial aspect. It is clear that if water tariffs are set at levels that do not allow the water company to recover costs, then it will either have to have recourse to subsidies or capital transfers from the government budget; or it will have to curtail operations, maintenance and investment activities with a negative impact on the level of service.

The second and more important aspect is the economic role of tariffs. We have seen that the tariff – the price of water – has a significant impact on demand. Therefore it has a fundamental role to play as a rationing device for a resource that is becoming increasingly costly to supply. If tariffs are set below the economic cost, water would be wasted, additional capacity made available by the project would be exhausted too rapidly, and new investments would have to be put in place prematurely. It is therefore necessary to assess what is the economic cost of producing water and compare it with existing water tariffs. A good operational approximation of the economic cost is the AIC which can signal to consumers the general level and trend of future costs, provided its calculation covers a sufficiently long time period; usually 10 to 15 years.[9] If tariffs are significantly below AIC, an increase in tariff appears necessary and a timetable of more or less gradual tariff adjustment based on the financial cash-flow analysis can be worked out.

Table 13.5 and Figure 13.4 compares the economic cost of producing water with water tariffs. Note that in the case in hand, there is no uniform national tariff. Tariffs can thus be set at the local level, so as to take into account cost conditions that vary from one region to another. We can see that

Table 13.5 Cost of provision and tariff (ECU/m³)

	Scheme 1	Scheme 2	Scheme 3	Scheme 4	Scheme 5	Scheme 6
Economic cost	0.68	0.57	1.13	0.5	0.66	0.55
Tariff	0.37	0.48	0.39	0.39	0.31	0.37
Cost coverage	53%	85%	34%	77%	47%	68%

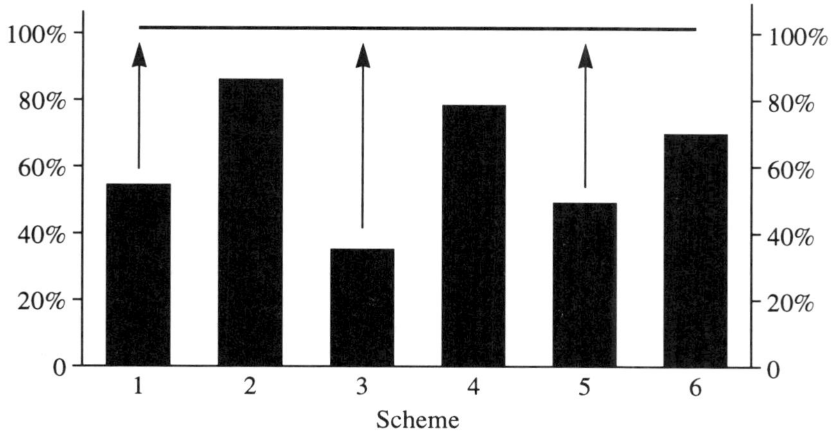

Figure 13.4 Cost of provision and tariff (ECU/m³)

in the six schemes water tariffs are below the economic cost of water. In the case of schemes 1, 3 and 5 the gap is especially large: tariffs cover only half or less of the cost of supply. In these three locations an increase in tariffs appears necessary in order to give consumers the appropriate signal on water scarcity and therefore lead to its more rational use.

On the basis of its analysis the European Investment Bank has recommended a gradual increase in tariffs over a period of five years so as to equal economic cost in 1998–99. A detailed timetable of these tariff adjustments has been introduced in the loan contract with the water company.

CONCLUDING REMARKS

Given the space available the description of what can be done in practice was necessarily rather sketchy. Nevertheless, it should have made clear that the main assumptions underlying the traditional, though still widely used approach, can no longer be accepted and that water-supply projects should undergo the same economic CBA as any other investment. To claim that benefits of this type of project cannot be quantified overlooks the fact that the WTP of consumers for improved service captures most of these benefits and that this WTP can be determined by looking more closely at what happens without the project. If this type of analysis were consistently applied in practice it should be possible to identify better potential investments in the water sector and to put more emphasis on the management of existing supplies.

The discussion should also have highlighted the importance of linking the project appraisal with an analysis of tariffs. By providing an estimate of the economic cost of water, project appraisal helps to identify the need for adjusting the price of water. In most cases water is still heavily subsidized, and use of water is higher than socially desirable. But not only is this a bad allocation of resources; it does not address the needs of the poor either. It is the rich, not the poor, who very often benefit disproportionately from this subsidy. Unserved people pay much higher prices for water than those fortunate enough to be connected to a public pipe. And it is the poor who are unserved.

Look again at the case study. Households not connected to the network are paying a price for water which is seven times higher than the tariff charged to connected households. There is ample evidence, as one might expect, that non-connected households are predominantly low-income ones. Even if the tariff is more than doubled to cover the costs of the extension of the network, the additional households that will be connected will end up paying only about a third of what they are now paying for water. If, on the other hand, tariffs do not cover economic costs, the water company will have to rely on budgetary transfers to finance and operate extensions of the system. But budgetary funds might be hard to find in the context of the adjustment policies being pursued by many governments. This would mean fewer new connections for low-income households, who would continue to pay water prices considerably higher than prevailing tariffs.

In other words, and to put it more generally, the approach described above can help reach the goal of a universal provision of water without relying on huge subsidies from the central government. It does so by helping to identify schemes users really want and are willing to pay for.

NOTES

1. Defined as the per cent change in quantity demanded for a 1 per cent change in price.
2. Whereas a reduction in physical losses reduces required production, reduction in non-physical losses (unrecovered bills) has an impact on demand only by way of an increase in the implicit tariff.
3. In this case and assuming a linear demand curve (and providing the change in volume is marginal) the consumer surplus (*CS*) can easily be expressed as a function of the prevailing tariff (*pt*), the price elasticity of demand (*E*), the proportionate change in consumption (Q') and the incremental change in consumption ($Q2 - Q1$). Thus $CS = -1/2\ (Q2 - Q1)\ Q'\ pt\ 1/E$. Under these circumstances *CS* generally lies between 5 and 10 per cent of additional financial revenues.
4. Defined as the average of all consumers already connected and those, presently unconnected, who will potentially connect to the piped system. The methodology presented assumes that all potential customers will eventually decide to connect.

5. Description of this approach, now known under the name 'ECOWAT', draws heavily on Lovei (1992) who first presented it.
6. These savings may for instance include the amounts spent on water sold by vendors, on the construction and repair of wells, handpumps, water storage tanks, and on the operation of diesel or electric pumps, time spent collecting and carrying water and operating handpumps (Lovei 1992, p. 10).
7. The weights are the consumed quantities.
9. In cases where the project only aims at satisfying consumption increases over a much shorter period, calculation of AIC has to include all other future investment costs during a sufficiently long period of time. Typically AIC is then based on the whole investment programme of the next 10 to 15 years.

REFERENCES

Al-Quanaibet, M.H. and R.S. Johnston (1985), 'Municipal Demand for Water in Kuwait: Methodological Issues and Empirical Results', *Water Resources Research*, **21** (4).

Bhatia, R., R. Cestti and J. Winpenny (1993), *Policies for Water Conservation and Reallocation: Good Practice Cases in Improving Efficiency and Equity*, Washington, DC: World Bank.

Lovei, L. (1992), 'An Approach to the Economic Analysis of Water Supply Projects', World Bank Working Papers, Water and Sanitation, WPS 1005, Washington, DC.

Martin, W.E. (1991), Water Pricing as a Policy Variable in Managing Urban Water Use: Tucson, Arizona, *Water Resources Research*, **27** (2), 157–66.

Martin, W.E. and J.F. Thomas (1986), 'Policy Relevance in Studies of Urban Residential Water Demand', *Water Resource Research*, **22**, 13.

Winpenny, J. (1994), *Managing Water as an Economic Resource*, London: Routledge.

World Bank Water Demand Research Team (1993), 'The Demand for Water in Rural Areas: Determinants and Policy Implications', *The World Bank Research Observer*, **8** (1).

14. The income-distributional effects of a mining project in Brazil

Alfredo Lopes da Silva Neto

INTRODUCTION

This chapter discusses the income-distributional effects created by the Carajás iron ore project. This undertaking was implemented in the 1980s by the Companhia Vale do Rio Doce S.A (CVRD), a Brazilian public enterprise that has a strong link with the mining sector and the international iron ore market. The Carajás project, located in Brazil's North region and designed to produce 35 million tons (mt) per year of high-quality iron ore is an integrated project formed by a complex of mine, railway, port and two townsites. This mining project came on stream in 1986 and its full capacity was achieved in 1989 when 34.5 mt of iron ore were exported and 0.5 mt were sold to local pig iron producers.

The Carajás project was appraised both at constant market prices and at shadow prices. This economic analysis identified and quantified the direct, indirect and the income-distributional effects that have resulted from the implementation and operation of this mining project (Silva Neto 1992).

The analysis of the income-distributional effects can be considered an additional step of the project's economic evaluation. In this case study, the analysis identifies the project's gainers and losers. As a result, it is possible to evaluate the positive and negative income effects generated by the Carajás project's operation.

METHODOLOGY

Two fundamental steps underpin the analysis of the income effects created by projects. First, one must identify the agents whose incomes are directly changed by the project. Second, the income changes of the identified agents must be measured.[1]

A project's resource flows estimated at constant market prices are the focal point for the income-effect analysis. However, to identify the economic agents that have their income affected by the project one must introduce financial flows into the analysis. This simplifies the identification task because these flows measure transfer payments from the economic agents to the project and vice versa. Therefore, income changes result from the difference between the value that an economic agent provides to the project and the value that comes from that project to the referred agent.

Project resource flows measured at shadow prices also help to analyse the relevance of the income effects. In this case, income changes result from the differences between the estimated benefits and costs at market and shadow prices (Curry and Weiss 1993, chap. 9).

DISTRIBUTIONAL EFFECTS: ANALYSIS AT MARKET PRICES

The Carajás project's resource flows estimated at constant market prices of December 1979 made up the base case for the distributional analysis. This choice is justified on the grounds that these resource flows incorporate the direct and indirect effects linked to the operation of the project (Silva Neto 1992, chap. 7).

Moreover, for the purposes of the distributional analysis not only the project's net present value (NPV) is estimated but also the present value (PV) of each cost and benefit of the project. Table 14.1 summarizes the PV of the Carajás project's main items that form the base case for the distributional analysis.

Table 14.1 PV of the project's resource flows (US$ thou. – Dec 1979 real terms)

Items		PV(1)
I	Benefits	2,736,223
II	Investment costs	1,887,846
III	Operating costs	649,054
IV	Working capital	49,633
V	Project costs (II + III + IV)	2,586,533
VI	Net present value (I – V)	149,690

Note: (1) Discount rate: 10 per cent representing the opportunity cost of capital.

Source: Silva Neto (1992, table 8.17).

The introduction of financial flows into the analysis shows that through transfer payments the project's NPV can be distributed among three economic agents. First, domestic and foreign financial institutions lent resources to implement the project and received interest plus capital repayment. Second, the government gets revenues from the profit tax payment and, third, the project's equity owners secure the surplus.

Financial Flows: Loans

The evaluation of the distributional effects adds a new dimension to the analysis that is being undertaken, since its focus shifts from the allocation of real resources to the distribution of the income changes brought about by the Carajás project. Table 14.2 summarizes the estimated PV of the loans, capital repayment and interest payments that form the mainstream of the Carajás project's financing plan negotiated by CVRD in the early 1980s.[2]

The two main domestic lenders are the BNDES and FINAME. On the domestic front, CVRD could also raise a substantial amount of resources through the issue of convertible debentures in the Brazilian capital market.

On the other hand, the main foreign financial agents are in Europe (KfW), US (World Bank, Morgan Guarantee Bank and Eximbank of US) and Japan (Eximbank of Japan and a syndicate of commercial banks lead by the Bank of Tokyo). The commitment of international financing agencies such as the World Bank and CVRD's customers (Japanese and European steelmakers) with this financial package were essential to CVRD's objectives.

As a result of this financing plan structure, the weighted average real interest rate that CVRD must pay for its loans is 9.5 per cent. This value is significantly below the LIBOR rate estimated for the period of analysis and even below the discount rate of 10 per cent (Zraick 1983, pp. 6–7 and Silva Neto 1992, table 6.13). This difference of 0.5 per cent (10 per cent – 9.5 per cent) is quite important in terms of the project's income effects. In fact, Table 14.2 shows that a net transfer from the lenders to the project's equity owners was created when both loans and loan payment (principal plus interest) are discounted at 10 per cent.[3]

From the point of view of the national economy, the negative flow of US$14,879,000, i.e. US$695,866,000 – US$710,743,000, is a transfer payment between nationals, in this case, a transfer from the two domestic financial institutions (BNDES and FINAME) to the project's equity owners. On the other hand, the loss experienced by the foreign lenders, i.e. US$724,000 (US$893,818,000 – US$894,542,000) has a different economic meaning that will be discussed later in the chapter.

Table 14.2 Project financing – loans (US$ thou. – Dec. 1979 real terms)

	Present value of foreign and domestic loans (1)		
	Loan	Loan payment (2)	Interest payment
Foreign loans:			
World Bank	212,715	227,925	121,936
EEC:	–	–	–
First tranche	48,719	37,940	8,429
Second tranche	40,660	36,467	9,286
Third tranche	33,454	28,256	6,568
Fourth tranche	50,729	43,667	10,460
KfW	60,331	71,794	34,656
Morgan Guarantee Bank	82,645	104,220	52,796
Japanese bond issue	14,876	14,394	4,054
Export-Import Bank of Japan	29,752	22,890	8,427
Nippon Carajás(3)	147,934	130,640	50,669
Bank of Tokyo	137,190	132,141	37,220
Export-Import Bank of USA	35,537	43,482	14,607
Subtotal	894,542	893,816	359,108
Domestic loans:			
BNDES(4)	454,545	409,455	187,688
FINAME(5)	106,612	111,571	56,621
CVRD – conv. debentures	149,586	174,840	91,709
Subtotal	710,743	695,866	336,018
TOTAL	1,605,285	1,589,682	695,126

Notes:
(1) Discount rate: 10%.
(2) Loan payments = capital repayment plus interest payments.
(3) Enterprise established by the following Japanese steelmakers: Nippon Steel, Nippon Kokan, Sumitomo Metal, Kawasaki Steel, Kobe Steel, Nisshin Steel and Nakayama Steel.
(4) National Bank for the Social and Economic Development (Banco Nacional de Desenvolvimento Econômico e Social – BNDES).
(5) The Special Agency for Industrial Financing (Agência Especial de Financiamento Industrial – FINAME).

Sources: World Bank (1982, pp. 57–8); Zraick (1983, pp. 1–13) and ECCA (1991, chap. 3).

Financial Flows: Profit Tax

The payment of profit tax transfers a fraction of the project's net income from the project's equity owners to the government.[4] The starting point for the analysis of the profit tax is the estimated operating profit (sales revenues – operating costs). In addition, depreciation allowances and interest payments

Table 14.3 Depreciation schedule (US$ thou. – Dec 1979 real terms)

Items	Years	PV(1)
Civil works	20	121,521
Equipments and machinery for:		
Mine	10	119,211
Railway	10	282,906
Port	10	66,770
Townsites	10	3,925
Other investments	10	48,542
Project management(2)	5	240,032
Mobile equipment for mine(3)	5	94,532
Replacement investments	5	124,627
Total		1,102,065

Notes:
(1) Discount rate: 10%.
(2) Pre-production capital expenditures for all project components.
(3) Trucks, shovels, drills, tractors, etc.

Source: World Bank (1982, p. 107)

are deducted from the operating profit so that the taxable income can be estimated, i.e. the profit before tax. The straight-line method was used to estimate depreciation charges based on the actual historic cost of the fixed investments. The items that are subject to depreciation were classified in three groups according to their expected operational lifetime, i.e. 20, 10 and 5 years, respectively. Replacement investments and pre-production capital expenditures were also depreciated since their cost estimates are available. Table 14.3 illustrates the PV for each of the three referred categories of items (World Bank 1982, p. 107).

Since interest payments were already estimated (see Table 14.2) the net profit (before tax) was calculated for each year of the Carajás project's operational phase (1986–2015). An effective rate of tax of 30 per cent was applied to the estimated flow of net profit before tax and the taxable profit was calculated on an annual basis (Hill 1980).

It is relevant to mention that the project benefited from a tax holiday during the first ten years of its operational phase (Brazil/PGC 1981). This was important for the project's financial viability since these years are characterized by heavy amortization of the contracted loans. Thus, the calculation of the value of the profit tax considered this tax holiday granted to CVRD.

Table 14.4 Profit tax (US$ thou. – Dec. 1979 real terms)

	Items	PV(1)
I	Operating profit	2,087,168
II	Depreciation	1,102,065
III	Interest payments	695,126
IV	Profit before tax (I – II + III)	289,977
V	Profit tax(2)	140,351
VI	Profit after tax (IV – V)	149,626

Notes:
(1) Discount rate: 10%.
(2) The PV of profit before tax (US$289,977,000) is equal to the PV of profits during the tax liability period (US$467,848,000) plus the PV of profits during the tax holiday period (US$104,681,000) minus the PV of losses incurred because of interest payment throughout the project implementation phase (US$282,552,000). The PV of profit tax is obtained as follows: $140{,}351 = 0.3 \times 467{,}848$.

Sources: Tables 14.1, 14.2 and 14.3.

Finally, Table 14.4 summarizes the PV of each of the flows that are required to estimate the profit tax.

Table 14.5 illustrates how loans, loan payments and profit tax interact with the original project's resource flows. The first three rows of this table show that the project was able to generate a positive NPV (US$149.7 million) although they say nothing about income changes. The distributional effects can only be visualized when financial flows are introduced into the analysis Thus, the next rows show the positive and negative transfers that resulted both from the project financing and profit tax payment. Finally, the last row illustrates how the project's NPV is distributed among the three economic agents that are being considered, i.e. the project's equity owners, the government and the lenders. The project's equity owners and the government are clearly better off as a result of the Carajás project's implementation and both the domestic and the foreign lenders are worse off.[5]

Yet, this result must be carefully considered because of property right relationships. First, 51 per cent of the CVRD's shares are held by the Brazilian government and the other 49 per cent belong to private shareholders. Therefore, the latter should also be better off if CVRD pays higher dividends in the future as a result of the Carajás project's operations. However, unlike interest payments, dividend payments are not subject to a contract between the enterprise and its shareholders. It is a well known fact that this income flow is a function of enterprise investment policy and, perhaps more important, it cannot be linked specifically to the results of a particular project.

Table 14.5 Income effects: analysis at market prices (US$ thou. – Dec. 1979 real terms)

	Equity owners	Government	Domestic lenders	Foreign lenders
RESOURCE FLOWS:				
I Benefits	(+)2,736,223			
II Costs	(–)2,586,533			
III NPV(1) (I – II)	(+)149,690			
FINANCIAL FLOWS:				
IV Loans				
Domestic lenders				
Loan	(+)710,744		(–)710,744	
Loan payment(2)	(–)695,865		(+)695,865	
Foreign lenders				
Loan	(+)894,542			(–)894,542
Loan payment	(–)893,818			(+)893,818
V Profit tax	(–)140,351	(+)140,351		
INCOME CHANGES	(+)24,942	(+)140,351	(–)14,879	(–)724

Notes:
(1) Discount rate: 10%.
(2) Loan payment = capital repayment plus interest payment.

Source: Tables 14.1–14.4

Second, both the BNDES and FINAME are public enterprises where the government holds 100 per cent of their shares. Therefore, the Carajás project created a transfer payment within the public sector, from one public enterprise to another.

From the national economy point of view what matters is that the balance between gainers and losers is still positive. This means that a project that is sponsored by a public enterprise can both improve the national income and reinforce the relative position of the public sector within the confines of that economy.

Since one of the main losers is a member of the public sector the Brazilian government has to decide how to manage such gains and losses. This is a project distributional effect that often arises when projects are financed and implemented by public agencies (Londero 1987, pp. 139–41).

INCOME EFFECTS: ANALYSIS AT SHADOW PRICES

The analysis that was carried out in the preceding sections showed some of the gainers and losers that resulted from the Carajás project's implementation and operation. In this sense, it illustrates how the project's NPV is transferred from the project's equity owners to the government and how the lenders transfer resources to the project's equity owners. However, this is only a partial picture of the income effects created by that project because financial flows can discern only income changes that result from transfer payments.

Transactions that involve the allocation of real resources also create income flows that are not reflected by the analysis at market prices. To measure these income changes one must compare estimates of the project's costs and benefits at market prices with the equivalent estimates at shadow prices (ODA 1988, p. 140; Londero 1981, pp. 7–37, Curry and Weiss 1993, chap. 9).

Therefore, the next sections compare the Carajás project's direct costs and benefits at market prices with their counterpart at shadow prices. Table 14.1 summarized the project's resource flows at market prices that form the basis for this comparison. The project's flows at shadow prices could be derived after the application of specific conversion factors (CFs) (Silva Neto 1992, chap. 7).

In comparing the PV of both flows (market and shadow prices) it should be realized that estimates at shadow prices are not simply equal to the product of their equivalent at market prices times the estimated CFs. This is because the discount rate applied to the evaluation at constant market price and at shadow prices differ. The former was estimated by the project's feasibility studies (10 per cent). The latter, the economic discount rate (EDR), is project-specific because its estimate (9 per cent) took into account not only the Carajás project's characteristics but also the available data (Silva Neto 1992, chap. 6).

Then, income changes that result from the comparison between market and shadow prices reflect different estimates for these two discount rates.

Direct Benefits

The estimated CF for iron ore (CF iron ore = 1.047) suggests that the shadow price of that commodity is higher than its domestic price because of the sales tax that is levied on the export parity price (EPP). This implies an income effect because part of the foreign exchange created by the Carajás project is appropriated by the government. It should be noted that this income change cannot be measured without a comparison between market and shadow prices.

The estimated transport service is a project's non-traded output. In this case, the estimated consumption conversion factor (CCF = 0.743) may be applied to convert the sales revenues created by this transport service from market to shadow prices. This is possible if the analyst can assume that the project's non-traded outputs substitute for a similar amount of traded goods, i.e. final consumption goods. In other words, at shadow prices the sales revenues of the project's non-traded outputs are equivalent to foreign exchange saved when a project produces a commodity that substitutes for imports (Ward et al. 1991, p. 97).

The government therefore loses tax revenues because fewer final consumption goods are imported due to the project's additional production of equivalent non-traded output. Table 14.6 illustrates the income effects that resulted from the differences between the market and shadow prices of the Carajás project's outputs, i.e. iron ore and railway transport.

Table 14.6 Income effects related to the project's direct benefits (US$ thou. – Dec. 1979 real terms)

Revenues	PV at(1) market prices a	Government b = (c – a)	PV at(2) shadow prices c
I Sales of iron ore (1 + 2)	2,680,235	(+)558,926	3,239,162
1 International market	2,634,483	(+)548,680	3,183,163
2 Internal market	45,752	(+)10,246	55,999
II Railway transport (1 + 2)	55,988	(–)6,255	49,732
1 Passenger transport	6,077	(–)712	5,365
2 Cargo transport	49,911	(–)5,543	44,367
Total = (I + II)	2,736,223	552,672	3,288,894

Notes:
(1) Discount rate: 10%.
(2) Economic discount rate: 9%.

Source: Silva Neto (1992, table 8.17).

Direct Costs: Traded Items

The starting point for the analysis of the income effects brought about by expenditures on traded commodities (capital goods and traded inputs) is the difference between their market and shadow prices. In the case of the Carajás project this price comparison shows that the former is greater than the latter. (This happens because the estimated CFs are always less than one, with the exception of imports of coal that will be analysed later.)

As far as capital goods expenditures are concerned this result suggests that the real cost to the Brazilian economy due to the use of such goods was less than the market value paid by CVRD. This means that the difference between market and shadow prices was appropriated either by the government or by the project's suppliers. On the one hand, no income change can be attributed to the government because all imports of capital goods were duty free. In addition, all the capital goods acquired from the domestic industry were also exempted from tax payment. Therefore, income changes created by expenditures on capital goods can be attributed only to the project's suppliers. These income changes are surplus profits, i.e. profits in excess of those that can be earned in other economic sectors (Brazil/PGC 1981, 1982; Curry and Weiss 1993).[6]

Table 14.7 summarizes the estimated PV of the positive income changes transferred to the Carajás project's domestic suppliers. This table shows that more than 30 per cent of the real cost of the capital goods were transferred to those economic agents. Therefore, despite the substantial resources that CVRD

Table 14.7 Income effects related to the project's traded items (US$ thou. – Dec. 1979 real terms)

Traded items	PV at(1) market prices a	Project's suppliers b = (a – d)	Government c = (a – d)	PV at(2) shadow prices d
Investment costs:				
Railway	399,640	135,348	–	264,292
Mine	196,899	33,013	–	163,885
Port	95,117	20,825	–	74,293
Townsites	5,696	453	–	5,243
Replacement investments	108,784	23,579	–	85,205
Imports of coal	65,846	–	(42,590)	108,436
Subtotal	871,982	213,218	(42,590)	701,354
Operating costs:				
Railway	161,507	–	47,496	114,012
Mine	124,694	–	8,354	116,341
Port	34,432	–	619	33,812
Townsites	29,618	–	8,321	21,297
Subtotal	350,251	–	64,790	285,462

Notes:
(1) Discount rate: 10%.
(2) Economic discount rate: 9%.

Source: Silva Neto (1992, tables 8.18 and 8.19).

managed to save with the acquisitions of capital goods this result reveals that the project's costs could have been still lower if these transfer payments could have been avoided.

Table 14.7 also shows the analysis of the income effects created during the project's operational phase due to expenditures on traded inputs. CVRD buys these commodities from the domestic industry and their acquisition is subject to tax payments. Therefore, the income changes that can be considered here are tax revenues and surplus profits. The latter can arise if licensing and quota restrictions are used to control the level of imports. For simplicity, the difference between market and shadow prices is assigned only to taxes that are charged when traded inputs are bought during the project's operational phase.[7]

Direct Costs: Labour

Central to the analysis of the income changes for labour is the difference between the PV of the market wage (MW) and the PV of the shadow wage (SW) at border prices. It should be remembered that the identification of the economic agents involved with these income changes is also an essential component of the analysis. This implies that the discussion must refer to the distinction between skilled and unskilled labour (Castagnino 1982, pp. 66–9).

Skilled labour

The structure of the labour force employed by CVRD to work in the Carajás project's operational phase is an important issue. It is assumed that the SW of skilled labour at market prices can be measured by their market wages, i.e. SW = MW. Furthermore, assuming that these workers can be withdrawn from every economic sector, the standard conversion factor (SCF = 0.629) was used to estimate their economic cost in the chosen numeraire of the analysis. Although SW = MW, the use of the SCF implies that the SW at market prices is different from the SW at border prices. This has implications for the income distributional analysis because the economic agents that get income changes due to the estimated difference between market and shadow wages (at border prices) cannot be identified. For example, if skilled labour were withdrawn only from traded sectors, then it would be possible to assume that the forgone production would be replaced by imports. In this case, the referred income changes could be attributed to the government that would get additional tax revenues.[8]

However, this assumption is not consistent with the use of the SCF since the forgone production is not always replaced by imports because the skilled labour can also be withdrawn from non-traded sectors. Therefore, in this case study the income effect of wages paid to skilled labour will be allocated to a special group called 'rest of the economy'. This group encompasses the three economic agents that get income changes due to the differences between market and shadow prices, i.e. unskilled labour, government and the project's suppliers.

Unskilled labour

The analysis is quite different where unskilled labour is concerned. The fact that these workers came from the country's regions characterized by high rates of underemployment and unemployment was taken into account in deriving the conversion factor for unskilled labour (CF_{ul}) and it was assumed that their SW at market prices is equal to half of the MW earned in the new job, i.e. SW = 0.5MW. The agricultural conversion factor (AgCF = 0.708) was used to convert this opportunity cost from market prices to shadow prices. This procedure resulted in a low CF_{ul} (CF_{ul} = 0.354)

Income changes linked to the difference between MW and SW (at border prices) can be divided in two segments. First, unskilled workers receive a positive income transfer that can be defined by the difference between MW and SW at market prices, i.e. MW – SW = MW – 0.5MW = 0.5MW. Second, the government can also get additional income if imports replace the output forgone by unskilled labour due to their move to a new job. In this case, income changes are brought about by tariffs on the extra imports.[9]

However, this possible income effect is not included in the analysis because there are no grounds for such an assumption. It has already been stressed that most unskilled labour employed by CVRD came from the rural areas of Brazil's North and Northeast regions. It is well known that rural workers in those areas are engaged in subsistence agriculture so that their forgone output is likely to be replaced by domestic production and not by additional imports.

The difference between the SW (at border prices) and the SW (at market prices) creates income changes whose beneficiaries could not be identified. They can be assigned either to the government or to the farmers. The former gets tax revenues from the domestic agricultural production and the latter get surplus profits due to the system of import control that prevails in Brazil, namely licensing and import ban. For this reason, these income changes will be allocated to the 'rest of the economy' group.

Table 14.8 shows the income changes experienced by labour as a result of the jobs created during the Carajás project's operational phase. It should be emphasized that this table shows a partial picture of this specific income effect because most unskilled labour was also employed during the project's implementation phase. However, the addition of these income effects was not possible because the available data for investment costs aggregate expenditures on labour together with other construction investment items.

Table 14.8 Income effects related to the project's labour costs (US$ thou. – Dec. 1979 real terms)

Labour cost	PV at(1) market price, a	Unskilled (3) labour, b	Rest of (4) the economy, c	PV at(2) shadow price d
Unskilled labour	45,760	22,880	4,362	18,518
Skilled labour	183,040	–	51,429	131,611
Total	228,800	22,880	55,791	150,129

Notes:
(1) Discount rate: 10%.
(2) Economic discount rate: 9%.
(3) b = 0.5 × (a).
(4) c = (a – b) – (d).

Source: Silva Neto (1992, table 8.17).

Direct Costs: Non-Traded Items

The differences between the shadow and market prices of the non-traded commodities used by a project can also be assigned to the economic agents affected by that project by splitting their cost structure into their main components. Such a detailed breakdown would bring about income changes for the government (tax revenues), project's suppliers (surplus profits) and unskilled labour (if the MW is greater than the SW), which will be assigned to the 'rest of the economy' group.

Table 14.9 indicates the income changes appropriated by this mix of economic agents (government, project's suppliers and unskilled labour). The

Table 14.9 Income effects related to the project's non-traded items (US$ thou. – Dec. 1979 real terms)

Non-traded items	PV(1) at market prices, a	Rest of the economy, b = (a – c)	PV(2) at shadow prices, c
Investment costs	1,015,863	408,324	607,539
Operating costs	70,002	23,297	46,705
Total	1,085,865	431,621	654,244

Notes:
(1) Discount rate: 10%.
(2) Economic discount rate: 9%.

Source: Silva Neto (1992, tables 8.20 and 8.21).

simplifying assumption adopted here implies a rough income distributional effect analysis that will be enhanced later on when an attempt will be made to split the 'rest of the economy' group.[10]

Direct Costs: Working Capital

The Carajás project's working capital is formed mainly by iron ore, spare parts and fuel. Accordingly, income changes will result if the shadow prices of these items differ from their market prices. It has already been stressed that iron ore is the project's main output, but this item is also a working capital component. In this case, iron ore is a cost for CVRD because it is held as an inventory both at the port and at the mine (Curry and Weiss 1993).

On the one hand, the government absorbs a negative transfer because it does not get the sale tax revenue equivalent to the difference between the market and shadow price of the iron ore. On the other hand, assuming that spare parts and fuel are imported at the margin, the government receives a positive income change because of the taxes that are levied on these additional imports. Table 14.10 shows that on balance, the positive income changes offset the negative transfers and the government income increases as a result of the project's working capital expenditures.

Table 14.10 Income effects related to the project's working capital (US$ thou. – Dec. 1979 real terms)

Working capital	PV(1) at market prices, a	Government b = (a – c)	PV(2) at shadow prices, c
Iron ore	25,734	(–)1,773	27,507
Fuel	113	16	97
Spare parts	23,786	3,050	20,736
Total	49,633	1,293	48,340

Notes:
(1) Discount rate: 10%.
(2) Economic discount rate: 9%.

Source: Silva Neto (1992, table 8.17).

Combining Income Effects

Throughout the last five sections, the Carajás project's direct costs and benefits estimated at market prices were compared with their counterpart at shadow prices. The differences between them form the basis for the income-

Table 14.11 Income effects: analysis at shadow prices (I) (US$ million – Dec. 1979 real terms)

	Equity owners	Govern-ment	Domestic lenders	Unskilled labour	Project suppliers	Rest of the economy	NPV shadow prices	Foreign lenders
RESOURCE FLOWS:								
Benefits	+2,736.2	+552.7						
Costs								
Investment costs	–1,887.8	–42.6			+213.2	+408.3	1,308.9	
Working capital	–49.6	+1.2					48.4	
Operating costs	–649.0	+64.8		+22.9		+79.1	482.2	
FINANCIAL FLOWS:								
Project financing								
Domestic lenders								
Loan	+710.7		–710.7					
Loan payment	–695.9		+695.9					
Foreign lenders								
Loan	+894.5						+894.5	–894.5
Loan payment	–893.8						–893.8	+893.8
Profit tax	–140.3	+140.3						
Income changes	+24.9	+716.5	–14.8	+22.9	+213.2	+487.4	1,450.1	–0.7

Source: Tables 14.6–14.10.

distributional effect analysis and, therefore, they should be carefully qualified and quantified.

Table 14.11 consolidates the income effects that have been analysed so far. Thus, the column ('NPV at shadow prices') shows the NPV of the foreign exchange that the project may generate during its lifetime (US$1,450.1 million). The row of totals of the other columns shows how these real resources may be distributed within the Brazilian economy. The project's main beneficiaries are the government (US$716.5 million), the project's suppliers (US$213.2 million) followed by the project's equity owners (US$24.9 million) and unskilled labour (US$22.9 million). Income changes obtained by the government, the project's suppliers and unskilled labour are sub-estimated due to the analytical constraints that have already been emphasized. The best evidence for this argument is the significant amount of foreign exchange (US$487.4 million) received by the 'rest of the economy' group that is formed by these three economic agents.

The income-distributional effect analysis shows how some market distortions affect the distribution of the income generated by the Carajás project. For example, tariffs on imports increase the financial cost of traded inputs and capital goods. Despite this, they neither change the project's costs nor the project's benefits (in terms of foreign exchange spent and generated by the project).

However, this tax payment implies an income effect because it changes the distribution of the foreign exchange created by that project. Now, part of this foreign exchange is allocated to the government. The same idea is valid when applied to an export tax, to the surplus profits received by the project's suppliers and to the difference between the MW and the SW that is paid to unskilled labour.

On the other hand, it has already been emphasized that transfer payments paid by CVRD (profit tax, interest payment, etc.) have no equivalent effect on the use of real resources. Therefore, in the evaluation at shadow prices these transfer payments have a shadow price equal to zero. Nevertheless, they can reduce (increase) the amount of foreign exchange that is left to the project's equity owners. In other words, although transfer payments neither increase nor decrease the amount of real resources created by the project, they affect its distribution within the economy. In the Carajás project's case, they shift foreign exchange from the project's equity owners to the government (US$140.3 million) and from the lenders to the project's equity owners (US$15.5 million).

Finally, Table 14.11 also illustrates a result that is already known, i.e. the project's losers are the domestic and foreign lenders (US$14.8 and US$0.7 million, respectively). It has already been highlighted that the losses absorbed by the domestic lenders are a transfer payment that does not affect the amount of foreign exchange created by the Carajás project.

However, the losses experienced by the foreign lenders have a different economic meaning. First, the foreign loans were negotiated directly by CVRD to finance specifically the Carajás project. This means that these resources are not part of a general budget available to finance investments in the Brazilian economy. This implies that this inflow of funds would not be available in a without-project situation (Curry and Weiss 1993, chap. 9).

Second, the analysis of the distributional effects is undertaken from the point of view of the national economy. In this sense, the foreign lenders' losses are real resources (foreign exchange) that in an economic analysis can be translated as a benefit created by the Carajás project. In other words, the project's NPV (at shadow prices) increases from US$1,449.4 million to US$1,450.1 million as a result of the sum of US$723,000 that is added to the project's income flows (Londero 1987, pp. 144–5).

INDIRECT COSTS CHANGE INCOME EFFECTS

Imports of coal can avoid the deforestation caused by pig iron production in the Carajás project's area of influence. Further, it was also estimated that the PV of these imports can achieve US$108.4 million (at shadow prices). This is the estimated price that should be paid by the present generation to overcome the worst environmental problem indirectly brought about by the Carajás project's implementation.[11]

Income effects change according to the economic agents who bear the expenditures with the imports of coal. One may earmark these costs to CVRD's equity owners on the grounds that deforestation is linked to the Carajás project. However, this assumption takes no regard of the fact already stressed that CVRD is a public enterprise owned both by the government and private investors (51 per cent and 49 per cent of its shares, respectively). This suggests that to keep the confidence of their private investors, CVRD has to define clear commercial objectives and an investment policy characterized by positive returns on equity (CVRD 1990).

Therefore, it would be unusual if CVRD's private investors had to absorb a cost that would bring positive income changes to shareholders of other enterprises, i.e. the pig iron producers. For this reason, it is proposed that the imports of coal should be paid by the pig iron producers themselves. Table 14.7 showed that the government also has to pay part of this price because imports of coal are subsidized in Brazil ($CF_{coal} = 1.389$).[12]

Accordingly, additional income changes are added to the project's income flows. The PV of the costs with imports of coal (US$65.8 million at market prices) is subtracted from the project's investment costs and allocated to the pig iron producers. As a result, the project's equity owners income increases

Table 14.12 Income effects: analysis at shadow prices (II)

	Equity owners	Govern-ment	Domestic lenders	Unskilled labour	Project suppliers	Pig iron producers	Rest of the economy	NPV at shadow prices	Foreign lenders
RESOURCE FLOWS:									
Benefits	+2,736.2	+552.7						3.288.9	
Costs									
Investment costs	–1,822.0	–42.6			+213.2	–65.8	+408.3	1,308.9	
Working capital	–49.6	+1.2						48.4	
Operating costs	–649.0	+64.8		+22.9			+79.1	482.2	
FINANCIAL FLOWS:									
Project financing									
Domestic lenders									
Loan	+710.7		–710.7					0	
Loan payment	–695.9		+695.9					0	
Foreign lenders									
Loan	+894.5							+894.5	–894.5
Loan payment	–893.8							–893.8	+893.8
Profit tax	–140.3	+140.3							
Income changes	+90.8	+716.5	–14.8	+22.9	+213.2	–65.8	+487.4	1,450.1	–0.7

Source: Table 14.11.

from US$24.9 million to US$90.8 million. Further, neither the income flow of the government nor the PV of the foreign exchange created by the Carajás project changes, i.e. US$1,450.1 million.[13] Table 14.12 summarizes these income changes.

INDIRECT BENEFITS CHANGE INCOME EFFECTS

The available evidence shows that the Carajás project brought some important indirect benefits to the skilled and unskilled labour employed by CVRD to run that project. These indirect benefits have resulted from the fact that social services such as health, education and housing are provided without any charge (Silva Neto 1992, chap. 7).

The point of departure to evaluate this indirect benefit should be the without-project situation. As far as housing service is concerned, in a without-project situation the workers employed by CVRD would either live in their own houses or pay rent. Thus, the housing service provided by CVRD creates an indirect benefit because real resources (houses) are freed for alternative uses.

To undertake this estimate one needs some hypothesis that links the economic value of the housing service to the wages paid to the labour employed by CVRD. Castagnino (1982, p. 92) estimated that free housing provided by mining projects in some Latin American countries is equivalent to 20 per cent of the wages paid to unskilled and skilled labour. Therefore, the same assumption is adopted here to evaluate CVRD's housing service.[14]

Table 14.13 shows the estimates that are based on the PV of the labour cost at shadow prices. The income effect brought about by this indirect benefit is twofold. First, it increases the amount of real resources created by the project.

Table 14.13 Townsites: housing service (US$ thou. – Dec. 1979 real terms)

Labour cost	PV(1) at shadow price, a	Housing service, b = 0.20 × (a)
Unskilled labour	18,518	3,703
Skilled labour	131,611	26,322
Total	150,129	30,025

Note: (1) Economic discount rate: 9%.

Source: Table 14.8.

Table 14.14 Income effects: analysis at shadow prices (III) (US$ million – Dec. 1979 real terms)

	Equity owners	Govern-ment	Domestic lenders	Skilled labour	Unskilled labour	Project suppliers	Pig iron producers	Rest of the economy	NPV at shadow prices	Foreign lenders
RESOURCE FLOWS:										
Benefits	+2,736.2	+552.7		+26.3	+3.7				3,318.9	
Costs										
Investment costs	−1,822.0	−42.6				+213.2	−65.8	+408.3	1,308.9	
Working capital	−49.6	+1.2							48.4	
Operating costs	−649.0	+64.8			+22.9			+79.1	482.2	
FINANCIAL FLOWS:										
Project financing										
Domestic lenders										
Loan	+710.7		−710.7							
Loan payment	−695.9		+695.9							
Foreign lenders										
Loan	+894.5								+894.5	−894.5
Loan payment	−893.8								−893.8	+893.8
Profit tax	−140.3	+140.3								
Income changes	+90.8	+716.5	−14.8	+26.3	+26.6	+213.2	−65.8	+487.4	1,480.1	−0.7

Source: Table 14.12.

Thus, in terms of the table, which displays the income-distributional analysis results, these estimates are added to the column 'NPV at shadow price' as an additional contribution of the project to the national economy.

Second, the free housing service increases the income flows received by skilled and unskilled labour. Therefore, the estimated income change will be added to the column 'unskilled labour'. In addition, a new column 'skilled labour' identifies the estimate of the indirect benefits received by those workers.

Table 14.14 displays the estimates of the income changes that could be quantified. The next section provides an additional refinement to the analysis because an attempt is undertaken to disaggregate the group 'rest of the economy'.

BREAKDOWN OF THE GROUP 'REST OF THE ECONOMY'

It was emphasized that this group includes income changes absorbed by government, unskilled labour and project suppliers. These income changes resulted from the differences between market and shadow prices of the expenditures on non-traded commodities and labour (skilled and unskilled).

Table 14.14 also shows that these income changes (US$487.4 million) are only surpassed by the government gains (US$716.5 million). Thus, a more detailed picture of the project's distributional effects can be obtained if this group can be split and income changes allocated to the group's respective components. This objective can be achieved through the cost structure breakdown of the non-traded commodities and the opportunity cost of labour. However, this attempt would result in new inputs that are non-traded and

Table 14.15 'Rest of the economy' group: weights and components

Resource flows	Rest of the economy(1)	Project suppliers		Unskilled labour		Government	
	a	Weight, b	c = a*b	Weight, d	e = a*d	Weight, f	g = a*f
Investment costs	408.3	0.5532	225.9	0.3488	142.4	0.098	40.0
Operating costs	79.1	0.5532	43.8	0.3488	27.6	0.098	7.8
Total	487.4	–	269.7	–	170.0	–	47.8

Note: (1) US$ million – Dec. 1979 real terms.

Sources: IBGE (1990, p. 105) and Table 14.14.

Table 14.16 Income effects: analysis at shadow prices (IV)

	Equity owners	Govern-ment	Domestic lenders	Skilled labour	Unskilled labour	Project suppliers	Pig iron producers	NPV at shadow prices	Foreign lenders
RESOURCE FLOWS:									
Benefits	+2,736.2	+552.7		+26.3	+3.7			3,318.9	
Costs									
Investment costs	–1,822.0	–2.6			+142.4	+439.1	–65.8	1,308.9	
Working capital	–49.6	+1.2						48.4	
Operating costs	–649.0	+72.5			+50.5	+43.8		482.2	
FINANCIAL FLOWS:									
Project financing									
Domestic lenders									
Loan	+710.7		–710.7						
Loan payment	–695.9		+695.9						
Foreign lenders									
Loan	+894.5							+894.5	–894.5
Loan payment	–893.8							–893.8	+893.8
Profit tax	–140.3	+140.3							
Income changes	+90.8	+764.1	–14.8	+26.3	+196.6	+482.9	–65.8	1,480.1	–0.7

Source: Table 14.14

subsequent income changes that cannot be allocated among the economic agents involved with the project.

Therefore, an alternative approach is to utilize the link of the 'rest of the economy group' with the shares of the respective economic agents in national income. Data provided by the Brazilian National Accounts show that, on average, in the 1980s the national income was appropriated as follows: (a) labour: 34.88 per cent; (b) private sector: 55.33 per cent and (c) government: 9.9 per cent (IBGE 1990, pp. 104–5).[15]

The National Accounts do not split remuneration paid to labour between skilled and unskilled labour but only the latter are components of the group 'rest of the economy'.[16] In addition, the private sector is represented by the project's suppliers that sold capital goods during the project's implementation and that sell inputs throughout its operational phase.

Table 14.15 illustrates how the mentioned weights can be used to split the 'rest of the economy' group.

Most of the income changes that are attributed to the group 'rest of the economy' were created during the project's implementation. During this phase the project employed a large amount of unskilled labour that received MW greater than their SW and, also, construction costs were the main item of the project's investment costs.

The results of the breakdown of the group 'rest of the economy' are consistent, therefore, with the analysis already undertaken. They show a substantial increment in the income received by project suppliers and unskilled labour. The small increment in the government's income flow is also consistent with the fact that capital goods used to implement the Carajás project were exempted from tax payments.

These additional income changes are added to the project's distributional effects already analysed. Table 14.16 displays the final results of the income distributional analysis.

CONCLUSION

This chapter has analysed in some detail the income changes brought about by the Carajás project to the economic agents that could be identified. These agents are the government, the project's equity owners, skilled and unskilled labour, domestic and foreign lenders, the project's suppliers and pig iron producers. The most important project users are the steelmakers that import the iron ore produced by the Carajás project. Their income changes were not considered because the distributional analysis is undertaken from the point of view of the national economy.[17] In other cases, due to analytical constraints, some economic agents could not be identified and, therefore, their income changes were incorporated in a special group called 'rest of the economy'.

The distributional analysis showed that the Carajás project's greatest beneficiary is the government despite the fact that the capital goods required to implement the project were exempted from taxes. The government receives positive income changes from taxes that are levied on the project's inputs and from profit tax. This result can be explained mainly by the project's long operational lifetime that more than compensated for the ten years' tax holiday awarded to the project.

Other important beneficiaries were the project's domestic suppliers that provided almost 90 per cent of the capital goods bought by CVRD to implement the project. This result suggests that the project's equity owners could get higher income changes if the prices paid for these capital goods were lower. This becomes clearer when the group 'rest of the economy' is broken down and the income changes that come from expenditures on construction and other non-traded inputs are estimated.

Unskilled labour also derives positive income changes due to the difference between the estimated MW and SW. This effect is enhanced after the split of the group 'rest of the economy' when additional income changes obtained by this category of labour during the project's implementation are included in the analysis.

Both the domestic and foreign lenders assimilate losses due to the fact that the average of the real interest rate paid by CVRD is lower than the discount rate. The pig iron producers are not really project losers because they are paying for an input that is consumed in their own plants. If the burden of this social cost jeopardizes the financial profitability of their projects the government will have to find alternative financing that will have other income effects.

Finally, the income effects linked to the project's indirect benefits were also considered in this analysis. These indirect benefits bring about income changes both to skilled and unskilled labour. There are important constraints to this evaluation but an attempt to estimate positive income changes derived from the free housing service was undertaken.

NOTES

1. A third step can be included in the analysis when the project's impact on low-income groups is important. In this case, a coefficient of distributional impact (CDI) can be estimated as follows:

$$\text{CDI} = \frac{\text{Present value of the net direct transfers received by low-income groups}}{\text{Net present value of the project}}$$

This third step is not considered here because it is implicitly assumed that a project highly intensive in capital such as the Carajás project cannot generate a relevant direct impact on low-income groups (Bayro 1981, pp. 76–81).

2. The Carajás project was funded by three different sources of financing: CVRD's own resources (46.15 per cent), domestic loans (21.69 per cent) and foreign loans (32.16 per cent) (Silva Neto 1992, chap. 6, section 6.5.2).
3. In a different situation, a transfer payment from the project's equity owners to the lenders would be generated if the real interest rate were greater than the discount rate (Londero 1987, pp. 134–8, Curry and Weiss 1993, pp. 267–70).
4. It should be remembered that the profit tax is only one of the financial flows from the project to the government. Due to the high expenditures with the acquisition of manufactured capital goods, the Carajás project was supposed to create important revenue taxes during its implementation phase. Instead of this, the Brazilian government exempted CVRD from all indirect taxes that are normally levied on the production and transport of goods and services, such as the value-added tax (*Imposto de Circulaçao de Mercadorias e Serviços – ICMS*). The same happened with the tax that is levied on the production of manufactured goods (*Imposto sobre Produtos Industrializados – IPI*) (Brazil/PGC 1981, 1982).
5. It can be verified that the sum of the last row matches the estimated project's NPV, i.e. US$149.7 million
6. The fact that transport costs and distribution margins could not be identified means that some of the project's suppliers could not be identified and the respective income changes could not be measured. Although this constraint is important because the project site is far from the nearest port, a sensitivity test could show that it does not change the main analytical results (Silva Neto 1992, chap. 7).
7. It would be necessary to improve the analysis to know in detail the structure of import control for each individual traded input. However, there is no point in such refinement since this structure is subject to variations both in the short and in the long term. Therefore, even if the knowledge of the import control pattern were available other simplifying assumptions would be inevitable.
8. This result is only valid if SW = MW. If CVRD had to pay higher market wages to attract skilled labour then this increase in nominal wage would create a transfer payment that would benefit those workers. This possibility is not introduced into the analysis.
9. However, income changes caused by payroll taxes (social security and other compulsory contributions) are not considered. It should not be forgotten that the analysis at market prices takes into account only resource flows.
10. These non-traded items could be identified and evaluated at shadow prices. Construction was the most important one for the project's implementation while electricity and water supply as well as some specialized services are used mainly during the project's operational phase.
11. Pig iron production in Brazil's Eastern Amazon is a forward linkage caused by the operation of the Carajás project. Details on the characteristics of this linkage and the related indirect cost (deforestation) are provided by Silva Neto (1994).
12. The impact of this additional cost on the financial profitability of the pig iron project is not examined here; such an analysis goes beyond the boundaries of this research.
13. Imports of coal are an indirect cost and their financing will always bring about distributional effects. It should be clear that there are other alternatives to solve this problem. For example, the government may decide to pay higher subsidies to import coal. In this case, this cost will be paid by the taxpayer and not by the pig iron producers' shareholders.
14. To evaluate the health and education services provided by CVRD to its employees one must estimate the costs of the resources saved elsewhere in the Brazilian economy. The basic data for evaluating these services are their specific operating costs provided that they were available in a without-project situation.

    It should be clear that an indirect benefit and, therefore, additional income changes would arise if the workers came from regions where there were no such services, or if there were, they could not afford them. However, the available data do not provide any grounds for a reasonable assumption that could create conditions for a rough evaluation of these services.

15. This is the decade in which the Carajás project was implemented and, therefore, when the project's important distributional effects were generated.
16. Skilled labour is excluded because it was assumed that MW = SW. This means that such workers do not get additional income due to the difference between market and shadow prices and, therefore, for the specific purpose of this analysis the share of labour in the National Accounts can be attributed to unskilled labour.
17. However, these steelmakers are also the project's gainers. Silva Neto (1992, chap. 4) concluded that the Carajás project depressed the iron ore price on the international iron ore market. Therefore, the steelmakers received a positive income change that would not be available in a without-project situation. The counterpart of this positive income change was absorbed by CVRD's competitors that had to sell iron ore for a lower price.

REFERENCES

Bayro, L.M. (1981), 'Guidelines for measuring the distributional impact of potable water supply programs', mimeo, Washington, DC: IDB.

Bayro, L.M. (1983), 'Guidelines for measuring the distributional impact of industrial investment programs', mimeo, Washington, DC: IDB.

Brazil/PGC (1981), *Declaration Act no. 01/81* (Ato Declaratório no.01/81, 30.08.1981), Brasilia: PGC.

Brazil/PGC (1982), *Declaration Act no. 15/82* (Ato Declaratório no.15/82, 17.08.1982), Brasília: PGC.

Castagnino, E.S. (1982), *Guidelines for measuring the distributional impact of mining sector credit programs*, mimeo, Washington, DC: IDB.

Curry, S.R. and J. Weiss (1993), *Project analysis in developing countries*, London: Macmillan.

CVRD (1990), Interview with CVRD's officials (May/June).

ECCA (1991), *Relatório sobre a gestão contabilistica e a gestão financeira da Comunidade Européia do Carvão e do Aço* (Portuguese version), Luxembourg: ECCA.

Hill, S. (1980), 'Financial model of the Carajás Iron Ore Project. Report to CVRD', mimeo, London: Samuel Hill Project Finance Ltd.

IBGE (1990), *Estatísticas históricas do Brasil*, 2nd edition, Rio de Janeiro: IBGE.

Londero, E.H. (1981), 'El Salvador' in T.A. Powers (ed.), *Estimating accounting prices for project appraisal. Case studies in the Little–Mirrlees/Squire–van der Tak Method*, Washington, DC: IDB.

Londero, E.H. (1987), *Benefits and beneficiaries*, Washington, DC: IDB.

ODA (1988), *Appraisal of projects in developing countries. A guide for economists*, London: HMSO.

Silva Neto, A.L. da (1992), 'A cost-benefit analysis of a large mining project in Brazil', mimeo, unpublished PhD thesis, Bradford: DPPC, University of Bradford.

Silva Neto, A.L. da (1993), 'The international effects of mining projects: the case of Carajás iron ore', *Resources Policy*, **19** (2), June, 124–30.

Silva Neto, A.L. da (1994), 'Environmental effects and the Carajás iron ore project, Brazil' in J. Weiss (ed.), *The economics of project appraisal and the environment*, Aldershot, UK: Edward Elgar.

Ward, W.A. et al. (1991), *The economics of project analysis. A practitioner's guide*, EDI Technical Materials, Washington, DC: World Bank.

World Bank (1982), 'Carajás iron ore project. Staff appraisal report', mimeo, Washington: World Bank.
Zraick, S. (1983), 'Equacionamento financeiro do Projeto Ferro Carajás', in *CVRD–Revista*, **4** (12), June.

15. Cost–benefit analysis in the project cycle: the example of French-speaking African countries

Jean-Pierre Foirry

INTRODUCTION

Considerable advances have been made in recent years regarding theoretical aspects of cost–benefit analysis (CBA) and its applications to project appraisal (Kirkpatrick 1994). Progress has been particularly significant in the analysis of linkages between macroeconomic policy and shadow prices, in the measure of non-monetary benefits and in the appraisal procedures of large projects.

However, theoretical advances have not clearly led to practical implementation by governments, ministries or organizations. This is true in most parts of the world. For instance, health economists from the World Bank Economic Development Institute (EDI) are trained in the use of CBA; however in many countries World Bank projects in the health sector are not selected according to the method set out in the training course. In France, some major ministries (for example, health and education) either do not use economic analysis, or do not always put its results into practice (for example in relation to roads). In some European countries, and even within the European Community (EC Commission 1993), project-cycle management has become more intensively used than CBA. Consider now evidence from French-speaking African countries: like most developing countries, they have introduced new methods in public investment programming, by using rolling three-year public investment programmes (PIP); moreover some of them have recently set up sophisticated public expenditure programs (PEP). But in any case CBA is neither widely nor rigorously used, and the use of CBA has not increased during the last years.

This gap between theory and practice has led to the development of the new public economics, which attempts to combine normative welfare economics (which projects are the best from a theoretical point of view) and positive economics (how projects are selected in the real world). The problem is finally to appreciate and perhaps to reinforce the credibility of CBA. One of our arguments is that some consensus among project analysts is required in order to improve usefulness and credibility of CBA. This consensus must be sought at all levels, in relation to both theoretical foundations and areas of implementation.

In this methodological chapter, we do not deal with the credibility problem of CBA in itself. We focus on the acknowledgement, the perception and the use of this tool by professionals and public managers. The question is how to make CBA feasible and useful. The analysis is useful if it serves its genuine purpose (choosing between alternative projects), and if it is not a mere alibi for decisions which have already been taken and have restricted the range of potential choices. The analysis is credible if there is a consensus about its usefulness.

On this basis one must speculate on factors that are likely to influence the usefulness and credibility of CBA. These factors include the reliability of information and the relevance of the economic theory used by the analyst: for example, if the 'effects method' is used, is it consistent with the foundations of public economics? Is it a credible alternative to the traditional shadow price method? These factors also include the applicability of instruments, the acceptance of instruments and results by the different actors, political and administrative constraints, and strategic aspects of public choices Such a multi-factor approach goes far beyond the determinism of pure single-factor approaches (optimal normative theory, public choice approach, institutionalism, and so forth), and it emphazises the synergism between conceptual analysis, ideological factors, interest group actions, political and administrative constraints and exogenous changes. It is hoped that from this perspective it is finally possible to understand the scope and the conditions for promoting and strengthening the role of rational analysis and the influence of cost–benefit methodology.

A CONCEPTUAL FRAMEWORK FOR ASSESSING THE USE OF CBA IN PROJECT APPRAISAL IN FRENCH-SPEAKING AFRICAN COUNTRIES

CBA is the rational examination of a decision (a project) in terms of its consequences for monetary costs and benefits. The analyst forecasts costs and benefits over the life of an investment and calculates synthetic indicators such as the internal rate of return (IRR). In this chapter 'CBA' is understood as 'sound efficiency CBA'. The qualifying term 'sound' is important: it means that the analysis and its results are not deliberately invented or distorted. Within the framework of project appraisal, an efficiency test is a simple decision rule which consists in measuring the net effect of the project on social welfare. The measure of this net effect involves a comparison of the economy 'with' the project with the economy 'without' the project. As the analysis of the project is necessarily associated with a state of the economy (i.e. a set of policies), the policies and the project should be designed (one may say selected) according to the same criterion (social welfare); thus the historical form of CBA in countries with strong imbalances is shadow-pricing analysis. In our approach, we therefore deal simultaneously with two questions: first, why should CBA not be used or promoted by agents in charge of project appraisal? Second, how can the image of CBA be improved and its role strengthened?

Textbooks usually indicate only the normative process of selection of optimal projects which maximize social welfare, whereas people in charge of appraisal often choose projects which are very different from the optimal ones. According to some economists, the reasons for this are lack of technical skills and imperfect information: in that sense, the decision process just has to be improved. According to other economists, the explanations have to be found in the objective functions of all people that are involved in the project cycle (governments, administrators, financial backers): their objective functions are likely to be quite different from the social welfare function. It is very important to combine these two approaches, as understanding whether and how theoretical ideas (what we call conceptual analysis) have consequences also depends upon the interest officials have in their use.

CBA is supposed to be conducted by a benevolent, well informed and wise planner; in this chapter it relates more particularly to physical productive investments. Although they observe a concrete investment process, it is obvious that decisions are in fact not always rational, centralized and normative. Moreover they do not mainly concern physical productive investments in developing countries. The rationality of CBA implies a progress within the project cycle following five successive stages:

1. Existence of a problem
2. Identification of the problem
3. Knowledge of alternative solutions
4. CBA
5. Decision.

But many decision processes do not follow this logical sequence. Some decisions precede CBA. Some solutions precede problems (for example imitation of neighbours, or sensitivity to suppliers). There are sometimes no alternative solutions. Centralization means that there is only one decision level in institutional organizations. But at least three problems arise within the project cycle that are related to the influence of politicians, the relationship between ministries and the influence of aid donors. Normative aspects of CBA imply, first, that there is a market characterized by two pillars: private rational agents and coordination through prices; second, that public interventions exist because of market failures. In fact there are also other kinds of coordination in organizations (through specific rules) and other kinds of market failures (in public interventions).

A significant and increasing part of African PIPs is made up of non-physical projects and includes more and more recurrent costs. As some countries are proving unable to meet current expenditures, their investment budgets are becoming instruments to find money instead of being used to allocate scarce resources appropriately. In these countries, some projects involve small-investment components which are used as alibis. Some project cycles are chaotic because people in charge of them are waiting for new financial backing. As soon as the investment budget represents a way of finding money and financing current costs, the credibility of CBA as an approach to investment decision making becomes, of course, questionable. In that context national agents are willing to accept all kinds of funding whatever the purpose of the project: they may even seek loans if one admits people are shortsighted or expect debt cancellation. Donors are therefore responsible for the choice of good projects. Nevertheless their ability to do so is questionable: first, there is some asymmetry in information, as the donor ignores the behaviour of other donors and lacks precise information on new projects or national requirements; second, there may be a hierarchy among donors about the use of CBA, so that the country is given some latitude regarding project choice; third, donors have their own objectives as organizations.

Rejection or distortion of CBA can be emphasized if variants of the public choice framework are used. Within this framework politicians select projects with a view to maximizing their chance of keeping political power by ensuring some social stability and implementing distribution rules in order to set up winning coalitions. It may also be worth noting that politicians are in a good position to select projects according to their benefits for their traditional partisans (status quo model) or to lobbies (pressure group model) or to important new voters (adding machine model).

Public decisions also reflect the institutional background of the country. According to the Institutional School, the two main points are the degree of fragmentation of political authority (to what extent are decisions centralized?) and the degree of independence of the administrations in charge of projects. As soon as projects are allocated among a large number of ministries, and central ministries have weak power over them, an important bureaucratic bias arises. In our model, technical ministries or sectoral bureaucrats stand at the heart of the process as they are in charge of project design:

for example, health ministries are in charge of projects in the health sector. In most African countries, even though bureaucrats have not necessarily the same duties or gains, they do not only aim at maximizing their budgets; above all they endeavour to maximize external aid, which implies projects or programmes. It may be in the interest of bureaucrats to avoid CBA for many reasons: the number of efficient projects is too low, some bureaucrats want to avoid possible intersectoral arbitration from planners, donors themselves do not always use CBA, and some bureaucrats include many hidden costs in projects. One way to improve this situation would be to adjust the ministerial organization chart to the structural evolvement of the PIP; another solution would be to allow some bureaucrats to manage projects in other sectors. These two solutions have been implemented in African countries; nevertheless it has often been done superfluously and has led to costly conflicts. The best solution would be an enforcement of coordination between donors.

PUBLIC INVESTMENT AND PUBLIC EXPENDITURE PROGRAMMES AND CBA

Planners represent an example of central ministries. In some countries there is a conflict between the planning agency and the budget agency. Often the power of the budget agency is very weak as a very high proportion of the PIP is financed by external donors. Consequently, planners are often responsible for PIP and PEP; their power has considerably increased over the last years, all the more since they have also been in charge of structural adjustment programmes (SAPs) and social programmes. As a result, they are in charge of promoting official guidelines for financial and economic appraisal of projects. Until now, actions in those fields have not proved successful for many reasons: first, some planning agencies have promoted one given method (e.g. the effects method in Senegal) which has been criticized by shadow price method experts; second, some planning agencies have promoted one method (e.g. the multi-criteria method in Mauritania and Ruanda) which had been recommended by one single donor, but this method was immediately criticized by other donors; third, many donors find it unnecessary to use this selection process because they have got their own method; moreover many planning agencies are still trying to make an inventory of projects in their countries (e.g. Chad is just creating PIP); some countries have undertaken sophisticated PEP (e.g. Burundi and Madagascar) which neglect the project appraisal methodology.

Multilateral aid donors comprise three kinds of influential agents: national government representatives, international bureaucrats and interest groups. International bureaucrats have their own objective function (budget, power, prestige, risk aversion) which may interfere with national Paretian choices; they are sometimes willing to develop their activities in new promising fields; thus they may come into conflict with all other parties, which may lead to a waste of resources. National governments' representatives may show ideological preferences and may play a leading role in project selection according to certain given factors: rules of vote, internal and external credibility, support of interest groups, existence of coalitions, and so forth. Within institutions, changes can occur: for instance some of their members may become more or less in favour of CBA for ideological reasons ('more': microeconomists, and 'less': Marxists and macroeconomists), psychological reasons ('more': economists, and 'less': sociologists, jurists) or any other reasons. Outside institutions, some interest groups with particular views on CBA may become more or less powerful (ecologists, women, consumers against producers). The role of CBA depends of course upon its ability to take into account new problems (environment effects, for instance).

The relationship between theoreticians (those in charge of conceptual analysis), professional analysts and other agents is problematic. Professional analysts know theories, but the way a project is appraised also depends upon the donor who required the appraisal; thus there is an implicit process of selection of the analyst. Success of a given theory is less based on its scientific quality or even on its applicability than on its ability to meet officials' objectives at a given point in time. In French-speaking African countries, one historical specificity has been that traditional CBA has been seriously called into question for ideological, political and practical reasons; thus French analysts have promoted the effects method rather than shadow-pricing methods. Paradoxically authors first criticized the role of the efficiency criterion (binding a voluntarist planner) at a moment when shadow-pricing methods became more sophisticated in order to take into account other criteria such as equity or industrialization; thus the main criticism of these methods was that they were much too sophisticated. However significant developments of the effects method have been achieved and these cannot be neglected for the future (see also Chapter 7 of this volume). It can now be stated that in almost any standard PIP of a French-speaking African country, 10 per cent of projects are analysed using the effects method and 10 per cent using shadow-pricing methods (the remaining 80 per cent are subjected to no economic analysis). As regards multilateral institutions, the effects method has never been taken into account by the World Bank; however, it is known by UNIDO and is now influential in the EC.

Though the extent to which ideas are influential depends upon the degree of convergence between theoretical progress and official interests, exogenous factors may also play an obvious role in changing behaviour. Technological changes may lead to new institutional rules or to modification of the scope of public projects; they may make easier the use of sophisticated CBA. External factors include evolution of external dependence and modification of aid conditionalities: among these is the implementation – ordered and financed by donors – of PIP and PEP.

In the 1980s, the crucial question in all French-speaking African countries was: since the old system of planning, programming and budgeting was not entirely satisfactory and did not guarantee sound resource allocation, what instruments should be used (Foirry 1988)? The old system comprised a comprehensive medium-term plan (five or six years) and an ordinary annual budget. The objective was to implement a system in which planning and budgeting would be treated as two facets of the same overall process; it would thus allow improved selection and programming of public investments. New programming methods should focus on three distinct characteristics: adaptability, coordination and selectivity. The new programming system included the setting up of three-year rolling PIPs.

What were the effects of the reforms on project appraisal? In spite of official recommendations, sophisticated CBA tended to be neglected in favour of two prevailing concerns of the 1980s: sector priorities and recurrent costs. The question is thus to understand how the introduction of these concerns can improve the choice of public projects.

Most countries have not succeeded in implementing all the elements for the reform. The reform comprises four stages: to improve information about public investments and expenditures; to change the size and composition of public expenditures; to increase marginal efficiency of public investments; and to increase efficiency of public expenditures. Distinguishing these four stages is useful: some countries have not gone beyond the first two stages and temporary changes in the size and composition of public expenditures do not necessarily involve temporary or permanent improvements in efficiency. The failure of the reforms can be explained by many factors (which differ among countries), for example:

- institutional matters and capacity to implement reforms are not appropriate;
- reaching the fourth stage too quickly (for example through too sophisticated PEP methodology) puts administration in inextricable difficulties;
- reforms are based on new instruments but they do not take into account process and behaviour (for example of bureaucrats, planners, politicians, donors);
- the financial resource constraint is a determining factor and intrasectoral choice is made according to a 'top-down' instead of a 'bottom-up' method.

Increasing the efficiency of public investment and expenditures in the long term crucially implies taking into account all these factors. We shall not go further on this matter, but just consider the difference between 'top-down' and 'bottom-up' methods.

The 'top-down' approach includes the following elements: identifying one global investment level in the macroeconomic framework; using sector priorities to generate new programmes for priority activities; and cutting down expenditures in other activities. The 'bottom-up' approach includes the following elements: considering the availability of financing and recurrent costs; and reviewing projects and programmes using project selection criteria. In some countries, classification of projects has been used as an application of the 'bottom-up' approach in order to reach a core programme. In the Ivory Coast, projects are divided into three categories: core projects, projects with a possible delay, and questionable projects. In Benin, a sequential screening is used: projects are first divided into feasible projects and non-feasible projects; second, feasible projects are divided into priority projects and non-priority projects; third, priority projects are ranked where possible, but not inevitably, using CBA. In most countries, there is relatively little reliance on CBA: sectoral bureaucrats and certain donors give greater importance to project conformity with sector strategies than to CBA. The other important scope of the reforms deals with the appropriateness of recurrent spending and cost recovery: this implies scrutiny of public expenditures using financial viability (including their productivity regarding the private sector, and the grant element of external financing etc.) and cost-effectiveness analysis rather than CBA. However, in our view, conformity with sector strategies and appropriateness of recurrent spending should not replace the use of CBA, but should rather be coupled with it in a multi-criteria approach which would please all participants. However, the question of the methodology and theoretical base of CBA needs also to be addressed.

THE USE OF CBA IN THE PROJECT CYCLE: TOWARDS A CONSENSUAL CONCEPTUAL ANALYSIS?

As mentioned earlier, CBA is the examination of a decision in terms of its consequences in monetary costs and benefits. The analysis is conducted by a benevolent, well informed and wise planner who evaluates a project either by assessing the value of inputs and outputs using shadow prices (this is the 'dual' method), or by analysing its general equilibrium effects and comparing the state of the world with and without the project in terms of social welfare (this is the 'primal' method). Benevolence and information issues obviously represent a crucial matter for the credibility of CBA and have been partly discussed above. Let us consider now the apparent absence of consensus about CBA methods.

Though the new effects method, which should not be identified with the traditional effects method that was strongly criticized in the 1970s (see Balassa 1976), is a primal method, it may be considered as equivalent to the dual methods (border-pricing method or domestic-pricing method): all of them are economic cost–benefit methods (see Franck, Chapter 7 in this volume). The difference between the old and new effects methods is that the new method takes into account opportunity costs through negative value-added and includes differences between domestic prices and international prices. The new effects method and the border-pricing or domestic-pricing methods tend normally to conclude with similar accept/reject decisions. The 'social welfare' function represents an objective function which reflects government preferences in the dual method and rough estimates of value-added in the effects method. The condition for equivalence is that the objective function should only reflect the efficiency criterion in its monetary expression, without including any interpersonal comparisons of welfare. If necessary, equity and other criteria may be considered in a second stage.

In Figure 15.1, equivalence between the effects method and the domestic-pricing method are described. At the theoretical level, the border-pricing method involves a refined set of procedures which have undeniable theoretical justification. However, it is easier to compare the domestic-pricing approach to the effects method as its numeraire is domestic prices.

With respect to the equity criterion, the effects method gives a practical approach which is worth considering: division of national net value-added among beneficiaries (agents or regions) is particularly interesting since it can be easily understood by administrators, thus avoiding value judgements regarding distribution across households. Note that for practical appraisal of a textile project in Pakistan, Weiss (1982) used a similar method and even went further by introducing multiplier effects which do not usually exist in the effects method. Likewise, Squire (1989) suggests that distribution effects should be set out in qualitative terms apart from shadow-pricing analysis.

When considering the two criteria, it appears that the effects method and the shadow-pricing methods should not be perceived as alternative or competitive methods: they are in fact complementary methods for analysing all large productive projects. As regards small productive projects, forward and backward linkages should normally be neglected; sophisticated economic approaches are useless. Note that for infrastructure projects such as the renovation of marketplaces, all forward and backward effects with price effects represent the main point of the appraisal: when using shadow-pricing methods, they must be considered as part of the project.

EFFECTS METHOD	DOMESTIC-PRICING METHOD
FINANCIAL ANALYSIS	
Financial analysis based on the French accounting system: Gross revenues – inputs costs = value added (VA) VA – labour costs – indirect taxes = 'excédent brut d'exploitation' (EBE) EBE – interest charges – direct taxes = 'capacité d'autofinancement' (CAF) CAF – contingencies = 'marge brute d'autofinancement' (MBA) Analysts estimate the net present value and the IRR using the CAF or the EBE less investment costs and less 'without-project' CAF or EBE	Financial analysis based on the English accounting system Gross revenues – variable costs = gross margin gross margin – fixed costs (including interest charges) = cash flow cash flow + interest charges = total cash flow cash flow – depreciation = net profit cash flow + loans – investments – less capital repayments = net cash flow Analysts estimate the net present value and the IRR using the total cash flow less investment costs and less 'without-project' cash flow
ECONOMIC ANALYSIS	
Economic analysis is based on the value-added less part of labour costs (those related to people still working without the project) THEN Indirect effects (backward and forward linkages) and other external effects are introduced: • backward linkages: values added on inputs when idle capacities exist (or all values when a follow-up investment is included in the project) • forward linkages: values added for the use of project output as an input in other activities (with a follow-up investment if necessary) • consumer rent if the consumer price is modified • economic valuation of environmental effects • loss of customs taxes	Economic analysis is based on the cash flow, which is equivalent to the net value-added when eliminating transfers (taxes) and using shadow-wage rate THEN Other shadow prices and external physical effects are introduced: • shadow pricing of inputs when idle capacities exist • shadow pricing of output including consumer rent if the consumer price is modified • economic valuation of environmental effects • shadow pricing of foreign exchange
SECOND STAGE After eliminating all transfers of revenues with foreign countries, net national value added is computed. Then its division among beneficiaries can be analysed	SECOND STAGE We then consider the equity criterion (historically, through the introduction of social marginal utilities of income or welfare weights in expressions involving shadow prices)
THIRD STAGE If necessary, other criteria are introduced: for example, industrialization, food availability, sustainability, recurrent costs in the government budget	THIRD STAGE If necessary, other criteria are introduced: for example, industrialization, food availability, sustainability, recurrent costs in the government budget

Figure 15.1 Equivalence of effects and shadow-pricing approaches

Regarding other effects (such as the effect of a project on sustainability, and recurrent costs), we suggest that multi-criteria analysis, shadow-pricing methods and the effects method should be combined. Other criteria should not be included in the IRR estimation in order to improve its transparency: when policy makers want to use the IRR criterion according to their own objectives, they may either change parameters and assumptions or they may introduce other criteria; thus economic interpretation of the IRR becomes impossible. Outcomes of the shadow-pricing method (regarding efficiency) and of the effects method (regarding equity) should be used as an input for multi-criteria analysis. Multi-criteria analysis has three advantages: it splits effects up into significant categories (the aim is to avoid double counting); it allows interaction between technicians and decision makers (the aim is to avoid long delays); and it is suited to the real world characterized by bounded rationality in which people choose feasible projects rather than optimal ones. Multi-criteria analysis allows various kinds of procedures: quantitative weights may be neglected when there are no trade-offs between aims or when there are acceptable limits for each criterion.

The problem of recurrent costs is often related to public fiscal constraints and public resources. Therefore a premium on savings is sometimes introduced. It should be underlined that in many African countries the issue is less that of promoting public saving than of overcoming its non-existence. So project appraisal in many social sectors should be based not only on the understanding of linkages between structural adjustment reforms and shadow prices, but on the identification of connections between macroeconomic changes (whether or not they result from reforms) and financial prices. Thus the value of a rigid benefit–cost ratio does not matter; demonstrating the possibility of funding the costs of activities whatever happens in the external economic environment is far more important. For example, investments in health sectors may depend on cost-recovery systems or flexible tariff policy. Cost-effectiveness methods are well suited to determine the minimum cost levels and the ways of funding them. For some classes of projects, it may be interesting to address these issues apart from other criteria, especially when measures of benefits are doubtful or when there is some difficulty in connecting specific benefits to specific costs.

Multi-criteria analysis is all the more convenient as it is satisfying for the Paretian decision maker who has many objectives and who is above all willing to keep some latitude for decision. He often thinks that CBA imposes choices and emphasizes efficiency too much. His aim is rather to ease social change, to avoid stupid decisions and perhaps to widen the scope of potential rational decisions. Combining efficiency (through shadow-pricing methods), equity (through the effects method), sustainability (through financial impact assessments) and cost recovery (through cost-effectiveness analysis) does not imply that these criteria have always the same importance for each kind of project. But it enables one to avoid two criticisms of CBA which weaken its credibility: its applicability and relevance of the information it provides.

CBA is not really controversial when applied to productive projects, for which assessing the monetary value of benefits and costs is relatively easy. However, during the two last decades, a decreasing number of productive projects has been earmarked for inclusion in PIP, due to reforms and private-sector development. On the contrary, PIP includes an increasing number of institutional, social projects and multi-sectoral projects for which appraisal can be very complex. There are two problems: identifying components of CBA, and expressing these components in monetary units. However the analyst may choose to select only the components that can be easily expressed in monetary units. The best way to avoid this problem is to require the analyst to demonstrate first an exhaustive impact assessment. Impact assessment aims at describing all the expected effects of the project and at selecting the best measures for assessing outcomes (Rossi and Freeman 1993). In such a framework, CBA comes at the final stage of impact assessment and represents a part of multi-criteria analysis.

CBA also requires a great deal of quantitative information, for example related to shadow prices, input–output matrices, and expected supply and demand. But first, there is no perfection in data collection; and second, analysts and organizations always use different data bases. In a poor French-speaking African country, as we have seen, only 10 per cent of projects are analysed with shadow-pricing methods in a standard PIP. Furthermore, economic analysis may be carried out using completely different shadow prices for projects in the same country; for example, in Mauritanian PIP, shadow-wage rates range between 30 per cent to 100 per cent of official wage rates for non-skilled workers; shadow exchange rates range between 100 per cent and 200 per cent of official exchange rates; life of projects range between seven and fourteen years for the same agricultural projects. All shadow-pricing methods in French-speaking Africa require an official internal rate of return (IRR) of 12 per cent after the conventional sensitivity testing (20 per cent increase in costs, 20 per cent decrease in benefits). In most cases, shadow-pricing analysis does not address equity issues, but it often includes some monetary measures of environment effects.

At this stage, it is important to keep in mind problems related to differences between the analyst, the theoretician and the planner. The analyst has to use existing information and is often obliged to be content with crude data. In the country, the planner should be in charge of evaluating shadow prices; but either they do not do this or they sometimes use estimates of one organization which are not accepted by others. The credibility of CBA would be increased if an agreement between international organizations could be reached or if the planners could give some guidance on what shadow prices to use nationally. Using special studies and sophisticated research, the theoretician may obtain some important results: for example, decisions vary if equity issues are introduced using a social welfare function or if specific conversion factors for non-tradeable goods are estimated through input–output analysis.

The planner may have valid reasons (time, money) to include projects in PIPs and investment budgets without revising economic analysis, but above all the main reason is that CBA plays no role in the process. Revision is useless for two reasons: first, the planner and the funding agency may have previously chosen the project; second, CBA has no influence on the next stages of the project cycle. Though this does not question the credibility of CBA itself, it puts a strong limit to its role as an aid to operational decisions. For analysts, CBA is too often an 'art of camouflage', since they are obliged to reach an IRR of 12 per cent whatever the project: for example, the main objective of low-traffic roads or other local projects is not efficiency but rather economic and political national integration; so, why not include this objective in a multi-criteria analysis?

The other reason must be addressed guardedly. *Ex-ante* CBA is important in itself for projects and programmes which cannot be abandoned or modified once they have been implemented. In PIP, most projects do not include significant physical investments and they are inserted in funding agencies' long-term expenditure plans; so evaluation during the life of the projects or programmes is crucial. The two prerequisites for good evaluation are first, that the objectives, costs and benefits of the projects have been well defined and articulated during the project design and appraisal; and second, that the projects are well implemented. This implies interdependence between project analysis, monitoring and evaluation and should increase the interest of officials in CBA and other methods.

In conclusion, a great many factors have to be taken into account in order to increase the usefulness and credibility of CBA in the project cycle. The normative economic methodology should not be questioned in itself; the problem is rather to know how it can be usefully applied in the real world. More generally, the economic theory of expenditure policy is more difficult to apply than other economic theories. Some issues are beyond the scope of economists; nevertheless other issues should be addressed and solved by economists themselves. One should also keep in mind that expenditure decisions require science and technique, but also vision and judgement.

REFERENCES

Balassa, B. (1976), 'The Effects Method of Project Evaluation', World Bank Staff Working Paper no. 231, Washington, DC: World Bank.

Bénard, J. (1989), 'Le calcul économique public: conflit des paradigmes et résistance des organisations et des mentalités', *Revue d'Economie Politique*, no.2.

Curry, S. and J. Weiss (1993), *Project Analysis in Developing Countries*, London: Macmillan.

Dreze, J. and N. Stern (1987), 'The theory of Cost-Benefit Analysis', in A.J. Auerbach and M. Feldstein (eds), *Handbook of Public Economics, Vol. II*, New York: Elsevier Science Publishers.

EC Commission (1993), *Project Cycle Management: Integrated Approach and Logical Framework*, EC Commission.

Foirry, J.P. (1988), *Public Investment Programming in African Countries: Experiences and Problems*, Washington, DC: EDI–World Bank.

Kirkpatrick, C. (1994), 'New Developments in Project Appraisal in Developing Countries', *Journal of International Development*, January–February.

Laffay, J.D. and J. Lecaillon (1993), *La dimension politique de l'ajustement économique*, Paris: OECD.

Rossi, H. and P. Freeman (1993), *Evaluation: a Systematic Approach*, London: Sage.

Sell, A. (1994), 'The Integration of Financial and Economic Analysis in Project Analysis', *Journal of International Development*, January–February.

Squire, L. (1989), 'Project Evaluation in Theory and Practice', in H. Chenery and T.N. Srinivasan (eds), *Handbook of Development Economics, Vol. II*, New York: Elsevier Science Publishers.

Van Pelt, M.F. (1994), 'Sustainability-oriented Appraisal of Agricultural Projects', *Journal of International Development*, January–February.

Weiss, J. (1982), 'Evaluation pratique de projets industriels', New York: UNIDO.

16. The evaluation of technical assistance projects for development in Eastern and Central Europe

Mark Gray*

INTRODUCTION

Since the dissolution of many of the former socialist state systems of the world began in 1989, there has been a strong desire in the West to aid the transition and stabilization process by offering technical assistance (hereafter TA) to support economic reform. A number of international agencies, including the European Union, the British ODA, the World Bank, the UNDP and the IMF have established programmes of technical support, education and training to equip the newly democratized countries of the socialist part of the world to undertake the technological and logistical reforms required – although there is no very clear evidence of how much TA has been placed in transition states (UNECE 1993, pp. 17–22). Familiarity with the economic conditions of these countries suggests that there may be problems in evaluating how successful TA actually is in delivering the benefits claimed for it.

For while the technical proficiency and integrity of the appraisers of these TA projects is beyond reproach, the practical difficulties in their way are not inconsiderable. Since the 1960s TA has grown significantly as a proportion of total 'first world' aid funding (see Cassen 1994; Santizo 1987; Berg 1993 on US TA; de Schaetzen 1985 on Swiss TA; Stokeld 1982, pp. 1006–8 on Japanese TA; Kabangu 1991 on Lomé Convention TA) giving added urgency to the need for some solution to the many impediments to maximizing value for money. The growing size of the direct financing budget of organizations like the World Bank and the IMF was the proximate cause of the rise of technical advice, cooperation and assistance in the 1980s (Helleiner 1992) – but the growing significance of TA in the overall expenditures of donor

*This chapter does not necessarily reflect the views of the College, the Cabinet Office or any other part of the UK government or civil service. Dr Gray was a TACIS programme expert in Ukraine in 1994–95; this chapter should not be taken to express the views of the programme, the Commission or any associated partner in the programme.

organizations has not produced any very discernible interest in the value for money and risk associated with TA projects nor any noticeable improvement in central control of remote TA programmes, a fact which has led some commentators on EU TA spending in Eastern and Central Europe, such as the *Economist* magazine, to assert that 'poor management of [programmes] has impaired their effectiveness and irked their recipients' (*Economist* 1993. See also House of Commons, Foreign Affairs Committee 1994, pp. xxxvi–xxxviii and xliv–xlv).

The variety of TA schemes in transition economies makes it difficult to define the 'typical' or 'average' TA programme – and consequently to define the benefits which such schemes might generally seek to capture. While the EBRD has funded bakery plant modifications in Ukraine, it has also funded bank supervision training; and while the EU–TACIS programme has supported the reform of the Ukrainian civil service, it has also provided hardware for computer support. In short, TA includes a mix of both labour-intensive and capital-intensive endowments, the benefits of which are often difficult to ascribe to one specific project. The 'spillover' benefits from previous projects within a programme may only be internalized, for example, when a later project is completed. Clearly the phasing of projects might be used to maximize project benefits by, for example, putting training TA in place before capital assets (Cassen 1994, p. 144; Cassella and Eichengreen 1994). Some assistance schemes have allocated capital assets before labour-augmenting training. Sometimes capital endowments are seen as preconditions for productivity gains *ex-ante* of human resource development; alternatively, training and education schemes are often regarded by international agencies as necessary to capture and extend the benefits of capital augmentation.

In general the higher profile given to the macroeconomic debate about the 'sequencing' of transition processes and the speed of transition has relegated the microeconomic analysis of optimal investment strategies for TA programmes to a lesser, supporting role. It is difficult to find in the very large post-socialist transition literature any very clear analysis of how TA strategies ought to be evaluated, apart from occasional generalizations concerning the extent to which programme success is likely to be contingent upon the co-ordination abilities of transition governments (McKinnon 1991; Dhanji 1991; Portes 1994; Sachs 1993; Blanchard et al. 1991). Moreover, the 'sequencing debate' – which has been a central issue for Western commentators on the progress of reform – has directed attention away from the vital question of evaluating the success of projects and programmes for the sponsors of those programmes.

This chapter explores some of the issues which face practical project and programme appraisers in assessing the benefits and costs of TA projects in the transition states. The extent of international aid and assistance to these states has been one of the most remarkable features of the last few years. A new awareness of the need for direct technical help in economies to which often inappropriate but extensive capital assets and labour skills have been bequeathed by socialist forerunners has led to the development of a large number of TA programmes, each of which has spawned several projects. This targeted aid is usually intended to help speed transition and stabilization; unlike other aid programmes, TA is also generally expected to augment (not replace) existing capital and skills. These general aims for TA projects and programmes should not be forgotten, for they provide a framework for the appraisal of the value for money and benefits of particular expenditures.

Whether the pace of reform, restructuring and transition is fast or slow, whether the sequencing of reform is direct or indirect, there will be a need for the agencies funding TA programmes to assess their projects. A number of problems seem to have arisen in relation to this apparently simple exercise for which, as yet, no experience among Western governments (either in giving bilateral, tied or gift aid) has supplied a satisfactory answer. Unique difficulties of identifying the terms for the *ex-ante* evaluation of project benefits, of shadow pricing the unaugmented assets and skills of transition economies, of determining project risk, of minimizing moral hazard and of valuing the wider 'development benefits' of TA schemes are all likely to cause difficulties for TA donor agencies, and strategies for dealing with them will need to be developed at an early stage in funding. This chapter will argue that some of these problems are genuinely insurmountable and that donor appraisers will need to appreciate this when undertaking case appraisals and post-project evaluations of project outcomes – whether they are using CBA, semi-input–output or general equilibrium methods. However, in other areas, it will be possible to devise a response to the realities of transition states which enhances the quality of appraisal and aids the decision process. This chapter offers a brief and general survey of problems the complexity of which deserve a more detailed and measured approach to the analysis of value for money in TA than space permits.

PROBLEMS WITH *EX-ANTE* EVALUATION

There is a fundamental problem inherent in evaluating the success of programmed TA for transition states. It relates to the fact that the *ex-post* welfare improvements measured by any CBA methodology will include costs and benefits resulting from the institutional transformation of the economy from one type to another – usually from a command type to a market type – to which the specific project only contributes at the margin. Some transition economists (memorably Brus and Laski 1989, and, recently, Balcerowicz 1994, and Portes 1994) have noted that the *ceteris paribus* assumptions required to allow programmes to be evaluated are unrealistic given the extensive nature of the reform process. There are two possible sources of difficulty here.

First, the full benefits of the programme may not be captured because of some systematic inconsistency in resource allocation due to the transition. For example, TA to establish skills in bank supervision may fail to deliver benefits in excess of costs because of the failure of independent reform to create a sufficiently strong banking sector. This leads to an undervaluation of the programme benefit–cost ratio.

Alternatively (and this is the issue specifically addressed by Balcerowicz 1994; pp. 19–20) there may be an equally serious problem in assessing *ex-ante* the cost savings (benefits) or 'efficiency gains' over the previous system. For instance, if programmed TA spending brings about a fall in sectoral welfare in comparison with the level of sectoral welfare before the reform process began, an evaluation would also reveal an undervaluation of the true benefit–cost ratio, all other things being equal. The guiding principle ought to be to compare *ex-ante* the benefit–cost ratio with the level of benefit yielded from an alternative reform-based programme at the same stage of the reform process. The opportunity cost of the TA programme is, therefore, properly assessed in relation to alternative uses of funds in a similar post-socialist state of the world, not by comparison with command economy welfare allocations.

The counterfactual problem here is more than merely semantic. The specification of a yardstick for the valuation of *ex-ante* benefits in terms of some alternative future without a particular TA project or programme permits judgements to be made about the success of reform programme support. What would be unacceptable, however, would be a counterfactual model which compared the net benefits from TA programmes with the costs and benefits of similar institutional arrangements under the preceding socialist state. It should be remembered, then, that the strict comparator must be the probable benefit–cost ratio from an alternative use of resources in the same newly liberalized economy. The results of choosing an alternative counterfactual model – for example, estimating the benefit–cost ratio from state expenditures on labour market information systems before transition and comparing it with the benefit–cost ratio of a single TA project in this area – is that it overvalues the use of TA resources in terms of their opportunity cost. At the same time, paradoxically, the TA project may appear to yield too little benefit in comparison with similar services provided before transition. After all, the cost of capital in state projects funded from the centre before transition had a lower shadow price than in capitalist states. The result may well be that it is impossible to place a relative value on the benefits yielded which fully reflects the conditions in a transition state.

PROBLEMS OF SHADOW PRICING NON-MARKETED OUTPUT IN TRANSITION

The shadow price of the non-marketed output of transition economies is an important stumbling block to the full evaluation of TA projects, particularly where capital-intensive investments are to be assessed. The theoretical problems of valuing outputs in non-market systems are too well known to require much rehearsal here. Ludwig von Mises's dismissive comment that '...in the socialist commonwealth every economic change becomes an undertaking whose success can neither be appraised in advance nor later retrospectively determined [and that] there is only groping in the dark' (von Mises 1972, p. 80) recalls the practical implications of directing economic resources by decree instead of rational market behaviour. Prices diverge randomly from opportunity cost and central direction is therefore an allocatively inefficient device. In the transition to a market economy, the 'marketization' of state output has proceeded at different rates and according to different trajectories in all the transition economies. The result has been that non-market distortions continue to affect the 'price' of assets, even after privatization.

It is frequently the case that TA projects are expected to deliver benefits in excess of the capital replacement cost of worn out or redundant technology. Not only is retired capital impossible to value at market prices; it is equally difficult to assign market values to the accumulated outputs of the non-marketed commodities left in stock or services 'on hold'. Several attempts have been made to find a valuation method which will allow the opportunity cost of such assets and stocks to be assessed (e.g. in the context of transition states, Hughes and Hare 1994, Curry and Guiping 1993). Most begin by trying to impute the opportunity cost of non-traded items by calculating conversion factors reflecting the differential between world prices and domestic values, following the Mirrlees–Little method (see Powers 1981; Weiss 1988; Saerbeck 1994). Very few economists have suggested the evaluation of non-market output by means of WTP or willingness to accept analysis – and for very good reasons. The extent of privatized marketed output in the transition economies is still relatively low and the dependency of consumers on the non-market sector is still considerable, despite waves of privatization. Consequently WTP is inappropriate since many assets and stocked outputs are still non-excludable and non-rival in consumption.

Moreover, all the available methods of preference revelation for non-rival goods (such as Clark's compensatory 'tax', the Clawson 'access value' measure, hedonic pricing and contingent valuation) suppose that the welfare consequences of intertemporal trades will be understood in terms of private utility.

The endemic problem here is one of insufficiently defined property rights and entitlements. In the Alchian–Demsetz theory of property rights (Alchian

1950, 1965; Alchian and Demsetz 1972), optimal systems of enforceable rights would possess characteristics of universality, transferability and exclusivity in property assets. Whilst economists seeking a method of measuring the value of non-market goods in transition states tend to concentrate upon absence of the last of these characteristics, the greatest hurdle to the operation of market signals in the transition period (and before full 'marketization' occurs) is surely the fact that public property and entitlements are generally not transferable and their value cannot be universally agreed.

The valuation process is impeded if, for example, the stocks of capital and other tangible assets are both exhausted and retired at a faster rate than the costs of the capital they embody. Some economists have suggested that the eradication of property rights problems is more than just the precondition for the 'marketization' and privatization phases of reform; the problem of the non-universality and non-transferability of property rights actually distorts the valuation of capital and non-capital assets (Blanchard et al. 1991, pp. xiv ff.; Murrell 1991; Jasincki 1992; Huntwork 1993, pp. 189ff).

The recurring indeterminacy of valuation of state assets through privatization suggests that it would be inappropriate to place money values on infrastructure assets in state-dominated economies by observing the market price for distributed shares. In those transition states with high personal-sector debt in which dissaving is widespread, voucher schemes to create transferable rights in state assets have generally resulted in a fall in the market price of secondary sales over issue prices. Moreover, there is no very clear evidence that the process of privatization has increased the transferability of former state assets, or that the universal acceptance of private ownership has been increased.

PROBLEMS OF DETERMINING THE RELATIVE PROJECT RISK

The evaluation of project risk through multi-way sensitivity analysis, simulation or the calculation of expected NPVs for project costs–benefits is usually carried out in large project-appraisal schemes to explore the relative likelihood of upside or downside effects resulting from the uncertainty of the project environment. In transition economies, of course, the political risk associated with the project is considerable and the need to incorporate some element of risk assessment is consequently greater. The assessment of political risk features is bedevilled by the fact that reform is a programme whose key features are determined outside a project framework and by the very real likelihood of a high turnover of decision-making personnel.

While the latter source of political risk is beyond the scope of formal appraisal (and TA project appraisers must rely upon the contractual and managerial features of the TA project for appropriate contingencies), there is scope to assess the effect of the former on the project outturn. It is not impossible (but certainly difficult) to evaluate outputs in terms of the host country's reform objectives or in terms of the objectives of major donors to the reform process. Yet precisely because of the uncertainty regarding property rights allocations referred to above, the most proximate cause of downside risk is likely to come from the indeterminacy of property rights. Contract risk is an endemic problem in many of the states of Eastern and Central Europe with TA and, until the law of property is set on a sound footing in many of these states, contract risk is always likely to be high.

The riskiness of TA investments is, therefore, directly proportional to the phase of transition during which the injection takes place. When political and legal reform has been achieved, it is likely that the net benefits of TA will be higher, all other things being equal. If they are not equal (if, for example, TA is concentrated in more backward or more developing sectors of the transition economy), then the relative riskiness of the project might be enhanced or reduced. Because these effects are unpredictable, risk analysis should concentrate upon the limitation of proximate project risk such as cost or time overruns.

PROBLEMS OF MORAL HAZARD

Economists have long been aware that a very large number of coordination problems involving bilateral bargaining between a principal (one who solicits a service) and an agent (one who provides it) occur where information asymmetry biases the welfare outcome from the allocation. Since most TA is delivered by means of some contractual arrangement (through tendering, for example), these problems are likely to have a very marked impact upon the net value of TA projects. In most bilateral contractual arrangements the principal and agent agree a fee (f) payable when the agent provides effort (e) to produce an outcome (x). If the principal undertook the task himself, he would know how much e is needed; but it is clearly in the interest of the agent to misrepresent the amount of e needed to achieve the task. Moreover, it is possible that some random element (R) may intrude to make the provision of x difficult. So,

$$f = f(x,e,R)$$

or, in words, the fee ought to depend upon the value of the outcome, the amount of effort induced in the agent and the untoward random effects. Since TA projects are delivered in large measure by contracting for private-sector service delivery, the scope for moral hazard, and hence for welfare loss, is potentially significant. Economists have begun to ask whether schemes of aid can be designed which assign the property rights in such a way that moral hazard does not result when principal–agent style contracts operate in TA projects (Pietrobelli 1992). If moral hazard is reduced, of course, the scope for maximizing *ex-ante* benefits with project costs is increased.

Simple Contingency Fees

One might make the value of f depend upon x directly. That is, the agent receives a flat rate fee f regardless of the benefit to the principal, and may be able to claim $x - f(x)$ for itself – that is, the excess between the value of the fee and the value of the outcome. This requires a very clear understanding of the valuation method for arriving at x (and a very clear idea for the principal of how to value $[f(x)]$. In the context of government-to-government assistance through TA schemes, a simple contingent fee model might be to permit contracts for TA programmes to reflect the estimated full cost of delivery, not the valuation of the marginal benefit of the TA project. The provider would then have a strong incentive to minimize the variable costs of the programme and maximize $x - f(x)$.

Simple Input-Related Fees

One might make the fee depend upon effort e directly, either by linking payments to some minimal display of increased effort $[f(e) = df(e)/de > 0]$ or by paying for at least some minimal effort revelation $[f(e) = f \text{ if } e > 0]$. This is tantamount to admitting that the monitoring costs for the principal are high above some minimal level of activity but are indeterminate for a broad range of activity or output $(1 > df(e)/e > 0)$. The simple input fee approach minimizes monitoring costs and ties the effort/reward to the contract.

Complex 'Performance Bonds'

One might make the value of f depend upon x where the risk-aversity of the two parties is differentiated. If the principal is more sure of the outcome than the client (the contractor has run similar training courses before; the commissioning TA donor has not), principal–agent theory predicts that it will be efficient for the agent to post a 'bond' for the fee f^* and take the excess of $x - f^*$ for him/herself. This is equivalent to the tender winner giving the TA donor a sum for the benefit x of the training and taking the difference (if any is observed) between the benefit and the fee. Whether the fee is less than or more than the benefit, the principal alone is likely to know because they have experience of *R* and, consequently, they can behave as risk-averse with respect to the 'unknown'. Moreover, because they are commonly providing the service of delivering *x* benefit, they can pool the risk over many other contracts. The advantage of this risk-reducing strategy for the TA sponsor is that the project fee *f* can be tied directly to an anticipated output (or benefit level), any private benefit in excess of which is internalized by the contractor.

By any or all of these means, the net value of a TA programme might be enhanced or maintained. It will be for project managers to decide whether the scope for moral hazard (as a result of the high costs of monitoring) warrants the creation of these sorts of arrangement to minimize loss from the implementation of the TA project.

PROBLEMS OF VALUING 'DEVELOPMENT BENEFITS'

In recent years, and particularly since the publication of the UNDP's 'Human Development Report' in 1990, the practice of measuring development benefits solely in terms of poverty reduction has been criticized by some economists, who argue that direct aid benefits are less important than the longer-term 'capabilities' or capacities which recipient countries receive. The argument, for those unfamiliar with it, is that aid purchases benefits which are long-lived and not merely transitional. If health care TA increases longevity, for instance, it also increases the potential level of economic activity by increasing the participation rate. In short, any assistance programme does rather more than merely ameliorate backwardness; it also stimulates development by reducing the barriers to the effective use of resources. Similarly, 'the capabilities approach would argue that the enhancement of people's ability to read and write ... should be considered ends in themselves, even if the conventionally measured economic return to investment in literacy ... is zero' (Anand and Ravallion 1993, p. 135).

Advocates of the 'human development' approach to assistance suppose, in short, that the benefits from (technical) assistance which directly affect the quality and quantity of human capital has longer-lasting benefits than traditional project-appraisal methods usually allow. Since TA is, in general, intended to 'build capacity' rather than deliver immediate welfare benefits (such as raising per capita income or reducing acute poverty) it may be that the rather different perspective of this 'capabilities approach' is relevant to measuring and evaluating TA programmes. The direct benefits from TA are, it might be argued, an improved capacity for self-sustained development. 'Value for money' measures might be constructed to reflect these benefits as outlined next.

Production-Based Measures

One class of measures might start by assuming that the self-sustained development benefit of TA lies principally in the creation of a capacity to maintain domestic production and build a capacity to compete with international competition in key product markets. If the ratio of the purchasing power parity basket value of national output as a proportion of total market consumption to the cost of TA were greater than 1, then one might legitimately claim that TA had been beneficial. Alternatively, if import penetration in intermediate goods markets fell, then some measure of the contribution of TA to the decline might be created from the value-added data recorded in input–output tabulations. However it is created, a production based measure will need to focus upon the effect of TA in freeing national economies from economic dependence.

Direct Welfare Measures

In their perceptive review, Anand and Ravillion (1993, pp. 135–6) point out that the appropriate measures of the contribution of assistance to development according to the 'capabilities approach' ought to be unambiguous. They note the human development approach thus leads one to 'ask [*ex-post* of assistance]: Do they live long? Do they avoid mortality during infancy and childhood? Do they avoid illiteracy? Are they free from hunger and undernourishment? Do they enjoy personal liberty and freedom?' (p. 135). TA is unlikely to deliver all these direct welfare benefits – but they may on occasion contribute some of them. For example, TA toward the development of new medical facilities or medical education may contribute to a reduced infant mortality rate. Judging the extent of this contribution and its value net of costs is complicated by the fact that TA alone is not usually the sole source of such direct welfare benefits. A contrived index might use a total factor productivity measure of inputs before and after TA-enhanced capital or labour factors. The ratio between the value of TA-related inputs and the value of the residual total factor productivity increase might then substitute for a more direct cost–benefit measure.

A 'HUMAN CAPITAL' MEDIATION MODEL

A third approach, following Saint-Paul and Verdier (1993), is to assume that assistance benefits are transmitted through an enhancement in human capital, that is, development assistance delivered by TA is eventually labour-augmenting. If TA is intended to develop systems and thereby build capacity, one measure of this improvement in systems will be the net value-added to human capital. One might, for example, try to isolate the impact of TA on money wage appreciation by holding other labour market forces stable in a cross-section model; an alternative method might be to establish a gross figure for human capital in terms of the opportunity cost of the 'unaugmented' labour and compare this with the *ex-ante* value of the TA-enhanced labour force. The disadvantage of this approach in the context of Eastern and Central Europe and the former Soviet Union is the relative inefficiency of unreformed labour markets and wage signals, which would necessarily overvalue the opportunity cost of unassisted labour.

CONCLUSIONS

This brief survey has suggested that many traps await the unwary evaluator of TA projects in the transition economies of Eastern and Central Europe and the former Soviet Union. The pace of reform, the level of stabilization and the degree of transformation will all play a notable part in making life difficult for the public-sector economist charged with identifying value for money in these projects. In addition to the substantive issues identified, other traps (such as the variability of inflation, the randomness of inflationary expectations, the apparent *ad hoc* nature of state asset sales and the relative degree of political uncertainty associated with coalition-based government) will make the task of the Western project appraiser considerably more difficult as the stabilization phase of reform gives way to fundamental transformation in these economies. An awareness of these evaluation pitfalls may, however, obviate criticism of the funding of transition economies and (by helping to make the case for assistance) may strengthen public support for the creation of independent market-based economies in a more inclusive Europe in which transition states enjoy, to quote the words of one of Ukraine's great national poets, membership of a 'great new family, the family of the free'.

REFERENCES

Alchian, A. (1950), 'Uncertainty, evolution and economic theory', *Journal of Political Economy*, **58** (3), 211–21.
Alchian, A. (1965), 'Some economics of property rights', *Il Politico*, **30** (4), 816–29.
Alchian, A. and H. Demsetz (1972), 'Production, information costs and economic organization', *American Economic Review*, **62** (5), 777–95.
Anand, S. and M. Ravallion (1993), 'Human development in poor countries: on the

role of private incomes and public services', *Journal of Economic Perspectives*, **7** (1), 133–50.

Balcerowicz, L. (1994), 'Common fallacies in the debate on the transition to a market economy', *Economic Policy*, **19** (Supp.): 18–50.

Berg, E. (1993), *Rethinking technical assistance and capacity building*, New York: UNDP.

Blanchard, O. et al. (1991), *Reform in eastern Europe*, Cambridge, Mass.: MIT Press.

Brus, W. and K. Laski (1989), *From Marx to the market: socialism in search of an economic system*, Oxford: Clarendon Press.

Cassella, A. and B. Eichengreen (1994), 'Can foreign aid accelerate stabilization?', CEPR Discussion Paper no. 961.

Cassen, R. and associates (1994), *Does aid work?*, 2nd edition, Oxford: Clarendon Press.

Curry, S. and C. Guiping (1993), 'Opportunity cost of labour in China', Research Paper, Development and Project Planning Centre, University of Bradford.

Dhanji, F. (1991), 'Transformation programs: content and sequencing', *American Economic Review*, **81** (2), 323–8.

Economist (1993), 'Good intentions, poor performance', 10 April, pp. 21–5.

Helleiner, G.K. (1992), 'The IMF, the World Bank and Africa's adjustment and external debt problems: an unofficial view', *World Development*, **20**, 779–92.

House of Commons, Foreign Affairs Committee (1994), *First report on monitoring of the European Community aid programme*, Session 1994–5: HCl1l.

Hughes, G. and P. Hare (1994), 'The international competitiveness of industries in Bulgaria, Czechoslovakia, Hungary and Poland', *Oxford Economic Papers*, **46**, 200–221.

Huntwork, J.R. (1993), 'Legal reform and economic freedom in Ukraine', *Ukrainian Quarterly*, **49** (2), 184–94.

Jasinki, P. (1990), 'Two models of privatisation in Poland: a critical assessment', *Communist Economies*, **2** (3), 373–401.

Jasinki, P. (1992), 'The transfer and redefinition of property rights and transformational privatisation in the post-STEs', *Communist Economies and Economic Transformation*, **4** (1), 1–22.

Kabangu, T.M. (1991), *La politica de desarrollo de la Comunidad Europea en Africa en el marco de los Convenios de Lomé*, Madrid: Agencia Espanola de Cooperacion Internacional.

McKinnon, R. (1991), *The order of economic liberalization: financial control in the transition to a market economy*, Baltimore, Md: Johns Hopkins University Press.

von Mises, L. (1972), 'Economic calculation in the socialist commonwealth' (1920) reprinted in A. Nove and D.M. Nuti (eds), *Socialist economics: selected readings*, Harmondsworth, UK: Penguin pp. 75–91.

Murrell, P. (1991), 'Evolution in economics and the economic reform of the centrally planned economies' in C. Clague and G.C. Rausser (eds), *The emergence of market economies in eastern Europe*, Cambridge, Mass: Basil Blackwell, pp. 35–53.

Pietrobelli, C. (1992), 'Inducing efficiency in the use of foreign aid: the case for incentive mechanisms', *Journal of Development Studies*, **29** (1), 72–92.

Portes, R. (1994), 'Transformation Traps', *Economic Journal*, **104** (426), 1178–89.

Powers, T. (ed.) (1981), *Estimating accounting prices for project appraisal*, Washington, DC: IDB.

Sachs, J. (1993), *Poland's jump to the market economy*, Cambridge, Mass.: MIT Press.

Saerbeck, R. (1994), 'Different approaches to the estimation of economic conversion factors to be used in Project appraisal', *Cahiers BEI*, **22**, 8–24.
Saint-Paul G. and T. Verdier (1993), 'Education, democracy and growth', *Journal of Development Economics*, **42** (2), 399–407.
Santizo, R. (1987), 'La oferta de cooperacion tecnica internacional', *Estado y Sociedad*, **3**, 45–64.
Schaetzen, Y. de (1972), 'La Suisse et l'Afrique', *Afrique Industrie*, **15**, 20–74.
Stokeld, F.W. (1982), 'Africa and foreign aid: using scarce resources wisely', *Orbis*, **6**, 993–1009.
UNECE (UN Economic Commission for Europe) (1993), *Economic survey of Europe in 1992–1993*, New York: UNECE.
Weiss, J. (1988), 'An introduction to shadow pricing in a semi-input–output approach', *Project Appraisal*, **3** (4), 182–9.

17. Cost–benefit analysis of privatization transactions in transitional economies: case study of Poland

S.I. Cohen and A.B. Czyzewski

INTRODUCTION

One of the salient features of the transition period from a planning-oriented economy to the market-oriented economy is the process of privatization of national productive real assets. There are many different opinions concerning how this process should be organized (Sarcevic 1992, Ajani et al. 1992; Lee and Nellis 1990), but most of them do agree on the crucial point that entrepreneurs in these economies have not enough resources or experience to finance and/or lead the process. Hence, a realistic solution to the problem is to attract foreign capital to join in managing or in taking over part or the whole of a privatized company.

We share the opinion that foreign capital is interested in directly investing in transition economies because it considers markets of the transition economies as being attractive from the point of view of future long-term profits. Therefore, we presume that the potential investor has considered his decision whether to invest in transition economies in terms of comparing his returns from investing in Poland or Hungary, or for that matter other East European economies, with returns from investing in existing market-oriented economies and found this to be positive. Having decided to invest, the foreign investor is going to compare expected rates of return for alternative investments in different sectors in alternative East European economies.

The aim of this chapter is to develop a framework for an *ex-ante* valuation examination of privatization transactions from the points of view of the foreign buyer, say a multinational company, and the seller – the government of an economy in transition. Our approach stands in contrast with OECD (1993).

The privatization transaction for a particular industry is examined in terms of:

1. The transaction value for the foreign buyer K_F.
2. The transaction value for the seller – the government K_G.
3. The negotiable transaction value between buyer and seller which would depend on the bargaining power reflecting demand and supply conditions in the international market for the industry in question.

The resulting model is based on the idea that the potential investor calculates for each sector (activity) the price of the transaction to be paid for access to the market of interest (including property rights of real assets). The price of the buyer is dependent on the discounted present value of future sales, additional investment costs which have to be made, and desirability of meeting competitive returns on investment. Since the transaction may take place only if it satisfies both sides, the buyer's offers are set against the seller's values of transactions which are based on the government's calculations of gains and losses from the privatization decision. Finally, the model includes a possibility of describing the process of negotiations by incorporating values of some exogenous parameters, which can be managed by the buyer and the seller in order to satisfy both of them.

At present the model considers only two periods: the period before privatization, indicated by O, and the period of transition during which privatization is settled and operation of the firm is normalized, indicated by T. The length of period T can be one or several years.

The model is demonstrated with parameters for several sectors of the Polish economy. Empirical results are reported in terms of ranks assigned to these sectors by the buyer and the seller, indicating their preferences for buying and selling real assets located in different sectors and values of several exogenous parameters, managed by buyer and seller in order to facilitate the transaction.

TRANSACTION VALUE FOR THE FOREIGN BUYER (K_F)

Let us consider a multinational company deciding to invest in Poland. The problem for this investor is to decide on which activity to choose for investing. The main elements of the privatization transaction considered by the buyer are brought together in Figure 17.1.

First take the upper curve of cumulated investments costs, denoted by K. At the beginning of the transition period, O, the capital stock has a book value of K_o which after scrapping a part of it, K_a, results in a productive stock of $K_o - K_a$. To this value renovating investment, K_b, is added in order to increase the capacity output of privatized activity to produce sales expected at the end of transition period T. There is also a required investment of

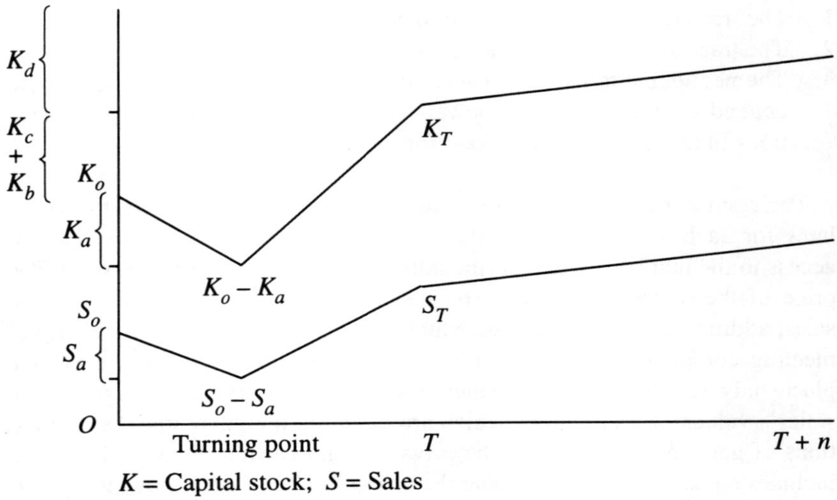

Figure 17.1 Main elements in a privatization transaction

amount K_c in delivering sectors, which will bring the capital stock at the end of the transition period T to $K_T = K_o - K_a + K_b + K_c$. Finally, after the transition period ends, the capital stock in the privatized activity K_T is increased each year in small amounts of K_d sufficient to meet replacement purposes.

Second, take the lower curve of sales revenue, denoted by S. The curve gives the sales revenue of privatized activity. It is assumed that sales revenue falls from S_o at the beginning of the transition period by S_a, then gradually recovers to reach at the end of the transition period the expected level of sales S_T (produced by assets K_T). Then sales continue to grow in line with demand conditions (absorbing replacement investments K_d). The profit curve P can be derived from the sales curve S via application of a profit rate π defined in terms of sales, thus $P = \pi S$.

Both the investments costs and the profits are discountable at the international discount rate δ.

The desired buyer's rate of return on the privatization transaction ($\bar{R}_F$) is defined by equation (1); τ is the rate of profit tax to the privatized activity. In order to meet a given target $\bar{R}_F$ the foreign buyer calculates the present value of K_F from the given parameters of equation (1).

$$\frac{\sum_t ((1-\tau)P)_t (1+\delta)^{-t}}{K_F + \sum_t (K_b + K_c + K_d)_t (1+\delta)^{-t}} = \frac{\text{Benefits}}{\text{Costs}} = \bar{R}_F \tag{1}$$

TRANSACTION VALUE FOR THE SELLER GOVERNMENT (K_G)

A definition of the seller's gain from the privatization transaction is not straightforward, since the government, the seller, has to consider many more indirect implications of the decision than the buyer. These implications cover such aspects as future growth, state budget, balance of payments, unemployment, environment and national wealth. To study all these issues one should use a model of the national economy, designed for the purpose of analysing privatization processes. In this chapter we shall consider a partial approach to approximate various elements of the seller's gain from a privatization transaction and compare them with the opportunity cost of forgoing the transaction.

The privatization transaction for the government consists in the conversion of real productive assets into financial assets. If the proper measure of real assets is their market value, the role of the government is to get, in exchange for privatized assets, their market value. The role of government is to aim at value equivalence in negotiating the transaction in order not to diminish the national wealth unnecessarily, and perhaps world wealth as well.

Because of the absence of capital markets in planning-oriented economies the government in such an economy usually does not know the market value of the candidate assets and the government's estimate of their value may differ substantially from that calculated by the foreign buyer. Usually the government's value of privatized real assets is closer to the book value of these assets (or replacement value) than to the buyer's evaluation based on a valuation of cumulated expected profits from sales of output produced by these assets.

Since the privatization of an enterprise is very likely to increase unemployment, the government will reduce its offer price by the minimum income transfers payable to unemployed persons that will result from lay-offs following a restructuring of the enterprise. But the act of privatization, which is meant to cause an increase in economic efficiency, should help the government to finance such transfer payments. The government will expect higher budget inflows from the taxation of a higher profit from the privatized enterprise than was the case without privatization.

On the basis of this reasoning one can define a measure of the efficiency of a privatization transaction by relating current and future discounted financial inflows to the value of real assets, which the government is desiring to sell. This measure is defined by equation (2):

$$\frac{K_G + \sum_t (\tau P - \text{unemployment benefits})_t (1+\delta)^{-t}}{K_o} = \overline{R}_G \tag{2}$$

The transaction value for government, K_G can be found from this equation given desired value of $\bar{R}_G$, or the seller's rate of return, which in turn depends on the community's valuation of the transition process and its patience towards achieving it. In the extreme case, if the government is very cautious in approaching the transition and is freely disposing of its public enterprises the denominator of equation (2) will be the book value of the public assets, and $\bar{R}_G$ will be set close to 1. At the other extreme, advocates of quick transitions will put $\bar{R}_G$ at a fraction of 1. Of course, the optimal value of $\bar{R}_G$ could be fixed at the ratio of market to book value, but as was stated earlier, the market value is difficult to determine in a situation where the number of privatization transactions taking place is small and the contents of the transactions are not transparent. The situation changes as more transparent transactions take place leading to the formation of reasonable expectations on $\bar{R}_G$.

THE NEGOTIATION PROCESS

Agreeing on the terms of settlement is best described as a negotiation process aiming at reaching a transaction value for the buyer K_F and the seller K_G which is close enough to satisfy the condition

$$K_F = m\,K_G \tag{3}$$

where m is a margin of the tightness of the private foreign investment market reflecting international forces of demand and supply. Stronger appetites by more and more Eastern European governments towards privatization via private foreign investment will push m downwards, which is comparable, in the terminology of Bhagwati, to a process of immiserization. It may be mentioned too that there is likely to be a greater degree of coordination between candidate buyers than among governments of the selling Eastern European countries, which may result in a further deterioration of the value of m to levels which shun the sellers.

In determining profit expectations from takeover, the potential investor will consider first of all the size of the market for their products, measured by the value of sales, which is expected at the end of the transition period, S_T.

To determine the value of expected sales the buyer takes into account an evaluation of the following factors:

1. Transformation of the initial demand structure towards a demand structure typical of free-market economies, which leads to a change of the market share for the concerned good from σ_o to σ_T at the end of the transition period.

2. A factor σ_a representing a competitive increase in the market share due to introducing higher quality by the investor. The competitiveness factor σ_a is dependent on the scale of modernization $K_b + K_c$.
3. Long-term rate of growth of demand, γ.
4. Length of the transition period, T.

The value of expected sales at the end of the transition period, S_T is expressed in equation (4):

$$S_T = S_o\,(\sigma_T/\sigma_o)\,(1 + \sigma_a)\,(1 + \gamma)^T \qquad (4)$$

After the transition period sales are expected to grow at the long-term rate γ:

$$S_{T+t} = (1 + \gamma)^t\, S_T \qquad t = 1,2,3 \qquad (5)$$

For the transition period itself it is assumed that the value of sales falls at the beginning of the period from initial value S_o to $S_o - S_a$ as a result of the necessary scrapping of a part of privatized real assets and a recessionary transition, and then gradually recovers to reach the expected value S_T at the end of the transition period:

$$S_t = [S_T/(S_o - S_a)^{1/T}]^t\,(S_o - S_a) \qquad t = 0,1,2,\ldots T - 1 \qquad (6)$$

Future profits are calculated on the basis of the expected value of sales, St:

$$P_t = \pi\,\varepsilon\,S_t \qquad t = 1,2,\ldots T, T + 1,\ldots \qquad (7)$$

where: π = profit rate in modern business, expressed in terms of sales; and ε = coefficient of inefficiency, particular to the transferred assets.

The current value of the cumulative discounted future profits determines the market value of the privatized productive real assets. This value is a sum of two geometric series. The first one concerns the transition period; the second is for the period after transition.[1]

DIRECT INVESTMENT COSTS

As a result of the privatization transaction the foreign buyer becomes the owner of a part of productive real assets located in a particular sector of activity. This gives them access to the particular market. Their next step is to reorganize and invest in order to create capacity sufficient to produce at the end of the transition period the value of sales S_T. To avoid details concerning capacity utilization and inventories we assume that sales = output = capacity output. We shall distinguish between three types of investments: K_b, K_c and K_d, for, respectively, investment outlays necessary to renovate and generate capacity output S_T, associated investment and replacement investment.

In determining K_b, which denotes investment outlays necessary to generate capacity output S_T in period T, we describe the production process in the privatized activity in terms of an empirically desirable vintage model of production:

$$S_o = (1/\kappa_1)\, K_1 + (1/\kappa_2)K_2 + \ldots + (1/\kappa_n)\, K_n \tag{8}$$

where K_t is a vintage of capital goods installed in period t and still in use in period O in the privatized activity; k_t is the capital output ratio of a vintage K_t and n is the age of the oldest vintage operating in period O.

Labour requirement is described in equation (9):

$$L_o = (1/l_1)\, Q_1 + (1/l_2)\, Q_2 + \ldots + (1/l_n)\, Q_n \tag{9}$$

where Q_t is a production capacity of a vintage of capital goods K_t in period O in the privatized activity, l_t is a labour-productivity coefficient for a vintage K_t, and L_o is the labour requirement for producing output S_o.

In the calibration to be reported below, empirical values of K_t, κ_t and l_t for the past were estimated on the basis of 1989 data concerning the average capital–output ratio for state enterprises in the privatized activity; the empirical age structure of state-owned assets in the privatized activity and the average labour-productivity coefficient for state-owned enterprises in the privatized activity; and experimentally chosen values of capital–output ratio κ_1 and labour productivity l_1, of the newest vintage in use before privatization. Search procedure was applied to find values of capital-augmenting and labour-augmenting technical progress coefficients ι and λ respectively, on the basis of following relations:

$$\kappa_{t-1} = \kappa_t(1 + \iota) \text{ and } l_{t+1} = l_\tau(1 + \lambda) \qquad t = 2,3,\ldots,n-1$$

The value K_b of investments necessary to produce S_T is found in equation (10) where χ_b is the capital–output ratio for a new vintage of capital goods K_b installed in period O to assure, after scrapping of inefficient vintages, a sufficient increase of production capacity required for reaching sales S_T:

$$K_b = \kappa_b[S_T + S_a - S_o] \tag{10}$$

The capacity lost due to scrapping of inefficient vintages is defined by equation (11):

$$S_a = (\phi_1/\kappa_1)\,K_1 + (\phi_2/\kappa_2)\,K_2 + \ldots + (\phi_n/\kappa_n)\,K_n \tag{11}$$

where ϕ is a dummy variable defined on the basis of a scrapping rule before 'technical death', which amounts to keeping a vintage of equipment in use as long as its quasi rent is positive, thus:

$$\phi_t = 1 \text{ if } p > W/l_t, \text{ otherwise } \phi_t = 0$$

where p is the revenue per unit of sales, W is the real wage and l_t is labour productivity of the vintage t.

The scrapping rule described in equation (11) leads to a decrease in employment LD, as equation (12):

$$LD = L_o - \left(\frac{1-\phi_1}{l_1}\right)Q_1 - \left(\frac{1-\phi_2}{l_2}\right)Q_2 - \ldots \frac{(1-\phi_n)}{l_n}Q_n \tag{12}$$

While new investments K_b lead to an increase in employment LI, dependent on the labour productivity of the new vintage l_b, as equation (13):

$$LI = (1/l_b)\,(1/\kappa_b)\,K_b \tag{13}$$

The net increase in unemployment associated with the privatization transaction amounts to UL, as in equation (14):

$$UL = LD - LI \tag{14}$$

The number of unemployed persons UL is multiplied by unemployment benefits (defined as a part of the wage rate W) to give the cost of unemployment benefits associated with the privatization transaction.

ASSOCIATED AND REPLACEMENT INVESTMENT COSTS

Modernization of equipment in a privatized enterprise increases both capital and labour productivity but full utilization of the modern capacity may be limited by an underdeveloped economic environment affecting the enterprise. In order to cancel external limitations regarding full capacity utilization in the privatized enterprise, direct investments in the privatized activity have to be followed by some additional infrastructural investment in delivering activities. For example, very modern equipment installed in a privatized car-producing factory has to be accompanied by additional capital investments in a factory producing modern tyres.

K_c is the associated investment in infrastructure necessary to assure production of $S_T + S_a - S_o$, we have thus:

$$(S_T + S_a - S_o) = \min [(1/\kappa_b) K_b, (1/\kappa_c) K_c]$$

Since K_c should not be the limiting factor, we therefore have equation (15):

$$K_c = (\kappa_c/\kappa_b) K_b \tag{15}$$

In analogy with the pattern of growth of sales as in equation (6) a uniform distribution of investment outlays $K_b + K_c$ is adopted in the transition period. The yearly outlay is discounted by the international discount rate δ, as in equation (7) above.[2]

The capital stock in the privatized activity in period T is shown in equation (16):

$$K_T = K_o - K_a + K_b + K_c \tag{16}$$

In order to continue the growth of sales after the transition period by the rate γ (see equation 5), K_T should grow each year by an amount sufficient to meet replacement purposes.

The size of replacement investments depends on the following factors:

1. Capital–output ratio of new vintages, κ.
2. Expected rate of growth of sales, γ.
3. Annual rate of depreciation of real assets, p.

If these factors are treated as constants then the necessary replacement investment in a year t is calculated from equation (17):

$$K_{d,t} = K_t + pK_{t-1} - K_{t-1} = (\gamma + p)K_{t-1} \tag{17}$$

For a year t after period T replacement investment is found from equation (18), assuming that the capital stock required to maintain a γ per cent growth of sales will have to grow by the same rate γ:

$$K_{d,T+t} = (\gamma + p) (1 + \gamma)^{t-1} K_T \tag{18}$$

The total discounted value of replacement investments is found along the lines of equation (7) discussed earlier.[3]

NET INFLOWS FROM PROFIT TAX

Net inflows for the government from profit taxation are calculated as the difference between the budget incomes from profit taxes imposed on expected profits P (equation 8) and the income the government would have if the activity were not privatized (status quo profits).

The status quo profits are calculated by the following assumptions:

1. Sales grow by a rate γ^1 which is less than γ.
2. The share of profits in sales is lower than in the privatized activity.
3. The profit tax is paid from profits diminished by reinvested profits.
4. Profits are discounted at the rate δ.
5. Reinvested profits are recalculated, whereby the rate of growth of sales γ is replaced by a lower γ' and the depreciation rate p by a lower p'.

PRELIMINARY EMPIRICAL RESULTS

The proposed model of privatization transactions was tested empirically on examples of five Polish industries: food processing industry (Food), light industry (Light), wood and paper industry (Wood), chemical industry (Chem), and electro-engineering industry (Elen).

Table 17.1 Economic and technical characteristics of selected Polish industries

	Food	Light	Wood	Chem	Elen
Whole sectors					
Sales 1989 (US$m)	2081.5	1168.1	460.9	900.9	2526.9
Real assets end of 1989 (US$m)	3256.4	2146.7	1486.0	3759.0	8524.1
Employment (thousands)	410.6	633.9	211.0	276.7	1300.7
Selected samples					
Sales (US$m)	208.2	116.8	46.1	90.1	252.7
Book value of assets (US$m)	290.4	197.8	141.4	362.7	789.4
Employment (thousands)	36.6	58.4	20.1	26.6	120.5

Table 17.2 Main characteristics of the privatizing enterprise and privatization transactions

	Food	Light	Wood	Chem	Elen
Buyer calculations					
1. Capital–output ratio κ	1.40	1.70	3.10	4.00	3.10
2. Labour productivity S per workers l	5686.00	1999.50	2294.60	3382.70	2097.60
3. Depreciation rate p	0.12	0.10	0.07	0.04	0.08
4. Expected profit sales ratio π	15.00	15.00	15.00	25.00	25.00
5. Efficiency index ε	0.70	0.80	0.80	0.70	0.70
6. Sales growth K_d/K_o	13.60	15.60	15.90	23.60	16.80
7. Scrapping rate $(S_T - S_o)/S_o$	0.35	0.54	0.38	0.42	0.36
8. Renewal rate $(K_b + K_c)/K_o - K_a)$	0.68	0.74	0.61	0.66	0.64
9. Discounted profits	593.40	287.30	166.40	218.50	73.20
10. Transaction value (US\$m) K_F	114.90	106.50	13.90	222.90	468.80
Seller calculations					
11. Net increase of employment, 1000s	0.60	7.20	1.30	0.20	3.00
12. Net unemployment/ employment, %	1.60	12.30	6.40	0.70	2.50
13. Discounted gain from profits, US\$m	38.50	23.00	13.10	38.00	90.30
14. Transaction value, US\$m, K_G	194.10	138.10	100.50	252.30	542.40
Buyer preference					
15. Endogenous R_F for given K_G	18.60	19.00	15.20	19.30	19.40
16. Buyer ranking	4	3	5	2	1
Seller preference					
17. Endogenous R_G for given K_F	52.70	64.00	18.80	71.90	70.70
18. Seller ranking	4	3	5	1	2
Buyer and seller preference					
19. Buyer offer/seller offer K_F/K_G	0.59	0.77	0.14	0.88	0.86
20. Buyer and seller ranking	4	3	5	1	2

Table 17.1 lists the basic economic indicators which characterize these industries. Values of these indicators were derived from statistical data for 1989 and 1990 concerning Polish state industry.

The subject of the privatization transaction is a hypothetical state enterprise with the level of sales in 1989 corresponding to 10 per cent of the market share of the sector. The value of sales, assets and employment are shown in Table 17.2.

A number of parameters are assumed to be the same for all five industries. These are:

1. Expected length of transition period T is five years.
2. The annual rate of economic growth γ is 2 per cent.
3. The structure of the market is not changed in the transition period.
4. Annual discount rate for future profits δ is 10 per cent.
5. W, which is the annual real wage rate per employee in the privatized activities at the end of the transition period, is 5.174 million 1989 zlotys (equivalent to US$545).
6. Profit tax rate τ is 25 per cent.
7. Unemployment benefits are equal to 60 per cent of the wage rate, ($0.6W$).
8. Exchange rate of zloty to US$ is 9500 zlotys per dollar.

Tables 17.2 and 17.3 report the solution, which was produced assuming a desirable rate of return for the foreign buyer, $\bar{R}_F$ equal to 20 per cent of total discounted costs. The rate of return for the seller government was defined according to equation (2) where the denominator is the book value of privatized assets. The desirable seller rate of return, $\bar{R}_G$, was set at the level of 80 per cent of the book value of privatized assets.

The analysis of the buyer and seller preferences is based on comparison of their rates of return, which would result if the offer of the other side were accepted. The results presented in Table 17.2 show the similarity of buyer and seller ranking of the assessed industries. The analysis of the feasibility of the transaction is based on the coefficient m in equation (3). This coefficient measures the relative discrepancy between the offers of the buyer and the seller. A buyer bidding at a value lower by more than 20 per cent of the offer of the seller indicates that partners are not going to reach agreement without major change in their positions. In such circumstances, only transactions concerning chemical and electro-engineering industries seem to be feasible.

The process of renegotiating for the other three industries, which is not reported in the results, would mean that both sides would have to weaken their initial positions. For example, the seller may accept a lower rate of return than the 80 per cent from the solution. The buyer, in turn, may revise their evaluation and assign higher weights to immediate incurred costs than to replacement costs, which consist of about one half of total discounted costs (Table 17.3).

Table 17.3 Structure of discounted buyer costs

	Food	Light	Wood	Chem	Elen
Transaction value	10.7	17.0	5.1	27.1	21.1
Direct investments	8.2	12.3	17.9	16.8	12.5
Associated investments	20.6	18.9	19.9	21.0	17.8
Replacement investments	60.5	51.8	57.1	35.1	48.6
Total costs	100.0	100.0	100.0	100.0	100.0

In this study we have assumed values of factor productivity coefficients at levels observed for 1989 because for this year the Central Statistical Office provided data for fixed assets evaluated in current prices of December 1989. Use of these data, and calculations in constant prices of 1989, in our opinion allows us to omit the problem of inflationary increase in prices of capital goods.

Results can be sensitive to capacity utilization. At the present stage of our research differences in the levels of capacity utilization were ignored, which results in a bias of capital–output coefficients.

Given average factor productivities, such factors as the rates of capital and labour-augmenting technical change, which are crucial for determination of scrapping and the level of direct necessary investments, are important in influencing results.

Some arbitrary values were fixed for factor productivity in the newest vintage of assets as well. Though some arbitrariness in fixing parameter values is unavoidable in such a model as that used here, their reliability can be evaluated by simulation experiments designed to check the sensitivity of the solution to parameter changes. Such an evaluation produced stable results.

CONCLUDING REMARKS

The chapter formulated the conditions under which a privatization transaction between a seller government and a foreign buyer takes place making use of a two-sided cost–benefit analysis by seller and buyer and considering the typical features of the transitional phase in which the privatization is supposed to take place.

An empirical application to five industries in Poland showed that the chemical and electro-engineering industries are better situated than other industries such as light manufacturing, wood and paper manufacturing and food processing for privatization transactions.

NOTES

1. The first geometric series is based on $P_1 + P_2 + \ldots + P_T$ and consists of a finite number of elements, dependent on the expected length of the transition period: $\{1 + [S_T/S_o - S_a]^{1/T}\}$ $(1 + \delta)^{-1}$. The second geometric series consists of profits over an infinite number of years after period T, thus $P_{T+1} + P_{T+2}$ etc. The value of this series is calculable for a ratio of $(1 + \gamma)/(1 + \delta)$ equalling less than 1, which is normally the case; see Cohen (1993).
2. The total value of discounted investment expenditures in the transition period is found as

$$(K_b + K_c)\text{disc} = \left[\frac{K_b + K_c}{T}\right]\left[(1+\delta)^{-1} + (1+\delta)^{-2} + \ldots + (1+\delta)^{-T}\right]$$

3. For instance

$$(\text{Sum } K_d)\text{disc} = \frac{K_{d,T+1}}{(1+\delta)^{T+1}} + \frac{K_{d,T+2}}{(1+\delta)^{T+2}}\text{etc.}$$

Substituting for $K_{d,T-1}$ the right-hand side of equation (18) we get the geometric series with a ratio $[(1 + p)/(1 + \delta)]$ less than 1. Hence, (Sum K_d) disc can be written as

$$\left[\frac{(\gamma + p)K_T}{(1+\delta)^T}\right]\left[\frac{1}{\delta - p}\right]$$

REFERENCES

Ajani G., B. Dallago, B. Grancelli (1992), *Privatization and Entrepreneurship in Postsocialist Countries: Economy and Society*, Basingstoke, UK: Macmillan.

Cohen S.I. (1993), *Patterns of Economic Restructuring for Eastern Europe*, Aldershot, UK: Avebury.

Lee, B. and J. Nellis (1990), *Enterprise Reform and Privatization in Socialist Economies*, Washington, DC: World Bank.

OECD (1993), *Valuation and Privatisation*, Paris: OECD.

Sarcevic, P. (1992), *Privatization in Hungary, Past, Present and Future*, London: Graham & Trotman.

18. Using project finance to minimize the state budget funding of essential infrastructure in emerging market economies

Ross Bull and Nicolas Lethbridge

INTRODUCTION

Governments in emerging markets are restructuring their economies to ensure future resource allocation is founded on market-based price signals rather than centralized control. Managing such structural adjustment is a difficult, two-part process, in which government must, first, stabilize the macroeconomy, particularly keeping the budget deficit under control, while sharpening the focus of public expenditure. The second part of structural adjustment requires government to create a commercial/contractual framework.

This chapter focuses on how governments in the emerging market economies of Central and Eastern Europe and the former Soviet Union can develop their national infrastructure, at the same time as managing this two-part process of structural adjustment.

The main option today in a resource-deficient economy is for the government to seek the participation of private business in the management of national utilities and public-sector economic/social infrastructure, as well as the financing of necessary investment requirements. Notable successes have been achieved internationally, often on the basis of joint ventures, where privatization and/or deregulation has introduced private-sector management and financing techniques to telecommunications, electricity, gas, wind power, health, water, sewerage, prisons, education and housing, as well as transport, covering bridges, toll roads, mass transit systems, ports and airports. Such wide experience suggests that it is possible for selected public utilities to be virtually self-financing, using private funds to the extent that the utility can be, or is allowed to be, marketed commercially, and private markets are prepared to underwrite the risks involved.

Table 18.1 Public versus private financing

Model	Type	Funds provided by	Risk allocation
I Public-sector financing (Public-sector ownership and financial support)	State funding	Government	Taxpayers take full risk
	State guaranteed (or quasi guaranteed)	• Banks • Bond investors • Lessors	Sovereign risk to lenders (taxpayer takes full risk)
	State subsidy	Government	Taxpayer grant
II Private-sector financing (Private ownership)	Share capital (quoted or unquoted)	Equity investors	Shareholders take full equity risk
	Debt finance	• Banks • Bond investors	Credit risk on the company
	Leasing	• Domestic lessors • International lessors	Credit risk on the company Security of the leased asset
	Government grant/credit support	Government	Taxpayers take full risk

Source: Adapted from Crowe (1992).

PUBLIC VERSUS PRIVATE FINANCING

Table 18.1 summarizes two ways of financing development. On the one hand, public financing is either provided directly by government, or sourced from private-sector investors against a government guarantee or quasi guarantee. Under this situation, it is the taxpayer, rather than the private-sector provider of capital, who takes the risk on an investment. Alternatively, private financing generally does not enjoy a state guarantee, and the providers of funds, whether equity or debt, will depend on an investment's future revenues to service debt and provide a satisfactory return to private shareholders. Whilst the distinction between public and private financing lies in the credit risk and security to which each is exposed, public and private finance can be mixed in a variety of ways for any given project or investment contract.

PROJECT FINANCE

There is, however, a third model with which to fund development – project financing. This is a financial engineering exercise which involves the creation of a finance scheme to suit the peculiarities of an individual investment. Such financing is only possible when there is a separately identifiable project, the net revenues and assets of which can be ring-fenced, and financed on a stand-alone basis. As project finance is funding secured only by the assets or cash flows of the project being financed, such finance is without recourse to any external guarantee or collateral. Each scheme of project financing is a unique combination of risks and benefits, which need to be optimized through finding the proper mix of financing structures. This requires knowledge of what can be created and placed in the financial market, what creative or new 'tricks' can be used, the best time to place a transaction in the market, awareness of any unusual market opportunities, the ability to analyse options, and skill at documenting contractual arrangements.

A variant of project financing is concession financing. This is the temporary or permanent granting of a licence by government to a project sponsor, consortium or joint venture, in relation to delivery of a particular service or services. Such a licence should be sufficient to permit the sponsor to raise necessary funds on a project-financing basis. Concession financing has many parallels with privatization, in that it involves the transfer by government of traditional state rights to a private entity, subject to the performance of minimum (volume and quality) standards of service. Concession financing will not necessarily involve 100 per cent private financing. This will depend on identifiable sources of revenue associated with the earmarked project, and may require some form of government payment/subsidy/guarantee. It is crucial, however, that whatever the source of revenue, its value, and risks in its variation, can be assessed and analysed.

Many international infrastructure projects are examples of joint-venture project financing. Table 18.2 outlines different financing schemes which have been used in recent years, particularly those which relate to the transport sector, all of which are variants of the DBOOT approach to project finance. In this case, the private sponsor/franchisee is invited (competes) to Design, Build, Own, Operate and, sometimes, Transfer back to government (after a given concession period) a selected infrastructure project. General issues surrounding DBOOT-type financing models are summarized in Table 18.3.

As a word of warning, project finance should not be confused with World Bank or Export Credit 'financing of projects', where all or part of the financing is secured by external guarantees.

THE PROJECT-FINANCE PROCESS

Whilst the process involved in obtaining project finance is simple, the detailed steps are not, and it can often take several years before all links in the chain have been successfully completed. This process, which applies in all countries, not just in emerging market economies, is as follows

1. An engineering/financial feasibility study of the proposed project is required. As banks do not like risk, this study should propose a low-risk project to lenders. The study should identify the proposed structuring of financing requirements, covering equity, loans, bonds and guarantees.[1]
2. In project financing, the equity rate of return (ERR) is the key issue. Tax efficiency is therefore sought to boost the proposed project's ERR through any tax-advantaged element of project financing, e.g. consortium tax relief (where tax relief on interest payments and capital allowances for depreciating fixed assets are set against taxable profits). Tax efficiency may also involve leasing.[2]
3. Revenue and cost streams of the proposed project must be analysed to ensure that sufficient revenues will be generated to cover raw material, operating and maintenance costs, and to service debt and reward equity.
4. Contract structuring is vital. Where a project has a limited number of construction/design risks, contractors are likely to offer a turnkey contract, guaranteeing a fixed price and completion date for the project. In this situation, liquidated damages will be available to cover the lender's risks of underperformance and late completion. In addition, a contract bid will be judged on the basis of the contractual guarantees and creditworthiness of the company offering them, with each party's obligations

Table 18.2 Different types of financing schemes

Methods of project financing	Key feature of method	Examples
1. Build–Own–Operate (BOO)	Used when infrastructure facility is brand new, rather than existing, requiring financing for construction/build. Sponsoring consortium finances construction and operation of the facility as owners without the need to consider facility transfer to the host government. Countries committed to private-sector development and liberalization can use this method as a major privatization strategy.	Bangkok Hopewell Rail Mexican Toll Road
2. Design–Build–Own–Operate–Transfer (DBOOT)	Used for new projects requiring financing, but where the sponsoring consortium is expected to transfer the ownership of the project to the host government (sometimes after a substantial number of years), normally, but not always, at zero cost. Government may extend the sponsor's operation of the project, which will be a function of time of transfer, performance of the sponsor and remaining economic life of the project. DBOOT projects can be turned into DBOO investments. A reason for asset transfer is government's attitude towards private ownership and control of sensitive/strategic activities.	Philippines power plant Philippines port terminal Pakistan Hab River power plant Malaysia Saba water supply Hong Kong second harbour crossing Channel tunnel Dartford bridge
3. Build–Transfer–Operate (BTO)	Used in cases where government is not committed to privatization. Here, there is no private ownership, and the operation resembles a franchise arrangement. Method may have public participation in funding. Government may also pay for the maintenance of the facilities. Method is	German toll roads Hungarian toll roads Polish Modlin airport

	preferable to BOOT where legal risk needs to be limited, as it is generally more difficult to sue government than a private concern.	
4. Buy–Build–Operate (BBO)	Used for projects involving existing facilities, where the sponsoring consortium can purchase assets from government, expand capacity, then operate. Used by governments committed to privatization, but wishing to expand the capacity of existing operations.	Philippines light railway system Pakistan telephone operations Dublin beltway
5. Build–Operate–Sell (BOS)	Public sector takes the risk that the ultimate sale value of the facility will not cover the costs of building and operating it.	Sheffield tram system
6. Lease–Develop–Operate (LDO)	Derivative of BBO, where full privatization is avoided through government's retention of ownership rights. Government receives cash flows as specified by the lease agreement, and existing facilities are financed by the lessee.	Toronto airport terminal Atlantic City international airport Kuala Lumpur/Kauntan road
7. Add–Own–Operate (AOO)	Derivative of BBO. Government retains ownership of existing facilities, but private-sector sponsor owns any expanded facilities it has financed.	Airport fuel facility
8. Contract–Add–Operate (CAO)	Derivative of BBO. Used where ownership is not allowed for private sector financed expansion.	Waste processing plant expansion

Note: Other acronyms are DBOOM (Design–Build–Own–Operate–Manage), BOTT (Build–Own–Toll–Transfer) and DCFM (Design–Construct–Finance–Maintain).

Source: Adapted from Rimpel (1993).

Table 18.3 General issues concerning DBOOT-type financed infrastructure projects

Characteristics likely to lead to project success	General problems	Negotiating issues
Lack of public funds	Availability of credible and experienced developers and investors	Government must accept partial loss of control to private sector
Pressing public need for project	Ability of government to provide adequate level of administrative support	Private sector must accept existence of public sector regulations
Public sector presumption that private sector will be more efficient in managing project and its associated risks	Formulation of workable corporate and financial structures to overcome complexity involving risk allocation and sharing	Allocation on negotiating and implementation responsibilities to a single authority
Private sector is efficient in managing project and its associated risks	High development costs	Need for flexibility, and need to allocate selected tasks (e.g. procurement) to the private sector
Sponsor should not compete with government	Conflict of interests between needs of project and financial return to suppliers/contractors	Government must be able to overcome negotiating disadvantages through recruitment of professional legal and financial advisers
Turnkey design/construction contracts with firm prices, terms and conditions		
Project financeable on a limited-recourse basis		
Substantial user fees generated and collected, with potential to create non-user revenues		
Binding agreement negotiated by single agency		
Back-up credit support provided by government		
Technical, economic and commercial elements should be closely integrated and coordinated, particularly where syndicated financing is involved		
Good management of cultural issues, particularly where personalities are involved		

Source: Adapted from Rimpel (August, 1993)

Packaging issues	Political issues	Project risks
Project consortia need to see project as a business: they are not simply offering to government technical, construction and consulting services with some project financing Length of negotiations to be kept to a minimum Availability of private- and public-sector staff experienced in BOOT-type operations is limited Project selection process should be fair, transparent and open to independent scrutiny, in order to avoid legal challenge by the losers, leading to delay in project implementation Project should be structured competitively to secure required funding: profit element has to be easily identifiable to project participants Projects need to be properly structured before negotiations to ensure full involvement of creditors during (generally) long project development and implementation stages Project partnerships should have exit provisions for incompatible or non-performing partners, and entry provisions for new participants	Must be inadequate public funds, and political will by government to support use of a properly resourced private-sector input Needs to be perception of low political risk (e.g. stability of government composition, laws and regulations) if international institutional investors are to be attracted Legal and regulatory policy framework for private foreign investment, BOT programmes and regulation of public utilities should be in place early if investors are to be attracted Communication between parties with vested interests (e.g. unions, consumers, government, politicians and investors) must be well coordinated	Risks should be shouldered by those most able to assume them Contractual documents should include mitigants to make the risks manageable to lenders Foreign exchange fluctuations, currency convertibility and remittance, as well as inflation variations, should be the responsibility of government, if investors are to be attracted Project commercial risk involves the effects of construction, operating and completion delays, which affect cash flow, so that, for a fixed price construction contract, price should be increased by a risk factor to compensate the contractor for risk taking Political and country risk is the responsibility of the host government Where possible, insurance should be taken out to cover risks, including potential commercial loss Uninsurable risks must be evaluated at the time of contract negotiation

carefully defined. Once construction has been successfully achieved, responsibility for performance is likely to pass to the manufacturer who will guarantee a certain level of performance over the debt term. The project must achieve expected levels of performance at all stages, because it is the sole source of cash with which to repay debt. The reason that individual risks must be separately identified, and transferred to a contractual guarantor, is to give lenders confidence that a single party is responsible for every element contributing to the project's cash flow. Finally, long-term fixed-price contracts will have to be agreed for raw materials and final outputs.

5. Obtaining key public/private planning consents and approvals, and undertaking environmental impact assessments, is essential.

Once the potential investor has completed this lengthy process, the lending banks will repeat the whole exercise. They will be less concerned about the project's upside potential, focusing on mitigation of downside risk. Lending banks will make (almost) certain that, if the project underperforms, they will be covered, even if investors receive nothing.

THE SINGLE-PURPOSE COMPANY

Project financing is always complicated, and usually relatively expensive when compared to other asset-backed or corporate borrowings. There are two basic motives for the use of project financing: first, when a sponsor cannot borrow in any other way; and, second, when a large corporation which could provide or procure the money does not wish to tie up its balance sheet. In both cases, it will be necessary to create a special or single-purpose company (SPC), the sole function of which is to carry out the project. This entity, often an international joint venture, will undertake and own the project, and receive loans from lenders. It is this feature which distinguishes project financing from other forms of funding. If the SPC fails to repay its debts, lenders will have nothing other than the assets of the SPC to fall back on. These assets are likely to have little value if the project itself fails.

In order to highlight the function of the SPC, it is worth noting the important distinction between corporate finance and project finance. Under corporate finance, a department/subsidiary of a company will identify a new investment opportunity by capital budgeting against a minimum rate of return. If the company's directors approve the proposed project's risk and return profile, least-cost capital will be injected to finance the investment. Funds will be procured as part of corporate financing requirements, and debt and equity markets tapped for the cheapest possible capital, the availability and cost of which will be unrelated to the proposed project's risk and return profile. When a company raises finance, the cost of debt will be determined by the overall perception of its corporate creditworthiness. When raising debt, the company will need to examine its gearing ratio, that is, the ratio of equity to debt. Equity capital protects lenders from the possibility that debt cannot be serviced from a company's net cash flow. So, for a company to maintain a high credit rating, increased levels of debt will often be supported by increasing amounts of equity because, if gearing deteriorates, the company's cost of funds will rise. Under project finance, however, the SPC does not have this relationship with the capital market. The SPC is not designed to raise balance sheet backed funding, but to attract finance on the strength of its expected future revenues. The project's earnings potential must be so secure that only a comparatively small equity investment will be needed from project sponsors.

RISKS

The difference between a project-finance loan and almost any other form of financing lies in the nature of the lender's security. When a company borrows, the lender normally has recourse to the company's overall balance sheet and income, and will only lend if satisfied that the company is not too highly geared, that is, the company does not have too high a proportion of debt, as opposed to equity, on its balance sheet. Under project financing, however, lenders rarely have security over anything that is worth much if the borrower defaults. Project financing is often called non-recourse (or off balance sheet) financing, precisely because it means the lender does not have recourse to anything other than the assets the loan has paid for, and the cash flow those assets may, or may not, generate. Project financing therefore is really only suitable when a sponsor wants to finance a long-lived and easily identifiable asset, and can ring-fence or marry a specific net income stream with the specific asset in question. The easier it is to predict the project's commercial prospects, the easier it will be to arrange project financing.

Most projects are sponsored and undertaken by groups of local/international private-sector companies, either as a joint venture or consortium, since the project development expenditures involved are large and risky, and diverse skills and experiences are required to make the project work. Whilst a joint-venture or consortium development will mean that risks can be spread among the various parties, it also tends to make decision making more complex.

A project sponsor in search of project finance will always want to see that private debt financing is maximized, because debt is bound to be the cheapest source of commercial, private funding available. Therefore, the higher the proportion of debt finance, the greater will be the potential return on the balance of required funding, i.e. equity or quasi equity. The gearing ratio is crucial to any project financing, and centres around negotiating the trade-off between equity and debt. When the costs and revenues of a project are both easy to predict, and can be relied upon, the gearing ratio can be high, with 90 per cent or more of the project's capital cost being debt-financed.

Lenders will want to be sure that the project can afford its annual (principal and interest) debt service obligations as they fall due, and that the term/maturity of debt is consistent with the type of project or life of its assets. The most common method used by commercial banks to assess how much, and in what form, to lend to a project SPC is to establish cover ratios for loan life and annual debt service. A cover ratio is the income available to the SPC from which it can service its debt divided by the debt service obligations of the SPC.

From the project's point of view, the SPC will want to arrange as long a loan as possible, generally with a back-ended repayment profile. This is particularly true where project demand is anticipated to grow over time, or inflation is expected to erode the real value of any outstanding debt. The shorter the maturity of the loan, and the less back-ended its repayment profile, the less the SPC will be able to borrow, because of the cash flow constraints imposed by the annual cover ratios.

A typical transport project, for example, will incur substantial construction and procurement costs over a prolonged planning, licensing and construction period. As no income will be received during this period, all funding will be by way of project equity and debt drawdowns, and interest on debt will have to be capitalized and rolled up. There will come a time, however, when equity and loan drawdowns will have reached their maximum, and it is this amount which will determine the project's total funding requirement and financing plan. The risk associated with this total amount outstanding will ultimately rest with the SPC, unless it is able to pass risks on to other parties through the various contracts it will make in order to carry out the project. Creation of the project-financing plan will therefore involve establishing which risks can be passed to parties outside the SPC, and determining the incidence of risk between parties within the SPC (namely equity investors and lenders). The key determinant of risk allocation in any project is its gearing target, since this determines the degree of project risk to which lenders to the SPC, rather than its owners, will be exposed. The greater the amount of risk which can be parcelled out to others, the higher will be the gearing of the SPC, since lenders will require lower cover ratios. In addition to gearing, any transport project will have to cope with the following risks:

1. Technology risk – the extent to which the SPC will be exposed to any risk of untried or untested technology or design.

2. Completion risk – the extent to which the SPC will be exposed to any cost overruns during construction, equipment procurement, or late completion/delivery.
3. Market risk – the degree to which the SPC will be exposed to market risks for the sale of its product (frequently avoided by the SPC making long-term off-take 'take and pay' or 'take or pay' contracts with creditworthy buyers).
4. Operating risk – the extent to which the SPC will be exposed to any costs or inaccuracies in operating-cost forecasts, and/or the risks of non-supply or unforeseen price increases of essential raw materials.
5. Other risks – the political situation, as well as changes in interest rates, exchange rates and tax rates.

Although the SPC will try to protect itself from as much risk as possible, the SPC's overall risk profile will determine the amount of debt relative to equity which it is possible to arrange. Whilst insurance is a key method of insulating the SPC against many of these risks, sensitivity analysis will be rigorously used to test the transport project's robustness to changes in key assumptions.

Finally, it is important to note that partial refinancing of the project from cheaper sources may be possible subsequently, once the construction period risk is over and revenues are starting to flow.

SUMMARY

So far, this chapter has concentrated on technical issues. General objectives associated with project financing a ring-fenced infrastructure project are the achievement of:

1. Maximum off-balance sheet financing – ensuring debt and any subordinated debt raised for the project will not be consolidated with sponsors' or equity investors' balance sheets (i.e. non-recourse financing).
2. Maximum gearing potential – achieving the highest proportion of non-recourse financing within total project-funding requirements.
3. Minimum cost of funds – procuring non-recourse financing at lowest available cost.
4. Maximum equity return – devising a financing plan which is expected to yield the highest return to shareholders' equity, consistent with financial viability and project competitiveness.
5. Maximum tax efficiency – boosting a project's equity returns through any tax-advantaged element of project financing.

6. Minimizing overall project risk – providing supportive contract terms and prices which will mitigate the risks of high gearing for lenders and investors.

USING PRIVATE FINANCE TO FUND ESSENTIAL INFRASTRUCTURE IN EMERGING MARKET ECONOMIES

Consider now the main focus of this chapter. What can governments do in emerging market economies to develop rapidly their national infrastructure, at a time of stringent control over public expenditure? One solution is for government to establish an immediate dialogue with local/international private sector business, using it to manage national utilities and public-sector economic/social infrastructure, as well as finance essential investment requirements.

There are a number of convincing reasons why government should access local/international private management and financing skills:

1. The private-sector financing of essential infrastructure investments will relieve pressure on government's budgetary requirements.
2. The private sector is generally perceived to be more efficient than the state.
3. The private sector is financially motivated to respond positively to profit-related incentives.
4. The private sector imposes discipline, through the profit motive. Project implementation is speeded up, and risk pushed on to project contractors (which may not happen when implementing publicly/concessionally funded projects).
5. Provided the legal regime exists, all privately held contracts can be enforced in the courts, through the lenders'/suppliers' access to liquidated and ascertained damages. However, if the full array of available financial instruments is to be used efficiently, it is essential that the tax regime in emerging markets should offer private/public joint-venture operators advantages which are similar to those available in other countries competing for private funds. Equally, because asset ownership must be beyond question, the legal regimes in all countries participating in the project must be accepted by all parties. This means that government must redraft tax laws and other legislation which will permit newly privatized enterprises and/or privately managed projects to take advantage of available private finance. Without such tax and legal consistency, negotiation for project financing will be difficult.

6. Ring-fenced projects with secure cash flows can be funded on an *ad hoc* basis, permitting terms and conditions to be negotiated with the private sector on a project-by-project basis.
7. Private involvement in individual project financings is not dependent on government policy towards privatization/deregulation.
8. The private sector is more varied in the financing schemes it is able to offer investors. For example, credit lines (possibly backed by IBRD/IFC, EBRD or EIB) can be used to purchase equipment that can be leased by financial intermediaries to either private enterprises (created out of restructured state-owned enterprises), or enterprises in the public sector. The introduction of the leasing instrument (see Annex 2) serves to deepen financial markets, to overcome the collateral constraint that many borrowers confront, and the legal constraint faced by lenders. The main difficulty with such an approach is finding suitably qualified financial intermediaries.
9. Private infrastructure projects can still work with subsidy programmes, provided a concession is granted by the state for a sufficient period of time, so that the owner/operator can repay debt and reward equity. As project usage cannot be guaranteed, the concession may partly mitigate this risk by providing in (say) the case of a transport project a lump-sum capital grant or per passenger/kilometre subsidy so that the project is not totally reliant on self-generating revenues to repay debt. (Another example might be a subsidy per unit of energy generated, with which to promote new technologies and make them commercially viable.)

Although government may find these convincing reasons for trying to access private management and financing skills in developing essential infrastructure, it is worth stressing the two main problems on which private sector partners will focus, particularly those invited to participate in an international joint venture. First, there must be reliable contractual arrangements over the (10–20-year) life of a project, and these must be enforceable through the courts. Second, a regular flow of project receipts can probably only be guaranteed where consumers are already used to paying for delivered services, such as those related to transport, power and water. In this regard, the lender is likely to look more favourably at revenue streams received in convertible currencies (for example, such as those that might be levied on international port movements).

Finally, it may be that public-sector agencies wish to use the principles of project finance, but not to introduce private management techniques. In this situation, the public sector is unlikely to benefit fully from private-sector skills and, at the same time, any gains from reducing the public-sector borrowing requirement would be lost.

PUBLIC/PRIVATE PARTNERSHIPS IN EMERGING MARKET ECONOMIES

Since the start of the 1980s, there has been a worldwide trend towards private provision and financing of services traditionally supplied through the public sector. Most commonly, this has taken the form of full-scale privatization, in which existing, publicly-owned businesses or utilities have been transferred or sold to the local/international private sector. However, in the many cases where large-scale, new investment is required, privatization as such is not necessarily appropriate. In this case, the challenge for government is how to procure the creation of a new, large, one-off public-service capital asset which can be owned and financed through the private sector.

The standard approach to obtaining private finance with which to fund new infrastructure projects has been for the public sector to design project requirements, and then invite local/international private companies to bid to meet them. Where the public sector has not necessarily wished to divest itself of the ownership of the new asset, it has invited tenders for a fixed specification. In this case, the private sector has not been able to contribute to the project's design performance or contractual structure. However, such an approach achieves competitive pricing, and ensures that the public sector predetermines exactly what it is going to get. In addition, the method can achieve transfer to the private sector of considerable risk ownership and financing burden, using various DBOOT-type concession arrangements of the type summarized in Table 18.2.

A drawback of this conventional approach is that it does not tap private-sector ingenuity, imagination and experience in the formulation of the project, asset or business itself. Accordingly, there is now a trend towards using private-sector talents before the nature of the business or the asset which is to be tendered/implemented has been fully defined. One method of achieving this is for the private sector to be brought in at an initial stage, with a view to achieving a project proposal which will assure commercial viability, based on the private sector's experience in assessing technical design, system costs and expected revenues. Such an approach permits the possible creation of a local/international joint-venture partnership between the public and private sectors, in which risks can be shared according to some predetermined formula. But, for the public sector to be certain it is getting value for money, competition can be introduced at a second stage, as follows:

- Stage 1. Private companies will form a development group, including the public promoter, to design project specifications and an underlying contract structure. At this time, it will be discovered how much project financing – debt and equity – can be raised on the basis of expected operating revenues. Any capital shortfall will require public support. If the gap is too large, the project will not go ahead, and the developers and public promoters will lose their initial design investment. This shared risk is a powerful incentive for all parties to create a commercially robust package from the beginning. If the gap is acceptable to the public sector, the second stage of the project can start.

- Stage 2. The finalized project will be tendered out to see if other private consortia can deliver the same project specifications at lower cost (thereby permitting, where appropriate, a lower level of state funding). If the bid of the Stage 1 consortium is undercut, its development costs will be reimbursed.

An alternative to this two-stage approach is to have a single competition, but invite the local/international private sector to participate very early. This is the approach being used for the Channel Tunnel Rail Link in the UK. Here, private-sector bidders have been invited to compete for a concession, and empowered to undertake a great deal of physical and institutional design. Clearly, the costs imposed on private-sector bidders of designing speculative investment plans against an uncertain future commercial and contractual background are likely to be very high, and bound to be greater than in a two-stage competition. Accordingly, if this method is adopted, it is likely that some or all of the bidders' project development costs will be reimbursed by the public sector or imposed as a cost to be borne by the winning scheme. In the case of the Channel Tunnel Rail Link, for example, four bidding groups have been pre-qualified and, so long as they produce conforming proposals, some of their costs will be reimbursed. Following valuation of the initial proposals, a final competition will probably be held between two shortlisted bidding consortia, and some or all of the final loser's costs are likely to be reimbursed.

Whatever method of competition is finally adopted, it will often be the case that the private sector cannot finance the entire cost of the public utility or transport infrastructure scheme. One way of financing the funding gap will be with a capital grant. Alternatively, government's financial contribution can be viewed as the purchase of externalities. Here, government will buy benefits on behalf of the taxpaying public which the project brings to society at large. In the case of transport, non-user benefits such as these might take traffic off the roads and put it on to buses or trams, thereby releasing road space, and providing quicker transport for remaining road users. As government can specify a price per passenger or train movement that it is prepared to pay in order to secure these non-user benefits, the private company can then make a revenue support agreement with government to supplement passenger revenues. This still leads to uncertainty, because of unknown market demand,

and funding will depend on the credibility that lenders ascribe to traffic forecasts, the project's marketing plan, and the operating strategy of the transport company. This is on the downside. On the upside, however, if the market exists, there is unlikely to be a natural or contractual limit to the income flow on which the project financing is based (even though, today, project financing tends to be confined to bank debt with a maximum life of about twenty years). Where a market can be established, with no limit to the revenue flow, this is likely to lead to better securitization of project-finance debt, and diversification of the sources of project financing. This deepening of the financial market away from commercial banks in favour of insurance companies, institutions and pension funds, will provide opportunities for fund managers looking for secure investment yields with long maturities.

CONCLUSIONS

Governments in emerging market economies need to construct new/rehabilitation infrastructure, in order to promote economic and social development. At the same time, for financial and policy reasons, they must minimize their involvement in the provision, financing and management of such investment. By using the project financing techniques outlined in this chapter, local/international joint venture projects can be structured to meet the needs of both public and private partners, thereby guaranteeing value for money for the public sector, and a return for the private sector. It does not take much imagination to see the advantages of injecting private funds into resource-deficient economies. Whilst it might take some time for governments in emerging market economies to come to terms with the conditions under which such private finance is available, they really have no option other than to start negotiating access to these funds. Otherwise, they will not be able to provide in the foreseeable future the essential economic and social infrastructure to which their populations aspire.

ANNEX 1 KEY POINTS CONCERNING ALTERNATIVE SOURCES OF FINANCE

All institutions involved in developing, owning or financing (infrastructure) projects want to know if they can use private-sector equity capital to their advantage. If so, where will it come from? Some of the more common sources of private finance are summarized below. The annex also briefly touches on the issue of co-financing.

1. Sponsor Equity

Project sponsors almost always contribute a proportion of a project's total cost as equity capital (preferably the smallest amount possible), to (a) match the project cash flow to the optimal amount of project debt consistent with the project's risk profile, and (b) provide psychological comfort to senior lenders (i.e. commercial banks), that project sponsors are committed, and have a reasonable stakes to lose. The form of sponsor equity will depend on the sponsor's ability and willingness to contribute, the project's tax position and dividend outlook, and the sponsor's tax position and investment objectives. There are different types of sponsor equity:

- *Share capital.* This is a cash contribution, the precise timing of which can be negotiated, which will have the effect of reducing interest charges during a project's construction phase. Since sponsor equity should carry the highest rate of return, and represents the most expensive form of finance, sponsors naturally aim to employ it last, and least.
- *Development capital.* Small developers without significant balance sheets will often try to make their equity contribution in the form of unreimbursed project development costs (or development fees for professional services rendered).
- *Asset contributions.* Providing equity in this way is difficult because of valuing the contributed assets. Whilst land is relatively straightforward to value, putting a price on operating facilities, such as plant, is not. Sponsors will want to check asset valuation, equality between shareholders' contributions, and the expected life and economic usefulness of the assets being contributed. There may be tax and earnings' impacts from the point of view of the sponsor contributing the assets.
- *Sponsor-supplied subordinated debt.* This can be used to maximize cash payouts to project sponsors as equity returns, or meet other investor/project needs, in the form of interest and principal, where dividends cannot be paid out because of accounting restrictions related to insufficient profits.
- *Preference shares.* These are on the boundary of debt and equity. They are used to offer a second-tier equity return to an investor wanting a debtor's priority. Preference shares do not typically have the beneficial tax impact on the project company associated with sponsor-supplied subordinated debt.
- *Convertible debt.* Some sponsors prefer the flexibility of a convertible instrument, since it can be classified as debt, but valued as equity. Such a situation may arise where a third party investor is included in a

partnership after the original sponsors have initiated project development.

2. Investor Equity

- *Third party equity.* Third parties are not project sponsors or original developers, but represent additional equity finance, such as knowledgeable industry insiders. There may be a conflict in this case between the sponsors' need for additional equity, and the third party's wish to share control and responsibility in project management and development. A way to overcome this is by obtaining (further) third-party institutional support.

3. Mezzanine Debt

- *Mezzanine (or subordinated) debt* is provided by entities other than project sponsors. True mezzanine debt is not strictly a source of equity capital, but is employed to enhance the equity rate of return, and meet the funding gap between available equity capital and senior debt. Mezzanine debt is uncommon in infrastructure projects, because initial financial structuring always strives to use as much senior debt as possible, thereby reducing mezzanine opportunities.

4. Senior Debt as Equity

This is commercial bank debt, which is generally the cheapest form of finance available. When conditions are right, commercial banks can be coaxed into providing some of what would otherwise be called equity capital.

5. Tax Equity

Tax capital is a form of negative capital, in the sense that the taxman expects a return on the project's tax base for which he did not contribute. Structuring the best finance plan for a project must include optimizing the project's after-tax rate of return, and therefore minimizing the project's tax capital. Two main options exist to reduce tax capital: first, the transfer of tax benefits between the project entity and sponsors/owners (i.e. the ownership composition that best exploits a country's tax and accounting rules); and, second, project leasing.

Finally, where the mix of financing an infrastructure project involves private equity and commercial debt, and possibly concessional loans, co-financing arrangements involving commercial banks and either IBRD/IFC, EBRD or EIB will very likely include mandatory cross-default clauses in loan agreements, putting pressure on the borrower to give equal priority to commercial and concessionary debt. A further possible financial instrument observed in recent World Bank lending policy (in China and elsewhere), is to guarantee private-sector investment in large co-financed infrastructure projects, subject to payment (by some institution) of a risk premium on the private-sector amount guaranteed.

ANNEX 2 KEY POINTS CONCERNING LEASING AND TAX ISSUES IN EMERGING MARKET ECONOMIES

1. Leasing

Substantial volumes of funds are available for investment in the emerging (and expanding) markets of Eastern Europe and the former Soviet Union, as well as in South America, Asia and Africa. Such investment can be used to support either infrastructure or direct production

In this situation, leasing is an obvious way to finance the purchase of new equipment. This is particularly the case for new small and medium-sized companies, which are unlikely to have acceptable balance sheets against which bank credit can easily be offered, making it difficult for such companies to raise necessary equity to fund equipment acquisition. The ability of leasing to offer 100 per cent asset backed financing is therefore crucial, more often for cash flow reasons than because of tax/accounting advantages.

Whilst emerging markets offer substantial returns, they can also involve extreme risks. Apart from political risk (which can be insured against), two basic risks for a lessor concern credit assessment, and asset repossession. Whilst the former is a function of local knowledge, particularly about the tax and accounting regimes, the second depends on knowledge of the law and agreements/contracts being carefully drafted. Development of leasing must therefore go hand in hand with legislation and commercial regulation. Uncertainties over such issues can prove to be insurmountable obstacles to leasing, as can *ad hoc* decisions by government.

As greater economic stability reduces (but does not eliminate) the risk of large currency devaluation, enabling local borrowers increasingly to access international finance markets, much cross-border funding of infrastructure to upgrade telecommunications, extend power, expand transport, develop natural resources and add to productive capacity has begun to flow from unsecured Euro-offerings, commercial bank loans backed by export credit agencies, and occasional cross border equipment leasing.

Companies funding working capital requirements with short-term loans from local banks find that these borrowings must be continually rolled over, creating administrative inefficiencies for both borrower and lender. This permits foreign-sourced leasing and asset-backed lending to compete with relatively expensive short-term lending. Leasing and secured lending inherently offer longer-term certainty, whether in fixed or floating rate form, but can be hampered by limited sources of funding, the imposition of local taxes, and legal systems not readily amenable to traditional Western asset secured financings.

As an example, consider aircraft leasing. Whilst the exact structure used will vary according to the financing terms, the basic elements of the structure will usually involve an offshore lessor and offshore lenders, as well as a guarantee by a local bank of the airline's lease obligations. Simply put, the offshore lessor will purchase the aircraft using funds borrowed from the lenders, and lease it to the airline for a period and a price exactly matching the term of, and payments to be made under, the loan. A mortgage of the aircraft and assignments of the lessor's rights under the lease (to insurance proceeds and against the guarantor), will be given as security for the loan by the lessor to the lenders. In operating leases, the financing of the aircraft by the operating lessor often involves the granting of a mortgage over the aircraft, and security assignments of the lessor's rights under the lease, guarantee and insurances, in favour of the operating lessor's financiers.

Leasing has shown itself to be a stable financial tool, and powerful instrument for repossessing assets. A lease effectively provides an equipment warranty, permitting easier recovery and sale of the leased asset.

Several factors determine whether leasing structures are economically attractive to emerging market importers. Generally, leasing is seen as a convenient means of achieving off-balance sheet financing. In addition, significant cost savings can be made by adopting leasing structures, due to trade regulations, custom duties and tax aspects. In many emerging market economies, leasing qualifies for considerable tax breaks, achieved through:

- customs taxes levied at the end of the leasing agreement;
- customs taxes levied on the residual value of the equipment;
- total/partial exemption from VAT; and
- significant exemptions on import duties for leased equipment.

2. Tax

Where possible, the tax treatment in a project financing should be optimized, since this can add considerable value, and often overwhelm the results of fine tuning interest rate margins and maturities. In particular, as a single-purpose company (SPC) will not in the early stages generate taxable profits, any available tax relief can be bought by domestic shareholders in proportion to their equity investment, and set against their stream of taxable profits. This will increase return on equity. Maximizing the scope and exploitation of opportunities to arrange tax-advantageous financing (both domestic and cross-border), is an important determinant of the scope and cost of the availability of project financing. Creativity through tax-advantaged financing can lower the cost of financing to the borrower/project, while preserving the yield requirements of the investor. This is because, usually, projects require large amounts of plant and equipment which can be rapidly depreciated for tax purposes in most sophisticated tax jurisdictions. To achieve this, the tax regime in the country where the project is to be financed must offer the operator certain tax advantages. If an SPC is unable to obtain consortium relief (either because the SPC is a subsidiary company, or its major shareholders do not have taxable profits in the project's country of domicile, or the SPC is not yet trading), project financing may still be able to provide tax efficiency through leasing. A project's capital assets may not necessarily be purchased with bank debt, but through a finance lease, where the SPC becomes a lessee renting capital assets from a leasing company. The lessor owns the assets, receiving tax allowances – depreciation plus interest expenses – and passes the bulk of them on to the SPC in the form of lower rental payments. However, because the ownership of leased assets must be beyond question, the legal regime in all countries participating in the lease must be accepted by all companies.

Financial leases have implications for credit status, the status of the taxpayer, the nature of the assets involved and the rates of tax allowance which are available. Such leases transfer all the risks and rewards of ownership to the lessee, who would, in particular, expect to retain a 100 per cent interest in the residual value of the equipment. Most project-leasing structures achieve this by providing some form of end-of-term fixed price purchase option in favour of the lessee. Whilst this is also true of operating leases, in this case the lessor participates in a significant amount of residual value risk in the asset (normally more than 10 per cent of the asset cost).

The financial benefits of leasing can be substantial. Typically, an operator can make an effective present value saving on its investment cost (over a sub-optimal design) of between 4 and 15 per cent. The ultimate benefit will depend, among other things, on the lease jurisdiction, the lease structure, the term of the lease, and the profile of the lease rentals. Where there is mixed public- and private-sector financing of projects, leasing by public entities should meet strict financial tests designed to ensure that the net position of government's finances, including tax revenues, is not adversely affected by any particular leasing scheme (bearing in mind that private-sector lessees are entitled to use whatever tax advantages are available under the existing tax system).

There is an overlap between domestic leasing and true non-recourse, off-balance sheet project finance. This is called project leasing, which aims to offer sponsors the best possible after-tax rate of return (given existing tax opportunities), combined with investment flexibility. This will depend on variables such as the amount of leasable equipment, depreciation life, tax rate and project profitability. Project leasing competes with other internal and external mechanisms for treating tax losses. As a source of finance, project leasing provides increased cash flow over a similar debt-financed project through lease rentals being less than the annual debt service payments for the same project. There is no simple one-stop shop for project leasing. Lessors are generally large commercial banks, financial institutions and corporate consortium leasing companies with sufficient taxable profits which they are prepared to sell for a fee.

Project leasing enables sponsors to make optimal use of a project's tax losses if the sponsor cannot efficiently transfer and use them. The intent is to minimize a project's tax capital within its own tax jurisdiction. It is also worthwhile to consider optimizing a project's after-tax internal rate of return (IRR) by taking advantage of tax benefits that arise in other jurisdictions. This is called cross-border leasing, which allows a project to reduce the purchase cost of equipment that originates from certain countries. The objective is to arrange a lease in one country that provides benefits to sponsors in another country. It depends on structuring a transaction where two companies are both considered owners of the same asset for tax purposes in their own jurisdictions, and able to gain from the same tax benefits. In the context of providing equity capital, cross-border leasing can reduce project costs, and thus increase sponsors' after-tax equity IRR.

REFERENCES

Adam, Christopher, William Cavendish and Percy S. Mistry (1992), *Adjusting privatisation: case studies from developing countries*, London: IRP/Heinemann.

Asset Finance and Leasing Digest (1993), 'Emerging markets: a special report', September.

Bull, Ross (1994), 'Using project finance techniques for transport infrastructure', paper presented to an international conference on 'Attracting private finance for transport infrastructure investments in Central and Eastern European countries', Brussels, 7–8 November, European Centre for Infrastructure Studies.

Conservative Transport Group (1993), *Getting Britain's railways right*, London.

Corporate Finance (1993), '1993 guide to the emerging markets', Special supplement, March.

Crowe, Norman (1992), *Debt and equity funding for Europe's railways*, London: Babcock & Brown, October.

Duff, Declan (1994), 'Private sector financing of infrastructure: IFC new approaches', paper presented to an international conference on 'Attracting private finance for transport infrastructure investments in Central and Eastern European countries', Brussels, 7–8 November, European Centre for Infrastructure Studies.

Duncan, Tim (1992), *Transaction analysis: assessing the parties' requirements*, London: Babcock & Brown, February.

Duncan, Tim (1992), *Recent innovations in project finance*, London: Babcock & Brown, February.

EC/PHARE (1994), *INFONOTE – PHARE general guidelines 1993 to 1997: a synopsis*, Brussels.

EC/TACIS (1994), *What is TACIS?*, Brussels.

Ernst and Young (1993), *Project finance in the 1990s: private financing of public infrastructure projects*, London.

Fayard, Alain (1994), 'The role of tolls and toll pricing policies in building new motorways', paper presented to an international conference on 'Attracting private finance for transport infrastructure investments in Central and Eastern European countries', Brussels, 7–8 November, European Centre for Infrastructure Studies.

Feldman, Roger D. (1993), 'Linking project finance to international infrastructure privatisation', *Transactional Finance*, **5** (2).

Frydman, Roman, Andrzej Rapaczynski and John S. Earle (1993), *The privatisation process in Russia, Ukraine and the Baltic States – Volume 2* (*Volume 1* covers the remaining Central and East European States), Prague: CEU Press.

Gaspard, Michel (1994), 'Financing needs and means for transport infrastructure in Central and Eastern Europe', paper presented to an international conference on 'Attracting private finance for transport infrastructure investments in Central and Eastern European countries', Brussels, 7–8 November, European Centre for Infrastructure Studies.

Getts, David (1992), *Equity sources*, London: Babcock & Brown, September

Green, Roy E. (ed.) (1991), *Enterprise zones: new directions in economic development*, London: Sage Focus Edition.

Haley, Geoffrey (1994), 'Basic steps for putting up projects for tender and contract negotiations', paper presented to an international conference on 'Attracting private finance for transport infrastructure investments in Central and Eastern European countries', Brussels, 7–8 November, European Centre for Infrastructure Studies.

HM Treasury (1992), *Private finance: guidance for departments*, London.

HM Treasury (1993), *Joint ventures: guidance for departments,* London.

HM Treasury (1993), *Leasing: guidance for departments*, London.

HM Treasury (1993), *Competition and the private finance initiative: guidance for departments*, London.

International Finance Corporation (1994), *Financing private infrastructure projects - emerging trends from IFC's experience*, Washington, DC: IFC.

International Finance Law Review (1993), 'Joint ventures: a legal guide to International joint ventures', Special supplement, February.

International Tax Review (1992), 'Project finance: a guide to the taxation of International project finance', Special supplement, May.

International Tax Review (1992), 'Joint ventures: a guide to tax-efficient international cooperation', Special supplement, November.

Lethbridge, Nicolas (1991), *Project financing, leasing assessment and allocation of risk*, London: Babcock & Brown, October.

Lethbridge, Nicolas (1991), *An investigative analysis of privatisation for Los Angeles airport*, London: Babcock & Brown, November.

Lethbridge, Nicolas (1992), *Finance for transport development*, London: Babcock & Brown, May.

Lim, Claire (1993), 'Project finance: an international guide – article on Singapore experience'. Special supplement to the *International Finance Law Review*, August.

Millot, Bertrand (1994), 'Risk and constraints in Central and Eastern European projects and how to overcome them', paper presented to an international conference on 'Attracting private finance for transport infrastructure investments in Central and Eastern European countries', Brussels, 7–8 November, European Centre for Infrastructure Studies.

Nevitt, Peter K. (1994), *Project financing*, 5th edition, London: Euromoney Publications.

Rimpel, Auguste E. Jr. (1993), *Infrastructure project financing in Asia: lessons learned*, Washington, DC: Price Waterhouse.

Roth, Gabriel (1987), *The private provision of public services in developing countries*, London: Oxford University Press.

Sacklen, Mats (1992), 'Negotiation investments in Central Europe', ABB Asea Brown Boveri Ltd, *International Financial Law Review*, March.

Smith, Warren F. (1993), *Project finance: principles and applications*, London: Euromoney Publications.

Timar, Andras (1994), 'The Hungarian motorway experience', paper presented to an international conference on 'Attracting private finance for transport infrastructure investments in Central and Eastern European countries', Brussels, 7–8 November, European Centre for Infrastructure Studies.

Watkins, Alfred J. (1994), 'Financing options for motorway projects', paper presented to an international conference on 'Attracting private finance for transport infrastructure investments in Central and Eastern European countries', Brussels, 7–8 November, European Centre for Infrastructure Studies.

Wilde Sapte (1993), *British Rail – privatisation or commercialisation?* London.

Wilde Sapte (1993), *British Rail privatisation – the insolvency regime*, London.

Wilde Sapte (1994), *British Rail privatisation update – putting the theory into practice*, London.

World Bank (1993), *MEBO privatisation programmes in post-socialist countries*, Washington DC: World Bank.

World Bank (1993), *Privatisation: the lessons of experience*, Washington DC: World Bank Country Economics Department.

World Bank (1993), *Aide Memoire concerning the identification of a World Bank project in support of financial and enterprise sector reform in Latvia*, Washington DC: World Bank.

World Bank (1994), *Latvia: public expenditure review*, Washington DC: World Bank.

World Bank (1994), *The World Bank's guarantees – catalysts for private capital flows*, Washington DC: World Bank.

19. Estimating shadow prices in a transitional economy: the case of Lithuania

David Potts

INTRODUCTION

Lithuania declared its independence from the former Soviet Union (FSU) in 1990 and gained admittance into the United Nations in 1991. The independent government inherited an economy that was heavily dependent on the FSU both as an export market for Lithuanian agricultural and industrial products and as a source of raw materials both for industry and more importantly for energy. The break-up of the FSU led to a disruption of trade relations both for Lithuanian exports and for imports. Particularly problematic was the substantial change in the price of raw materials for energy generation consequent on a move from the heavily subsidized prices of the FSU to world prices.

Independence also meant the establishment of new government institutions and the reform of existing institutions to fit in with the transition from a predominantly state-owned centrally planned economy to a mixed economy. An important part of the process of economic reform was the establishment of a public investment programme (PIP) through which priorities for public-sector investment could be determined in the aftermath of the rapid economic decline that accompanied independence. GDP fell by 54 per cent in the first three years of independence and inevitably this had a substantial effect on the capacity to fund public investment from internal sources. As a result it has been necessary to seek external funds to finance much of the PIP and it has also been important to ensure that those funds that are available from internal sources are used as effectively as possible.

The first stage in establishing the PIP was to obtain a systematic database recording all the ongoing and proposed projects of the different ministries and organizations. It was then necessary to established a standardized form of reporting and to ensure that projects were costed properly. A major training programme was undertaken to allow the introduction of cost–benefit analysis techniques into the analysis of the larger projects. In the first instance, analysis of projects has been undertaken at market prices, but it was recognized that, partly as a result of the heritage from the FSU, the prices of some goods and services diverged significantly from their economic value. The PIP Unit therefore decided to commission a study (Potts 1995) on the aims and scope of economic analysis and the estimation of economic prices. This chapter describes some of the main features of the study and tries to identify some of the similarities and differences between shadow pricing in a relatively industrialized economy in transition and shadow pricing in a typical developing economy.

PROCEDURE

The procedure used to estimate shadow prices for Lithuania was a variant of the semi-input–output approach using a world-price numeraire.[1] The process of calculating the conversion factors was similar to the 'extended' semi-input–output procedure used by Tan (1994) for Malaysia in that labour categories were treated in the same way as economic sectors although, in the Lithuanian model, domestic resources was treated as a separate primary factor and the standard conversion factor was derived by iteration.[2] The inputs into labour in this approach were defined by the opportunity cost of labour and depended on assumptions about the sectoral source of the different categories of labour. A separate calculation using conventional A and F matrices was also undertaken to indicate the breakdown of sector output values into the normal primary factor categories.[3]

The extended A matrix used for estimation of the conversion factors consisted of six main sectors, 54 sub-sectors and four labour categories. The Leontief inverse of the A matrix was multiplied by an F matrix consisting of two primary factors (foreign exchange and domestic resources) and five categories of transfer payment (taxes and subsidies, operating surplus, changes in income to semi-skilled labour, changes in income to unskilled labour and changes in income to the rest of the economy). The conversion factors were derived by constructing a 2×1 vector (P) containing the economic values of foreign exchange (1.0) and domestic resources. The value for domestic resources was a seed value for the first round but was determined by a weighted average of sector conversion factors in all subsequent calculations. The vector P was multiplied by the first two rows of the F matrix (called PF for primary factors) to derive a vector of conversion factors (S) for sectors, sub-sectors and labour. Three iterations were enough to achieve convergence to three decimal places. A standard conversion factor of 0.92 was obtained indicating a relatively low general level of protection consistent with a fairly open trading economy.

The treatment of the operating surplus, particularly for non-traded goods, was as a residual after the deduction of an adjusted value for capital costs. Most values for capital costs were derived by adjusting accounting values for depreciation. From an economic point of view accounting values suffer from two major defects. First, they are usually based on historic cost and therefore bear no relation to replacement cost under conditions of high inflation. Fortunately many of the non-traded sub-sectors in Lithuania experienced a major asset revaluation in 1994. For example, this led to the value for depreciation in the rail sector increasing by a factor of 13.6. The second major defect of accounting values is that they do not allow for any return on capital. To adjust replacement-cost depreciation estimates to allow for a return on capital it was necessary to estimate the average life of capital assets and to multiply the depreciation value by the ratio of the capital-recovery factor for the asset life to the reciprocal of the asset life. This ratio was described as an asset-revaluation factor. As discussed below, the discount rate assumed for these calculations and recommended for use in economic analysis in Lithuania was 8 per cent.

Once the depreciation estimates had been adjusted they were treated as part of the overall costs for the sub-sector in question and included in the estimation of the coefficients in the A matrix. As a result, the residual difference between the value of the output of the sector and the total value of costs estimated in this way was treated as a pure operating surplus and categorized as a transfer payment. In many cases the value of the operating surplus was negative, indicating either negative or sub-normal profits.

The approach to estimating the discount rate was to assume that the marginal source of investment funds was borrowing from abroad. It was also assumed that public sector investment should be able to earn a rate of return at least equal to that of the marginal private-sector investment. Information was therefore obtained on the terms of loans to the private sector for which loan guarantees had been approved and the discount rate was assumed to be defined by the upper end of the range. For Lithuania most such loans were denominated in US dollars or Deutschmarks and based on LIBOR plus a margin or a similar fixed rate. The resulting estimate was for a discount rate of 8 per cent.

THE OPPORTUNITY COST OF LABOUR

Conventional approaches to the opportunity cost of labour in developing countries look to casual wages in the agricultural sector because this sector is the largest single source of employment and is usually assumed to have an excess labour supply. The situation in Lithuania shows some similarities with, but also some differences from, that of most developing countries.

There is strong evidence for the existence of underemployment of labour in Lithuania in both the agricultural and the industrial sectors. Underemployment is reflected in the low levels of earnings of some workers, but overt unemployment was still relatively low in 1994/5. There was actually an increase in the size of the agricultural labour force, but this was largely a reflection of land restitution and the break-up of the former collective farms into smaller units. It can be assumed that many of the people currently working in the agricultural sector would move into other occupations if they had the opportunity.

There are some problems in following the conventional approach to estimation of the shadow wage both because the market for casual labour is relatively undeveloped and because existing information systems do not collect data on casual labour rates. It was therefore necessary to look to other sources to try to establish estimates of the opportunity cost of labour.

The agricultural sector is the biggest single employer of labour with 24 per cent of total employment in the third quarter of 1994. However, the agricultural sector does not dominate employment in the same way as in most developing countries. Furthermore, the skill composition of the labour force is different because Lithuania is a fairly industrialized economy with a high level of urbanization and education. For this reason the majority of the labour force cannot be classified as unskilled. In fact, in a recent Statistics Department survey of the labour force, only 25 per cent of the surveyed workers were in categories that could be regarded as unskilled. This proportion is almost certainly an underestimate because it is likely that the agricultural sector is underrepresented in the survey due to the high proportion of self-employed unskilled workers in the sector. Nevertheless the proportion of unskilled workers in the total labour force is unlikely to be more than 45 per cent.

Due to the relatively high level of urbanization and education a large proportion of the labour force can be defined as semi-skilled. It is therefore important to include semi-skilled labour as a separate category. In the Statistics Department survey labour categories that could be described as semi-skilled took up 46 per cent of the total labour force and, even allowing for the under-representation of agriculture in statistical surveys, the proportion is at least 30 per cent. This category of labour is particularly important in the industrial, transport and construction sectors.

The relative importance of skilled labour is also greater in Lithuania than in a typical developing country. In the Statistics Department survey 30 per cent of the workers were in categories that could be described as skilled. After allowing for the under-representation of agriculture the proportion is still around 25 per cent. Skilled labour is rarely given much attention in economic analysis on the grounds that it is a relatively small cost item and that, since it is relatively scarce, the shadow price is unlikely to diverge significantly from the market price. In Lithuania the process of transition has led to a substantial decline in the real value of earnings of all categories of labour and a movement of workers from the public to the private sector. Where workers are relatively scarce, earnings in the private sector tend to be higher than in the public sector. This indicates that the opportunity cost of public-sector skilled labour may be above the market wage. The Statistics Department survey indicated that the average earnings of labour categories classed as skilled in the private sector were about 18 per cent above those in the public sector. The differential is higher the higher the level of skill required, reaching 28 per cent for the highest skill category. This differential between public-sector and private-sector skilled labour earnings is also a common feature of the experience of developing countries undergoing structural adjustment and would suggest that more attention could be given to the economic cost of skilled labour in developing countries.

The information outlined above and derived from Statistics Department surveys was used to try to estimate the opportunity cost of labour. Other sources of information on earnings levels by category were also used to supplement the main source.

In the case of unskilled labour, the average level of earnings suggested that the vast majority of the workers in the agricultural sector could be classified as unskilled, particularly in the private sector. It was therefore assumed that the main source of unskilled labour (85 per cent) would be the agricultural sector. In addition there was evidence of a decline in employment levels in the industrial sector. It was therefore assumed that part of any extra unskilled labour required (15 per cent) would be derived from the industrial sector. It was further assumed that such workers would be drawn from the lowest-paid occupations in the industrial and agricultural sectors on the grounds that low pay would encourage workers to move and that the existence of low rates of pay provided an indication of underemployment. Average earnings in private-sector agriculture were estimated to be 150 Litas per month and for low-paid industrial workers they were estimated to be 240 Litas per month. The national opportunity cost of labour was therefore assumed to be 127.5 Litas (150×0.85) in agricultural output and 36 Litas (240×0.15) in industrial output to give a total of 163.5 Litas. Average earnings for unskilled workers were estimated to be about 280 Litas per month. After taking account of the conversion factors for agricultural and industrial output this gave a conversion factor for unskilled labour of 0.60.

A similar approach was taken for semi-skilled workers, except that in this case the majority of workers were assumed to be derived from the industrial sector (89 per cent) and only a minority (11 per cent) from agriculture. Average earnings for low-paid semi-skilled workers were estimated to be 270

Litas per month compared with average earnings for all semi-skilled workers of 450 Litas per month. The resultant conversion factor for semi-skilled labour, taking account of relevant sector conversion factors, was 0.57.

Skilled labour was divided into public and private sectors. It was assumed that the opportunity cost of private-sector skilled labour was equal to the market wage but weighted by the relative importance of different sectors in private-sector skilled labour employment using the employment proportions and conversion factors for these sectors. This gave a conversion factor for private-sector skilled labour of 0.89. Public-sector skilled labour was assumed to have an opportunity cost at market prices that was 18 per cent higher than the market wage. This value was weighted in a similar way by the relative importance of different sectors in public-sector employment. After adjusting by the standard conversion factor of 0.92, this gave a conversion factor for public-sector skilled labour of 1.09.[4] It should be noted that this value may be an underestimate, particularly for the highest skill categories because it does not take account of the cost of training replacements.

THE RELATIVE IMPORTANCE OF DIFFERENT SECTORS

The relative importance of different sectors and commodities in shadow price estimation in Lithuania is influenced by the relatively high level of industrialization and urbanization, which explain the importance of the energy sector, whilst geographical location as a transit route to other countries of the FSU contributes to the importance of the transport sector. Geographical location is also a contributory factor to the relative importance of livestock and dairy products in the agricultural and agro-industrial sectors.

The energy and transport sectors are also important because of the extent of the differences between shadow prices and market prices which are partly caused by the inheritance from the FSU of subsidized energy prices and capacity geared towards the needs of a much larger market. The variation of conversion factors within the sub-sectors also illustrates the dangers of using average conversion factors where there is extensive cross-subsidization.

The Energy Sector

The electricity sub-sector is dominated by the Ignalina nuclear power station which has a capacity far in excess of the medium-term requirements of Lithuania. Although electricity is exported to neighbouring countries, the capacity exceeds any likely demand. This leads to the curious situation of a good that is actually traded being treated as a non-traded good on the grounds that any extra domestic demand would lead to increased power generation rather than a reduction in exports. The existence of excess capacity also means that the marginal cost of electricity generation is well below the market price because most of the costs associated with nuclear power generation are fixed. This situation will continue as long as the Ignalina power station continues to operate with its existing capacity. However a complication arises due to the strong pressures on safety grounds to decommission the plant as soon as possible. The long-term cost of electricity generation may therefore be very different from that in the short and medium term depending on decisions on the future of Ignalina and the nature of its replacement.

Heating is an important sub-sector in Lithuania because of the relatively cold climate. District heating companies supply heat to both industrial and domestic users. Since most domestic users live in flats and individual flats are not metered there are no strong incentives for energy conservation. Subsidized fuel prices in the past also contributed to energy inefficiency. With the move towards world prices for fuel the cost of heating rose considerably while the economic decline reduced the capacity of the users to pay for it. The result has been a situation where it has been necessary for industrial users to subsidize domestic users because domestic users would be unable to pay the full cost of heating their flats. Although the extent of cross-subsidization is being reduced there is still a significant difference between the conversion factors for domestic heating (1.42) and industrial heating (0.60). A similar though less extreme form of cross-subsidization exists in the electricity sector.

The Transport Sector

The transport sector in Lithuania as in most countries is dominated by road and rail transport. While road freight operates on competitive market principles, there is considerable cross-subsidization in the rail sub-sector. In particular passenger traffic and internal freight are subsidized by transit traffic, particularly transit to the Russian enclave of Kaliningrad. Conversion factors for the four different categories in the rail sub-sector range from 0.28 to 3.18. With such variation an average conversion factor for the rail sub-sector should be treated with caution.

In the case of the road freight sub-sector there are also some differences from the typical situation. In most countries fuel is taxed quite highly and in many cases so are vehicles. This usually leads to a relatively low road-freight conversion factor.[5] In Lithuania fuel taxes are relatively low, as are taxes on vehicles. The decline in economic activity in the countries of the FSU has also led to a situation of temporary excess capacity in the road-freight sector with the result that profit margins do not cover fully the cost of vehicle replacement, leading to a negative value for the operating surplus. The effect of inflation on conventional accounting for depreciation may also contribute to charges that do not cover full costs. The result of all these factors is a relatively high conversion factor for road freight.

The Agricultural Sector

The agricultural sector in Lithuania is dominated by livestock and milk production. Together they account for about 64 per cent of the value of the output of the sector. Although the agricultural sector is quite highly protected with typical import duty rates of 20–30 per cent, the overall level of protection of the sector is quite low because the two major products are exported at the margin. It is only in the cases of sugar beet and grains and related processed products that relatively low conversion factors are obtained.

The conversion factors for some products are very sensitive to changes in producer prices. This is particularly true for indirectly traded outputs like milk and sugar beet where the economic value is derived from the border price of the processed product (dairy products and sugar respectively) less the cost of processing. A change in the ratio of the border price of the processed product to the value of the producer price for the raw material input has a substantial effect on the conversion factor for the raw material. In the case of dairy products the cost of purchasing milk fell from 73 per cent of total costs in 1993 to 59 per cent in 1994. If profit margins over total costs were similar in both years the conversion factor for milk would have increased significantly.

ENVIRONMENTAL ISSUES

Lithuania has a system of environmental taxes related to factors such as the level of omissions of pollutants. In principle the taxes are supposed to represent compensation for environmental damage although the current levels are insufficient to have a substantial impact. If these taxes are sufficiently closely related to environmental costs they could be regarded as a proxy for environmental resource costs rather than a transfer payment. This approach was taken in estimating conversion factors for Lithuania on the grounds that, where such taxes can be identified, environmental costs are at least large as the tax. Although this is a minimalist approach, it establishes the possibility that environmental costs could be included in the estimation of shadow prices as long as environmental taxes can be related to environmental costs. Eventually this could be a significant issue in the valuation of projects that are geared towards the replacement of environmentally damaging activities and materials with cleaner alternatives.

SHADOW PRICES AND EXCHANGE RATE POLICY

Lithuania has a policy of maintaining an exchange rate that is fixed in relation to the US dollar. This policy is being maintained as an anti-inflation measure in a situation where internal inflation is expected to decline but will still be well above international levels for the next four years. Existing policy will therefore lead to a substantial appreciation of the real exchange rate for the Litas.

World Bank forecasts for the Lithuanian economy assume that real wages will grow at the same rate as the growth of the economy (World Bank 1994). This therefore means that real wage costs will rise in relation to the value of traded goods since productivity gains are passed on proportionately to the workforce. In the meantime the value of the opportunity cost of labour, particularly where this consists mainly of the output of traded goods, will not rise at the same rate as the market price for labour. The effect of a real appreciation of the Litas will therefore be a decline in the conversion factor for labour and also for those non-traded goods in which labour features as a significant item. An attempt was made to include this effect in projections of conversion factors over the next four years by multiplying the opportunity cost of labour by a ratio reflecting the assumed change in the value of the opportunity cost of labour and the assumed change in the market price for labour.[6]

The results indicate a decline in the conversion factor for unskilled labour from 0.60 in 1995 to 0.37 in 1999. A similar decline is observed for other categories of labour.[7] These results are consistent with the expectation of increasing levels of overt unemployment. Significant declines are also recorded in the conversion factors for relatively labour-intensive sectors like construction (0.85 to 0.72) and finance and trade (0.79 to 0.70) The standard conversion factor falls from 0.92 to 0.88.

These changes are probably underestimates of the likely changes to the conversion factors of some non-traded goods because they do not take account of the likely change in the proportionate composition of costs consequent on an increase in wage costs. Nevertheless they do indicate clearly that macroeconomic policy assumptions have significant implications for economic analysis if changes in relative prices are included in constant price estimates of costs and benefits. It is not enough to assume that conversion factors will remain unchanged if macroeconomic policy suggests otherwise. It is also important to review the estimates periodically (preferably every year) to check that the original assumptions are still valid.

USING THE ESTIMATES

The conversion factor estimates were prepared for the PIP Unit. It is therefore intended that they should be used for projects put forward for the PIP for 1996–98 and also for loan guarantee requests for the same period. Given the limited project analysis capacity in Lithuania it is worth considering which projects are most likely to show significant differences between the results and the results at market prices.

Ideally shadow prices would be applied in a consistent manner to all projects. However it is unlikely that the capacity will exist for this and for some projects it may not be necessary. Rates of protection in the industrial sector are relatively low and for traded manufactured products conversion factors are all above 0.9. It is therefore unlikely that there will be a substantial difference between results at market prices and at shadow prices for commercial manufacturing projects. In the health and social sectors benefit estimation is quite difficult and it is unlikely that shadow pricing will improve the quality of decisions except for cases of choice of design between alternative ways of achieving the same objective (i.e. cost-effectiveness analysis in project design). For small technical assistance projects the benefit of doing the analysis is unlikely to justify the cost.

The most important areas where shadow prices might be used are in projects in or making substantial use of the energy and transport sectors and in loan guarantee projects in the agricultural and agro-industrial sectors where protection is relatively high. Cost-effectiveness studies in energy conservation, alternative energy sources and environmental protection are particular areas where the estimates might be useful. These are also priority areas for the PIP.

CONCLUSION

The methodology for systematic application of shadow prices was originally developed in the context of highly protected import-substituting manufacturing industries in developing countries. Particular concerns were the effect of underemployment in the rural areas on the opportunity cost of labour and the maintenance of an overvalued exchange rate.

In Lithuania the general level of protection is low and the exchange rate is not particularly overvalued although the maintenance of a fixed exchange rate is becoming an issue, particularly for the industrial sector. Shadow pricing for most manufacturing projects is unlikely to have much effect and the focus is more towards energy, transport, and agro-industries. It is possible that the estimates will be as useful for cost–effectiveness analysis as they will be for cost–benefit analysis, particularly in the areas of energy conservation and environmental improvement.

Surplus unskilled labour in the rural areas is a relevant consideration for Lithuania, but surplus semi-skilled labour in the industrial sector is equally significant. The effect of transition on the relative scarcity of skilled labour in the public sector is also an important consideration.

The stability of conversion factors over time is an important question and relates to assumptions about macroeconomic policy. The usefulness of the estimates depends on their accuracy and durability and on the adaptability of the model used for calculation. This will become apparent as attempts are made to use and update them.

NOTES

1. A review of existing practice is given in MacArthur (1994).
2. Tan (1994, chap. 3) uses an approach in which the A matrix is extended to include all labour categories and average conversion factors. The F matrix then only includes foreign exchange and various categories of transfer payment (income changes). Since foreign exchange has a value of 1.0 and transfers a value of 0.0 there is no need for the use of seed values and iteration. Tan goes on to introduce income-distribution weights for the income changes. No attempt was made to introduce income-distribution weights for the Lithuanian model and the value of the SCF was left out of the A matrix in order to focus attention on the relative value of foreign exchange and domestic resources. A review of the 'Extended SIO' approach is given in Tan and MacArthur (1995).
3. This procedure does not involve significant extra effort – simply the inversion of a smaller matrix excluding the labour categories and multiplication by a bigger F matrix in which the labour categories are included. It has the advantage of indicating the effect of the use of particular commodities on the employment of labour. The extended approach indicates the effect on labour incomes so, by showing both approaches, information is generated on both employment and income effects.
4. The conversion factor for skilled labour can be expressed in the following formula:

$$CF_{SL} = \frac{OC_{SL}}{MP_{SL}} \cdot \sum_i CF_i \cdot P_i$$

   where CF_{SL}, is the conversion factor for the skilled labour category under consideration; OC_{SL} is the opportunity cost of the same skilled labour category at market prices; MP_{SL} *is* the market price of the skilled labour category; CF_i *is* the conversion factor for sector i; P_i is the proportion of skilled labour in the category under consideration employed in sector i. For private-sector skilled labour $OC_{SL}/MP_{SL} = 1.00$; for public-sector skilled labour $OC_{SL}/MP_{SL} = 1.18$.
5. MacArthur (1994) gives examples of conversion factors for road freight generated by SIO studies. With the exception of Egypt they all lie in the range 0.6 to 0.9. The CF for road freight calculated for Lithuania was 0.99.
6. The change in the ratio of the opportunity cost of labour to its market price over time was estimated on the following basis:

$$\frac{OC_{n+1}}{MP_{n+1}} = \frac{OC_n}{MP_n} \cdot \frac{(1+WI_{n+1})}{(1+DI_{n+1})}$$

where n and $n + 1$ refer to years, *OC* refers to the opportunity cost of labour, *MP* refers to the market price of labour, *WI* refers to world inflation and *DI* refers to domestic inflation.

Changes in other conversion factors were then estimated by running the model with the new values for the opportunity cost of labour.

7. For skilled labour the opportunity cost was assumed to be derived from various sectors, not all of which are traded. The factor by which the ratio of skilled-labour opportunity cost to its market price was multiplied was therefore a weighted average of the factor indicated in note 6 (for traded sectors) and 1.0 (for non-traded sectors). The conversion factor for skilled labour categories therefore declines more slowly than that for unskilled and semi-skilled labour.

REFERENCES

MacArthur, J.D. (1994), 'Estimating efficiency prices through semi-Input–Output Methods – A review of practice in available studies', *Journal of International Development*, **6** (1).

Potts, D.J. (1995), 'Economic Analysis for the Public Investment Programme in Lithuania', mimeo, University of Bradford: Development and Project Planning Centre.

Tan Tok Shiong and J.D. MacArthur (1995), 'An extended semi input–output method for estimating shadow prices', *Project Appraisal*, **10** (1), March.

Tan Tok Shiong (1994), 'Shadow Prices for Malaysia with an Extended Semi-Input–Output Method', unpublished PhD thesis, University of Bradford: Development and Project Planning Centre.

World Bank (1994), *Lithuania Public Expenditure Review*, Washington, DC: World Bank.

Index